Rave reviews for Loren Coleman's colorfully informative guide to the nation's inexplicable wonders and mysterious creatures . . .

"There are a lot of strange 'things' happening in these United States, and a goodly number of them are described in Loren Coleman's *Mysterious America*. . . . It contains not only accounts of such well-known crypto-critters as Bigfoot and Champ, but a host of other reports of high strangeness. . . . In short, it's a potpourri, with something for almost any lover of the strange and the unusual."

—*Cryptozoology*

"Coleman has done more than sit in a library reading room; he has collected information in the field. . . . I recommended it to everyone who is interested in the strange, bizarre, and unusual."

—*Fate* magazine

"The lists are worth the price alone."

—*Critique*

"Objective, painstaking, exhaustive."

—*London Times*

***Mysterious America* is also available as an eBook**

Selected Books by Loren Coleman

True Giants (2007)

Weird Virginia (2007)

The Unidentified/Creatures of the Outer Edge: The Early Works of Jerome Clark and Loren Coleman (2006)

The Field Guide to Bigfoot and Other Mystery Primates (2006)

Weird Ohio (2005)

Copycat Effect (2004)

The Field Guide to Lake Monsters and Sea Serpents (2003)

Bigfoot! The True Story of Apes in America (2003)

Tom Slick: True Life Encounters in Cryptozoology (2002)

Mothman and Other Curious Encounters (2002)

Mysterious America: The Revised Edition (2001)

Cryptozoology A to Z (1999)

The Field Guide to Bigfoot, Yeti, and Other Mystery Primates Worldwide (1999)

Child Maltreatment and Abuse Investigations for Law Enforcement Officers (1998)

Creating Kinship (1996)

Working with Rural Youth (1994)

Tom Slick and the Search for the Yeti (1989)

Working with Older Adoptees (1988)

Unattended Children (1987)

Suicide Clusters (1987)

Curious Encounters (1985)

Creatures of the Goblin World (1984)

Mysterious America (1983)

Creatures of the Outer Edge (1978)

The Unidentified (1975)

Mysterious America

The Ultimate Guide to the Nation's Weirdest Wonders, Strangest Spots, and Creepiest Creatures

by LOREN COLEMAN

PARAVIEW POCKET BOOKS
NEW YORK   LONDON   TORONTO   SYDNEY

PARAVIEW
191 Seventh Avenue, New York, NY 10011

POCKET BOOKS, a division of Simon & Schuster, Inc.
1230 Avenue of the Americas, New York, NY 10020

ISBN-13: 978-1-4165-2736-7
ISBN-10:   1-4165-2736-2

This Paraview Pocket Books trade paperback edition April 2007

10   9   8   7   6   5   4   3   2   1

POCKET and colophon are registered trademarks of
Simon & Schuster, Inc.

Manufactured in the United States of America

For information regarding special discounts for bulk purchases,
please contact Simon & Schuster Special Sales at 1-800-456-6798
or business@simonandschuster.com.

Dedicated to my friend, editor, and co-author
Patrick Huyghe

Contents

PHANTOMS AFIELD. . .

FIRESIDE THINKING. . .

THE LISTS. . .

Preface to the 2001 Edition

Cicadas sing sweetly in the distance, the smell of the willows finds its way nearby, and the fan-shaped leaves of ginkgo flicker from the trees. I'm walking slowly through the memories of a long-ago Midwestern day, searching again.

I started simply. Asking people questions. Reading the latest news article or book on the inexplicable. I scrolled microfilm files for old cases. Then I ventured out into the field. Many, many times I walked the walk. Trekking through an Illinois farmyard with a game warden, I wondered if he was serious when he told me the report of a black panther was merely a beaver. Getting scratched on the face with itchy weeds, as the spring peepers played the music of the hunt, I looked for tracks and found some. And then I went on the next quest, and the next.

This eventually led to my first solo book, *Mysterious America.* Now, almost a quarter of a century and several books later, *Mysterious America* has become a Fortean classic and it appears I have become a celebrity of sorts. The Center for Bigfoot Studies honored me as their "Bigfooter of the Year" in December 1999. During 2000, I was named the Senior Series Consultant for a new "In Search Of" series. Mostly, I remember the personal kudos spoken in quiet conversations with the folks from Alton, Illinois to Newcomerstown, Ohio, from San Francisco to Rangeley, Maine.

Indeed, it is sometimes hard to grasp what has happened to me since *Mysterious America* first appeared in 1983. I had been doing fieldwork since 1960, as well as chronicling my investigations and appearing on television programs discussing unexplained and cryptozoological matters since 1969. When I wrote *Mysterious America,* the idea was merely to gather in one place some of my adventures along the way, and give a few insights into my treks into the unknown. The book has become a popular introduction for people who wish to understand the many mysteries that lie just beyond their living room and backyard.

Today, I live in Maine, not Illinois or California, and teach courses in research, cryptozoology, and documentary film at New England universities. And, yes, I am also a devoted father of two boys, a partner to a wonderful woman, a baseball coach, and a soccer dad who happens to take every chance I get to chronicle and investigate Nessie at Loch Ness, prehistoric stone walls in Illinois, giant snakes in Missouri, mad gassers in Illinois, panthers all over eastern North America, sea serpents off Nova Scotia, Skunk Apes in Florida, and hairy hominid sightings everywhere, all for fun and enlightenment. I have a great deal of passion for what I do; that's why I do it.

Readers have told me for years how much they still love *Mysterious America*, first published by Faber and Faber in 1983 with a black and white cover, then later reprinted in 1989 with a colored one. Many of these folks have wanted another copy to share with a friend, but to no avail. The book has been out-of-print for so long that I thought it would be great to see it back in print and available for a new generation of searchers. Thanks to Paraview Press, here it is. The edition you are reading is the first major revision of *Mysterious America* since 1983. I have made corrections, added material, inserted new chapters, deleted inappropriate material, and located new illustrations. But I have left most of the book "as is" for historic reasons and because much of what I said in 1983 is still sound today. I hope you enjoy your journey with me, a little more seasoned and hopefully a lot wiser, as we travel through Mysterious America.

Loren Coleman
October 1, 2000

This 2007 Paraview Pocket Books–Simon & Schuster version of *Mysterious America* displays a cover that is in tribute to my readers. In addition to the faithful fans of my articles and books, I send out a special tip of my hat to the millions of readers who have discovered me via my daily blog at Cryptomundo. The cover serves as a special appreciation to you and other readers such as Phyllis Mancz of Ohio, who contributed the "mystery fish" postcard dated to 1904–1918, to Joe Citro, who took the great photo of me with the Crookston Bigfoot, and to my friends at Cryptomundo—Craig Woolheater, Eric Reed, John Kirk, Rick Noll, and Duncan Hopkins. Thank you all!

Loren Coleman
December 8, 2006
Portland, Maine

On the Road Again...

Introduction

The damned data Charles Fort gathered covered so many marvels, mysteries, and monsters—including unidentified aerial objects, frog falls, disappearances of ships, red rains, earthquake lights, lake monsters, animal mutilations, psychic explosions, and much much more—that if I were to name them all, the list would go on for pages. Indeed, Fort is even credited with inventing the word "teleportation." Today, the people who study the wonders examined by Fort are called "Forteans." The strange and unusual phenomena we Forteans research and write about is often referred to as "Forteana." Such associations as the International Fortean Organization just outside of Washington, D.C., and the journal *Fortean Times* of London have sprung up in the wake of Charles Fort to carry on his work.

Charles Fort, who died in 1932, probably would be embarrassed by the subculture of followers which has grown around his work. He even refused to join the original Fortean Society of the 1920s which was begun by the likes of Ben Hecht, Booth Tarkington, Tiffany Thayer, Theodore Dreiser, Alexander Woollcott, Buckminster Fuller, Oliver Wendell Holmes, Clarence Darrow, Burton Rascoe, John Cowper Powys, and other intellectuals. Fort would have laughed not a little that annual conferences are now held entitled "Fortfests" and that seminars on cryptozoology (the study of hidden animals, i.e., monsters) are commonplace.

I discovered the works of Charles Fort in the late 1950s and soon joined the leagues of Forteans. In the 1960s, I began a ten-year correspondence with the late zoologist Ivan T. Sanderson who once wrote: "I am a 'Fortean' and very proud to be labeled as such." Like Sanderson and scores of others I have worked with in this field, I am quite happy Charles Fort has influenced my life as he has. Fort was one of the first true intellectual investigative reporters; he had honed his craft long before Watergate was a household word. Through the 1960s and 1970s, as I jumped into the thick of the pursuit of the unknown, Fort's humor and skepticism served me well. We Forteans of today are carrying on his tradition in an intense fashion—and have added fieldwork to the laborious bibliographical tasks he started in the British Museum and the New York Public Library.

In *Mysterious America,* I have set down my personal insights and experiences as a Fortean traveling around North America during the first twenty or so years of my investigations. I have chased monsters and mad gassers; tracked down teleported animals; interviewed scores of people who have seen creatures from mysterious kangaroos to black panthers, or viewed entities from phantom clowns to lake monsters, and more. To pursue Fortean phenomena, my travels have taken me to the four corners of the country, from the Pacific Northwest to the U.S. Virgin Islands, from New England to the Southwest. My car has crisscrossed the Midwest so many times that sometimes I think I could turn it loose and it would steer itself to the latest Bigfoot or panther sighting. I find myself going to places like Fort Mountain, Georgia, and Mystery Hill, New Hampshire, to examine strange structures built by ancient unknown peoples, or to various wooded areas in the Northeast to run down the latest phantom feline account.

Every day I open my mail (and now email) and hear about a new Fortean or cryptid event happening someplace in this nation that deserves my attention. The material rolls in an ever increasing wave, and this searcher into the unexplained can barely keep up with the demand on his investigative time. It is a strange world out there, and some people may be too busy to stop and notice. Since I have made so many treks on the trail of the inexplicable, I present this book to you, to share with you some of my excursions and adventures in *Mysterious America.* I hope it helps you to look beyond the horizon. If it does, and you would like to exchange information and ideas on the subjects explored, please write me.

Loren Coleman
Post Office Box 360
Portland, Maine 04112

Email: MA@lorencoleman.com

CHAPTER 1

Reflections of a Traveling American Fortean

Our thoughts often turn to moving, weekend treks, taking vacations, going on holiday, and visiting family and friends in other parts of the country. If your thoughts also have a Fortean bent to them, if you mix your pleasure with furthering your own personal inquiries into the unexplained wonders around you, then some helpful hints toward making your next trip a worthwhile phenomenological adventure might interest you.

You can do many things at home before you travel to your destination. A hefty amount of background research, before your journey, can save you hours of wasted time in the field. I always discovered that it was important to find out what the specific locales I was going to, and through, have to offer. All researchers must ask themselves specific questions which apply to their own interests, but in general, I like to know if there are runes, mounds, monster-inhabited lakes, spook lights, Bigfoot sightings, haunted places, ice caves, panther-frequented valleys, and a whole host of more-or-less permanent Fortean wonders in the vicinity of my route or its predetermined end.

Finding these fixed unexplained locations by way of the Internet today is, of course, extremely easy, and search engines can help you put your fingertips on wonderful sources. The Fortean literature also provides some references of great assistance…if you can put your hands on them. George Eberhart's *A Geo-Bibliography of Anomalies* and Jim Brandon's *Weird America* are two of the best books with individual locale listings. Eberhart's expensive book might be available in a few libraries, and Brandon's quality paperback should be almost as difficult to run across in some used-book stores. Both are worth the effort of the search, however.

Brandon's *Weird America* is especially good since it is compact and offers a rather complete rundown on the individual Fortean sites. Since he used his own files as well as the items in the *INFO Journal* and *Fate,* Brandon was able to give a rather nice cross-section of what each state has or has had to offer. *Weird America* is a true Fortean guidebook, and Brandon's 1983 book, *The Rebirth of Pan,* adds another chapter in his unique analysis of the cryptograms written on the face of America. *Amazing America* and other books and websites like *Roadside America* are less helpful in terms of weirdness and Fortean activity. These books are exaggerated collections of the biggest, shortest, oldest, usually man-made attractions along the way. In fact, it serves as a good negative guidebook for it lets you know some things to avoid.

You might also be tempted to refer to *Space-Time Transients and Unusual Events* by Michael A. Persinger, but the book is a teaser; while listing some spots from the author's computer printouts, it really leaves a lot out. And be on your guard, too. The database is slanted towards Fortean phenomena, as seen through the pages of *Fate.* Because a couple of active writers (myself and Jerry Clark) did many pieces on Illinois mysteries, the book has a map demonstrating the especially active nature of Illinois Forteana, which is probably not really the case.

Salvatore Trento's *In Search of Lost America,* Barry Fell's *America B.C.,* and others are good starting places if you are looking for ancient anomalous sites. Trento's works, all of them, are very good sources for geographical mysteries, and are recommended highly. The National Geographic's *Guide to Ancient Treasures* is excellent for its detailed highway route and byway travel tips to archaeological wonders. Also, as I discuss elsewhere (Chapter Three), ancient sites labeled "devil" should be at the top of the list of sites you should seek out.

On certain other topics, such as where Bigfoot has been seen, John Green's *The Apes Among Us* gives an easy state-by-state breakdown to follow. *The Field Guide to Bigfoot, Yeti, and Other Mystery Primates Worldwide* and *Cryptozoology A to Z* are useful, of course, in this realm. Peter Costello's *In Search of Lake Monsters* does a fairly complete job of indicating where to find the watery beasts, and the novice will find it of assistance. *Mysterious America's* Chapter Nine and Appendix VI give specific data on monster-inhabited lakes. Articles with seed catalogue-type presentations can be treasure troves of information on specific locations of particular phenomena. Mark A. Hall's spook light listing (see Appendix II) still ranks as my favorite; it is very detailed concerning what to expect to see and where. Patrick Huyghe's *The Field Guide to Extraterrestrials,* and his and his co-authors' other books in the series *(The Field Guide to UFOs* and *The Field Guide to Ghosts and Other Apparitions)* are likewise extremely helpful for narrowing your focus.

Falls of strange items from ice to frogs, for example, appear to be one-shot affairs, but it is always good to understand a locale in terms of its total Fortean history. Falls, strange appearances, and permanent phenomena are natural candidates for lists, and *Fortean Times* and the *INFO Journal* articles on these topics pinpoint the sites of the occurrences. The Appendices of this book contain a good collection of Fortean lists. For example, Appendix III, on the appearance of out-of-place crocs and 'gators, is an illustration of a seed catalogue worth having; another is David Fideler's old, enjoyable, but hard-to-find listing of kangaroo sightings in the *Anomaly Research Bulletin.* Tom Adams' *Stigmata* has had many articles and maps on the mystery of the cattle mutilations, for those interested in pursuing such stories. You just can't beat a good list.

Overall, these books and articles should give you a fairly good idea about where to target some of your efforts on your trip, as should *Mysterious America.* After going through the literature, you may wish to contact researchers who have done extensive fieldwork in the locale of your interest. The best way to locate such individuals is by taking a deeper dip into the vast underground pool of Fortean organizations, newsletters, and journals. Contact through the Internet is fast today and links can be made via *Fortean Times, Fate, The Anomalist, INFO, NEARA,* and others. Personally I enjoy finding out about the most recent activity in an area I am heading for. Colleagues and associated researchers can often give me a lead, but another way to discover if anything unusual is hopping is by reading the local area's newspapers before I take my journey. Today, this is much easier with online access. On the road, I also often stop at the regional weeklies to inquire about any local folklore or any local, well-known wonder like the Devil's Tramping Ground, the Lake Champlain Monster, etc. These Fortean fishing trips are lots of fun. Sometimes I am casting out a line for a Bigfoot account, and I reel in a close encounter with a giant snake. It's amazing what a Fortean investigator can come up with; it certainly keeps me on my toes.

While getting to and going through an area, I try to pick up books written by local people on the regional folklore. (See the Bibliography for the names of some of these classic books.) Sometimes I come across some intriguing maps which have captured local legends in little pictures with quaint names, like the Cape Anywhere Sea Serpent, the Buried Treasure of Someplace Canyon, or the Headless Horseman of This Valley or That. These legends are often new to me because they are part of the local people's traditions which have not yet been widely publicized in books or on television programs. Undiscovered wonders still do exist. Finding such a Fortean gem can make a trip very worth your time and toil.

Another resource for finding out what unexplained happenings and places abound in any given province is simply talking to the local folks. Full-service gas station attendants and the employees of locally-owned sandwich shops are a gold mine of information, if you take the time to get out of your automobile or SUV and chat with them. The people at flea markets, craft shops, and yard sales know a good deal about the countryside, and often are willing to share with you some unique incident or story if you are friendly and unjudgmental.

The worst possible source of Fortean knowledge, I have discovered, is located at the so-called "Information Bureaus." These sandtraps of the American vacationer give out little more than some insights into the nearest or newest tourist attraction. If you go to them with anything more than a specific question about a specific location, don't expect much satisfaction. They have been able to tell me where, for example, a well-known haunted house was, but frequently an information bureau has not been able to direct me to an interesting creek close at hand; I had to get that information from a service station operator. I should also warn you about "Mystery Spots." In nearly all cases, these tourist attractions are optical illusions. Unfortunately, some completely worthwhile and top-notch Fortean sites have been labeled a "mystery" something or other. The most famous example of this is the 4000 B.P. megalithic structures at North Salem, New Hampshire, entitled collectively "Mystery Hill," a spot well worth a detour. A word to the wise will save you some time, either way.

Well, with all these hints and warnings in mind, it is time to take your trip. Get your laptop, tape recorder, camcorder, digital camera, paper, pen, and money and take a Fortean adventure. With careful planning, a little research, and some friendly questions along the way, your journey anywhere in Mysterious America can be rewarded with some interesting Fortean and cryptozoological discoveries. Enjoy yourself. And help enlighten others after your return.

CHAPTER 2

A Couple of Side Trips into the Unknown

For the decade I lived in the Boston area, I sometimes would forget how driving from the urbanized East Coast of the United States into the Midwest is a culturally shocking event. The megapolis of the Washington–New York–Boston complex often stymies life and the natural world, as well as the imagination of man. Despite some articles in recent years about the encroachment of wildlife into North American cities, these fingers of urban nature are generally nothing more or less than the occasional raccoon, opossum, or deer. Only when you get away from the overcrowded, concrete jungle do you find the kind of space, the corridors of vegetation, that allow the creatures of the netherland to roam freely. New England is beautiful and wild, but the temperate climate and open territory of the Heartland has reserved a special place in its soul for the kind of unknown animals I love to pursue. Be they ape-like, feline-formed, or thunderbird-shaped, the beasts of the Midwest make a Fortean's drive through Ohio, Indiana, and Illinois an exciting trek. From just such a journey, here are some stops along the way.

Phantom Panthers

Westerville, Ohio, is a mere mile from Interstate 270, the vast ring of highway that keeps the sprawl of Columbus so neatly contained. Interstate 270, like the others of its kind in America, serves as a barrier separating wildlife from man, and suburbs from the city. But Westerville is not a suburban community of square little houses and clipped lawns; rather, Westerville is a gathering of cornfields, of country roads where speed limits are difficult to enforce, of homes and farmhouses here *and* there, and, of course, trailer courts.

Most cities in the U.S. move their corporate limits into an area and along with the new sidewalks, stop signs, and sewage systems, they also introduce zoning laws that quickly eliminate trailer courts. This forces mobile home parks to move beyond the new city limits. In a way, the residents of trailers are becoming the new pioneers of our civilization. They relocate on the edges of the country, often with nothing more than a thin sheet of metal between them and the unknown. As quite a few researchers have discovered, many occupants of trailer courts find their confrontations with the unexplained more frequent than they desire. My travels have led me to quite a number of trailers and their owners.

Following up on a lead supplied by David Fideler and enhanced with information from Mark A. Hall, I stopped by the Lake Estates Home Park in Westerville, Ohio, to check on the recent accounts of a panther seen thereabouts in June 1979.

Elusive, phantom panthers are nothing new to central Ohio. Back in 1947, Stanley Belt saw one near Kirkwood. The reports have come in periodical waves since then. Black panthers have been seen in virtual flaps in 1955, 1962, and 1973, in the Urbana-Springfield region of the state, and the Bluffton area was the site of some activity in 1977. Ron Schaffner's investigations of 1978 revealed sightings near Minerva. Not too surprisingly, the phenomena continue still.

Starting in late May 1979, Delaware County Sheriff Bill Lavery began getting calls from residents who claimed to have spotted a large cat-like animal, a "cougar." In the village of Delaware, a big feline had killed some sheep, and in nearby Sunbury, some people had actually spied the cat. As with the Bluffton, Ohio, panther reports I investigated in 1977, [see *Creatures of the Outer Edge* (Warner 1978) pp 209-217; or "Phantom Panther on the Prowl," *Fate* November 1977, pp 62-67] the pattern of livestock kills, sightings, and footprint finds was repeated in Delaware County, Ohio, in 1979.

In the midst of all of this "cougar" activity, the animal made a visit to the Lake Estates trailer court. Charles and Helen Marks, co-managers of the court for three years after having moved from Toledo, did not think they were going to get involved in "cougar tracking," when suddenly on June 10, 1979, they found huge footprints at their doorstep.

This is the way Charles Marks described the course of events to me:

"Someone had called the police, and said that the night before, they were fishin' out here (at the little lake next to the trailer court). See we got a lot of good fish in this lake here. It's stocked. He was out fishin' and he'd seen these prints. Then he called the Delaware sheriff, and they came down Sunday morning. The guy showed them the prints; he'd staked them all out. Then we hightailed it out here to see what was going on." Helen Marks added: "We didn't know if it was a dead body or something. But it was these prints, some with claws, some without."

Charles Marks had some plaster of paris from the time he had repaired a broken leg of a pet, and Marks tried his hand at making some casts. His wife, in the role of "operations director," told Charles to make a cast of the more exciting clawed tracks, and thus these were the ones shown to the police. The authorities quickly labeled them "dog prints," an excuse familiar to anyone interested in mysterious feline accounts.

The Markses found over 200 prints in the small muddy and grassy fields across from their trailer and next to the little lake. They are convinced they had discovered "cougar" prints, for they also came upon a patch of vegetation with clear signs of where the animal had lain. Helen Marks recalled: "And you could even see the tufts of grass sticking up between the place the head had rested, and the five-foot-long depression where the body was."

Later on that eventful Sunday, three boys were out playing in their "fort" behind the trailer court, the discovery of the prints unbeknownst to them. Quite suddenly, they encountered a large, tan panther in a tree. Donnie Grady, 12, said the cat jumped from the tree, landed on all fours, and fled. Ricky Smith, 10, obviously taking the encounter very personally, told of how the thing "looked at me and jumped from the tree." Travis, Ricky's eight-year-old brother, said, "When it growled, I saw those BIG front teeth." The boys, residents of the trailer court, later saw the "cougar" on a nearby roadway, and then learned of the Markses' discovery of the prints.

More reported encounters with the panther took place the following week in June. A woman on nearby Fancher Road was taking out some trash when she met the big cat—and promptly fainted. Other sightings filled the newspapers for a few days, but like many elusive creatures of the borderland Midwest, this one too faded from the view and the minds of the residents of central Ohio.

The percipients of such incidents, however, do not so quickly forget the events which touched their lives. This came clearly into focus in Illinois.

Big Birds

On July 25, 1977, as 10-year-old Marlon Lowe played outside his family home along open fields near Kickapoo Creek, two giant birds passed over. One suddenly swooped down to grab the boy, carrying him a few feet before dropping him, apparently because of his frightened mother's screams. The incident occurred in front of seven witnesses, all of whom described exactly the same thing: two huge, coal-black birds with long, white-ringed necks, long curled beaks, and wingspans of 10 or more feet. [See *Creatures of the Outer Edge* pp 225-227; and *Fortean Times 24:* 10-12.] My brother, Jerry Coleman of Decatur, Illinois, had been able to interview Marlon, Ruth and Jake Lowe on two occasions in 1977, within hours of the incident. During my 1979 trip I planned to reinterview the Lowes and inquire into the occurrences since the time of their encounter.

Their trailer had not changed any since the photographs Jerry had taken in 1977, and the prophetic black eagles on the mobile home's shutters were still there to greet us.

Ruth Lowe was cautious, to say the least. This was a woman who had obviously been hurt, but I was soon to hear the surprising depths of this sorrow. And harassment.

After Marlon Lowe was lifted into the air, and the media had carried the story, individuals started leaving dead birds on the Lowes' front porch. Right after the first press mention, Ruth Lowe found a "big, beautiful eagle" spread out at the foot of their door. The next day, a circle of six birds was placed there. The authorities seemed unable or unwilling to help the Lowes.

The dimension of the human tragedy was great for this family. Turning to my brother, Ruth Lowe asked: "You know how red Marlon's hair was? He had the reddest hair you'd ever want to see on a kid."

Lowering her tone, she continued, "Well, he wears a hat all the time now. For a year the kid won't go out after dark. I started coming home early before he got off the bus to clean off the front porch. I had hawks, owls, you name it, I had 'em on the front porch here. And I started coming home early from work just to clean off that front porch. Now that's when I started getting hysterical when I found all the birds, the little notes, and got all the telephone calls. But about a month after it happened, I was washing his head, and I mean to tell you, the only red hair he had on his head was just the top layer. It was just as gray as could be."

After the initial shock, and her mistake of telling Marlon sent him into hysterics, Ruth Lowe cut his hair short and debated whether to put a color rinse on it. She reflected: "It grew out. It's not a red. It's not a blond. It's a gray." And the reason for the change was not shadowy to Marlon's mother: "It was the shock of it. And we are still putting up with a lot. The poor kid gets in one or two scraps a week."

Subdued, Ruth Lowe observed: "They called him 'Bird Boy.' He's quite a fighter now."

The event itself still haunted her. "I'll always remember how that huge thing was bending its white-ringed neck, and seemed to be trying to peck at Marlon, as it was flying away," Ruth Lowe commented, in a new detail which did not come out two years before. Although she said the massive size of the bird reminded her of an ostrich, the bird itself looked like a condor. She had spent some long hours in the local library looking for a clue to what she had seen. She was certain that it was not a turkey vulture, as an area constable would have her believe.

"I was standing at the door, and all I saw was Marlon's feet dangling in the air. There just aren't any birds around here that could lift him up like that," Ruth Lowe told us.

And then there were the other sightings, which had continued quietly in the Lawndale area. In nearby Lincoln, one of the big birds was flying down the middle of the main street, when the cab company's dispatcher yelled over the radio: "There goes that son-of-a-gun now." But his report was silenced.

A December 1977 account of the killing of one of the birds was similarly kept under wraps for fear of ridicule. Apparently a woman was on her way to work in Beason when she saw something like a "man standing in the road with something over its arms." (A description which conjures up the images of Mothman.) The woman collapsed, was hospitalized, and recovered some time later. A group of men, hearing of this report from the local grapevine, went out to the spot, killed a large bird, and burnt it. Whether it was one of the big birds will never be known, but this kind of story demonstrates the level of emotion these creatures can activate in such generally calm Midwestern towns as Lawndale.

Ruth Lowe's sister-in-law was even involved in a frightening big bird run-in at Belleville, Illinois. A large bird landed on top of one of the mobile homes in the trailer park where she lives. The thing flapped its wings once, took off over the trailers, and left many residents gasping in disbelief at its 18-foot wingspan. Needless to say, this creature was the talk of the trailer court for some weeks thereafter.

The local reports and the memories have given the Lowe family many haunted moments, for as Ruth Lowe knows and quietly told me: "They're still around here!"

The Lawndale, Illinois, incident is a modern, real-life enactment of a kind of episode portrayed in folklore all over the world: the attempted abduction of a child by a thunderbird. Today, this remarkable sighting is regarded as one of the most important avian cryptozoological events ever to have been investigated.

CHAPTER 3

Devil Names and
Fortean Places

When Western Europeans landed in the New World and began spreading across what was later to become America, they discovered what the Amerindians already knew…there were some strange places in this new land. Certain locations were "strange" because the early explorers and settlers would see, hear, smell or feel strange things—weird globes of light, eerie screechings, sickening sweet odors, cold drafts of air as well as unknown aerial phenomena, mystery animals and other "inexplicables." The interface between these newcomers and the decidedly unexplainable phenomena produced place names that attempted to reflect the notion that the locales were special, different and, indeed, strange. The names can take many forms, but I have long noticed an American historical acknowledgment of Forteana-ridden places by the use of the word "devil" in the naming of these locations. A few examples will illustrate this point.

Some of the more frequent sightings of California's phantom black panthers occur in the Diablo (Spanish for "devil") Valley east of San Francisco. The Las Trampas Regional Park booklet notes the black cat is referred to as "The Black Mountain Lion of Devil's Hole" because it is frequently seen on the slopes of Mt. Diablo and in the Devil's Hole area of the park. Mystery lights also turn up in the Mt. Diablo–Diablo Valley area frequently.

In 1873, a live frog was found in a slab of limestone in a mine on Mt. Diablo, and in 1806, Spanish General Vallejo encountered a man-like apparition (which had exotic plumage and made "diving movements") while battling the Bolgones Indians. Monte del Diablo is a very strange place.

The territory known as Devil's Kitchen in southern Illinois was avoided by the region's Amerindians because of their awareness of its sinister nature. Southern Illinois, in general, is a frequent host to mystery animals and UFOs as well as the site of pre-Columbian stone walls which form a rough alignment between the Ohio and Mississippi rivers.

Near Grand Tower, also in southern Illinois, is a small rocky hill known as the Devil's Bake Oven. South of that prominence is a longer hill known as the Devil's Backbone. Speaking of the Devil's Bake Oven, folklorist John W. Allen observes: "On those nights when the hill was flooded with gentle moonlight, visitors would report that they had seen a weird and mistlike creature...floating silently across their pathway to disappear among the rocks or in the dense bushes on the hillside. This disappearance was often followed by moans, wails and shrieks such as only a ghost can make."

Devil's Lake of Wisconsin has its share of geological oddities such as glacier scratches on unusual rock formations and petrified sand waves of an ancient sea, but it is the Amerindian mounds that are especially interesting. Three major effigy mounds are located in Devil's Lake State Park. One in the shape of a bear and another, which resembles a lynx, are at the north end of the lake. A bird-shaped mound is at the southern end. Did the moundbuilders wish to acknowledge real animals or phantom creature forms that haunted the shores of Devil's Lake?

From nearby Baraboo (a mere three miles north of Devil's Lake on Wisconsin 123), stories were circulating in the seventies of giant ghost elephants. Or were they mastodons? August Derleth, author and follower of H. P. Lovecraft, likes this area of south-central Wisconsin because he felt it contains "Cthulhu power zones."

During the summer of 1970, campers at Devil's Lake complained of shadowy "somethings" prowling around their tents. Department of Natural Resources personnel stated that no bears are found in the area. However, Bigfoot accounts are well known from Wisconsin. Devil's Lake is also the location of an 1889 lake monster report. Additionally, the surface of the lake is broken with the ghostly wake of a phantom canoe seen in the mists of cold, still nights. The place does have an aura about it. Folklore tells of an Indian maiden and her lover leaping to their deaths. In general, the site is said to be a "place of many dead."

Devil's Lake, Wisconsin, is a spooky spot.

* * *

One of my favorite examples of the reflection of Fortean phenomena via a "devil name" comes from one corner of the inland town of Chester, New Hampshire, on Rattlesnake Hill. A cavern there of "great notoriety in all the country round" bears the name Devil's Den. According to local legends, the path leading to the cave "was always kept open, in summer and winter, by the passing to and fro of the evil spirits who frequented the place, though themselves invisible to the eyes of mortal men."

The poet J. G. Whittier put the Devil's Den traditions into verse, and the following two stanzas from his poem "Devil's Den" give deep insight into bedeviled places in general:

'Tis said that this cave is an evil place
The chosen haunt of a fallen race
That the midnight traveller oft hath seen
A red flame tremble its jaws between,
And lighten and quiver the boughs among,
Like the fiery play of a serpent's tongue;
That sounds of fear from its chambers swell
The ghostly gibber, the fiendish yell;
That bodiless hands at its entrance wave,
And hence they have named it The Demon's Cave.

* * *

Yet is there something to fancy dear
In this silent cave and its lingering fear,
Something which tells of another age,
Of the wizard's wand, and the Sybil's page,
Of the fairy ring and the haunted glen,
And the restless phantoms of murdered men:
The grandame's tale, and the nurse's song
The dreams of childhood remembered long;
And I love even now to list the tale
Of the Demon's Cave, and its haunted vale.

Simply stated, the strange events of the past are often remembered in the geographical names of the area. Place names can be a Fortean's clue

Devils Tower, Wyoming

to the "haunted vale." By 1983, I had found one hundred and twenty-five places with "devil names" in the United States, and I am finding more correlations with this list and Forteana every day. (See Appendix V.) I suspect many more etymological connections exist. My list of "devil names" is just the tip of the pitchfork. Indeed, Henry Franzoni, a researcher living in the Pacific Northwest with a remarkable names database, told me that as of 1998, he had found 2,635 places named (or which were named) Devil, Diablo, or Diabla in the United States.

In a related vein is the native Algonquian word for the Devil—"Hockomock"—which I have written more about in *Curious Encounters*. Franzoni has found a total of ten places in the U.S. named "Hockomock": six in Maine, where I now live, two in Massachusetts, one in New Jersey (Hockamik), and one in Minnesota (Hockamin Creek). One of these, the Hockomock Swamp in the Bridgewater (Massachusetts) Triangle, is discussed in the next chapter. It is a place where people vanish and creatures like giant snakes, Bigfoot, Thunderbirds, and phantom panthers are seen. I first talked to Hockomock-area residents and Native Americans about the meaning of the name "Hockomock" to discover its link to the word "Devil." Then I looked in a Depression-era Writers Project Administration (WPA) guide, the one on Massachusetts, and found it defined the variant name for the swamp, "Hoccomocco," as "evil spirit."

By the way, the WPA guides are wonderful books for tracking down the origins of place names. One of my favorites is the story behind Lake Manitou, Indiana. "Manitou" is an Indian word demonstrating some power and connection to the unknown—"The Great Spirit," similar in a fashion to what we are talking about here regarding "devil." According to the WPA guide for Indiana (page 436), Lake Manitou was inhabited by three "monster devilfish" that began destroying all the fish there after arriving from Lake Michigan. "They even drove the wild game away, for when the buffalo, elk, deer, and other animals came to the lake to drink, fearsome serpentine tentacles shot out and dragged them beneath the surface of the murky water." The prayers of the Natives exterminated the monsters and out of gratitude, they named the lake after the Great Spirit. While the exact details of the encounters may be shrouded in folkloric overtones, the underlying nature of such stories are an intriguing bit of evidence for some historical links to real events, as we have seen over and over again. The land reveals its secrets for those who wish to look.

The United Kingdom, likewise, abounds with fertile devil sites for the curious researcher. Evan Hadingham in *Circles and Standing Stones* writes: "There are countless names and stories connecting ancient sites with giants and devils, such as the Devil's Arrows alignments at Boroughbridge, Yorkshire, or the name Devil's Quoits associated with Stanton Drew."

Geographical "devil names" worldwide may indicate, as they seem to in America, locales high in Fortean energy and strangeness. These places deserve some extra attention, for from the stray sod to the fairy ring, from the haunted glen to the Devil's Den, there lies many a riddle to unfold.

CHAPTER 4

Things That Go Bump in the Bay State

The Bay State's heritage of hauntings, both real and imagined, goes back nearly three centuries to the Salem witch hunt of 1692. That brief hysteria of accusations, trials, and twenty executions has been documented and analyzed so often that the phrase "Salem witch trials" has passed into household usage. The same cannot be said of Massachusetts' myriad other recorded incidents of hauntings, cursed apparitions, and unusual phenomena. Yet one need not look far to find a rich harvest of the mysterious.

The Hoosac railroad tunnel that runs through the Berkshire Mountains has been associated with spooky incidents for more than a century. Its construction cost more than $15 million and 200 lives, and legend has it that the tunnel's dead do not rest easy.

On March 20, 1865, two explosives experts, Ned Brinkman and Billy Nash, were buried under tons of rock when their foreman, Ringo Kelly, accidentally set off a blast of dynamite. Kelly disappeared immediately after the accident. Exactly one year later he was found strangled to death deep inside the tunnel at precisely the spot where Brinkman and Nash had died. Since then, many people have reported ghostly encounters with all three of the dead men.

In 1872, executives of the Boston and Maine Railroad were frightened by a moaning figure carrying a lantern through the darkened corridors of the Hoosac. In 1936, Joseph Impocco, a railroad worker, reported that he was saved from being run over by an express train when a spooky voice called out, "Hey, Joe. Joe, jump quick!" He leaped from the track just seconds before the train roared by.

Many people have mysteriously disappeared in the Hoosac Tunnel. In

1973, Barnard Hastaba set out to walk through the tunnel from North Adams to Williamstown. He was never heard from again.

Retribution is the motive attributed to Goody Hallet, the Witch of Wellfleet. Seduced at fifteen by pirate Sam Bellamy, she was later charged with murdering the child born of the union. While awaiting sentence, so the legend goes, she signed a pact with the devil and escaped from jail. From then on, she haunted the dunes, summoned hurricanes, stirred up thick fogs, and set out false lights to lure ships onto the shoals.

In 1717, Bellamy's ship the *Widdah* was wrecked and his body cast ashore near Goody Hallet's ruined cottage. Still not satisfied, her ghost continued to plague the waters of Cape Cod for the next eighty years, and on occasion she was sighted late at night dressed in red, dancing demonically on the Wellfleet village green.

Mad Meg Wesson, the Witch of Cape Ann, did not fare as well as the Witch of Wellfleet. Mad Meg wore a necklace of eels and kept as her familiar a raven with a peculiar jagged white marking under one wing. She heaved a multitude of curses in her time prompting hens to stop laying, fishnets to break, and pigs to devour their piglets.

In 1745, Sir William Pepperell led a military expedition against the French fortress of Louisburg on Cape Breton. On the night before setting out from Cape Ann, Pepperell's troops gathered for a celebration at a local tavern. Mad Meg appeared at the door and cursed the campaign. Thereafter all military pursuits failed miserably.

One day the troops spotted a raven, its underwing zigzagged with white. One of the soldiers fired twice at the bird. His first shot broke the raven's leg, his second shot killed it. Two days later, the army triumphed at Louisburg, and when the soldiers returned to Cape Ann, they later learned that Meg had fallen down and broken her leg. Two days later, the day of the Louisburg victory, she had died.

More than two hundred years later such ghostly goings-on can be dismissed as local legend or embellished half-truths. But dozens of other phenomena simply cannot be explained away so easily. Many inexplicable incidents have occurred in two "window areas," the Quabbin Reservoir near Amherst and the Hockomock Swamp in southeastern Massachusetts, near Brockton.

On August 13, 1819, there was a huge blast and a flash of light in the sky above Quabbin. Afterward a bowl-shaped object, dubbed a *whatsis,* was found in the front yard of an Amherst professor. The object was about eight inches across, covered by a velvety nap of buff color, and full of a stinking pulp that turned blood red and liquefied on exposure to the air.

College authorities judged the *whatsis* to be an unknown form of freshwater nostoc algae. Several more of the saucers were found soon afterward and similarly dismissed as nostoc, which forms blue-green colonies embedded in jelly. Nostoc, however, has never been known to arrive with a blast and a flash of light. Nor has it been known to stink and to dissolve red on exposure to air.

Other Quabbin oddities include mysterious beehive-shaped caves in Pelham, Leverett, and Shutesbury, and the sightings of crocodilian creatures in the Dismal Swamp near Ware. Crocodiles between six and eight feet long were spotted in 1922. Since then, three crocs ranging in size from one to three feet have been captured in the swamp. Crocodilians are generally found only in tropical or semitropical climates, of course. Unless you take into account the notion that Mysterious America's colder climes have frequently been visited by out-of-place crocs. But more on that later.

On June 14, 1972, several fat, four-foot-long eels were pulled from the water pipes in a house in Medford after residents complained of low water pressure. The eels are believed to have swum more than 100 miles through the pipes from the Quabbin Reservoir.

The Hockomock Swamp area claims its own share of strange occurrences. Because of its long history of evil, bedeviled, and ominous occurrences, residents have recognized this area of the state for its strange and often sinister character and have, over the years, dubbed it "The Bridgewater Triangle." This Hockomock Swamp region covers an area of approximately 200 square miles and includes the towns of Abington, Freetown, and Rehoboth at the angles of the triangle, and Brockton, Taunton, the Bridgewaters, Raynham, Mansfield, Norton, and Easton within the triangle. Historically, residents of areas such as this one have acknowledged the haunted or bedeviled nature of these places by giving them names such as Devil's Kitchen in Illinois, Devil's Den in New Hampshire, and Diablo Valley in California, as I pointed out in the last chapter.

In recent times, areas of strange unexplained activity—UFO sightings, mysterious disappearances, creature sightings, and a high incidence of accidents, violence, and crime—have been labeled "Triangles." The most famous of these is the "Bermuda Triangle." The term "Triangle" is now a commonly accepted way of describing what researchers of strange phenomena call a "gateway" or "window" area, that is, a location of focused unexplained activity. The Bridgewater Triangle seems to be one of these focal areas.

For thousands of years, the local Indians have recognized the extraordinary character of the Hockomock area. Indian history figures prominently in the lore of Hockomock. The Indians viewed the area as especially sacred and sometimes evil. Several years ago, an expedition of Massachusetts archaeologists discovered an 8,000-year-old Indian burial site on Grassy Island in the Hockomock Swamp. When the graves were opened, the red ochre within the tombs allegedly bubbled and dissolved mysteriously, and every photograph taken of the site failed to develop. During the 1970s, while clearing a path for Interstate 495, workers in Norton discovered arrowheads, stone tools, pottery and other remains of prehistoric Paleo-Indians who may have moved into this area after the glaciers receded more than ten thousand years ago. Archaeologists were not surprised by this significant discovery because this area of Massachusetts has one of the highest densities of prehistoric sites in New England.

The question of exactly who were the first new inhabitants of this area is a matter of local controversy. On a site thirty miles up the Taunton River at the edge of the Hockomock Swamp, there is a mysterious forty-ton sandstone boulder, which has been used by various nationalities as proof that they were the first "pilgrims." Dighton Rock, as it is called, sits on the riverbank directly across from the Grassy Island Indian burial grounds. This rock is covered by a tangled pattern of carvings and hieroglyphics. Various national groups have interpreted these carvings in a manner that supports each group's contention that pilgrims or explorers of their nationality were the first to settle the area. Today, Dighton Rock is the main attraction of Delabarre State Park. It sits in a temperature controlled house, the walls of which are covered with exhibits that support first pilgrim theories of various nationalities including Egyptians, Phoenicians, Vikings, and Portuguese.

Many Portuguese-Americans live in the area, and lately the inscriptions on Dighton Rock have been most cited by adherents of the theory that the first settlers were Portuguese. In Lisbon, there are royal charters indicating that in 1501 Gasper Corte Real embarked for the New World and was followed in 1512 by his brother, Miguel. Neither ever returned. However, among the spidery scrawls on Dighton Rock, there appears to be the date 1511, with the abbreviated name "M - COR" near it. To adherents of the Portuguese pilgrim theory, these signs indicate that Miguel Corte Real arrived in mid-1502 and stayed for nine years. During that time, it is further theorized, the Portuguese and Indians interbred and this intermingling is supposedly the reason why the Indians of this region were remarkably light-skinned. European explorers such as Verrazano and Roger Williams later remarked upon the light skin of these Indians, known as the Wampanoags or "People of the Dawn Light." The present day Portuguese-American residents of the area believe this characteristic was passed on by the crews of Miguel Corte Real, and that he and his crew were the first pilgrims. There is, however, no certainty to this theory. The solid carved and cross-hatched forty tons of Dighton Rock is but one of the many mysteries on the landscape of the Hockomock and the Bridgewater Triangle.

The swampy landscape, full of quicksand, rivers, and murky reed-infested pools, is not the only thing mysterious about the Bridgewater Triangle. The skies of this area also abound with strange appearances and disappearances. From colonial times comes the report of "Yellow Day" when the skies above the area shone all day long with an eerie sulfurous yellow light. In more recent times, many reports of strange lights and noises in the sky above the massive power lines that run through the swamp have been recorded. Every January, "spook lights"—unexplained elusive balls of light—have been seen over the railroad tracks that run beside the Raynham Dog Track and through the swamp. In 1973, in Rehoboth, patrons of Joseph's Restaurant on Park Street believed they were visited by a UFO. The restaurant experienced a short power failure; when the lights came on, two large perfect circles were found imprinted in the dirt behind the restaurant. During the summer of 1978, many UFO sightings occurred throughout the months of July and August. Another major flap occurred during the spring of 1979. One of the most spectacular unidentified flying objects was seen then by Jerry Lopes, a radio newsman at WHDH in Boston. Lopes encountered his UFO on the 23rd of March. He described it as shaped like home plate on a baseball diamond, with a bright red light on its top, a powerful white "headlight" at the point on the bottom, and rows of white and red lights around the edges. Jerry Lopes saw this strange aerial apparition at the junction of Routes 24 and 106 near the center of the Bridgewater Triangle.

Finally, in the skies of the triangle, there have been sightings of large unknown birds. The most dramatic sighting of one of these huge birds took place at 2 a.m. on a late summer's night in 1971. Norton police sergeant Thomas Downy was driving along Winter Street in Mansfield toward his home in Easton. As he approached a place known as "Bird Hill" in Easton at the edge of the swamp, he was suddenly confronted by a tremendous winged creature over six feet tall with a wingspan of eight to twelve feet. As Sergeant Downy drew to a stop at the intersection, the bird flew straight up and, flapping its massive wings, disappeared over the dark trees into the swamp. Downy reported the sighting to the Easton police as soon as he reached home. A patrol car searched the area, but the huge bird was not sighted again. For weeks after, this policeman with the feathery name was teased by his fellow officers who called him "The Birdman." Downy stuck to his story. Of course, he is not alone in sighting these tremendous birds or bird-like creatures.

Again and again, these enormous birds appear in human history and folklore. They figure in the Indian legends of Hockomock and of many other areas throughout the Americas. Known as Thunderbirds in Indian mythology, these creatures were large enough and powerful enough to carry off a man. In recent times, these huge birds have been sighted by people in Texas and throughout the Southwest. They have been reliably reported from the Midwest since 1948. In Lawndale, Illinois, I investigated the 1977 report that one of these huge birds carried a ten-year-old boy for a distance of thirty feet through the air (See Chapter Two). Thunderbirds have also been seen in Northern Pennsylvania, in an area known

as the "Coudersport Triangle." These Thunderbirds are not the only creatures of the Netherland to have appeared in the Hockomock Swamp region. Several other creatures that occur repeatedly in human folklore and
legend have manifested themselves in the Bridgewater Triangle.

The most famous creature to appear in the Bridgewater Triangle is
the notorious Bigfoot. During the 1970s and 1980s, all kinds of sightings of Bigfoot, ranging from almost certain hoaxes to incidents involving eminently responsible witnesses and organized police hunts, have
been reported. In Bridgewater, in 1970, heavily armed state and local
police, along with a pack of hunting dogs, tracked what was reported to
be a huge "bear." Since the creature was not found, police were never
certain what it really was. Although bears have not been seen in the
Bridgewater area for many years, they are certain that whatever the
creature was it was not a hoax. Several very reputable citizens had had a
good look at the huge creature before it lumbered off into the woods,
and large definite tracks were found there. In other parts of the country,
people trying to make sense of the unexplained have often labeled these
large hairy creatures "bears."

Around the same time, in April 1970, there were several other reports
of a large hairy creature walking upright in other places in the Bridgewater vicinity. Farmers reported killed and mutilated pigs and sheep. Another Bridgewater resident complained to the police that a large hairy
creature walking upright was thrashing about in the backyards and woods
of the neighborhood. Police investigated several times. One officer, lying
in wait in his patrol car, reported that, entirely without warning, something picked up the rear of his car. The policeman spun the car around and
when he flashed his searchlight, he saw something that looked like a huge
bipedal "bear" running away between the houses. Then on April 8, police
officers reportedly found tracks after a seven-foot-tall creature was seen.
Nothing was found in further searches.

However, there were several other sightings in the area during 1973-
1974. In Raynham, a night security guard at the Raynham Dog Track reported a series of horrible screams and screeches that frightened him and
upset the dogs. Huge footprints, fifteen to eighteen inches long, were discovered in the snow south of Raynham. I discovered in my interviews
with local authorities that on separate occasions several residents had re-

ported seeing a tall, furry, man-like creature in the Elm Street/Bridge Street area of Raynham, and near the Hockomock Swamp.

In the Hockomock Swamp is Lake Nippenicket (locally called "The Nip"), a few miles northeast of Raynham. During the summer of 1980, several local men in a canoe on the Nip sighted a small, red-haired, chimpanzee-like ape, which reportedly walked upright on the lake's island. They told me in a subsequent interview that they had landed their canoe and searched the island but had found nothing.

In 1977, outside of the triangle area in Agawam, Massachusetts, near Springfield, footprints were discovered in the snow, and again tales of Bigfoot circulated. This time police determined that the incident was almost certainly a hoax. Previous sightings within the Triangle, however, could not be explained as hoaxes. Many area observers and even the police have by now become firm believers in the weird creatures of the Bridgewater Triangle. As one police officer said in 1970, "Nothing surprises us much anymore. Last week, a motorist ran over an eight-foot boa constrictor. We still haven't learned where that came from."

Huge mystery snakes have been sighted before in the Hockomock region. In 1939, Roosevelt-era CCC workers, completing a project on King Phillip's Street at the edge of the swamp, reported seeing a huge snake "as large around and black as a stove-pipe." The snake coiled for a moment, raised its spade-like head and disappeared into the swamp. Local legends claim that a huge snake like this one appears every seven years.

In addition to legendary serpents, great cats—"lions" or "phantom panthers"—have been sighted regularly in places throughout the Bridgewater Triangle. In 1972, in Rehoboth, Mass., a "lion hunt" was organized by local police. Residents of the area had been terrorized by what they said was a large cat or mountain lion. Cattle and sheep in the area had been mysteriously killed, and carcasses were discovered raked with clawmarks. Police took casts of the animal's tracks and used dogs and a helicopter in an attempt to track it down. Nothing was caught. But similar incidents involving phantom cats have occurred in other places throughout the Bridgewater Triangle and across the nation. None of these mysterious felines has yet been captured. In 1993, a series of reports of a "large, light tan cat the size of a Great Dane," labeled "The Mansfield Mystery Cat," issued from the area. Local officials took the sightings very seriously, especially after Fire Chief Edward Sliney had a mystery felid encounter of his own.

Huge black dogs, as well as black panthers, have been reported within the Bridgewater Triangle. Both of these "creature-forms" have a long history in human mythology and folklore. Sir Arthur Conan Doyle's *Hound of the Baskervilles* has its roots in the many legends of the Hounds of Hell and the Irish Pooka, those huge black ghost-like dogs with eyes of fire. In 1976, a huge black "killer dog" was reported in Abington within the Bridgewater Triangle. The "dog" ripped out the throats of two ponies. Local firefighter Phillip Kane, the owner of the ponies, saw the "dog" standing over the bloody carcasses gnawing at their necks. He said that the "dog" eluded extensive police searches and, for a period of several weeks, terrorized the community.

During the three days following the killing of the ponies police received a thousand telephone calls. Schoolchildren were kept in at recess, and many home owners and storekeepers armed themselves with rifles. The last time this "dog" was seen was when police officer Frank Curran sighted it along some railroad tracks. The officer fired a shot but "missed." The "black dog" merely turned away and walked off slowly in the other direction. And perhaps into another dimension.

The coastal areas of Massachusetts are also fecund territory for weird phenomena. The sands of Singing Beach in Manchester keen strangely when walked upon; all attempts to recreate these sounds under laboratory conditions have failed.

Twice during the last century, in 1819 in Nahant and 1817 at Cape Ann, hundreds of North Shore residents reported sighting a forty-foot-long chocolate-brown sea serpent. More recently, in 1964, a sleek unidentifiable creature about the size of a seal was reported to be haunting St. Mary's Cemetery in Quincy. The creature, described as being black with short legs and dragging tail, uttered shrill cries and always appeared near running water.

There have been a host of other random oddities in other towns around the state. On September 7, 1954, in Leicester, frogs and toads fell from the sky and landed on rooftops and gutters throughout Leicester center and on Paxton Avenue. In Pittsfield, during February of 1958, patrons of the Bridge Lunch Restaurant were surprised to see an old-time steam engine with half a dozen coaches go clattering by on the railroad tracks outside. Railroad officials said that steam engines have not operated on that line for many years. On October 22, 1973, a Sudbury woman noticed sparkling fibers gathering on wires and tree branches. When she looked upward, she saw a shiny globular object disappearing in the clear sky to the west. She collected many of the strange fibers which have been found in other places and are known to ufologists as "Angel Hair." She then quickly sealed them in a jar before they evaporated. Scientists at the University of Massachusetts confirmed that the fibers were not spiderweb but could not determine further what this Halloween substance was.

One can devise all sorts of explanations for unusual events. They might be the result of hoax, coincidence, or natural forces that have yet to be understood. Psychic energy, the power of suggestion, and the fertility of imagination may be contributing factors. One might concede that supernatural or extraterrestrial forces are at work.

The public still treats such phenomena with a healthy skepticism. But there are indications that people are beginning to accept that there may be more to our haunted heritage than meets the eye. In 1974, for example, the director of the Barnstable (Massachusetts) Housing Authority allowed a family to move from one public housing unit to another. The reason: the tenants had complained that the rooms were haunted.

Creatures Aplenty...

Nape

CHAPTER 5

A Case Study:
The Dover Demon

People often ask me what happens when I investigate a sighting; how do I hear about it, what steps do I take to verify the status of the witnesses in the community, and several other related questions. All accounts are different, of course, and require a variety of investigative methods, but in essence, Fortean fieldwork is a form of investigative reporting and scientific inquiry. To get an insider's look at one such examination of an outbreak of sightings, I asked Walter Webb, then the Assistant Director of the Hayden Planetarium at Boston's Science Museum, for his kind permission to publish his sterling report on the systematic investigation of the Dover Demon.

Walter Webb, the first researcher to hear about and examine the details of the Barney and Betty Hill UFO abduction case, completed the Dover Demon report in September of 1977. I follow Webb's remarks with some of my own observations, given here, for the first time, almost a quarter of a century after the sightings.

Introduction and Background
In April of 1977 the town of Dover, Massachusetts, provided the setting for one of the most baffling creature episodes ever reported. Generally recorded as the wealthiest town in Massachusetts, Dover (pop. 5000) is a heavily wooded community situated just 15 miles southwest of Boston. During a 25½-hour period on April 21-22, four teenagers claimed to have made three independent sightings of a small gnome-like entity with an enormous head, large round glowing eyes, and long spindly limbs. In all three circumstances the bizarre creature—tagged the "Dover Demon" by investigator Loren Coleman—was allegedly spotted within a two-

mile-long zone along narrow paved roads. The vegetation in this rural-suburban area alternates between wooded land and pasture, and houses generally are spaced several hundred feet apart. No UFO was reported by the witnesses.

On April 28, one week after the sightings, Loren Coleman happened to be at the Dover Country Store when a store employee, Melody Fryer, told him about William Bartlett's sighting and his sketch of the creature. Mrs. Fryer promised to get Coleman the sketch. Two days later the investigator obtained two of Bartlett's drawings. The following day, May 1, Loren interviewed Bartlett, and on the 3rd he questioned John Baxter and

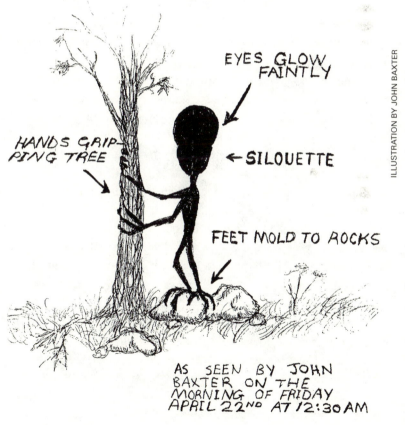

Dover Demon

Abby Brabham (Will Taintor was quizzed about two days after that). Also on the 1st Coleman gave the Dover Police Department a copy of one of Bartlett's sketches in case other witnesses should come forth. On the 4th Loren contacted *The Real Paper* in Cambridge. The newspaper interviewed Coleman as well as Bartlett, Baxter, and Dover Police Chief Carl Sheridan on the 7th.

It was on May 12 that the Framingham radio station WKOX, searching for local news stories, happened to call the Dover police station and thereupon was informed about the creature sightings. WKOX/WCVF-FM aired the story the next day. On the 14th the Associated Press and the *South Middlesex News* (Framingham), having heard the WKOX report, also called Coleman for more information. Finally, the first newspaper accounts appeared— the *South Middlesex News* and *The Real Paper* on the 15th and the *Boston Globe, Boston Herald American, Patriot Ledger* (Quincy), and other New England newspapers on the 16th. Local and national television picked up the story.

I actually was aware of the Dover affair on May 14. My informant, a Needham resident, only made brief mention of it, and I passed it off as a probable hoax. Three days later, however, my administrative assistant (at Boston's Charles Hayden Planetarium) and a visitor (a witness in another UFO case) almost simultaneously brought my attention to the newspaper stories.

Since there appeared to be several observers of the creature and the sightings occurred as close as four (air) miles from my home in neighboring Westwood, I could hardly pass this one up. I visited the Dover police station on the evening of the 17th and obtained the addresses and telephone numbers of Bill Bartlett and Loren Coleman. When I called Loren, he suggested I join him and two other local UFO investigators in sort of a "pool coverage" operation.

The four of us represented five UFO/Fortean organizations, and we happened to be from four different towns surrounding Dover. The team consisted of Coleman, who is consulting editor of INFO (International Fortean Society), an honorary member of SITU (Society for the Investigation of the Unexplained), and co-author of *The Unidentified* (Warner Books, 1975); Joseph Nyman of Medfield (MUFON/APRO); Ed Fogg of Foxboro (New England UFO Study Group); and myself (APRO). Loren proved especially valuable to our joint effort not only because of his initial investigation into the Dover sightings but also because of his knowledge of and rapport with young people. He is a social worker at a school for emotionally disturbed boys.

Together, on May 21, we interrogated witnesses Baxter, Brabham, and Taintor as well as Baxter's mother and Taintor's parents (Bartlett was confined in a hospital with mononucleosis). Afterward Loren led us to the three sites where the "demon" was alleged to have been seen. At these places we took photographs and measurements. On June 11 we finally questioned Bartlett and his parents.

Additional information concerning the youths' reliability was obtained from the police, teachers, and the principal of the school. I concluded my own investigation on August 7, with interviews of Bartlett's two companions (non-witnesses in his car at the time of his sightings) and with a telephone call to one of the teachers.

The Bartlett Sighting

On the evening of April 21, William Bartlett, 17, of Dover, was driving around in his VW with two friends, Mike Mazzocca, 17, and Andy Brodie, 17, of Sherborn. Bill recalled that the sky was clear and stars were visible (confirmed by the National Weather Service at Boston's Logan Airport; temperature was 55°F at the time of the sighting, according to Blue Hill Observatory located ten miles from Dover). Although Bartlett hadn't been drinking, he said he had smoked a little marijuana in Norwood about an hour before his sighting. He emphasized, however, he had only a few puffs and was positive his head was clear during the crucial moments of the encounter.

About 10:30 p.m. (EST) the trio was driving northward at about 40 or 45 miles per hour on Farm Street, approaching Smith Street, when Bill said he spotted what he at first thought was a dog or cat creeping along a low wall of loose stones (the wall was about two feet high) on the left side of the road. (The site is almost opposite the L. B. Taylor mailbox on Farm Street. Immediately next to the wall is a single row of trees, and beyond is an open field.) The figure appeared to place its hands and feet carefully on the stones as if it weren't sure of its path over the wall.

Bathed in the car's high-beams, according to Bartlett, the creature grabbed onto a rock with long fingers, slowly turned its head toward the approaching car, and stared into the light. In the next instant, the witness said he realized it wasn't a dog or cat. The entity possessed an unusually large head shaped like a watermelon and about the same size as its trunk. In the center of the head glowed two large, round, glassy, lidless eyes, shining brightly "like two orange marbles" in the glare of the headlights. No other features were detected on the head; there was no discernible nose, mouth, or ears. The head seemed supported on a thin neck.

The creature's body, according to Bartlett, was thin with long spindly arms and legs and large hands and feet. The shape reminded the witness of a "baby's body with long arms and legs." Its skin was hairless, with something like dirt smudged on it, appeared to be the rough texture of a shark ("like wet sandpaper"), and was a peach color —"an exaggerated skin color, like Fred Flintstone in the Sunday comics" (quote from *The Real Paper* interview). The tint was lighter, almost whitish, near the hands. The entity's size appeared to be about that of a monkey, three and a half to four feet tall. Although no tail was visible, Bartlett admitted one could have been present but hidden behind the figure.

The following two paragraphs quoting Bartlett were taken verbatim from *The Real Paper* interview and best describe what happened next (parenthetical remarks are mine):

"I really flew after I saw it. I took that corner at 45, which is pretty fast. (In several timed re-enactments, the sighting lasted a maximum of five or six seconds. By our actual tape measurement, his vehicle would have passed within about 20 feet of the creature.) I said to my friends, 'Did you see that?' And they said, 'Nah, describe it.' I did and they said, 'Go back. Go back.' And I said, 'No way. No way.' When you see something like that, you don't want to stand around and see what it's going to do. (Continuing nearly a mile beyond the site, Bill turned left on Glen Street and then turned around.)

"They finally got me to go back, and Mike was leaning out of the window yelling, 'Come on, creature!' And I was saying 'Will you cut that out?' (He said he was still shaking at this point.) Andy was yelling, 'I want to see you!' I was trying to get them to shut the windows." (The entity was gone.)

I questioned both Mike and Andy separately. I asked them why neither saw the alleged creature. Mike, who was sitting in the front seat beside Bill, said he was looking at his own side of the road. Andy, on the other hand, was in back and said he wasn't sure but thought he was talking to Mike at the time. Mike said Bill was "pretty scared" after seeing the creature and didn't want to go back. Andy agreed that Bill "sounded genuinely frightened." At first the two youths didn't believe their friend's description of a big-headed creature with large glowing eyes, long fingers grabbing the rocks, etc. But Bartlett's fright was convincing, and both Mazzocca and Brodie soon accepted the witness's story. They urged Bill to make a drawing of the creature when he got home so they could see what it looked like.

As soon as he returned home, Bill said he took out his sketchpad and drew the figure as he recalled it. (Quote from *The Real Paper:* "I draw a lot. I train myself to remember what I see as soon as I see it.") He is an excellent amateur artist and showed us some of his work; he is a member of Boston's Copley Art Society. Mr. Bartlett told us his son was upset when he came home and described to his father what he had seen. Both Mr. and Mrs. Bartlett are convinced Bill saw "something," that he is "very honest and open," and not the kind to play pranks or make up stories. He is not a drama student nor is he a science-fiction buff.

The Baxter Sighting

The second encounter reportedly occurred about two hours later (April 22) 1.2 (air) miles northeast of the Bartlett location. Around midnight John Baxter, 15, of Dover, left his girlfriend's house (Cathy Cronin) at the south end of Millers Hill Road and proceeded to walk north toward the end of the street where he hoped to hitch a ride home.

After a half hour, he had walked nearly a mile (.95 mile by our speedometer) up the left side of Millers Hill Road when he said about 50 yards away (100 feet by our measurement) he glimpsed the silhouette of someone approaching him on his side of the road (paved).

As he got closer, John said he could see that the figure was very small and thought it might be a kid he knew who lived on the street, M. G. Bouchard. He called out, "M.G., is that you?" There was no response. Both the witness and the shadowy figure continued to walk toward each other.

When they were about 15 feet apart (about 25 feet by our measurement), the figure stopped. Baxter also halted. The witness said he again called out, "Who is that?" It was very dark, and he could barely see the figure. (Logan Airport reported scattered clouds at 25,000 feet at midnight becoming overcast by 1 a.m. The temperature remained at 55°F at Blue Hill.)

As John took another step toward the figure, suddenly it scurried very rapidly to the left down a shallow wooded gully, across a low wet spot, and up the opposite bank. The witness said he could hear the creature's footfalls on the dry leaves as it ran.

Baxter scrambled down the slope after the creature for about six to eight feet and then stopped. Across the gully he could see the being (about 30 feet away by our tape) standing with both feet "molded" around the top of a rock a few feet from a tree. It was leaning toward the tree, the long fingers of both hands gripping the trunk for support (the tree's diameter was about eight inches). The digits of the feet, according to Baxter, could be seen in the dark curled around the rock because of the rock's lighter color. He was unsure of the exact number of digits on each hand and foot.

The figure was now clearly outlined against an open field providing the witness with his best view. The dark silhouette resembled that of a monkey except for a large "figure-eight" head. The creature's eyes showed up as two lighter spots in the middle of the head and peered straight ahead at the observer.

After staring at the entity for what seemed like a few minutes, Baxter said he began to feel uneasy about the situation he was in. He said he didn't quite know what sort of creature or animal confronted him, and it looked as if it might be ready to spring. At this point the witness said he backed up the slope, his heart pounding, and "walked very fast" down the road (another .15 mile or 800 feet) to the intersection at Farm Street. There he was picked up by a Dedham couple who dropped him off at his home (about 1 a.m.). He estimated observing the figure less than ten minutes (probably considerably less).

John said as soon as he got home, he drew a sketch of the creature (as Bill had done) allegedly before he knew of Bartlett's own sighting. Although *The Real Paper* implied that John's mother doubted the creature existed, she told us her son "never made up stories" and she believed "he saw something." We were unable to talk to Mr. Baxter, who was recovering from a brain-clot operation. *The Real Paper* stated that Mr. Baxter didn't believe his son made up the story.

However, he was also quoted as saying: "The only thing that bothers me a bit is that he's an avid science-fiction fan." John readily admitted his sci-fi interest which includes writing his own stories. But he denied this had anything to do with his sighting report.

When we visited Baxter's claimed encounter site, we spoke to the owner of the nearest property, Alice W. Stewart. She was aware of the Dover Demon stories. We asked her if she had noticed or heard anything at all peculiar near her house that night. She replied she hadn't. Her dogs were inside the house at the time.

The Brabham-Taintor Sighting

Bartlett said he was unaware of Baxter's confrontation with the demon until five days later (April 26). At that time John, who had heard about Bill's sighting, showed Bill his own sketch of the entity. Bartlett said he was "amazed" because it was the same creature he had seen. Although Bill didn't see John until the 26th, on the 22nd he did tell his close friend, Will Taintor, 18, of Dover, about his strange experience.

That night, about midnight on the 22nd (almost 24 hours after the Baxter sighting), Will was driving Abby Brabham, 15, to her home in Sherborn. They were about a quarter mile out of Dover center on Springdale Avenue when Abby said she saw something in the headlights in the left lane of the road. (The site is atop a culvert crossing the east branch of Trout Brook 1.2 miles east-northeast of Baxter's location and 2.3 miles northeast of Bartlett's.) A creature of some kind was crouched on all fours facing the car and looked like a monkey or small ape, with several important exceptions: its head was very large and oblong; the body appeared hairless and tan or beige in color; and there was no nose, mouth, ears, or tail. The facial area appeared somewhat lighter around the eyes, which were round and glowed bright green in the headlights. (Abby was questioned closely about the eye color, and she felt positive about the green hue.)

Taintor's car was traveling about 40 miles per hour, and by the time he said he noticed the creature in the road, he managed to catch only a fleeting glimpse (for perhaps a few seconds). He recalled having the impression of something with a large head and tan body crouched in the road, with its front legs raised in the air. He was certain it wasn't a dog. Will thought it might have been as large as a goat, and Abby guessed it was the size of a German shepherd. Apparently neither witness noticed hands or feet.

As the vehicle drove past the creature (perhaps as close as eight feet away by our measurement), Abby asked Will to speed up and get out of there. Although she thought she had viewed the creature for as long as 30 to 45 seconds, a timed re-enactment placed the length of Abby's observation at only about five seconds.

As they drove on, Will said he suddenly remembered the Bartlett sighting and only then did he begin to question Abby more closely about specific details, features he was aware of from his conversation with Bill (Will's own sighting proved brief and unspectacular). Taintor said he deliberately asked Abby leading questions about the creature's appearance—about details he knew were not true—in order to check her story and description against Bartlett's. According to Will, he divulged nothing to Abby about Bartlett's sighting until after theirs had occurred. Abby agreed she hadn't known about the other sighting reports.

Cloud conditions during the third sighting, according to Logan Airport, were overcast at 20,000 feet, with broken clouds at 7,000 feet. The temperature at Blue Hill Observatory was 65°F.

When we interviewed Will and Abby, Will's parents were present. Like the parents of the previous boys, Will's parents believed their son and Abby were telling the truth and they saw something real. Mr. Taintor tended to think a conventional animal of some kind was mistaken for the demon, while Mrs. Taintor speculated an unknown creature might be involved.

Evaluation

After hearing the four teenagers tell their stories, the four of us who conducted the investigation agreed unanimously about the witnesses: we were impressed by them, especially Bill Bartlett and Abby Brabham. Bartlett, who claimed the first sighting and who became the central figure in the case due chiefly to his widely publicized sketch, was overwhelmingly endorsed by townspeople. The following represent typical responses:

Dover Police Chief Carl Sheridan described Bartlett as an "outstanding artist and a reliable witness."

Science teacher Robert Linton, one of the first adults to talk to

Bartlett outside Bill's parents, said the youth "seemed extremely sincere and I had to believe him."

Mike Mazzocca and Andy Brodie, Bill's two companions during the sighting, agreed their friend was "pretty scared" (Mike) and "sounded genuinely frightened" (Andy) after seeing the creature. Although they themselves didn't glimpse the demon, they became convinced Bill's account was true.

Mr. Bartlett testified his son was upset when he arrived home. After hearing Bill's story, he said he believed Bill saw "something," an animal of some kind. Bill's parents assured us their son was "very honest and open" and not the type to make up stories. As also pointed out before, he was not a sci-fi fan nor a drama student.

Loren and I questioned Bill's science teacher on separate occasions. Robert Linton, 35, has taught at Dover-Sherborn for seven years and is greatly liked and respected by the students. On April 25—four days after Bartlett's encounter and also the first day back to school following spring vacation—the teacher said he overheard Bill discussing his sighting with students as they entered the classroom. He asked Bill about it, whereupon the youth described his experience and drew a picture of the creature. Linton told us Bartlett was convinced he saw the creature, that it "scared the hell out of him," and that the others later saw the same thing, too. The instructor asked his student if he had anything to smoke or drink beforehand. Bill replied, as he had to us, that he puffed a little marijuana that evening but felt he was "straight" during the sighting. Linton accepted Bartlett's story.

In the midst of all of the endorsements for Bill Bartlett's reliability, we came across only one curiously negative opinion. It was expressed by one of Bill's teachers who desired that his name not be divulged. Joe Nyman received the name through another teacher. When Joe telephoned the anonymous instructor (his name is on file), this individual implied that Bartlett was a troubled frustrated kid with very low credibility, that he cut classes, hung around the students' smoking lounge with John Baxter, and belonged to a clique that included Baxter. The teacher summed up his low opinion of the witness by stating: "If I had to pick someone to pull something like this, it would be Bartlett."

Loren confronted Bill with these charges, saying they came from a "source" at school. The youth denied the accusations. He said the smoking lounge happens to be a central meeting place for students whether they smoke or not (both Bartlett and his parents said Bill doesn't smoke cigarettes although he does puff pot out of school occasionally). He said Baxter is only one of his friends, and he was detained only once this year for cutting a class.

Loren went back to the teacher with Bartlett's denials, but he refused to change his opinion and stuck to his remarks. Because this individual is the only person we uncovered who held an unfavorable view of this witness, and since it was such a total contrast to the opinions of others, we believe the teacher's motives may be suspect. Our reasons for thinking this have to do with things that can't be revealed without giving away the instructor's identity. In addition, he was the only person who refused to allow his name to be published. Of all the witnesses, we were most impressed by Bill Bartlett—as a healthy well-adjusted teenager, as a careful observer, and as an excellent artist.

Regarding John Baxter, Loren Coleman felt some uneasiness about his testimony during Loren's May 3 interview. The investigator thought John might have been a bit defensive owing to some initial resistance he may have received to his story. However, we all agreed he appeared much more relaxed during our interview on May 21. Baxter's mother told us John "never made up stories," and she believed "he saw something." Although Mr. Baxter apparently agreed, it will be recalled he told *The Real Paper:* "The only thing that bothers me a bit is that he's an avid science-fiction fan." John admitted writing sci-fi stories for fun but rejected the notion that this played a role in his sighting claim. While we all agreed Baxter's account of his experience had the ring of truth as we listened, to what extent his sci-fi interest might have influenced his sighting, or his account of it, is a troublesome feature that can't be completely ignored.

In the case of Abby Brabham and Will Taintor's assertions that they also witnessed the Dover Demon, Abby's story proved quite convincing to us, especially when she declared adamantly: "I know I saw the creature and don't care what happens!" It will be recalled that Will was already aware of the Bartlett sighting and yet failed to "capitalize" on it by embellishing his own observation. In fact, his own description was meager compared to Abby's because he caught only a fleeting glimpse of the creature.

This lends credibility to Will's account. At the time Abby claimed she didn't know about the earlier sightings until Will mentioned Bartlett's *after* their own encounter.

Other comments from Dover residents concerning the witnesses in general:

High school principal Richard Wakely told Loren: "I don't think these kids got together and invented it." Were they troublemakers? "No. They're average students."

Michael Dowd of the Dover Country Store: "I'm a sucker for anything. But the kids trust me and they're really upstanding kids. I don't think they're making this up" (Dover-Sherborn *Suburban Press*).

An unidentified officer at the Dover Police Department: "At first I was going to ask one of the witnesses to give me whatever it was he was smoking, but I know all four, and I know that, to all of us, they're very reputable people" *(South Middlesex News)*.

What arguments, if any, support the hoax hypothesis? A skeptic might draw up the following scenario: all four youths were either close friends, acquaintances, or knew of one another at school. The teenagers seemed to agree there is little for kids to do in Dover, especially during spring vacation when the alleged sightings occurred. Perhaps inspired by a science-fiction film or by Tolkien's little goggle-eyed creature known as Gollum (suggested in a letter to the *Boston Globe*) or even by a creature in one of Baxter's own fictional yarns, Bartlett might have got the others to go along with a little prank, aided by sketches from Bartlett and Baxter, to "liven things up" around town. Alternatively, perhaps they themselves were the victims of a hoax perpetrated by other equally bored youths. In any case, there can be no denying the youths received a lot of attention, both locally and nationally in the press, as a result of this incident.

Loren Coleman reported Bill and John became quite popular at school, and Bill enjoyed recognition as an artist by having his sketch published in the newspapers. Abby and Will were invited to appear on Television Channel 44's "Club 44," where they described their encounter. However, equally logical counter arguments balance or even outweigh the hoax scenario. Perhaps first and foremost, Bill Bartlett's emotional upset during and immediately following his sighting was attested to by both the two companions and his father. His fright appeared genuine, not staged.

While John Baxter's sci-fi interest tends to complicate his sighting claim, both Bill and Abby appeared quite convincing in our presence. Loren was the first investigator to interview all four witnesses when their stories were still rather fresh and before the media coverage. He was especially impressed at that time by Bill and his testimony (Loren's insight as a social worker proved extremely helpful in this regard).

None of the four was on drugs or drinking at the time of his or her sighting so far as we were able to determine. As students at the same high school, it would be surprising if the witnesses were not at least aware of each other. None of the principals in this affair made any attempt to go to the newspapers or police to publicize their claims. Instead, the sightings gradually leaked out. Finally the teenagers' own parents, the high-school principal, the science instructor, and other adults in Dover whose comments were solicited didn't believe the Dover Demon was a fabrication, implying the youths did indeed see "something." (The sole doubter we encountered was the teacher whose damning remarks were somewhat suspect.)

As for the idea that the witnesses were victims of somebody else's stunt, this seems most unlikely, chiefly due to the virtual impossibility of creating an animated, life-like "demon" of the sort described. If these young people saw "something," what sort of creature did they see?

Theories have ranged all the way from an escaped monkey to an unknown animal or extraterrestrial visitor. Mr. Bartlett's belief was that although the creature could have represented something supernatural or extraterrestrial, he was certain it had a "more plausible explanation," such as an escaped laboratory animal of some sort. Mrs. Bartlett told us her neighbor suggested a sick fox because there is a disease that makes a fox swell up grotesquely and lose all of its hair. Joe Nyman asked a veterinarian about this and discovered in such cases where the hair falls out and the body swells, the skin of the fox becomes *dark* (the Dover creature possessed a light color). However, the greatest objection to the sick fox-escaped monkey/lab animal hypothesis is the simple fact the demon bore absolutely no resemblance to any of these animals (sick or healthy). All of the witnesses agreed their creature was hairless *and* lacked a nose, mouth, ears, and tail. Besides, if the animal were someone's escaped monkey or lab animal, it seems strange that no one came forth to identify it.

Interestingly, all four witnesses thought the most likely explanation for what they saw was that the creature must have been an unknown terrestrial animal that, until now, managed to escape detection in Dover's dense woods. Bill and Abby believed it must be a water creature of some kind since it was seen not far from water in all three instances. John said it wasn't like any creature he'd ever seen. He thought an unknown earth creature "seems a little more realistic" than the notion it might have come from space. He considered, then rejected, the idea that a "very misshapen monkey" could have been the source of the sightings. It seems very unlikely to this investigator that any unidentified earthly creature the size of the Dover Demon could dwell so near large population areas and remain hidden from the eyes of science until now—and then be glimpsed three times in one 25.5-hour period, only to disappear back into oblivion. However, the fact that all the observers preferred an earthly explanation to an extraterrestrial one provides further credibility for their reports.

Loren was the first to note some resemblance between the Dover entity and the famous Kelly, Kentucky, "little men" incident of 1955 (the subject of Chapter 19). Yet major differences abound, not the least of which were the Kentucky creatures' large floppy ears. Like the Dover Demon, the Kelly being has never been reported before or since. I asked Ted Bloecher, co-chairman of MUFON's Humanoid Study Group, if he recalled anything in his humanoid file that matched the description of the Dover Demon. He replied in the negative. The Dover occurrence is a Type E event in the Bloecher classification system, that is, "no known association between entity and UFO." Using Ted's witness credibility scale (0-9), I assign a 4-5 rating to the Dover Demon case.

In some respects, the Dover entity resembles some of the gnome-like critters of fairy folklore. For example, the Cree Indians of eastern Canada have a legend about the Mannegishi, who are supposed to be "little people with round heads and no noses who live with only one purpose: to play jokes on travelers. The little creatures have long spidery legs, arms with six-fingered hands, and live between rocks in the rapids . . ." (Sigurd Olson, *Listening Point,* Knopf, 1958)

The Dover Demon is a disturbing, bizarre affair. There are many frustrating, troublesome aspects about it. Like the Kelly encounter, it is without apparent precedent. But despite the doubts and questions this episode raises, I believe a hoax is unlikely and the report should be classified as a low-weight unknown.

Thus ends Webb's report. Since 1977, a few have wondered about the Dover Demon, and one or two people have called it an outright hoax. This seems hardly the case. Walt Webb's report stands the test of time, and I still today, in 2000, agree with his conclusions. As to their credibility, here is my professional (investigative and psychiatric) reading of the best witnesses.

Bartlett remains a pillar of society today, as he was then. I accept the reality of Barlett's first sighting as an actual, unknown encounter of some type. I do not feel it was ufologically related or something "paranormal." It seems like a real, biological event, but I am not certain of the source or animal involved. Bartlett got caught up in the media hype produced by the sightings, but is that a surprise to anyone?

Baxter encountered something too. However, Baxter was developmentally younger than Bartlett, and may have been influenced in the weeks following the initial sightings by the media. His presentation of self appeared youthful to some but not as if he was overtly lying. He seemed very anxious when discussing the matter with Nyman, Webb, and the media. If anyone slightly elaborated later their version of events to "perform for the media," it may have been Baxter. This may have soured later reporters on Baxter, but must be separated from the initial interviews. Baxter, to me, seemed sincere but not as convincing as all of the other witnesses. I think Baxter picked up on this skeptical attitude from the investigators, and almost became more dramatic in his retelling, as he really wanted to convince folks he wasn't lying. This may have reflected a less-than-happy home situation. Rumors circulated in later years that Baxter did not take well to the whole public exposé, got in minor trouble (a rumor was mentioned that he threw a brick through a window), and really didn't deal with his uninvited "fame" as well as the calm, good-boy-next-door Bartlett had.

Brabham was a very good witness. As the only female, she was not interested in being put into some kind of "witness club" with the boys. Whereas Baxter and Bartlett were always linked by reporters, sometimes interviewed together, Brabham was not interviewed as much but came across very well to the investigators. She would not change any details of her story to please anyone, even though the green eyes of her creature were so different than the reportedly bright orange eyes seen by Bartlett. At the time, we all were very struck by the sincere nature of her sighting.

Taintor was a good confirming witness of "something in the road" to Brabham's encounter. I doubted his account of the timing of the event, his mentions of the "together talks" of the witnesses, and the fact he saw anything too clearly on the road, at the time, and do now.

A few other points: Smoking a joint an hour before the incident was known and not considered significant. Hallucinations are not generally associated with marijuana; Bartlett reported he did not have hallucinations; and I doubt the Dover Demon was a hallucination. I am skeptical it was a newborn horse, a school prank, or a homeless person, all theories I have heard and looked into regarding the Dover Demon.

Bartlett's later reports of "in-sync feelings with animals" have little or no influence on my sense of the reality of his 1977 sighting. In the 1970s, before the New Age era really got underway, people were experimenting with thoughts on all kinds of things. They have little bearing on the Dover Demon sighting. Bartlett was in the horrible position of trying to make sense of what he had seen, and he and the others often said some pretty silly things in retrospect. These witnesses were interviewed nonstop by four investigators, the police, their parents, school officials, their friends, several reporters, several TV stations, and others, during an intensive four-week period. They began to think that they should "know" why these sightings happened, and often felt forced to answer questions as if they had all the answers. Of course, they didn't, but the investigators and reporters kept asking until they sometimes became frustrated and developed theories and statements that had absolutely no bearing on the facts of the sightings. Such is the life of a witness. But people still come up with interesting theories to try to debunk the case.

Not a Demon Moose

At the time of the incident, we, the investigators, did not have any frame of reference for what this creature might have been. As an easy moniker, I, Loren Coleman (not the newspapers as has been recorded by some), dubbed the thing the "Dover Demon." While Japanese toymakers and

Fortean authors have celebrated the story down through the years, the "Dover Demon" has resurfaced repeatedly in different contexts. In *Passing Strange: True Tales of New England Hauntings and Horrors* (Boston: Houghton Mifflin, 1996), Joseph A. Citro, for example, finds the Dover Demon one of the most intriguing cases he has ever run across, and tries to put it in the context of ghost stories. In the recent book by Janet Bord, *Fairies: Real Encounters with Little People* (Michael O'Mara Books, 1997), she places the creature in the context of the fairies and little folk she chronicles.

Then late in the 1990s, there appeared a new attempt to discredit various elements of the case by Illinois farmer and ufologist Martin S. Kottmeyer. In 1998, he wrote an article called "Demon Moose" for the Fortean journal *The Anomalist* (Issue 6:104-10), which attempted to explain away the Dover Demon as a mere moose. While I believe Kottmeyer is in error, he at least returned to the original sources for his critique, and does attempt to find an animal-based answer to the mystery, rather than seeking a UFO or fairy connection.

Kottmeyer suggests that the Dover witnesses were seriously mistaken about what they saw, and using two general animal encyclopedias and a good field guide for his sources, he concludes that the Dover Demon may have been a young moose. He points out that the sightings lasted only seconds, except for Baxter's, and that all of them occurred in darkness. He notes: "Bartlett's placing of the eyes matches the placement of eyes just above the hip of the muzzle on a moose's head. The lack of a discernible nose and mouth is easily laid to the fact that nostrils and mouth are very far down on the muzzle. A drawing of a young moose presents the ears swept back along the line of the head and would not discernibly stick out, thus accounting for the absence of visible ears." The drawing in *The Anomalist* was clever, but it does not show how a yearling moose would look in April.

Saying that the Dover Demon is nothing more than a moose *(Alces alces)* is unfortunate. Kottmeyer's faulty conclusion could be ignored if his debunking was not already becoming the last pivotal point from which writers now construct their new Dover Demon insights. For example, Jerome Clark in his second edition of *Unexplained!* (Visible Ink, 1999) has redone the Dover Demon entry to include this fashionably skeptical approach. Clark writes: "Because nothing like the Dover demon has been reported since, Kottmeyer's theory that the incident grew out of a misperception—though not perfect—is hard to discount."

But Kottmeyer is just dead wrong on this one. A skinny, four-foot-tall, upright (coming down on all fours sometimes), sandpaper-skinned, five-huge-fingered, bright orange "baby moose" would be more of a wonder than the Dover Demon itself, I'm afraid. When Walt Webb and I were on-site investigating the Dover Demon, we checked out numerous "baby animal" theories. At the time, one of the favorites was that the Dover Demon was a newborn baby horse (foal). On the surface of it, a newborn foal would be much more available than a young moose. There are more horses in Dover than people, a well-known local fact that caused our investigating team some pause. But the police, the witnesses, and the investigators found absolutely no evidence of animal remains, tracks, afterbirth, or missing newborn foals at the sighting locations or anyplace around Dover, Needham, or Newton.

Midwestern farmer Martin Kottmeyer may know cows, but his moose zoology and ecology is simply off-base. Kottmeyer writes that the Dover Demon "faintly reminded me of a moose. The small size and absence of horns would mean it had to be quite young, perhaps a yearling recently weaned in advance of the mother giving an April birth." First of all, moose have antlers, not horns, as cattle do. Secondly, mothers chase away their large yearling moose only two weeks before giving birth, if at all. Thirdly, the sightings took place the third week in April, in rural, highly populated eastern Massachusetts and new moose are born at the end of May or early in June. And finally, Kottmeyer overlooks the fact that moose are not creatures of the night. Moose are active at dawn, dusk, and somewhat during the middle of the day, but not at ten or near midnight. They are diurnal not nocturnal animals. The Dover Demon exhibited very active nocturnal behavior two nights in a row.

Kottmeyer is also incorrect about the small size of a year-old moose. They are relatively huge—much taller and bulkier than the little Volkswagen that Bartlett was driving that night—and not this small, thin animal seen on the 21st and 22nd of April 1977. Having lived in Maine for almost two decades now, I have seen over 50 moose, including a family group of 17 at one time. They are not small animals, even the young. A bull moose can weigh up to 1,600 pounds. A newborn moose weighs 30 pounds when first born, and grows to weigh 300 pounds or more within five months. By the time they are a year old, they can be more than 650 pounds—and physically, quite tall. I know moose, and this was no yearling moose.

Moose are very, very rare in Massachusetts, and those that do appear are not mothers with young moose but usually juvenile males that are interlopers. I've been forwarded the records of all moose dealt with in the state of Massachusetts in 1976-1977. Moose are seen infrequently, and to restate this point, most "travelers" are almost full-height juvenile males, two years old and older. Here's what I received from the wildlife agency of Massachusetts: "We had one moose killed in Holden, Mass. on 9/30/76 as a public safety measure, likely it was in or along a road. We had one moose moved on 9/29/77 from the city of Worcester and relocated. These were the only moose records for those years you specified." These cases took place in western and central Massachusetts, and please note—in September. September is the rutting season, and juvenile males routinely move around, over vast areas, from Vermont, New Hampshire, and Maine, but rarely into Massachusetts. The moose population has exploded in the last 20 years, and was not as much on the move as they are today. A mother moose and her calf would have been a major media event in eastern Massachusetts in April, and there were no such events in 1977.

Kottmeyer's "Demon Moose" article falls short on other points as well. He completely ignores and never addresses the bipedal sighting of the Dover Demon. The Dover Demon did more than lean against a tree. It was standing on two legs, ran down to a gully, and then propped itself toward and on the tree with its right arm. This is very un-moose-like behavior.

I also found Kottmeyer's explanation of the long and thin digits of the Dover Demon as vines stuck in the moose's hooves more wishful thinking than scientific conjecture. And his comments about the young moose's ears being pressed back against the head and that it may have been coming out of water, all to explain the "look" of the Dover Demon head, flies in the face of typical moose looks and behavior. Moose generally have their ears out to survey the sounds in their environment, especially when coming out of water. The ears are held back when they are physically confronted in close quarters, and are angry, usually at another moose with whom they are competing for a mate (in September) or when threatening their newborn calf (from May through August).

So overall, the size difference, the middle of the night appearance, the location in Massachusetts, and the dates of the sightings all argue against this being a yearling or newborn moose. Biologically, zoologically, forensically, the evidence for the Dover Demon being a moose is just not there.

Personally, because the Dover Demon is such a strange case, I have entertained and explored my own doubts about the sightings. Down through the years, I have asked myself many difficult questions about what was behind the sightings. Was it a schoolboy prank inspired by drawings of the stonewall creeping Gollum from J. R. R. Tolkien's *The Hobbit* (first published in 1937)? Could it have been a newborn horse foal, a hoax, or a wet dog? Today, I continue to reject all of those, based on what we know and discovered during our onsite 1977 investigations. And, so too, despite Martin Kottmeyer's creative idea, the Dover Demon certainly does not match the biology of a young moose. Nor does it fit the known patterns of ghosts, fairies, or ufonauts. The Dover Demon is a true enigma, an animate anomaly that intersected the lives of four credible young people that lonely week in April, 1977.

During June 2000, Mark A. Hall added a new twist on the theories swirling around the Dover Demon by suggesting that the creature might be a member of the long-neglected Merbeings. In Hall's "A Primer on Mermaids" (*Wonders,* Volume 6, No. 2), he writes: "An example of a pygmy mer-being is the so-called 'Dover Demon,' which was seen in Massachusetts along the Charles River in 1977. It has similarities and some differences with the gray mer-being reported elsewhere....There are traditions of such small water-dwelling creatures known to the American Indians across North America."

And so, perhaps, a new chapter in the Dover Demon saga is yet to be written.

CHAPTER 6

Teleporting Animals and *Magnolia*

The look to me is that, throughout what is loosely called Nature, teleportation exists, as a means of distribution of things and materials...

We shall pick up an existence by its frogs.

Charles Fort in *Lo!*

Charles Fort invented, coined, and used the word "teleportation." Today, we take the word for granted, as a transportation process found in science-fiction novels and movies. Within Fortean studies, Ivan T. Sanderson and others have discussed "out-of-place" (OOP) animals in their works, for example, discussing the movement of giant leaf-eating queen ants from one nest to another. Others have casually mentioned teleportation as the means by which various biological specimens pop up in one place or another. Fort talked of falls of toads, frogs, and fish. Teleportation, Fort felt, was real. Today, we are closer to seeing he may be right.

In 1998, via an apparatus at California Institute of Technology, physicists at Caltech, Aarhus University in Denmark and the University of Wales accomplished the actual teleportation of a beam of light, creating a replica some distance away. Quantum teleportation is now known today to be a reality. "We claim this is the first bona fide teleportation," says Caltech physics professor Jeff Kimble, one of the researchers. The October 23, 1998, issue of the journal *Science* reported the advance could help with sophisticated cryptography and possibly ultra-powerful "quantum computers." In December, 1997, two research groups, one in Austria and one in Rome, reported successful teleportation experiments. The earlier experiments, however, were limited to teleporting information about whether a photon was polarized in the up or down position. Kimble's group extended the theory and technique to work more broadly. It was the first to verify that what goes into the transporter is the same thing that comes out of it.

According to an ABC News report, the experiment took advantage of one spooky aspect of quantum mechanics to circumvent one of its constraints. The constraint is the Heisenberg Uncertainty Principle, which states one cannot precisely measure where something is and how fast it is moving, at least not at the same time. In essence, if you look too closely, you inevitably bump the object you are looking at, and it is no longer where you thought it was. That would appear to be a problem if you're trying to teleport something. If you cannot precisely measure a photon or an atom (or a frog), how can you tell someone else how to make an exact copy? Surprisingly, the way to get around the Heisenberg Uncertainty Principle is to mess up the information so badly that it is meaningless. Did someone say chaos?

The magic comes from the fact that under certain, carefully constructed circumstances, two particles or beams of light become "entangled"—perturbations to one instantly affect the other, even if they are separated far apart. Albert Einstein once described entanglement as "spooky action at a distance."

Now teleportation becomes simple. The sender—who physicists insist on always naming "Alice"—takes the original item to be transported and combines it with her special "entangled" encoder, producing what looks like gibberish. Since it's gibberish to her, she has not disturbed the item's underlying quantum mechanical state.

Alice then sends her gibberish to the recipient—who is always named "Bob"—and he combines that gibberish with his "entangled" decoder. Bob puts them back together, and out pops this same quantum state. Teleportation is thus complete.

In principle, teleportation could be used to send information to create replicas of objects, not just light beams. Researchers are already looking to teleport atoms. Forteans merely have to look at old records. I would guess that Charles Fort might wonder what all the fuss is about: Hasn't "something" already experimented with teleportation? Doesn't the "damned data" reflect these "experimentations" on a broader scale?

Frogs Do Fall

The theater of life is dark. Finally, we hear the uncredited voice of anomalist and actor Ricky Jay, telling a story of strange circumstance, even before we see the first flicking images: "In the *New York Herald,* Nov. 26, 1911, there is an account of the hanging of three men, for the murder of Sir Edmund Berry Godfrey, on Greenberry Hill, London. The names of the murderers were Green, Berry, and Hill. It does seem that this was only a matter of chance. Still, it may have been no coincidence, but a savage pun mixed with murder."

The passage may be slightly different, but this quotation from Charles Fort's *Wild Talents* (Chapter 2) serves as the beginning of *Magnolia,* director Paul Thomas Anderson's newest film. This former documentary filmmaker has created the world's first Fortean fictional documentary—a cinema few understand on that level, except for those that are attuned to the fact "these things do happen."

While "critically acclaimed," nevertheless, quite a few movie critics were confused by *Magnolia*'s storyline of nine Los Angeles characters whose lives intertwine. The reviewers love the acting, can believe those stories, the coincidence of overlapping relationships, but several have been confused by the finale's explosion from the sky.

For example, here's what some reviewers wrote in January 2000:

"The film is defined into three acts, separated by weather reports that lead to perhaps the oddest precipitation sequence ever filmed." (George Zabolski, *Oklahoma Daily*)

"Just when it seems that no more tears can be shed and no more problems can possibly unravel, Anderson throws in a shocking ending that literally comes out of nowhere." (Kirsten Orsini-Meinhard, *Mustang Daily*)

"The final hour of *Magnolia* tops off the insanity with a 10-minute downpour. (Hint: it's not water falling from the sky.) This scene does successfully manage to shock the audience, but possibly only because it makes no sense whatsoever." (David Yen, *Guardian*)

No sense to whom? *Magnolia* has many Fortean clues peppered throughout the film, foreshadowing the now well-known downpour of frogs. One occurs when a member of the game show audience holds up a sign that says "Exodus 8:2." The passage, not shown, reads: "If you refuse to let them go, I will plague your whole country with frogs." The placard is confiscated quickly by one of the floor managers. I count at least three characters that talk about the movie's earlier afternoon shower as a time when it is "raining cats and dogs." Other subtle indicators are there. The Masonic symbols placed in the background of scenes, the script full of twenty-threes and fives, the Masonic ring coyly shown being worn by the Ricky Jay character as he comforts the Philip Baker Hall game show host.

When Paul Thomas Anderson was interviewed by National Public Radio's Terry Gross, Gross just could not believe that frogs really fall from the sky, and thought Anderson was pulling her leg. The director calmly remarked that Charles Fort documented such cases, and commented that veteran character actor Philip Baker Hall told of how he was in a shower of frogs in Italy.

You do not have to wait to the end of the film to see the "thank you" addressed to the lower-cased "charles fort." Or watch the slow pan over the child prodigy's books—which include Charles Fort's *Wild Talents,* Ricky Jay's *Learned Pigs and Fireproof Women,* a William Corliss book, a Ripley's *Believe It or Not* book, and *The History of Freemasonry*—to know you are watching a special film.

Few films have gone where *Magnolia* takes its audience. Even though the Fortean significance of Peter Weir's *The Last Wave* (1977) has been mentioned in *Fortean Times* twice, its fall of frogs is unnoted in both of those discussions, although its ice fall, black rain, and other Fortean phenomena are. But in reality, frogs do fall from the sky. (And by the way, one of the shortcomings of the "waterspout" debunking that these reports so routinely receive is the simple fact that only one species of frog, toad, or fish usually rains down at a time. Why would not the twisters dump all matter of algae, water weeds, fish, and amphibians from the heavens?) Fort's books are filled with records of these incidents. Fort discovered 80 documented instances of frogs falling from the skies (Damon Knight, *Prophet of the Unexplained,* 1970, page 173). And they continued doing so after Fort died. Frogs fell out of the skies of my hometown of Decatur, Illinois, in 1937 (*Fortean Society Magazine,* Number 3). On September 23,

1973, tens of thousands of toads fell on Brignoles, France (Jerome Clark, *Unexplained!,* 1999, page 101).

These things do happen. As *Magnolia* began its screenings in America, head-scratching scientists were confronted by 30 blocks of basketball-sized chunks of ice that fell out of the skies all over Spain. Some were pranks, but the first few were definitely not, said Spanish officials. *Magnolia* is about several things, but one it highlights is what Marcello Truzzi calls "cryptometeorology," a very Fortean kind of new science.

It is nice to have a film that knows that the oneness in all things can even be measured in its frogs.

CHAPTER 7

Alligators in the Sewers

Alligators have fascinated me for years. Charles Fort was delighted by the croc reports also, and some of his most interesting words on tele-portation can be found in his passages on the crocodiles in England. From 1836 through the 1860s, Chipping Norton and Over-Norton in Oxford-shire were visited by young, usually foot-long crocs. Along with Fort's work, and my list of some eighty-odd accounts that I compiled in 1983 (Appendix III), the concept of the "crazy crocs" (as Bill Grimstad labeled them) has been firmly planted in the sphere of Fortean study.

California's central valley has a long history of strange animals and cryptozoological wonders. The Trinity Alps Monster (apparently a giant salamander?) and Folsom Lake's "alligators" stand out. In the Tulare Lake Basin, Corcoran, California, a six footer was sighted during the summer of 1930. And in nearby Folsom Lake, a series of sightings of 'gators oc-curred between September 1957 and June 1958. In recent years, I've been told of the reported finding of a dead alligator on the shores of Folsom Lake.

Folsom Lake's elusive alligators once had to share their watery retreat with another enigmatic beast we Forteans have had to deal with now and then. In April of 1972, a penguin was stolen (by "pranksters," the reports say) from the Sacramento Zoo. After its alleged theft by these alleged jokesters, the penguin was found swimming and feeding in that Fortean hot spot, Folsom Lake. It took six months for officials to end its freedom, and the animal died three weeks after its return.

Not so strangely, another gateway of Fortean creatures, Loveland, Ohio, had a penguin incident. During a late summer's hot spell in Septem-ber of 1978, two penguins supposedly escaped from a safari exhibit on Kings Island, ten miles from Loveland. One penguin was struck by a car and killed in Foster, but the other black and white creature caused havoc in

Loveland for several hours. Darrell Merritt, a service station attendant, said: "I walked in here about 7 o'clock in the morning. Then this guy came to the door and said there was a penguin behind my station. I thought he must have been drunk. I went out and looked. I had to see for myself, you know." What Merritt saw was a penguin. After waddling around town a bit, the penguin was finally captured by two volunteer firemen.

Loveland, Ohio, is perhaps best known for the frog-mouthed "trolls under the bridge" sighted in March 1955, and investigated by Leonard H. Stringfield. Ron Schaffner and Richard Mackay interviewed the police officers involved in the March 1972, Loveland incident in which a four-foot-tall creature described as a frog, or lizard, was seen. Loveland does seem to be one of those focal points we need to watch. Whether for frogs or penguins, who knows?

But back to penguins of late. As the summer of 1981 came to an end, a strange visitor appeared on the shore of Monmouth Beach, New Jersey—a South American rockhopper penguin. On Saturday, August 29th, the skinny creature was spotted on the beach, and spent the next several days, first in jail, then with the humane society, next at the Bronx Zoo, and finally at San Diego's Sea World. The bird's origin remains unknown and a deep mystery to officials who have been unsuccessful in theorizing an explanation to answer all the questions the rockhopper raised.

Sewer 'Gators

The story of alligators haunting the sewers of major American cities is a modern urban mystery. Most people have heard the rumors about alligators in the sewers, in large part, because of Thomas Pynchon's 1963 novel, *V.* Pynchon wrote of the cute little pet alligators purchased as Florida souvenirs, eventually discarded, then growing and reproducing in the sewers of New York City. Moving through the underground system, Pynchon told us, they were big, blind, albino, and fed off rats and sewage. Pynchon envisioned an Alligator Patrol going into the depths of the sewers, working in teams of two, with one man holding a flashlight while the other carried a twelve-gauge repeating shotgun. As no one before him had, Thomas Pynchon wove the rumor of alligators-in-the-sewers through the fabric of his fascinating work of fiction. But where does Pynchon's fiction end and fact begin?

The reworking of the alligators-in-the-sewer legend in the 1960s only served to further confuse its origins. Folklorist Richard M. Dorson repeated the oft-told tale that marijuana harvesters in pursuit of the elusive strain "New York White" (what did you think happened to all those seeds flushed down toilets by nervous pot users?) were experiencing difficulties because of the alligators swimming around in the sewer system.

The last word (supposedly) comes from the realm of science. The herpetologists Sherman and Madge Rutherford Minton, in their book *Giant Reptiles,* inform their readers that "One of the sillier folktales of the late 1960s was that the New York sewers were becoming infested with alligators....We...would assure New Yorkers that alligators are not among their urban problems."

But alligators and other crocodilians are one of the most frequent creatures involved in Fortean events, and to find actual records of alligators-in-the-sewers is an easy task. Finds of out-of-place crocs cover more than a century and continue into this new century.

Accounts of alligators falling from the sky would seem to be a rarer and less defensible form of crocodilian mystery, but no less an authority than the U.S. Weather Bureau related such a fall for July 2, 1843, on Anson Street, Charleston, South Carolina. Also, the *New York Times* carried an item on a fall of alligators; they fell on a turpentine farm in Aiken County, South Carolina in December of 1877.

Alligators, caimans, and crocodilians have materialized in cottonbins in Texas, express trains in France, hot water ditches in Illinois, and basements in Kansas. Some of these alleged discoveries are unusual, as, for example, the "alligator five and a half feet long ... found near the bank of the Rock River, at Janesville, Wisconsin, frozen to death," in 1892. I compiled a list (see Appendix III) of eighty-plus encounters with erratic alligators for the years 1948-1983. Though a supposedly true finding of an alligator in a sewer proved to be a rare occurrence, I was able to discover just such an event, recorded as fact from, not surprisingly, New York City. It is no wonder the reports of alligators slithering and slinking through the New York City sewer system are more than baseless rumors.

Surprisingly, the origins of the New York stories go back to the 1930s. On June 28, 1932, "swarms" of alligators were seen in the Bronx River, and a three footer was found dead.

On March 7, 1935 a three-foot alligator was caught alive in northern Yonkers while at Grass Sprain a six-foot 'gator was found dead. A barge captain at Pier 9 on the East River captured an alligator four feet long on June 1, 1937. Five days later, at the Brooklyn Museum subway station, a New Yorker caught a two footer.

Perhaps the most exciting story of alligators in the sewers in the 1930s, therefore, is the one told in the *New York Times* of 1935. Some teenagers living on East 123rd street encountered and killed a seven-and-a-half-foot-long, 125-pound alligator. That chilling account gives one pause about current urban problems.

The incident may or may not have taken place, but its publication in a no-nonsense fashion in a highly regarded and respected newspaper must have lent much credibility to the story. The *New York Times* of February 10, 1935, carried this article, and is given here in its entirety:

ALLIGATOR FOUND IN UPTOWN SEWER
Youths Shoveling Snow Into Manhole
See The Animal Churning In Icy Water.
SNARE IT AND DRAG IT OUT
Reptile Slain by Rescuers When It Gets Vicious

Whence It Came is Mystery.
Salvatore Condulucci, 16 years old, of 419 East 123rd Street, was assigned to the rim. His comrades would heap blackened slush near him, and he, carefully observing the sewer's capacity, would give the last fine flick to each mound.

Suddenly there were signs of clogging ten feet below, where the manhole drop merged with the dark conduit leading to the river. Salvatore yelled: "Hey, you guys, wait a minute," and got down on his knees to see what was the trouble.

What he saw, in the thickening dusk, almost caused him to topple into the icy cavern. For the jagged surface of the ice blockade below was moving; and something black was breaking through. Salvatore's eyes widened; then he managed to leap to his feet and call his friends.

"Honest, it's an alligator!" he exploded.

Others Look and Are Convinced.

There was a murmur of skepticism. Jimmy Mireno, 19, of 440 East 123rd Street, shouldered his way to the rim and stared.

"He's right," he said.

Frank Lonzo, 18, of 1743 Park Avenue, looked next. He also confirmed the spectre. Then there was a great crush about the opening in the middle of the street and heads were bent low around the aperture.

The animal apparently was threshing about in the ice, trying to get clear. When the first wave of awe had passed, the boys decided to help it out. A delegation was dispatched to the Lehigh Stove and Repair Shop at 441 East 123rd Street.

"We want some clothes-line," demanded the delegation, and got it.

Young Condolucci, an expert on Western movies, fashioned a slip knot. With the others watching breathlessly, he

An alligator from the sewers

ILLUSTRATION BY BILL REBSAMEN

dangled the noose into the sewer, and after several tantalizing near-catches, looped it about the 'gator's neck. Then he pulled hard. There was a grating of rough leathery skin against jumbled ice. But the job was too much for one youth. The others grabbed the rope and all pulled.

Slowly, with its curving tail twisting weakly, the animal was dragged from the snow, ten feet through the dark cavern, and to the street, where it lay, non-committal; it was not in Florida, that was clear.

And therefore, when one of the boys sought to loosen the rope, the creature opened its jaws and snapped, not with the robust vigor of a healthy, well-sunned alligator, but with the fury of a sick, very badly treated one. The boys jumped back. Curiosity and sympathy turned to enmity.

"Let 'im have it!" the cry went up.

Rescuers Then Kill It.

So the shovels that had been used to pile snow on the alligator's head were now to rain upon it. The 'gator's tail swished about a few last times. Its jaws clashed weakly. But it was in no mood for a real struggle after its icy incarceration. It died on the spot.

Triumphantly, but not without the inevitable reaction of sorrow, the boys took their victim to the Lehigh Stove and Repair Shop. There it was found to weigh 125 pounds; they said it measured seven and a half or eight feet. It became at once the greatest attraction the store ever had had. The whole neighborhood milled about, and finally, a call for the police reached a nearby station.

But there was little for the hurrying policemen to do. The strange visitor was quite dead; and no charge could be preferred against it or against its slayers. The neighbors were calmed with little trouble and speculation as to where the 'gator had come from was rife.

There are no pet shops in the vicinity; that theory was ruled out almost at once. Finally, the theories simmered down to that of a passing boat. Plainly, a steamer from the mysterious Everglades, or thereabouts, had been passing 123rd Street, and the alligator had fallen overboard.

Shunning the hatefully cold water, it had swum toward shore and found only the entrance to the conduit. Then after another 150 yards through a torrent of melting snow—and by that time it was half dead—it had arrived under the open manhole.

Half dead, yes, the neighborhood conceded. But still alive enough for a last splendid opening and snapping of its jaws. The boys were ready to swear to that.

At about 9 p.m., when tired mothers had succeeded in getting most of their alligator-conscious youngsters to bed, a Department of Sanitation truck rumbled up to the store and made off with the prize. Its destination was Barren Island and an incinerator.

Teddy May, the Superintendent of the New York City sewers during the 1930s, began hearing reports of alligators from his inspectors, but May did not believe them. May refused to approve these 1935 reports with the inspectors' notations on alligators. Indeed, Teddy May hired extra men to watch the inspectors and tell him how they were getting their liquor down in the sewers. The word came back to the "King of the Sewers" that his men were *not* drinking, but the reports of narrow escapes from alligators persisted. Bound and determined to lay the claims to rest, Teddy May decided to go down and have a look for himself.

A few hours later, May returned, shaken. His own flashlight, Robert Daley wrote in *The World Beneath the City,* illuminated the truth behind the rumors. Teddy May had seen alligators two feet in length and longer. Avoiding the dangerously fast currents in the main sewer lines under the major avenues, the alligators had taken to the smaller pipes in the backwash of the city. The alligators had settled in, and Teddy May was now faced with the task of ridding his sewers of the 'gators. Within months Teddy May felt he had finished that task. The methods he used were unorthodox, but then his prey was rather unusual. Rat poison got rid of some as did forcing some onto the main trunk lines where they drowned or were swiftly washed out to sea. A few alligators were hunted down by sewer inspectors with 22s on their own free time. Teddy May rid New York City of its alligators in the sewers—or so he thought.

In 1938 five alligators were caught in New Rochelle, New York, and sightings of alligators-in-the-sewers in New York City were recorded for 1948 and 1966.

Alligators in the sewers are neither rumor, folktale or myth, but a real part of the underground world of some of our larger urban centers. For, although this discussion has focussed on New York City, recent accounts seem to indicate that alligators are also prowling the sewers of other cities. The widespread nature of this phenomenon remains to be seen. But hints continue to be found.

University of Utah's Professor of Folklore Jan Harold Brunvand first read of my alligator-in-the-sewer interests in the 1983 edition of *Mysterious America,* and mentioned my discoveries in his books, *The Vanishing Hitchhiker, More of the Straight Dope,* and *Rumor!* This led to two decades of exchanges between Brunvand and myself, most of which have had to do with alligators in the sewers. His readers have been very interested in finding early examples of the 'gators. Some have been most intriguing.

In 1999, Russell L. Martin III, Curator of Newspapers at the American Antiquarian Society, passed along this information to Brunvand: "In the course of our work, we recently discovered what may be the earliest example of the classic urban legend, 'alligators in the sewers of New York.'"

Martin continued, "Filed away with our bound volume of the *New York Evening Post* was a single issue of a previously unknown newspaper. The title is *The Planet,* published in Union Village, N.Y., July 18, 1831. It is unclear whether it survived beyond vol. 1, no. 1. At any rate, in the midst of the news and anecdotes is this curious item: 'A live Alligator, it is said, was seen on Friday in the slip between Murray's and Pine street wharves, New York.'"

During 2000, Brunvand sent me an old record of an alligator in a sewer other than one in New York. Ms. Phyllis Harrison was searching old newspaper files for advertisements and references to auctions, a particular interest of hers, when she came across the following article in the September 28, 1927 (Vol. 5, No. 8) issue of the Bloomfield, Indiana, *Democrat:*

ALLIGATOR FOUND IN SEWER
Employee of Pittsburgh Bureau of
Highways and Sewers
Pulls Out 3-Foot Saurian

Pittsburgh—The North side has been famed for many things. Now it is the habitat of the alligator.

If you don't believe it, ask George Moul, a perfectly reliable employee of the Bureau of Highways and Sewers. He has the proof on exhibition at his home in Lockhart street. He got it yesterday when he was sent to fix a sewer in Royal street.

He had lifted the manhole and was prodding to remove the obstruction, when a strange face, with rather evil-looking eyes, bobbed in his range of vision.

After the first shock Moul grabbed the head and drew forth a 3-foot alligator. He got a rope and led it to his home and is trying to dope out how the Florida native got this far North.

The history of alligators in the sewers, throughout its Fortean range, is far from being completely written.

CHAPTER 8

Giant Snakes

Mystery animals have long held the interest of humans, and specifically the tales of giant snakes have captivated audiences since prehistoric times. Snakes and serpents were very prominent in the religions of the early civilizations of the Old and New World. The snake appears to have been widely worshipped as a source of supernatural power. From ancient Chinese literature, we have the stories mentioned by Shan Hai King of the giant Pa Snake, a fabulous monster capable of swallowing whole elephants and ejecting the bones three years later. In the ancient cultures of the Americas, hints of the extent of the influence of giant snakes in the religions of these peoples is seen in the cult of Quetzalcoatl, the feathered serpent of the Aztecs, as well as in the monumental earthworks of the giant Serpent Mound of Ohio. Carvings of great serpents are often found on the monuments and temples of the Toltecs, Aztecs, and Mayans of ancient Mesoamerica. One excellent carving from Mexico shows a large snake in the act of swallowing an elegantly costumed woman who appears lacerated and crushed in the snake's jaws. The ancients were in touch with the importance of giant serpents in their lives.

Giant snakes, the Bigfoot of the reptile world, tend to have characteristics almost ghost-like in nature on the one hand, yet are frighteningly physical on the other. To complicate the picture even further, some cases of real out-of-place oversized snakes do surface from time to time.

During the winter of 1959-1960, for example, I found people discovering huge, flesh-and-blood snakes in three spots in North America—all in places where they should not have been. Late in September, 1959, William Hayden of the Bronx, New York, found a five-foot-long black snake in his backyard and popped it in his bathtub for safekeeping. Not too surprising perhaps, but the next day, on September 29th, Hayden found a five-foot-long boa constrictor curled around an ash can outside his apartment. Meanwhile, Reid Trail decided to have the twelve-foot python he ran over and killed near Roanoke, Virginia in December of 1959, stuffed because people would not believe him. And from Montreal, during this snake-filled winter, apartment tenant Marc Rivard was shocked to come home one February evening and discover a seven-foot-long boa in his front living room.

Exotic animals do escape. People's pets do roam. Some native specimens do grow large. Incidents, involving out-of-place big snakes such as the five-foot-long boa captured in Champaign, Illinois, in 1972, are far more common than one might suppose.

But on a totally different level of reality, something besides pythons in toilet bowls have crept from the fringes of the borderland that separates mystery animals from actual zoological specimens. What are we to make of the old report of the 16-footer killed in a field in Lock Springs, Missouri, in 1897?

Giant snakes, creatures of the outer edge of zoology like Sasquatch, phantom panthers, giant salamanders, and thunderbirds, have been seen in this country and elsewhere for centuries. The giant serpents and snakes of the shadow world of cryptozoology have many of the same characteristics as their brethren—namely, they are generally described as monstrous in size and dark in color, are never caught, and exhibit behaviors much more aggressive and daring than one would expect of these normally timid and retiring reptiles.

The history of incidents with giant snakes is a long one and can best be examined through a few highlights from the Western Hemisphere. Some of the most intriguing accounts have issued from Brazil, and some of these have been brought back from the Amazon hinterland by the extremely colorful character, Major Percy Fawcett.

In 1906, twenty years before he vanished without a trace in the Amazon, Major Fawcett was sent by the Royal Geographic Society to make a thorough survey of the Rio Abuna and Acre Rivers. Thirty-nine at the time, Major Fawcett, as Ivan T. Sanderson once observed, was known for two sometimes contradictory character traits: he was a dreamer whose dreams led him to envision lost jungle cities of fantastic wealth and splendor; he was also a scrupulously matter-of-fact military man who reported exactly what he saw in detailed and down-to-earth observations. His memoirs, striking for their contrast of visionary dreams and earthy rankness, relate many strange adventures—including an encounter with a giant anaconda of the Amazon.

Fawcett ran across the giant snake in 1907. He was drifting along the Rio Negro with his Indian crew, when he spotted the snake. Fawcett reported that a great triangular head appeared at the bow of the boat, and when he shot the creature in the spine the body of the snake thrashed the water all around the boat. With great difficulty Fawcett convinced his crew to approach closer to the bank where the great snake lay. The Indians feared that the injured reptile would attack the boat or that its mate, as often happened, would come to destroy the hunters.

Fawcett then stepped onto the shore and cautiously approached the snake. According to Fawcett, the snake measured 45 feet out of the water and 17 in it, for a total of 62 feet. Considering its length, the snake's diameter was surprisingly small, only about one foot. The beast was not dead and emitted an awful odor from its mouth. Fawcett was told of many such stories, including one about a super giant of more than 80 feet long that was said to have been killed by the Zrajchan boundary commission. The common length of the anaconda does not usually exceed 25 feet. Yet Fawcett's tale is only one of many made by South American jungle guides and explorers who have reported giant snakes varying from 75 feet to even 150 feet in length. These giant creatures are said to have eyes the size of plates and weigh several tons.

Closer to home, far from the teeming jungles of the Amazon, in the summer of 1944, a huge snake known as the Peninsula Python caused excitement along the Cuyahoga River in the wooded valley between Akron and Cleveland, Ohio. The creature first appeared on June 8, 1944 when Clarence Mitchell saw it sliding across his corn field. The Peninsula Python left a track the width of an automobile tire, and Mitchell reported the creature to be about 18 feet in length. Two days later, Paul and John Szalay reported a similar track in their fields, and two more days later, Mrs. Roy Vaughn called out the fire department when the giant reptile attacked her hen house. The snake had climbed the fence to her chicken coop and devoured a chicken.

Now that the snake was accepted as fact, theories abounded as to where it had come from. Two years earlier, a carnival truck had supposedly smashed up in a cemetery in the valley and it was speculated that the python might have escaped from this wreck. As I have discovered many times before in my investigations of "circus train wrecks" as the source of any given mystery animal report, the story could never fully be tracked down.

The Cleveland and Columbus zoos offered rewards for the live capture of the Peninsula Python, and the news services began to carry the story, which aroused overseas interest from servicemen whose families lived in the valley.

On Sunday, June 25th, the sirens blasted to report the creature had been sighted near Kelly Hill. The town emptied as countless residents headed off to the hill in search of the Python. The hunters trampled through tangled thornbush and burrs only to learn later that it was a false alarm.

Two days later, on June 27th, the snake leaped down out of a dead willow and frightened Mrs. Pauline Hopko. It so frightened her milk cows that they broke their halters and ran off across the fields, while her dogs cowered under Mrs. Hopko's skirts. Mrs. Hopko was left holding the milk pail. The snake was also sighted by Bobbie Pollard and some other boys at this time, but it disappeared before the mayor's posse arrived on the scene.

After another two days, Mrs. Ralph Griffin saw the snake rear up man-high in the middle of her backyard. Again, the creature avoided the posse. Then Mrs. Katherine Boroutick saw it in her backyard; it came crashing down out of her butternut tree when she was out by the river throwing out some trash. The posse found broken tree limbs and another track to the riverbed. Professional searchers came into the area and the snake was reported a few more times in the fall. However, hunters said they never got word fast enough to get a shot at the snake. By first frost, residents waited for the buzzards to find a huge carcass of a snake dead of the cold, but the Peninsula Python was never sighted again, dead or alive.

Accounts of giant snakes have circulated throughout the United States. Reports from the area around Bridgewater, Massachusetts, as mentioned earlier, tell of CCC workers encountering huge coiled serpents along the pathways through the Hockomock Swamp. And from Hastings, Michigan, come tales of the twenty-foot-long Carter's Snake, so named because it was always seen near Carter's Lake. Near another lake, Reynold's Lake in Kentucky, local people began to take their hogs inside for fear that their giant snake would devour their livestock after it got its fill of frogs. The era of a snake as "large as a stovepipe" is gone only because nobody uses stovepipes any longer, but the reports of giant snakes continue.

The 1970s and 1980s had their share of monster snake accounts. The old alternative service, the Zodiac News Service, reported in January 1975 that hikers in the northern Appalachian mountains had sighted a 40-foot-long giant snake. The slithering monster had reportedly been seen by more than a dozen hiking parties since it was first viewed in 1919. Legend has it that the giant snake, which witnesses have seen on Broad Top Mountain, survives Pennsylvania's harsh winters by crawling into warm coal mine shafts. Researchers who checked out one sighting claim the monster left behind a long trough in the earth four to six inches deep.

Curtis Fuller, the late editor of *Fate,* wrote of a giant snake report in the May 1979 issue. Fuller detailed Eileen Blackburn's and her daughter's (October 1978) experience near Cascade, Montana. The giant 20- to 30-foot-long snake reportedly had coils at least three feet across. Cascade Police Chief Earl Damon said he had other giant snake reports from area people. Like so many other mystery animal encounters, the Blackburns had their run-in while they were traveling in their automobile. Mrs. Blackburn was not sure if she hit the giant cobra-like creature, or if it struck her car.

In days past, the giant snakes attacked not cars, but horses. One of the classic accounts is given in John Keel's *Strange Creatures from Time and Space.* The Kenton, Ohio, individual out horseback riding was Orland Packer (not Parker, as given in Keel's book). On June 9, 1946, an eight-foot-long snake with a diamond shape on its flat head bit at Packer's horse, taking off a patch of the horse's hair. Packer was thrown and broke his ankle. His wife reported in 1970 that her husband used crutches for two years and suffered from excessive sweating and fever long after that.

What are we to make of all of this? The investigation of giant snake sightings is a compelling challenge to modern cryptozoologists.

In *Wonders,* Volume 3, no. 3 and no. 4, Mark A. Hall chronicled all the incidents of giant snake sightings in North America he could find. He listed many noteworthy locations, including near Nashville, Tennessee (29½ feet in length, and spotted like a rattlesnake); "The Drowned

Lands," New York, where giant snakes were seen in the marshlands south of Lake Champlain; the Ottawa Valley, Ontario, in Ottawa River, Chats Lake, Green Lake; Lake Ontario; Ohio River, West Virginia; and the Minnesota River. Hall points out several good 19th century cases from Illinois, Kansas (one killed in Fredonia, measuring almost 40 feet in length); Lake Minnetonka, Minnesota (a 30-foot "sea serpent"); Vincennes, Indiana (looked like it was 60 feet long); Big Swan Pond, Indiana (20 to 25 feet long and carried its head high above the water when swimming); Loudonville, Ohio (20-foot snake killed in barn); and Nebraska (15- to 18-foot snake seen in field).

Hall's work is worth following. He summarizes that of the reports from after 1940, there are eight reports from Indiana; one each for Ohio, Georgia, Oklahoma, Alabama, North Carolina, Montana, and Texas; and two for Kentucky. He clearly agrees with me that "there is no evidence" to dismiss these very old reports as all circus, zoo, and pet escapees.

Could a temperate forest pattern underlie the more reliable reports? Is there a common denominator in the ecology of these unknown giant terrestrial snakes? Could there be a possible aquatic link?

Even our critics are open to the possibility of giant snakes. Cryptozoology email list moderator Chad Arment, for example, who feels most of the cases are feral snakes or pranks, has written that "there are a couple of cases which warrant further investigation."

During July 2000, a media report out of Foreman, Arkansas, showed that giant snakes can still, even if rarely, make the news. Tales of a huge snake that had been eating animals in Little River County, Arkansas, caused local officials to take notice. An animal rescue group, the Arkansas Wildlife Rescue and Rehabilitation Association, was summoned from Pulaski County to try to catch the reportedly 30-foot-long snake. While Arkansas Game and Fish Commission officials remained skeptical, residents of Foreman and nearby communities reported that something definitely was eating small animals in the area. One resident reported that a pet goose named "Miss Daisy" died after being bitten by a snake under her right wing. Bullfrogs have vanished in a pond; fish in two more. Cranes and herons that once perched on the edge of Terry and Wedia Landsell's pond have relocated. Mrs. Landsell said some of her cats have disappeared, too. "When you get asked at the Taco Bell about it, you know something is up," said Jim Williamson, editor of the weekly *Little River News.*

Although Game and Fish officials have suggested that what residents have seen is an oversized cottonmouth, Mrs. Landsell said this is no normal snake. "I've seen a lot of snakes, but nothing this big," Mrs. Landsell said, who has seen "it early in the morning or late in the evening."

Last word was the snake has gone uncaught. Like so many other mystery animals.

A Discovery Channel exposé claiming that this giant snake was merely a Burmese python still left many questions open, like how they seemed to have not really caught the "big" one.

CHAPTER 9

Lake Monsters

Technology will soon catch up with North America's Lake Monsters. Dennis Jay Hall of Vermont's Champ Quest is ready to follow the lead of sonar-sonic scientists who are currently tracking various watery European cryptids. During 2000, exciting new sonic surveys have revealed that the Loch Ness monsters may be a distant relative of the walrus, according to Official Loch Ness Monster Fan Club director Gary Campbell and other European lake monster researchers and sonar-sonic technical scientists. They found that a series of unidentifiable sounds in the loch fell into a frequency (747-751Hz) matched only by the walrus, the elephant seal, and the killer whale. The sounds were analyzed by marine laboratories and the Swedish intelligence agency known as FOA65.

The sounds were described like a pig grunting or a person snoring. They were recorded by highly sensitive hydrophones lowered to a depth of 65 feet in two spots where sightings have been reported. The Swedish team, which carried out the research in March on Loch Ness's western side, said the sounds were similar to those found in Swedish and Norwegian lakes also rumored to be populated by water monsters.

"Most of the noises we picked up in the loch we can identify as eels, pike, or trout, but this noise was a sort of grunting, very like sounds we recorded in [Norway's] Lake Seljordsvatnet, although shorter and sharper," noted the Swedish team. "Let's say these sounds were from Nessie—she could be a relative, a sub-species."

Meanwhile, also at Loch Ness during the summer of 2000, pleasure cruise boss Ron MacKenzie fitted a trawler sonar to his pleasure boat, the Royal Scot. He felt the £10,000 machine for hunting shoals of fish would be a monster hit with Nessie hunting searchers. Tourists can watch the screen aboard the Royal Scot. MacKenzie said he tested a more basic system and "got two strange readings of large soft objects," which was reported by the *Scottish Daily Record* on August 18.

Later during the summer, other researchers were busy in Ireland at Sraheens Loch, and then on to south Norway where they set a trap for a lake monster.

"This is the first sea serpent trap of its kind in the world," the Swedish group told the media. The team, comprised of seven Swedes, three Norwegians, a Canadian, and a Belgian, plan to lower the 18-foot-long tube-shaped trap, comprising a metal frame with nylon netting, into Seljord Lake. It will contain live whitefish for bait to catch an elusive beast known locally as "Selma." With two biologists at the University of Oslo, on standby to fly in by helicopter and take tests if the trap worked, the group hoped to take a DNA sample, document the serpent, and then release it into the lake.

In 1999, I traveled with my sons Malcolm and Caleb to Loch Ness. I was happy to speak at the first cryptozoology symposium ever to be held there and to meet some colleagues like Gary Campbell, Robert Rines, Henry Bauer, Gordon Rutter, and others. The lake is grand, the people are generous, and the Scottish air is clear. It is the epicenter of cryptozoology, and we in America have much to learn from Loch Ness.

But as I have been telling people for years, we do not have to cross the Atlantic to uncover "Loch Ness monsters." We have plenty of our own in North America.

Canada has several native monsters, the most famous of which is Okanagan Lake's "Ogopogo" in British Columbia. The same province lays claim to "Caddy" in Cadboro Bay, as well as an unnamed creature lurking in the depths of Cowichan Lake north of Victoria. Ontario has "Hapyxelor" in Muskrat Lake, and Manitoba "Manipogo" at the northern tip of Lake Manitoba. The monster of New Brunswick's Lake Utopia is still being seen regularly. During July of 1982, Sherman Hatt told of sighting the creature, which he said was "like a submarine coming out of the water with spray on both sides. It was about ten feet long and put me in mind of the back of a whale."

The United States has a long tradition of lake monster legends that stretches back to the folklore of its first residents, the Native Americans. One of these tales, related by David Cusick in a pamphlet, "History of the

Six (Indian) Nations," published in 1828, was collected from the Oneida branch of the Tuscaroras. The legend tells how long ago a great reptile, the "Mosqueto," rose from Lake Onondaga (near Syracuse in upstate New York) and slew a number of people. The Indians also said that "2200 years before the time of Columbus" a great horned serpent appeared on Lake Ontario and killed onlookers with its overpowering stench.

A strikingly similar beast figures in legends of the Indians of Nebraska, who told the first white settlers that a monster lived in Alkali Lake near Hay Springs. The accounts seem to have some truth in them, if we are to credit the testimony of one J. A. Johnson, who is quoted in the July 24, 1923, *Omaha World-Herald:* "I saw the monster myself while with two friends last fall. I could name 40 other people who have also seen the brute.

"We had camped a short distance from the lake on the night before and all three of us arose early to be ready for duck flight. We started to walk around the lake close to the shore, in order to jump any birds, when suddenly, coming around a slight raise in the ground we came upon this animal, nearly three-fourths out of the shallow water near the shore. We were less than 20 yards from him.

"The animal was probably 40 feet long, including the tail and the head, when raised in alarm as when he saw us. In general appearance, the animal was not unlike an alligator, except that the head was stubbier, and there seemed to be a projection like a horn between the eyes and nostrils. The animal was built much more heavily throughout than an alligator. Its color seemed a dull gray or brown.

"There was a very distinctive and somewhat unpleasant odor noticeable for several moments after the beast had vanished into the water. We stood for several minutes after the animal had gone, hardly knowing what to do or say, when we noticed several hundred feet out from the shore a considerable commotion in the water.

"Sure enough the animal came to the surface, floated there for a moment and then lashed the water with its tail, suddenly dived, and we saw no more of him."

Another of America's long-lived monsters belongs to Lake Champlain in the Champlain Valley of Quebec, New York, and Vermont. The first white man to see it was the lake's namesake, explorer Samuel de Champlain, who in July 1609 observed a serpent-like creature about 20 feet long, as thick as a barrel, and with a head shaped like a horse's. Today, many sense this may have only been a sturgeon. Down through the years, however, folks have reported "Champ" animals (as they are called) that seem nothing like a big fish. The work of such people as Joseph Zarzynski and Dennis Jay Hall suggests that Champ requires serious consideration.

So seriously, in fact, that the animals ought to be protected. During the summer of 1982, the Lake Champlain Monster was the focus of resolutions passed by the Vermont House and the New York Senate protecting the lake monsters "from any willful act resulting in death, injury or harassment."

That something exists in Lake Champlain, I, at least, am not prepared to dispute. But one of the oddest aspects of the whole affair is not the identity of the animals, but the baffling query raised by Marjorie L. Porter in *Vermont Life* magazine: "If the unknown creature is a huge aquatic mammal or a reptile, the question remains: how could it survive when the lake is locked solid with ice?" as it is almost every winter. (More on Champ in Chapter 11.)

Alaska's Iliamna Lake, 80 miles long, hosts a number of monsters of various sizes, all described as possessing broad, blunt heads; long, tapered bodies; and vertical tails. Witnesses usually state that the monsters' color is similar to that of "dull aluminum."

These things, whatever they are, have been around for quite a while. The Aleut Indians have been familiar with them for many years and display a healthy respect for the creatures. This "respect" sometimes has escalated into downright fear. Earlier in the century, according to Aleut testimony, a monster upended one of their boats and swallowed up a crewman. For some considerable time afterwards the Indians conscientiously skirted that section of the lake.

Since then several fishermen have hooked the beasts with extremely heavy tackle, and bush pilots flying over the lake have seen them at, or just beneath, the surface of the lake's clear waters. No one has yet been able to formulate a satisfactory explanation for these beasts, though some theorists have speculated they may be beluga whales, which have entered the lake from the sea via the deep Kvichak River. Longtime residents of the Iliamna region scoff at this notion, however, pointing out that beluga whales, common enough sights in the area, have paper-white backs, tapered heads and horizontal tails.

At one period in the last century Lake Michigan also claimed a mysterious watery inhabitant. In its August 7, 1867, issue the *Chicago Tribune* went so far as to assert, "That Lake Michigan is inhabited by a vast monster, part fish and part serpent, no longer admits of doubt."

The *Tribune* reported that not long before crews of the tug George W. Wood and the propeller boat Sky Lark had seen the creature lashing through the waves off Evanston. They said the thing was between 40 and 50 feet long, with a neck as thick as a human being's and a body as thick as a barrel. On the morning of August 6th, fisherman Joseph Muhike encountered the same, or a similar, animal on the lake a mile and a half from the Hyde Park section of Chicago.

During the summer of 1879 another monster appeared in Illinois, this time in Stump Pond in DuQuoin. One night a man named Paquette had been fishing on the lake when something rushed through the water creating enough disturbance to rock his boat. Unnerved, Paquette headed for shore, vowing not to venture out on the water again during the late hours. A year later, in July 1880, two miners reportedly saw a 12-foot "serpent," its body the thickness of a telegraph pole and dark green in color, heading their way from one-eighth of a mile out. They chose not to avail themselves of the opportunity for a closer look.

Reports of a monster in Stump Pond continued until 1968 when the body of water was partially drained and its fish cleared out with electric stunners. The largest fish weighed 30 pounds apiece; impressive as fish go, but certainly not big enough to be mistaken for anything else. Needless to say no monster showed up; but still witnesses stuck to their stories. One of them, 66-year-old Allyn Dunmyer, had a frightening experience several years before. "I was in my boat fishing for bass when it happened," he said.

"Something came up from the bottom, struck the boat underneath so hard I nearly tipped over."

Dunmyer had seen the monster—or monsters—before. "I think there are more than one of the critters in the pond," he told a reporter. "I've seen them so near the surface that their back fins were sticking out of the water."

One man, wading in the pond's shallows, stumbled onto something sleeping underneath the algae which covered part of the water. He thought it looked like a large alligator.

The monsters that supposedly inhabit Lake Waterton in Montana are called "Oogle-Boogles" by local people, though no one knows just how that name got started. Flathead Lake in the same state boasts similar beasts, which have been described variously as between 5 and 60 feet in length. This is not the only inconsistency in the reports—there are enough inconsistencies to give any conscientious researcher a severe headache. But then consistency is not a virtue found in most monster lore. That does not have to mean, however, that therefore monsters do not exist. The vast majority of witnesses are obviously sincere and stand to gain little, aside from ridicule, for coming forth with their stories.

While some monsters, as we have seen, are longtime residents of certain lakes and rivers, others appear only once or twice and disappear. The creature observed in Michigan's Paint River in 1922 was apparently a one-timer. In the words of a lady who saw it, "I was walking down the hill toward the river to visit a girlfriend who lived at the bottom of the hill. A Mrs. Johnson was walking up the hill and we met on the knoll about halfway, which was very near the river. We got a very good look at this animal—both saw it at the same time, and stood stunned, speechless, watching it till it went out of sight. Mrs. Johnson, as if to check on her sense, asked me in Swedish: 'Did you see what I saw?' I assured her that I did. She went on ejaculating in Swedish, very excited, saying: 'It had a head bigger than a pail.' She then made me walk up the hill to our house, and I had to verify everything she said to my mother.

"My report? Yes, it did have a head much bigger than any pail I knew of; the head stood straight above the water; the body was dark color; the body did not move like that of a snake, but in an undulating motion. We could see humps sticking out of the water, and I recall counting six of them. How long? This is difficult to recall. It was swimming north up the river between two bridges. This distance could be the length of a city block, and this monster must have been nearly half of that bridge, but we followed its wake on up the river."

The monster of Big Chapman's Lake, near Warsaw, Indiana, evidently was also a one-timer. On August 16, 1934, H. W. Scott was fishing from a boat when the head of something rose from the water not far away. The head was two feet across, Scott reported, and it had "large cow-like eyes." That unfortunately is the extent of the description given in an *Indianapolis News* account of the sighting. The same source lists two other witnesses who allegedly saw the creature about the same time: Scott's wife and a Mrs. George Barnwell.

Another one-timer, a black fish about six or eight feet long with no visible appendages, rammed a fisherman's boat and dented its fiberglass body one day in the summer of 1970. Ronald J. Haller was floating down the Missouri River between Fort Benton and Lewistown, Montana, when the collision occurred. Haller swung his boat around and followed the fish upstream with a movie camera.

To the best of my knowledge Haller's film has never been released, but the witness and his lawyer are known to have shown it to wildlife authorities, who so far have not identified the creature.

The monsters of inland America cannot be disposed of easily. (See Appendix VI to see the extent of the accounts.) Have zeuglodons and plesiosaurs survived hundreds of millions of years in our lakes and rivers? Are long-necked unknown seals part of the mix? Are some just folklore, phantoms, and archetypes of another plane? As in the case of black panthers, common sense and our knowledge of the workings of the natural order unequivocally dictate that these things cannot be—yet they are.

In a sense they are the watery flying saucers of the natural order. They share with panthers, Bigfoot, and other related biological but anomalistic phenomena a kind of nebulousness, appearing from time to time within our vision but seemingly forever beyond our reach.

Lake Monster Latitudes

Is there an underlying pattern to Lake Monster reports from North America and elsewhere in the world?

The great Fortean zoologist Ivan T. Sanderson commented on this topic in his book *"Things"* (Pyramid Books, 1967): "From what has been said thus far, don't think for a moment that fresh-water monsters are confined to our northern latitudes. There are numerous other 'horrors' reported from our south central states and from Florida, and from all around the tropics. Then again, they also crop up in the cold temperate regions of the Southern Hemisphere. But here is a funny thing. When you come to plot the scores of lakes and rivers in which 'monsters' have been reported in the northern belt, which encircles the Arctic polar area, you will note that all of them fall within the vegetational belt known as that of the Boreal Forests, or in southward extensions of this which enter the U.S. due to high altitude—such as the Adirondacks, Montana, and Idaho."

Bernard Heuvelmans, in his book *In the Wake of the Sea-Serpents* (first French edition, 1965; English edition, 1968), further commented on this interesting correlation. In Chapter 14, "Disentangled and Classified at Last," he details his observations on the "Geographic Distribution" of his various types of Sea-Serpents. "A careful study of this type of animal, which is found in many steep-shored lakes in cold temperate regions in both Northern and Southern Hemispheres, show that its sight is rather poor," writes Heuvelmans on page 559. His footnote to that sentence notes that his careful study is a treatment "Which will appear in a separate book on 'monsters' of lochs, lakes, marshes and rivers—freshwater unknown animals." (Unfortunately, Heuvelmans never got around to writing this book.)

French cryptozoologist Michel Raynal has pointed out that in private correspondence Heuvelmans routinely acknowledges Sanderson for various theories throughout this Sea-Serpent book. Raynal and I see many examples (e.g., breathing tubes and humps) throughout, but regarding these observations and thus the theories associated with the study of Lake Monster distribution, Heuvelmans was first.

Certainly, Bernard Heuvelmans formalized his thoughts on the whole matter of how such cryptids as Champ and other Lake Monsters fit in when he wrote in *Cryptozoology* (1986): "Attention must be drawn to the fact that all these long-necked animals [so-called "Lake Monsters"] have been reported from stretches of freshwater located around isothermic lines 10°C; that is, between 0°C and 20°C (i.e., 50°F, between 32°F and 67°F) in both Northern and Southern hemispheres. One could hardly wish for better circumstantial evidence of their existence."

CHAPTER 10

Giant Catfish

There was always one creature, that was said to dwell right here in De-catur, and it was a particular favorite of mine. It was the giant catfish that was said to live below the Lake Decatur dam. For years, I heard sto-ries of huge, mutated catfish that lived in the mud below the dam. These catfish, according to reliable witnesses, were said to have grown to the size of cows! —Troy Taylor, *Haunted Decatur Revisted,* 2000

Swimmers still get scared as they plunge into parts of Lake Decatur, Illinois. But it doesn't stop there. Ohio River welders refuse to work on bridges underwater, children playing on the shore of the Mississippi River disappear, and Kentucky divers boycott going underwater by the power dam because of what they say they saw down there. Many forms of water-dwelling mystery creatures exist but perhaps some of the strangest are those said to look like "giant catfishes"—so familiar yet so weird. Urban folklore, rural folklore, watery folklore, yes, perhaps this is. But, then again, it is a hint of what may lie behind the murky surface of some American aquatic habitats.

Think of it. You are boating and look over the side to view the fish while talking to your boat mate about doing a little fishing. And all of a sudden, you are confronted by a reddish fish, over nine feet long, weigh-ing a half a ton. Now that's a scary moment, and you suddenly realize, no one will believe this fish story of yours!

Then consider what's happening routinely in North America.

Quebec is the location of many lakes said to be inhabited by mon-sters. Michel Meurger and Claude Gagnon wrote an important 1982 book in French about the Canadian province, entitled *Monstres des lacs du Quebec* (which was rewritten and reissued as an English edition, *Lake*

Monster Tradition, in 1988). The book details a few examples of giant catfish-like lake monsters.

In interviewing Quebec residents about Lake Massawippi (Abernaki for "deep water"), Meurger and Gagnon spoke to Paul Simard, vice president of the Massawippi Fishing and Game Club. Simard, 65, said that when he was fifteen, his parents told him and his thirteen siblings "when we were swimming, not to go too far because there was a monster in the lake. There was a time during the 1920s when people were afraid to go fishing because of the monster, the Serpent of Lake Massawippi, who was six or seven feet long, with the head of a catfish."

Intriguingly, Meurger and Gagnon point out that many Lake Monster reports which speak of "whiskers" on the cryptids may be describing instead the wattles that can be found on a "giant catfish." The Lake Champlain Monster (Champ of New York and Vermont), the Loch Ness Monster, and others have shown this trait in a few sightings. The so-called "Champ's Younger Brother," the Lake Brompton Monster of Quebec is said to be at least six feet long with "an evil-looking head" and "something like a moustache." Are these the wattles of the catfish again?

But giant catfish are not supposed to exist in North America. Charles Paxton, the British zoologist who bravely wrote a paper in 1998 saying that all the marine animals have not been discovered yet, is in the process of writing a similar one about freshwater forms. However, he is cautious about giant catfish in the United States and Canada. He tells me that there "could be no giant species" of catfish in North America that are over 6 feet. He also points out that eyewitness reports may not be common because "big catfish are (with the exception of a few tropical species) pretty much benthic so they rarely come to the surface (although some breathe air occasionally and come to the surface more often)."

Author Burkhard Bilger, writing in the *Atlantic Monthly* in 1997, summarizes the short "ancient" history of giant catfish accounts in America thusly: "Jacques Marquette and Louis Jolliet, canoeing down the Mississippi in 1673, were warned of a demon 'who would engulf them in the abyss where he dwelt.' Mark Twain, two centuries later, claimed to have seen one more than six feet long and weighing 250 pounds. 'If Marquette's fish was the fellow to that one,' he wrote in *Life on the Mississippi,* 'he had a fair right to think the river's roaring demon was come.'

When pioneer mothers did their wash by a stream, another story goes, they sometimes heard a splash and a muffled yelp. Where a little boy had been playing, only a few bubbles were left."

Such was the sinister fear instilled by the stories of giant catfish. In straight zoology, of course, catfish do not get that big in North America. Maybe over 100 pounds, but 500 pounds and six feet long? Not according to the official fish people.

Ichthyologist Lucas Negus notes: "The blue catfish is North America's giant of the freshwater. The record in the United States for blue catfish is 111 pounds. Another very large catfish in North America is the flathead catfish. This fish does not get quite as large as the blue but makes up for it with its looks. The blue catfish is not attractive by most people's standards but the flathead is even uglier."

Bilger feels that the catfish are growing larger, all over the United States, due to neglect. Are deep-dwelling catfish growing bigger in the dark of the undiscovered corners of some of America's lakes? Perhaps so.

It is certainly true that the reports of giant catfish persist.

When Jay Sullivan lived in Arizona, he told me, there were common rumors of giant (9 feet) catfish in Saguaro Lake, an artificial recreational lake east of Phoenix. It was said that they lived undisturbed in the deep water near the upstream dam, and that was why people were warned against swimming in that area. Ron Schaffner of Ohio passes on the stories of Ohio and Mississippi welders working on bridges who refuse to go underwater after giant catfish are seen. Another Ohio researcher, Marc DeWerth writes that when he was growing up, his grandfather told him about a friend fishing the Ohio River in a 20-foot fishing boat and hitting a 25-foot log close to shore. It ended up that the log was a dead catfish of some kind. The way it was explained, it was some sort of channel catfish. Ken Wilkinston mentioned to me that he heard of giant catfish in Lake of the Pines, east Texas. George Stoecklin, DVM, forwarded word to me of giant catfish at Bagnell Dam, Lake of the Ozarks, Missouri, and near Hoover Dam at Lake Mead.

Eyewitness accounts, in the midst of cloudy watery folklore about giant catfish, still come my way about these critters. In August 2000, Cynthia Fairburn told me her story: "Back in the summer of 1971, when I was a teen growing up in Fresno, California, a girlfriend and I were enjoying the sun at Lost River and Lost Lake just north of Fresno. I had been there many times before, wading in the icy waters of the river that feeds into Lost Lake. It was a favorite picnic area among locals, but off the beaten track; it wasn't very well known to many. My friend Mary and I were sitting on the shore of the river, when all of a sudden Mary screamed 'Oh my god!!!!' I looked up to see a tail fin at least two feet wide splashing back into the water, and a shadow that made me estimate a total length of about 8 to 10 feet. It must have breached out of the water about 5 feet. Now I could believe such a monster in the lake, but the river was only about 20 feet wide, and only 3 or 4 feet at its deepest. The fish was headed for the lake downstream maybe 1 or 2 miles. Mary said it was a catfish that looked shiny black, rather than scaly. The water at the river was very clear, although the lake itself was murky and deep, and we never swam there. It was enough of a scare that I never again went swimming in Lost River."

And Mark Twain did claim he saw a catfish "more than six feet long and weighing 250 pounds" even though they aren't suppose to exist in North America.

Giant Catfish Around the World

Cryptozoology, around the globe, accepts that at the root of certain accounts of Lake and River Monsters may be giant catfish. Bernard Heuvelmans spends a good amount of space in his classic book, *On the Track of Unknown Animals* (1958), discussing giant catfish-like monsters seen in Lake Victoria and the Upper Nile River of Africa.

William Gibbons, who planned to lead a dinosaur-hunting expedition to Africa in 2000, reports that Missionary Eugene P. Thomas once caught an enormous catfish (weighing over 200 lbs.) from the Oubangui River in the Congo. It fed him and ten pygmy families for 10 days.

In his 1986 checklist of cryptids, Heuvelmans mentions a mysterious animal of the Paraguayan Chaco, South America, said to look like a "slug-like snake," which he believes is a giant catfish called the *manguruyu*. This beast is said to be 18 feet long and a half a ton huge. Heuvelmans points to *Black Jack's Spurs—An Autobiography* by Charles Craig (London: Hutchinson, 1954) as his source.

The late Loch Ness Monster researcher Tim Dinsdale recounted in his books the disappearances of people pulled under in South American rivers. Dinsdale suggested the events could have been caused by giant catfish.

There are actually rather large catfish in the Amazon River. Six different species there reach over 100 pounds. The locally-named piraiba grow to an amazing 300 pounds or more.

Killer Catfish

In Europe, researchers Ulrich Magin and Karl Shuker have written of very real giant catfish (sometimes described as "Lake Monsters") seen in Lake Zeegrzynski, Poland, and Lake Zwischenahn, Germany.

In August of 1998, a Slovenian fisherman drowned trying to land a giant catfish. At a Ljubljana, Slovenia, lake, Franc Filipic, 47, hooked a sheatfish, a type of catfish, and refused to release it when it pulled him under. A friend of Filipic quoted his last words as "Now I've got him!"

Police and divers found Filipic's body two days later. The fish was not recovered. How large was it? Filipic's friend swore it had to have been more than six feet long and weighed upwards of 110 pounds.

Meanwhile in Asia, giant catfish are seen in the Mae Khong River, Thailand, and reported from the Tali Lake, China.

Every year, from the middle of April to the end of May, natives near the Mae Khong River try to catch the giant catfish called Pla Buek *(Pangasianodon gigas chevy)*. Armed with large nets, the men in long wooden boats seek to capture supposedly the world's largest freshwater fish. This catfish is native only to the Mae Khong River, the longest river in Asia.

The Pla Buek can weigh as much as 300 kilograms and can be as long as nine feet in length. These catfish were nearly extinct during the 1990s, and still not much else is known about them. There is a theory that these giant fish travel up the Mae Khong to spawn in southern China's Tali Lake, but no data exists to support this notion.

Ichthyologist Lucas Negus comments on the other Asian giant catfish rumors: "Another not only giant catfish but also a man-eating one is the *Wallago attu* found in parts of Thailand, Java, India, and Burma. This catfish is actually known as the giant, or man-eating, catfish. These catfish grow to about five feet in length, but what makes them dangerous is the fact that they are pure carnivores. It is not totally uncommon for human remains to be found in these giant catfish."

So yes, giant catfish do exist around our Mysterious World, but whether they are to be found in Mysterious America is still not known.

CHAPTER 11

Champp

"I still have nightmares about the monster," the witness told me. "The thing is chasing me, and I'm running to get away. After I saw the monster and took his picture, I had the dreams all the time, but then I got in touch with Zarzynski and the nightmares went away for a while. Now, with all the public pressure and people saying I didn't really see it, the dreams have started again. It's frightening, and sometimes I wish I hadn't told anyone about the picture, or I hadn't seen the monster."

This is Sandra Mansi, soft-spoken and matter-of-fact, telling me about her life since she had become an instant celebrity thanks to the *New York Times* and *Time* magazine. I spoke to her in late August of 1981, following a stimulating day at the first scientific seminar devoted to a study of the monster that has been reported lurking in the waters of Lake Champlain the past 300 years.

"I have been very careful about the people I tell about my experiences," Mansi said. "Someone recently was amazed when I told them I was going to the seminar, and began asking me if I believed in ESP, UFOs, and the tooth fairy. I didn't even tell that person I had seen and photographed the monster."

I have interviewed hundreds of witnesses who have had encounters of the monstrous kind—Bigfoot, mystery felids, sea serpents, or lake monsters. However, in all the research and fieldwork I have done since 1960, the story that unfolded at Lake Champlain is one of the most fascinating I have investigated. The Lake Champlain monster, or "Champ" as it is called, is not a new story, but developments at the lake in the 1980s, including the Mansi photograph, made the area a hotbed of unexplained-phenomena activity and media attention.

The first white man to be credited with seeing the Lake Champlain monster was the lake's namesake, explorer Samuel de Champlain, who in his journal entry for July, 1609, told of having observed a serpentine creature about 20 feet long, as thick as a barrel, and with a horse-like head. Champlain wrote that the Indians called the animal a *chaousarou*. Today, we know what he probably saw was a sturgeon.

Between the time of Champlain's sighting and the 1800s, there were no known EuroAmerican records of Champ sightings, perhaps because the area was sparsely settled until just before the War of 1812. Previously, the only Europeans in the Champlain Valley were mostly Jesuits and soldiers, and they left no stories of any missionary or military encounters with the creature. By 1810, however, monster sightings show up in various records, as about 150,000 settlers looking for inexpensive land had found their way to the lake

The early pioneers discovered they had quite a lake to conquer. Lake Champlain is the United States' largest body of water other than the Great Lakes, occupying portions of what is now Vermont, New York, and the Quebec province of Canada. It is almost 110 miles long and 13 miles wide, with a maximum depth of 400 feet. The surface area is 436 square miles. The action of ancient glaciers carved out the lake, and as the ice sheets retreated they left behind a finger of inland sea that at different times was connected to the ocean. Like Loch Ness in Scotland, Okanagan Lake in British Columbia, and scores of other deep, cold-water lakes in the northern temperate zone, Lake Champlain appears to be an ideal home for monsters.

The early inhabitants soon found that the lake was indeed the residence of a monster of its very own. After Champlain's recorded encounter, there was a void until July 24, 1819, when pioneers sighted a lake monster. Accounts of the time, published in the *Plattsburgh Republican,* tell how in that year pioneers were alarmed by the beast as it stuck its head above the surface of Bulwagga Bay, near what is now Port Henry, New York.

Between the arrival of the steamboat, around 1870, and 1900, according to one historian, the lake's creature was reported on at least twenty occasions. Noteworthy in reviewing this series of sightings is the fact that in all but two incidents, the monster was seen by a number of people at the same time, and that the witnesses included men and women of unimpeachable character.

On August 30, 1878, for example, the yacht *Rob Roy* was becalmed off Button Bay Island; soon the yacht's party of six saw a large monster (although, of course, the incorrect moniker "sea serpent" was used by the papers) swimming rapidly by, its head occasionally projecting through the "smooth as glass" surface of the water. On November 5, 1879, three University of Burlington (now Vermont) students saw the monster—15 feet of it visible above the water—travel gracefully from Appletree Point, near Burlington, around Rock Dunder, and head for Essex. On July 9, 1887, the creature made a spectacular appearance as a group of East Charlotte, Vermont, picnickers saw it come around a bend, its flat snake-like head visible above the water, and make straight toward them. As it grew closer at a terrific speed, several people screamed, and the monster whirled to the right and disappeared under the waves. On August 4, 1892, the American Canoe Association's annual outing, at Willsborough, New York, abruptly ended when the monster surfaced near their gathering and the canoeists scattered in panic.

The ridicule experienced by today's witnesses was not found during the "monster scare" of 1870 to 1900. People came forth readily to tell of their encounters. P. T. Barnum was so struck by the idea of possibly corralling the monster and adding it to his traveling exhibits that he offered $50,000 for the "Champlain Sea Serpent" carcass. No one produced a body, although the sightings continued.

In 1915, according to a subsequent *New York Times* account, several observers saw the monster stranded in the shallows at the entrance of Bulwagga Bay near the Crown Point fortifications. The animal, said to be 40 feet long, lashed the waters in an attempt to escape its fate. Soon it released itself, swam for the Vermont side, and finally sank "submarine fashion, leaving a wake which was well defined on the glassy surface of the lake."

The next series of monster sightings occurred in the 1930s and 1940s. Mr. and Mrs. Langlois, who were fishing in their motorboat off Rouses Point, New York in August, 1939, had an especially close encounter when the monster headed for them and the couple hastily veered to avoid being hit. As they fled for shore, the monster disappeared below the lake's surface. In 1943 Charles Weston watched through binoculars as a large animal churned up the water off Rouses Point. In 1945, one

Winooski, Vermont, woman aboard the *SS Ticonderoga* described how she and other passengers witnessing a bridge dedication saw the beast raise its head from the nearby water.

Through the 1950s, 1960s, and early 1970s, sightings of the Lake Champlain monster were infrequently reported. But that all changed with the arrival on the scene in 1971 of Joseph Zarzynski, a dynamic investigator, lecturer, and social science instructor at a junior high school in Saratoga Springs, New York. He organized the Lake Champlain Phenomena Investigation and made the search for Champ his passion for almost twenty years. Zarzynski's no-nonsense approach to monster hunting meant that those who for years had been ridiculed because they saw something strange in the lake had a sympathetic ear during this new era of cryptozoological investigations at Lake Champlain. He was very active in the 1980s; for example, he noted that the Lake Champlain Monster was seen by 21 people in 1981, but that the sightings had dropped off to only 10 incidents in 1982. But his presence and research documented the old and the new. By the end of the summer of 1982, he told me, Zarzynski had recorded 170 sightings.

Dennis Jay Hall and his Champ Quest continued the search in the 1990s and into the new century. The years regularly produce an average of more than a dozen sightings of large animate objects that might be Champ. The most recent sighting Hall has chronicled involves one on August 14, 2000. A Port Henry resident was traveling north along the "rock cuts" of Port Henry, around 4:00 p.m., when he happened to look over the railroad tracks and saw something that looked like a *huge* snake, in a coiled swimming position, making waves on all sides. The witness tried to convince himself that it was a log. But he could not shake the fact he had indeed seen something moving like an animal in the lake. He told Hall it was almost black or a very dark green, with a body about a foot in diameter, and at least 15 to 20 feet long. The quest for Champ continues.

Luckily, Hall has the legacy of Zarzynski on which to build.

I knew "Zarr," as he was known to his friends, throughout the 1970s and 1980s, and found his research thorough, his method enthusiastic. At six-foot-six, a towering presence, Zarr had a friendly manner and confident style that made him one of the most trusted cryptozoologists in the country. His nature induced witnesses to confide in him; they quickly

Champ

learned that Zarr understands because he has cruised the lake, sonared its depths, and dived its bays.

Zarzynski has also talked to the scores of witnesses who have seen Champ, becoming the lightning rod that monster sighters needed to comfortably tell of their encounters.

A case in point is Sandra Mansi, a 34-year-old tinsmith and amateur photographer with no previous exposure to the world of cryptozoological controversy. Largely because of Zarzynski's stewardship, Mansi has been able to navigate some choppy waters on her way to sharing with the public what Zarzynski calls "the single most impressive piece of evidence" for Champ. Indeed, without Zarr, Mansi's incredible photo might have never been made public.

Mansi's adventure began on July 5, 1977, as she, her husband-to-be, and two children, were picnicking and sightseeing along the Vermont side of Lake Champlain, north of St. Albans. The group decided to get a closer look at the lake and cut across a farm field. The day was bright and sunny, and the water shimmered royal blue, luring the family to the lake's shore.

As Mansi sat there, watching her children play in the water, she saw an object near the middle of the lake. At first, she thought it was a large fish, then the hand of a diver surfacing, but finally she realized it was the grayish brown head and long snake-like neck of a creature breaking the lake's surface. The thing's head seemed to be twisting around, scanning the countryside, Mansi later told me. Although scared to death, she rushed to get her Kodak Instamatic camera from her car, and snapped one shot of the beast. Once the photograph was taken, she grabbed the children and hightailed it out of there.

Mansi had observed that the monster had skin "like an eel" and was "slimy looking," but still had a hard time explaining it to herself in terms of any known animals. Therefore, Mansi and her family cautiously began to joke about the sighting, as a way of living with their strange experience. "We had trouble rationalizing it, so we decided to call it a 2,000-pound duck," she told participants at the August seminar I attended. "It's easier to live with a 2,000-pound duck than something you don't know."

Fearful of the jokes and ridicule she might be subjected to outside her family, Mansi hid the picture for three years. Finally, encouraged by friends and the growing interest in Champ promoted by Zarzynski and his investigation, Mansi, by now living in Winchester, New Hampshire, produced the photograph for scrutiny by some academic types allegedly interested in the monster. The fact that Mansi had lost the negative, and had never known the exact location of the sighting, led to some difficult moments—until Mansi was introduced to Zarzynski.

After interviewing Mansi, Zarzynski contacted other figures in the field of cryptozoology to help him evaluate her evidence. Dr. Roy Mackal, a University of Chicago zoologist famed for his Loch Ness work, and J. Richard Greenwell and Dr. B. Roy Frieden, both of the University of Arizona, examined Mansi's photograph and subjected it to computer analysis (not an easy procedure in the 1970s). According to Frieden, a professor of optical sciences, no evidence of a montage or superposition could be found. Greenwell and Mackal were similarly convinced that

Mansi had snapped a picture of an unknown animate object in the lake.

Since the Mansi photograph's first publicity, Zarzynski has been deluged by witnesses, bringing forth new and old sightings. Among them: spring, 1980, near Fort Ticonderoga, two dark humps were seen swimming by in the lake; in April, 1981, something 25 feet long and dark was sighted near Port Henry, New York; on July 6, 1981, a cake-decorating class in Panton Cove, Vermont, was disrupted when a 20-foot blackish hump was seen moving toward some children playing in the water. Said one class member: "It was exciting. I've never believed in the monster before."

As the interest in Champ increased over the summer of 1981, sparked in large part by the publication of Mansi's photograph in the *New York Times* and *Time* magazine, Zarzynski and others decided a serious conference was needed to examine all the evidence for the existence of Champlain's beast. The "Does Champ Exist?" seminar took place on August 29, 1981, in Shelburne, Vermont.

In the morning session, Zarzynski ran down the historical background of the Champ sightings and introduced the audience of 200 people to the Mansi photograph. Projected on a wall-size screen in an old barn on the shore of Lake Champlain, the vivid blues and browns of the photograph presented an image few conference members will soon forget. The showing was coupled with Zarzynski's impassioned plea for state governments and environmental groups to help protect the monster.

Next, Mansi, despite being visibly nervous about speaking before a large group, told the story of her experience. Conference goers knew the details, but it was the first time Mansi, who now lives in her native Vermont, had spoken publicly. She stirred the audience when she forcefully answered the question raised by the title of the conference: "You don't want to ask me if I think Champ exists. I've seen him, almost on a first-name basis. I've photographed Champ."

The afternoon's session presented analyses by cryptozoologists Mackal and Greenwell, as well as their theories about what the creature might be. Two major camps have developed to explain Champ. The leader of one, Greenwell, is convinced that Champ is a plesiosaur, an extinct marine reptile, not unlike the Loch Ness monster. He feels that both creatures, and others in Northern Hemisphere lakes, were trapped in the inland lakes formed at the end of the last ice age. In frank disagreement with Greenwell's theory is Mackal, who is certain that these temperate-zone lake monsters are relics of an early era, related to zeuglodons, primitive whales thought to have died out 20 million years ago; he also senses they have access to the oceans via waterways.

Despite debates over what exactly the Lake Champlain monster may be, the seminar did introduce a new period of credibility to Champ watching. Although Mansi is often afraid she has opened a Pandora's box for herself and other monster researchers by releasing her photograph, Zarzynski, who has investigated more than a hundred sightings, believes her picture has put a nice cap on the issue. The Mansi photograph is the one piece of evidence that Champ researchers have needed to compel the broader public to open its eyes to some rather strange goings-on.

As I left the first scientific seminar on the Lake Champlain Monster, and headed back down the road again, I turned on the radio to find the song "Puff the Magic Dragon" by Peter, Paul and Mary playing. In the past, such conferences would have left me feeling as if my time had been wasted on examining something as elusive as a puff of smoke, but after Zarzynski's pioneering work and Mansi's photograph, the Lake Champlain Monster appears to be an actual creature frolicking in the autumn mist.

CHAPTER 12

The Phantom Panthers

P hantom panthers seem to have an unusually high attraction to automobiles, especially those with people in them. In 1948, a couple of Indiana wildlife officials told of a 350-pound mystery feline that lunged at their car, crashed into the car's side, and then fled into the woods near Quakertown. Matt Bille, who writes about cryptozoology, remembers the story of his father, Don Bille, who encountered an unusual black feline that leapt right in front of his car in rural east-central Maine in 1955. Three years later, near Rome, Georgia, a big black panther jumped up against a motorist's car and left muddy pawprints on its side.

One of the first attacks on an automobile and its passengers happened early in the 1900s near a city which has hosted several phantom panther accounts. Many pages could be spent recounting hundreds of American mystery felid cases found in my files or in the collections of other dedicated researchers, such as Mark A. Hall, John Lutz, Bruce S. Wright, Todd Lester, Ted Reed, Ron Schaffner, Ivan Sanderson, and Dan Manning. Let me, however, dwell on the phenomenon reflected through the "window" of Decatur, Illinois, my base of operations from 1947 through the early 1970s. Phantom panther sightings often occur in waves or flaps in specific locations. Decatur will serve as our convenient, well-researched petri dish.

Nellie

The creature which terrified the Decatur, Illinois area in July 1917 was called "Nellie the Lion," an oddly affectionate nickname for a creature whose nasty temper made her anything but lovable.

Nellie, or her male companion (there were two giant mystery cats, not just one, around and about), first angered and frightened the public by attacking Thomas Gullet, a butler at the Robert Allerton Estate, southwest of Monticello, while he was in the garden picking flowers. Gullet only suffered minor wounds but a furor swept central Illinois nonetheless.

The affair had actually begun around Camargo a few days earlier, but the Gullet attack got all the press attention. It led to a 300-person posse that tramped through the woods most of July 15. While the hunters engaged in this fruitless endeavor, the lion nonchalantly reappeared a quarter-mile away from the Allerton mansion and Mrs. Shaw, the chief housekeeper, got a good look. As chance would have it, she was one of the few people in the vicinity not carrying a gun at the moment. Like Gullet, and this is an important detail that we shall run into often in other cases, she referred to the animal as an "African lioness."

The drama moved to Decatur on July 17 when searchers found tracks five inches long (12.7 cm) and four inches (10.16 cm) wide. Two fourteen-year-old boys, Earl Cavanaugh and Glyan Tulison, saw the beast the same day, walking along Allen's Bend of the Sangamon River, a short distance east of the city.

A sort of hysteria overtook the region. Silliness, too. On a number of occasions people mistook collies for one of the lions, and one farmer distinguished himself by shooting a hole through the radiator of an approaching car; he had mistaken the headlights for the beast's shining eyes. The newspapers, of course, had a good time with this kind of fear-filled foolishness, and convinced puzzled readers to dismiss the other reports as jokes.

But another attack got everyone's undivided attention again.

Chester Osborn, Earl Hill, and their wives were driving near Decatur when the lion pounced on their car as they were motoring west on the Springfield road. The startling encounter took place at 10:30 p.m., on July 29. Hill and Osborn, sitting in the front, saw Nellie standing in the weeds next to the road. It leaped twenty feet, struck the car's side, and fell onto the highway. Osborn and Hill rushed back to Decatur to summon the police. The lion was still there when they returned. But it quickly disappeared over an embankment, and further search parties could not find it.

On July 31, at about 3:00 p.m., James Rutherford, a farmhand, was driving a hay wagon past a gravel pit when he spotted a "large yellow, long-haired beast." As he gaped in terror, the animal regarded him without interest, then wandered off into a clump of bushes near a small creek. When the inevitable armed posse rushed to the scene, they found only its tracks, which, strangely enough, had claw marks in them. This extremely odd detail turns up over and over again, and appears to have nothing to do with the fact that most felines (except for the cheetah) usually do not leave claw marks. ("Usually" they do not, but sometimes the larger cats, when running in pursuit of prey or in slippery or otherwise less than perfect footing, do leave clawed tracks.)

Soon after that "Nellie" disappeared forever. Or so it seemed. Perhaps her offspring stayed in the area.

More Illinois Panthers

After Nellie departed, several years passed before the reign of the panther would return to central Illinois—or so the gap in our records indicates. Instead, the 1940s would see the sightings of many black panthers and maned cats in Indiana, with reports of two black panthers together at Oquawka, Illinois, in September 1946, and a black panther spied in Jasper County, Illinois, during August 1949. Black panther stories began circulating in the Decatur area after September 13, 1955, when a woman saw one slinking along a road. The next evening, two truck drivers spotted the "black cat" in the vicinity of Rea's Lost Bridge. Other people reported hearing its scream in the night. The animal was described as "long, lowslung and jet black with gleaming eyes."

Then, on the 25th of October, 1955, game warden Paul G. Myers surprised a black panther near Decatur and shot at it. Despite the fact that he, like scores before and after him, thought he had wounded it, Myers never found a body.

The year 1963 had barely begun when a giant cat began frightening residents of Fisher, Urbana, and Mahomet in Illinois' Champaign County. Sheriff Everett J. Hedrick of Urbana said reports described something about five feet long "and very dark, possibly black," adding, "it's just about impossible for the animal to be a panther. It might be a mountain lion that somehow got loose in this area." This time, around 300 men joined another Illinois posse. Needless to say the animal eluded them but its tracks, between a large dog's and a mountain lion's, were baffling.

Sightings of the animal continued well into 1963. One of them, made by farmer Bill Chambers of Mahomet, is sufficiently detailed to be worth quoting in full. Here is the letter he sent me:

In regard to the Mahomet cougar, I have seen it twice. The last time was just a fleeting look at daylight before it was light enough to shoot. The first time was the day before, just before sunset on June 2, 1963.

The cat was hunting in clover and was unaware of me, apparently. I was about 300 yards from him when I first saw him, or it. I was on the road in my pickup and the cat paid no attention to the truck so I drove into a lane and coasted down a little grade to within what I estimated to be 190 yards.

I had a set of sandbags that I use on my shooting bench and I put them on top of the truck cab to give me a steady shooting position.... (Through the scope) the head was visible but seldom still enough for a target and the head is a poor place to shoot a cat anyway.

The cat spent several minutes near a big weed clump with little showing until he jumped on something in the clover. When he did this I had laid my rifle down and was watching with my 8x binoculars and the tail was clearly visible.

A little later, he sat up facing straight at me and with the sun down and directly at my back, I was looking at the lighted side all the time and he appeared jet black except for two tawny streaks under the jaws extending two or three inches down his neck. Before I could get the rifle on him again, he settled back down in the clover. I was within an ounce of getting the shot off three different times in 10 or 15 minutes but the cat kept moving and I never got my shot off.

The next day, I stepped the distance from the truck tracks to the weed clump and got 187 steps. The clover there averaged 12" tall which would make him about 15" tall at the shoulder. The fact that I was looking down on him a little might bring his shoulder height to about 14". Tail and all, I would say he was between four-and-a-half and five feet and probably closer to the four-and-a-half feet. The only tracks I could find measured two-and-five-eighths inches in soft wet ground and had no claw marks like a dog would make.

Strangely, in May and July of 1962, near Urbana, *Ohio,* which happens to be in Champaign County, a major "black panther" flap was occurring. Over a dozen people said they saw the "all black, big" cat "with a long tail and big eyes." In the midst of the sightings, one individual came forward to say he had seen a black panther in 1955 when he was driving west of Urbana. Of the 1962 accounts, one incident involved Mr. and Mrs. Darrell Goffs viewing the panther jumping eight feet from a tree, and leaving behind tracks with "distinct claw marks." What is incredible is the interesting fact that in separate Champaign Counties, near separate Urbana's—in Illinois and Ohio—two major mystery feline flaps could be so closely timed. Hancock County, Indiana, also had some black panther sightings in September-October 1962.

Returning to the survey of the central Illinois flap, during the early morning hours of June 30, 1963, George W. Davidson of Decatur, Illinois, aroused by the sound of dogs barking in the neighborhood, chased a "large cat" into a tree. As he approached, however, it leaped on him, scratched his face, and dashed away over a five-foot fence. He said the animal was three feet long and dark in color. Perhaps it was nothing more than a fisher? Or a small black "panther"?

The identity of the creature seen two years later appears much less mundane. A black panther reappeared in Decatur, Illinois, at 2:00 a.m., June 25, 1965. Mrs. Rogers was pulling into her driveway when a "black, big cat-like animal" suddenly loomed in her headlights. Before the witness could move, the thing had escaped into a field close to her home. According to the sheriff's report, "the animal stood higher than her car's headlights. She showed (an investigating officer) a pawprint in the dust of her driveway which was made by the animal. . . . The print (was) about four inches across and apparently made by a member of the cat family as opposed to the dog family."

Three days later a large mystery cat startled three children at an outing in Lincoln Park on the south end of Decatur; as they took off running, it gobbled up a sack lunch one of them had dropped.

A "mountain lion" loped rapidly across the road in front of Anthony Viccone's car at dawn of June 27, 1967. Viccone told me he knew it was a "mountain lion" because he had seen them on television. Driving south of Decatur, Viccone said that at a "conservative" estimate the creature was six-and-a-half-feet long and its color was a shiny "metallic" bronze. "It wasn't a bobcat," Viccone insisted. About twenty sheep had been killed in the area in prior weeks.

Then, in 1970, an "invasion" of mystery animals began throughout Illinois. It started and ended in Decatur. In January, west of Decatur, an employee of the Macon Seed Company saw a large black animal he described as a "cougar." William F. Beatty, president of the firm, told me that he had found tracks left by the animal, which he said had twice torn down his electric fence. Two days later game warden James Atkins, investigating along with me on site, concluded that the animal was a beaver— a most unusual beaver to be sure, since the large felid tracks that Beatty found didn't look at all like a beaver's!

Alexander County, in southern Illinois, had a series of black panther sightings from 1966 through 1970. The edge of the Shawnee National Forest kept up its reputation as a high sighting area, highlighted by the Mike Busby case of 1970. On April 10th, Busby was driving along State Road 3, outside of Olive Branch, on the edge of the bottomlands forest, when his car experienced engine problems. In looking to see what was wrong, he was attacked by a semi-upright six-foot "tall" monster feline, covered in steel-wool-like black fur. Busby and the cat rolled around on the ground, until a big semi truck passed and scared the cat away. Busby, who was taken to a local hospital by the truck driver who had stopped, was covered with wounds. These were still visible when I interviewed him a week later. Edwardsville, Illinois, also had black panther sightings that year.

Finishing out 1970, a large black panther and its half-grown cub appeared in a field outside of Decatur on December 11th, and were observed twice during the day by members of the Clarence Runyon family. The Runyons thought the animals may have been the reason forty chickens disappeared from their farm during the summer. The Illinois Department of Conservation's investigation produced no results.

My days of investigating the state's phantom cats had me trekking all over Illinois. In addition to the felids, of course, the 1960s and 1970s brought reports of mystery animals ranging from Momo-like hominid beasts and ape-like creatures to so-called "kangaroos" seen near Decatur and elsewhere in Illinois. Those will be discussed in other chapters. When

I left Illinois in 1974, my investigations ranged from black panther reports from Marin County, California to the melanistic Van Etten Monster of Elmira, New York. Finally, a couple years later, I relocated to New England. It was time for someone else to come forth and look into the Illinois sightings.

Troy Taylor, author of many books on Illinois mysteries, including *Haunted Decatur Revisited* (2000), first became interested in black panthers after he saw one running through the bush in Moweaqua, Illinois, a small town near Decatur, in the spring of 1984. Taylor would soon discover that his personal family "folklore" told of the night in 1960 when his stepfather's mother saw a big black cat cross the road in front of her car near Decatur.

The black cats would keep any Illinois investigator busy. On December 18, 1986, in East Carondelet, Illinois, a phantom feline was roaming about and killing pet dogs. A footprint measuring three and a half inches long was obtained by Thomas Amlung from the St. Clair County Animal Control. An East Carondelet man was driving home at 3:00 a.m. when what was described as a "black leopard" struck the front of his bumper. The driver believed he saw a patch of white on its chest. Mayor Herb Simmons and police chief Skip Mize found some good tracks, but there was no evidence of blood or hair on the car bumper. Simmons and Mize both claimed to have seen this animal a few weeks earlier using a spotlight from a police cruiser, clearly noticing that it was coal black.

Then in February 1987, in East Carondelet, Illinois, a woman saw the same creature under a street light outside her home, and then near Cahokia, Frank and Rosie Armstrong were driving home when they saw the cat eating on a dead carcass in the middle of Stolle Road. The couple were surprised at the animal's lack of fear of humans and automobiles. But we weren't.

Troy Taylor began to collect reports in the mid-1980s and continues to do so to this day. One series he examined included black panther sightings during the fall of 1995. During one of these incidents, a giant melanistic cat attacked a Decatur family's dog. The pawprints that it left behind were reportedly huge.

The Decatur area reports continue, just as they do throughout the country. During April 1999, nearby Clarksdale experienced a close encounter of the panther kind. "Early one morning, I was standing looking out my window when I saw a big black, panther-like animal walking across my yard," Bev Ray, 48, told Decatur journalist Tony Reid. "It was jet black, and it was just calmly walking along, not running or anything. And it was big. I saw it from less than a few hundred feet away, and it was really, really big. It walked through my yard and disappeared into some timber nearby. The point is, I know what dogs and coyotes and other animals look like, and this black creature I saw wasn't one of them. It moved like a big cat, not a dog; you know, kind of slinking along. I'd say it was about one and a half times the size of my biggest Rottweiler. I wasn't too frightened at the time but later I got to thinking 'Did I really see that?' And I kept thinking about it, and I knew I really did see it and then it was like 'Oh, wow.'"

Both Bev Ray and her husband, Mike Ray, 54, found tracks close to their home which they measured at four inches across. Heavy rain destroyed the prints before the Rays could make casts, but during the spring of 1999, they were all set to take plaster imprints if the big cat came back. They also had their camcorder and camera ready.

"You need something for people to believe you," said Ray, a retired truck driver. "Bev contacted the county sheriff, and he told us to just call the dog pound. People blow stories like this off, but we've really got something big living out here."

Joe Khayyat, a spokesman for the Illinois Department of Natural Resources, said state experts were pretty skeptical, but added: "We know you can't just completely and absolutely rule out that those folks did see something."

Last word is that the Rays did not have another visit, and were not able to get the kind of casts or photographic evidence they wanted. Too bad.

Back in 1976, when another black panther was sighted in southern Macon County where Decatur is located, one man did get one important piece of proof. Louis Jockisch of Boody managed to make an audio recording of the cat's cries.

One could examine any number of hot spots in this country, such as Waldo County, Maine; Alexander County, Illinois; or Oakland County, Michigan, and find similar routine flaps of black panther reports issuing from those locations. Folks are encountering these animals, some with surprise, some matter-of-factly, because they happen to be part of their environment.

Black Panthers

People often could care less if others do not accept that they are seeing black panthers. The witnesses are often remarkably credible people who have had extraordinary experiences. Like Betty Ann Cushman, the wife of one of Maine's Baxter State Park rangers, who in 1981 encountered a large melanistic cat and said:

> There is absolutely no doubt in my mind that what I saw was a black panther. We were driving between Harrington Lake and the Sourdnahunk gate when this handsome animal appeared in the road. It had the wide head of the cat family, the long tail, and its every motion was one of grace. It took a long look at the truck, then seemed to glide over the road bank and into the woods.

The whole subject of melanistic or black felines is shrouded in mysterious happenings supported by statistical data and sincere sightings. Early investigator Bruce Wright reported 20 good encounters with "black panthers" from his New Brunswick fieldwork from 1951-1970, recording them in his *The Ghost of North America* (1959) and *Eastern Panther: A Question of Survival* (1972). Gerry Parker's *The Eastern Panther* (1998) noted that "approximately 15-20 percent of sightings [of eastern panthers] from most regions are reported to be black." Elsewhere in his book, he comments that maybe as high as a quarter of all reports appear to mention black cats.

Old black panther sightings occurred in Florida in 1929; Louisiana in 1945; New Hampshire, Massachusetts, Indiana, and Ohio in 1948; Nebraska in 1951; and Michigan in 1952. That's just a sampling; the list is a long one. Mark A. Hall has shared with me and written extensively on this matter, especially in his "The American Lion *(Panthera atrox),"* *Wonders* (3(1): 3-20, 1994). Hall is to be credited with discovering records of many old sightings, as have I and others. (Hall's important list of 70 *selected* cases is the foundation of the American Lion list, an appendix in this book.) Hall has also heard of the killing of three of these cats:

In the early 1970s Walter DeYoung was living on his farm near Bemidji, Minnesota. One night he saw a long black cat in his corral and he watched it leap the fence. He thought it must be a puma. So did the local conservation officer he talked to who already knew about the cat. He asked DeYoung not to talk about it. The cat was seen for about 3 months until a local paper ran a picture of the dead cat after it had been shot.

A second occurrence appears to have happened in early 1960. Sallie Ann Clarke of Fort Worth, Texas, told me in 1970 that a "black panther" had been routinely seen along a creek beside her new home. Finally a farmer shot and killed the animal, according to a newspaper report.

The most involved incident is documented in Atlanta, Georgia, newspapers for the year 1975. The story began with an 18 Sept. report from Stockbridge with the title "Something Screams at Night." From the woods came sounds "that'll turn your blood cold." People reported a "sleek black cat with a long tail" and eyes the size of silver dollars. A penned-up goat was killed.

Three days later it was reported that five residents around Stockbridge had seen the same black cat. A trap was put out by officials of the Game and Fish Division of the Georgia Department of Natural Resources. At this time it surfaced that a local resident, James Rutledge, had shot and killed an animal during the previous spring. He was plowing in his garden when he spied what looked like a young black panther in a tree. He shot it three times. According to the *Atlanta Constitution* "he said he buried it without telling anyone because he was afraid of upsetting local residents."

At this point officials gave their views on black panthers. Dr. Ernest Provost of the University of Georgia (Forest Resources Dept.) said, "There may be panthers here but they are not black. This black business has never been proven. No one has ever gotten a black panther." Ron Jackson, curator of mammals at the Atlanta Zoo, said a black panther was not a biological impossibility but no zoo had one. If reports were correct he thought it would have to be a leopard, saying, "As far as I know there would be nothing like that unless someone released it. It's possible that some circus had it and it escaped."

Terry Johnson, a biologist with the state DNR, wanted to dig up any skeletal remains of Rutledge's kill. And it was reported that this would happen within a week's time.

On 6 Oct. the *Atlanta Journal* reported the outcome of the interest in the corpse. Rutledge decided against revealing the location. He told the DNR that he could not remember where it was. According to the *Journal:* "Rutledge is reportedly afraid of being prosecuted for killing an endangered species, which carries a maximum fine of $20,000 and two to five years in jail." An unnamed U.S. official was reported to say that such prosecution was unlikely. The newspaper concluded "apparently Rutledge will not lead officials to the site unless he has a written document granting immunity from prosecution, a document that officials say they cannot legally provide."

How widespread are the eyewitness reports of these black mystery cats? From the data of the 615 "eastern cougar" sightings collected by John and Linda Lutz of the Eastern Puma Research Network (1983 to 1989), Richard Greenwell ("The Eastern Puma: Evidence Continues to Build," *The ISC Newsletter,* 1989) found that 37 percent of the total reports involved black felines. According to John Lutz, who is headquartered in Maryland, the majority of these black cat reports were in Maryland (40 sightings), Pennsylvania (37 sightings), and West Virginia (29 sightings), with accounts also reported from New York (13), Wisconsin (12), Virginia (6), Michigan (6), Kentucky (5), Maine (5), Florida (4), Illinois (4), Ohio (2), Indiana (1), New Jersey (1), and Alabama (1).

For the 1990s, John and Linda Lutz of the Eastern Puma Research Network, gathering what he thought were eastern USA reports of "pumas," found the "blacks" showed up in these numbers:

1990——total = 149 ....black.....46, tan....103, cubs....46
1991——total = 567 ....black...176, tan....391, cubs....52
1992——total = 507....black.....133, tan...374, cubs.....55
1993——total = 435.....black.....95, tan...340, cubs.....21
1994——total = 245.....black.....39, tan....206, cubs.....20
1995——total = 510.....black.....94, tan....416, cubs.....47
1996——total = 460.....black.....87, tan....373, cubs.....45
1997——total = 323.....black.....63, tan....260, cubs.....29
1998——total = 355.....black.....70, tan....285, cubs.....26
1999——total = 397.....black.....62, tan....309, cubs.....25

Additionally, he recorded in 1999 a total of 14 rust, 1 grey, and 9 milk chocolate-colored cats.

Todd Lester's Eastern Cougar Research Center recorded, from 1995 through 1999, a total of 673 individual "eastern cougar" sightings. Hidden within these reports are "melanistic panther" reports. His state-by-state breakdown reflects the bias of his base of operations being in West Virginia, in the same fashion that the Lutz-Maryland link does. Here is Lester's data on black panther sightings for 1995-1999: West Virginia (122), North Carolina (17), Virginia (16), Kentucky (6), Pennsylvania (5), Ohio (2), Georgia (2), Maryland (1), Florida (1), Tennessee (1), Kansas (1), New Brunswick (1), Louisiana (1), and Maine (1).

All of these reports seem to bring into doubt the theory that these mystery cats are merely the eastern subspecies of the mountain lion or puma, *Puma concolor couguar,* repopulating its old niches. The puma is extremely shy and does not routinely attack automobiles or humans. But perhaps most importantly, the puma is tawny in color, not black.

These cryptids, the mystery cats of North America, are, more often than not, described as "black panthers." Generally, one thinks of the melanistic leopard of Africa and Asia as the black panther, but it is the puma of the New World that is the skeptic's usual flesh and blood rebuttal to these accounts of large, black cats. To confuse matters even further, "panther" is a term synonymous with mountain lion, puma, cougar, or painter; all supposedly denote, at least in North America, the same animal, a tawny (not a black) felid.

The problem remains, however, that besides being behaviorally worlds apart from the phantom felines, the record of a black puma displaying the melanistic color phase is so rare that the one or two cases seemingly accepted are in dispute. In 1843, an allegedly melanistic puma supposedly was killed in the Carandehy River section of Brazil. There is no record of what became of the body. Perhaps it was a black jaguar, after all. "Black pumas" have attained almost folkloric status. The most significant proof appears to be that noted by J. B. Tinsley in *The Puma: Legendary Lion of the Americas* (1987) who published a photo of a black feline labeled: "Black puma, or *pantera negra,* killed by Miguel Ruiz Herrero in 1959 in the Province of Guanacaste along the north Pacific coast of Costa Rica." Still, these instances remain in question. No scientifically verified melanistic *Puma concolor* of any subspecies is accepted.

Zoology texts indicate melanism in the Felidae, the family of cats, apparently runs the highest in the moist tropics and subtropics. The most frequent numbers of black mutations appear to occur in the jaguar *(Panthera onca)* of Latin and South America, and the leopard *(Panthera pardus)* of Asia, and less so of Africa.

The black jaguar found in Central and South America is comparatively rare. During the 1980s, when I conducted a global survey of captive melanistic felid holdings, not more than thirty jaguars populated the world's zoological gardens. Of these, a large percentage found in zoos today continue to be related zoo-bred animals. Black jaguars, therefore, are not that common in the wild, and seem frequently to be concentrated in specific areas such as the jungle of Guyana Massif. As far as I have been able to determine and as Gerry Parker notes in his eastern panther book, no black jaguars have ever been captured or killed in the United States, although the spotted variety infrequently has been known to range into some parts of the Southwest. The black jaguar is a stocky beast, and quite different from the descriptions of our melanistic phantom felines, or so-called "black panthers."

The black leopards of Africa and Asia are referred to as black panthers, and therein lies a good deal of confusion among people seeing the "panthers" of America. Within any litter of spotted leopards, the chances are high that one of the kits will be black. Among leopards of Asia, especially, the frequency of births and survival of black offspring is common. Among African leopards, the black ones are rarer. It's notable that these tend to come from the mountains of Kenya, the site of other anomalistic and melanistic felid sightings, especially the cryptid spotted and black lion reports, as well as those of accepted black specimens, such as the black serval.

Some laymen have wrongly viewed the black leopard as a separate species and labeled them "black panthers." Since most people sense that a majority of the mystery cats are reported to be black, the phantom felines are thus tagged "black panthers" by the press and the witnesses. Because of such semantic games, the Illinois Department of Conservation, for example, can make ridiculous statements like the following:

> Now and then, rural communities in Illinois have a panther scare that reduces normal, thinking individuals into children that are afraid to step out in the dark. Usually, the alleged animal is said to be a black panther, not a cougar (puma). Cougars are not black, and black panthers are not native to the Western Hemisphere. In Africa and Asia where panthers do roam, the black panther is a rare animal because it is a freak, a melanist.

California Dreaming

But it is not so easy to dismiss the "black panthers" of North America. Take, for example, the "black panthers" of California. California is a state where recent estimates claim about 2,500 mountain lions may roam. But some intriguing "black panther" reports are found within the range of the California puma. The problem of "real" mountain lions and the allegedly "unreal" mystery or phantom cats is brought into clear focus in California.

For several years, large black cats have been sighted near Ventura, in the Conejo Valley. A full-fledged hunt for two of these full-grown black panthers was conducted in 1964, but things did not come to a peak until 1967. During the afternoon of the 12th of December of that year, Henry Madrid of Montelvo was installing a fence around the Ventura County sewer plant. Henry spotted a black panther pacing restlessly back and forth on the steep mountainside near the treatment facility. He and fellow workers Dick Simmons, Fred Salinas and Manuel Portillo kept an eye on the panther while the county sheriff deputies were notified. Taking in the situation quickly soon after they arrived, the deputies pointed their squad car in the cat's direction, and bounced off in hot pursuit toward the hillside. The obligingly flat field stretched out before them, but it proved to be merely a thin, dry crust over a bed of sludge. The chase ended with the police car plunging hood-deep into a sea of sickening muck. By the time a tow truck arrived to rescue the deputies from their smelly predicament, the black panther had long disappeared.

This was the first in a series of incidents that led many to sense that the Ventura County black panther was a sinister omen. Soon after the deputies' disaster, Kenneth French and his wife saw the black cat on January 9, 1968, near a mountainside while they were out driving. The couple debated whether to report it. "Finally my husband stayed to keep an eye on it, while I went to get a sheriff's deputy," Mrs. French later told reporters. "Apparently, the cat ran away just after I left. My husband and I aren't the type to report weird things, and it's pretty embarrassing to have people think you go around seeing black panthers! Whatever kind of black cat it was, it was bad luck."

The "bad luck" of this black panther even trapped an airman on a sheer, six-hundred-foot cliff on the 23rd of December, 1967. It took rescuers four hours to get him down after he went hunting for the panther. Ventura County's black panther was never caught, despite efforts by the airman and many others.

Not to be outdone in claims to phantom pantherdom, the accounts from Northern California far outweigh those from the southern portion of the state. All of the sightings from the north are centered around the San Francisco Bay area.

One of the investigations I conducted while living in California during the mid-1970s was a survey of the Marin County's San Rafael newspaper, *The Independent Journal,* for the years 1957-1975. In an area that was not supposed to have a population of pumas living there, my search revealed thirty separate sightings of large, mountain lion-like animals. More often than not (75 percent of the total), the color of the creature is not given, but in 15 percent of the reports, the cat is said definitely to be black. What is being seen: "black panther" or puma? Adding to the mystery is the incident in June 1963, when two women collecting watercress at a creek were chased home by a "panther," its behavior quite unlike *Puma concolor*. In March of 1975, a large powerful-looking "panther" sauntered through downtown Fairfax, California, and jaywalked across busy Sir Francis Drake Boulevard, leaving townsfolk shuddering in its wake. The Humane Society of Marin attempted to track it down and capture it, but gave up empty-handed. Roubert L. Dollarhite, Director of Operations of the organization, called the Fairfax sighting "extraordinary," saying it is unusual for mountain lions to approach urban areas.

Mystery feline or common mountain lion? These panther accounts merge into those from Mt. Tamalpais and Mill Valley, also in Marin County, of a chattering five-foot-tall, "earless mountain lion" and Bigfoot seen in 1963, 1975, and 1976. What are we to make of this swirling phantasmagoria of mysteries? But things get crazier way out west.

South of Marin and San Francisco, a flurry of reports of a five-foot-long, 150-pound, "dark black" (how dark can black get?) panther made it into the papers in December of 1973. Navy Lt. Comdr. Thomas Mantei's collie, Cleo, supposedly even treed the cat in a eucalyptus in a gully behind Mantei's San Jose hillside home.

Meanwhile, east of San Francisco, in what is generally known as the East Bay area, a series of black panther sightings was coming to an end. It started in the spring of 1972, when in the space of three days two men called Gary Bogue, Curator of the Alexander Lindsey, Jr. Museum in Walnut Creek, to tell him of sightings of black panthers. Neither knew the other, and no press coverage had stimulated the reports. One man watched the cat through binoculars when he was at home for lunch. The other witness was walking his Irish setter when his dog started barking at a large black cat up in a tree. The five-foot-long beast jumped out of the tree and ran off.

About twelve miles from the first reports and three weeks later, a woman and her neighbor reported they were looking out the back window, watching a black panther chase cattle. The panther also strolled over to her pool and took a drink. (This daytime pool-drinking behavior was also reported of other mystery felines seen by witnesses in Southern California in 1972, and Ohio in 1977.)

Without any publicity, East Bay's cat continued to be seen. A month after the swimming pool incident, the Concord Naval Weapons Depot Commander called authorities to report a black panther on the grounds of his facility. Animal Control officers and several military personnel observed the mystery feline through binoculars. All agreed it was black and puma-sized. When they called out one of the officers with his .357 magnum rifle, the cat vanished.

During the fall of 1972, a rancher living at the base of Mt. Diablo ("Devil's Mountain") noticed that his ducks and geese had begun disappearing. The fowl were not being ripped apart like a dog would do, but were totally devoured. The rancher and his wife also heard what sounded like heavy guttural purring outside their bedroom window. Then one midnight, there was a loud thump on their roof, their horses started fussing, and the family German shepherd scratched to be let in. The rancher grabbed a flashlight, went outside, and saw a large black panther turn, look at him, and walk calmly away. Tracks about five inches across were found.

Three months later the naturalist at the Las Trampas Regional Park was the next person to see "it." The naturalist and others frequently saw the black panther in the company of a tawny-colored cat-like animal chasing deer. This is not the first time two different colored mystery cats have kept company. We are reminded of the August 7, 1948, Turner boys sighting from Richmond, Indiana. The patterns of the mystery felines were, and are still, being played out in California.

The Bay area's phantom panthers have also had their random encounters with automobiles. For example, on Wednesday morning, the 19th of December, 1973, Larry Rephahn told Fremont police that he almost struck a black mountain lion as it dashed across Niles Canyon Road near Joyland Park.

Indeed, stepping back from the California accounts, what we see is part of that circle we can start measuring anywhere. The "black panthers" do not seem to be "black mountain lions." The Californian mystery cats reflect and repeat patterns. These cat sightings occur in waves ("flaps") and in specific locations ("windows"). The year 1973 appears to have been a big year around the San Francisco Bay area for sightings of large, black panther-like creatures; it was also the "year of the humanoids," to use David Webb's phrase, elsewhere in America.

As for "windows," I have already stated my long noticed American historical acknowledgment of weird phenomena by way of place names including the word "devil." Interestingly, some of the more frequent flap-related sightings of the Californian black panthers have taken place in the Diablo (Spanish for "devil") Valley. One booklet on the Las Trampas Regional Park noted the black cat was referred to as "The Black Mountain Lion of Devil's Hole" because it was frequently seen on the slopes of Mt. Diablo and in the Devil's Hole area of the park.

So, in a smoke screen of actual *Puma concolor* in California, something else appears to be creeping about. Flaps and window areas exist where people are viewing creatures unlike mountain lions. Mountain lions are not black. Mountain lions do not usually chase people. Nor do they prowl during the day. These mystery cats do.

This Mystery Feline Has History

A good phantom panther report cannot be shrugged off easily. The conventionalists, unwilling to admit they are stumped, usually try to ignore the mystery cats, or explain them away in terms of the escape of known animals. Yes, the exotic pet trade is very real, and some animals are escaping, living in the wild for a time, while others return or are killed. The fact that the pumas or mountain lions *(Puma concolor)* are still to be found in scattered parts of the New World makes it easy for the rationalizers to dismiss individual sightings of the "black panthers" or related mystery felids as hoaxes, mistakes, or descriptions of normal pumas stepping briefly outside of their usual territory. In the Northeast, in northern Maine, in the Appalachians of New York State, and in the Great Smokies of the Southeast, *Puma concolor couguar,* the eastern puma, appears to be making a comeback. However, knowing the characteristics of our phantom felines, I am not easily distracted by such flimsy explanations.

Circus train wrecks have been a classic "wipe"—the ending for mystery animal stories for years. The pattern is typical. A strange beast is seen around, sightings are recorded, search parties are dispatched, tracks or dead livestock are discovered, but no animals like the ones being seen can be caught or killed. A news reporter or local sheriff then comes forth with the rumor that a "wrecked circus train" is responsible for an escaped black leopard or African lion. Quickly the story dies away, the sightings cease, the ridicule factor quiets all, and the wave is dead. Hollywood even captured and promoted this mythical answer to mystery animal reports with Cecil B. DeMille's 1952 movie, *The Greatest Show on Earth,* with a dramatic circus train wreck and the escape of many wild cats.

I sense that the escapee theory for these cases, which is favored by my colleague Karl Shuker, is a case of *deus ex machina la Felidae.* Shuker believes it's an example of Occam's Razor, which I understand, but disagree with. Sadly, the escapee explanation is too frequently used by people (rural law enforcement and local news media) not open to any "unknown animal" hypotheses. While we know that many more felid releases and escapes are occurring than reported, we are also conscious of the fact that many unchronicled sightings of large mystery cats are happening in locations where few escapees have ever even left a pawprint. Ridicule keeps an even higher number of these cats from being reported.

Another criticism heard is the so-called "historical problem"—that there is no good evidence for the presence of large black felines in North America prior to the 1940s. What is happening, of course, is that the widespread use of the word "panther" in historical records is unfortunately not linked to any discussion of the "color" or actual description of the cats called "panthers." Under these situations, how would we know that there are no records of black cats in the past?

What are we to make of the report from the Jesuit explorers Louis Joliet and Jacques Marquette, when in June 1673, they reached the mouth of the lower Wisconsin (in what is today Grant County) and reported seeing "a few monsters: big catfish, a spadefish, a panther." Wisconsin's Objiway called the local large feline *mishibigin.* Do we know what these panther and *mishibigin* looked like?

Consider the similar situation concerning the *onza,* a panther-like mystery cat reported in the Sonora region of Mexico. Historical research in which old records of the *onza* have been found are often frustrating because once the word *onza* is used, often no description is given. Neil Carmony in *Onza: The Hunt for a Legendary Cat* (1995) finds that several names for large cats were used in old Mexico, including *tigre, leon, leopardo, pantera,* and *onza.* "Exactly what cat is being considered is often impossible to ascertain [sic] for the writers rarely gave adequate descriptive details," Carmony notes. For example, world-famous wildlife artist Arturo Imaz Baume, who knew his country's wildlife in some detail, was stalked by, and encountered, an *onza* in May 1930. As Robert Marshall observed in his *The Onza* (1961), Baume never described what the *onza* was in his memoirs because as soon as Baume used the word *onza,* he assumed everyone knew what he was talking about. Writers in early America using the word *panther, painter,* and other terms often did not describe what they were actually seeing. How many were black? We have no way of knowing.

In general, what one finds in looking for black panther accounts historically is a lack of reports of anything that is a cryptic black felid before the advent of cryptozoologists, romantic naturalists, and, yes, popular outdoor and men's magazines of the early 1900s in America. Think about the historical context. The year 1850 is the beginning, but not the end, of the extinction threshold for the eastern puma; some states declared the puma extinct as late as 1920. You had two world wars, and a depression to distract people. Finally, after WWII, and in spite of the fact no mountain lions were supposed to be around, you get people seeing black, tan, and maned felids in the east. Nevertheless, the folklore from the black forests of Indiana and Pennsylvania suggests older reports of black felids are to be found.

Chad Arment's rebuttal is that "early newspaper records (1850s to early 1900s) did in fact note strange animals that were reported at that time. During this period there was a boom of amateur naturalists who attempted to describe and explain various sea monsters, natural phenomena, and other odd natural events, oftentimes doing so in their local newspapers. Travelling menageries carried curious exotic animals from town to town, numerous small natural history journals were started (most disappeared), and local newspapers routinely mentioned reports of strange critters that had been shot while trying to get into a farmer's chicken-coop."

Routinely? And who has searched these for mystery feline accounts? Only a handful of people have spent any time in the libraries looking. Besides interviewing witnesses and investigating sightings in the field, a few of us spent long hours in the late 1960s and early 1970s, in library microfilm newspaper archives, searching through local dailies' old news morgues. I looked mainly in Missouri and Illinois papers; Mark A. Hall searched several including the *Richmond* (Indiana) *Palladium-Item* and *Sun-Telegram* in 1970, where he discovered articles on many old mystery felines in Illinois, Indiana, and Ohio.

Yes, all of what Arment says may be true, in part, but let's look at the tip of the iceberg, as well. Pennsylvania histories mention records in 1797 and 1901 relevant to our discussion; Russellville, Kentucky's "tiger of brindle color" was reported in 1823; Rising Sun, Indiana's Black Forest great cat with six-inch tracks, attacked Mary Crane in 1877; Angelo Capparella's remarkable digging unearthed records of the "Santer," the local name for mystery cats seen during the 1890s in the mountains of northwest North Carolina; Mark A. Hall's incredible bibliographical searches have revealed the black panthers' march down through historical records, peaking with the concentrated accounts of the hunts of the "varmints" (the local Indiana name for their mystery black and maned felids) in the 1940s; and Bruce Wright's writings tell of the 700-person "Critter Hunts" in pursuit of a black panther in Lycoming County, Pennsylvania during 1953-1954. There are also old surprises in the next chapter that have come our way in the last twenty years.

If you dig, you will find. But most people looking for sea serpent and hairy wildman accounts in old papers have overlooked the black and mystery cat reports as merely more mundane mountain lion accounts.

Enduring Enigma

We have here the bare hints of an enigma that is extremely vast. When I began researching the accounts of phantom panthers almost four decades ago, I was shocked to learn the subject had been so ignored by Forteans and even by most budding cryptozoologists. Through efforts by Mark A. Hall and myself, the vast importance of these cases came to the fore in recent years via the work of people like John Lutz, Todd Lester, Chris Bolgiano, and a dozen others. Old-timers, researchers like Frank Weed of Florida, Harold Hitchcock of Vermont, Bruce Wright of New Brunswick, Spencer Kraybill of Pennsylvania, and Herbert S. Sass of the Carolinas, were mostly interested in collecting eastern cougar stories. In the early days of mystery felid research, the few that granted its relevance to our area of interest were perhaps not able to grasp its magnitude. Today, we are apparently dealing with thousands of sightings, spanning at the very minimum, two centuries of records of large and highly enigmatic cat-like creatures.

From my studies of mystery felines, I have come to see that they sort themselves via specific behaviorally predictable patterns and descriptions. To confuse the picture, a few appear to leave pointed toe or clawed prints with otherwise felid features. The black panthers are extremely dangerous to human beings, and destructive to livestock and dogs, in contrast to pumas, whose attacks are less frequent and almost nonexistent. In all of North America, there are only a little over a dozen recorded cases in which *Puma concolor* has attacked people; with phantom panthers, unprovoked assaults are the rule. Perhaps within the realm of cryptid cats, we are seeing a reflection of the more aggressive melanistic behavioral patterns found among leopards that are black (as discussed by R. J. P. O'Grady in his 1979 study, "Melanism in Breeding Wildcats" in *Symposium 4 Proceedings, Association of British Wild Animal Keepers*). As I will detail in the next chapter, black panther reports may be related to a relict population that definitely has a two-toned split personality. The whole notion of tawny pumas still existing in the East, black panthers getting into the mix, and tan "African" lionesses being seen has made for a confusing picture. Perhaps we can straighten it out a bit, and organize what is occurring.

The phantom felines are so oddly elusive that inevitably they remind one of Ivan T. Sanderson's dictum about Fortean phenomena: "We'll never catch them." Witnesses have shot at them without apparent effect, wildlife officials have set traps, sheriffs have conducted "safaris," and many people have done everything possible to bring a specimen in for examination. The mystery cats possess that weird tangible intangibility that makes understanding so difficult and investigation so frustrating. Their intelligence seems to be something we have underestimated and only recently are beginning to comprehend.

As a *Toronto Star* editorial writer once expressed it, black panthers are the "flying saucers of the animal world." When talking about reports of mystery "pumas" in New York, a State Conservationist called them "feline flying saucers." It is in the United States and Canada, as opposed to England or Africa or Australia, where I have been able to examine the subject the closest, and have come away perplexed but pondering some possibilities. In America, there are large felids—the cougar or mountain lion—but in spite of this known great cat, the reports of phantom panthers and mystery cats float above the normal animal background, and give notice to the world that something cryptid is taking place.

CHAPTER 13

Maned Mystery Cats

An "African lion" loose in California? The November 1979 sightings of a fully maned cat serve as our entry point into this chapter of the elusive phantom feline mystery.

Fremont, California, the site of past reports of black panthers, is across the East Bay from San Francisco, but fringed by some of the wilder regions of Northern California. At 5:27 p.m., on the night of November 10, 1979, Fremont residents near the Coyote Hills Regional Park relayed to police the disturbing fact that a large male lion was roaming loose. One caller told the authorities, after swearing he was not drunk, that he heard roaring at the corner of Alvarado and Lowry boulevards.

Soon a massive search was organized. Based on the 6:28 p.m. reports of several residents who saw the lion near Alvarado Boulevard and Whitehead Lane, the "safari" began in the Alameda Creek area. More than forty policemen, firefighters, animal control workers and East Bay Regional Park District personnel were involved in the unusual chase. At one point, tracking dogs and a Bay Area Rapid Transit helicopter were included.

Shortly after 9:00 p.m., Fremont Police Officer William Fontes came face to face with the big cat under the Fremont Boulevard/Nimitz Freeway overpass, as the feline meandered down the Alameda County Flood Channel. When Fontes shined his flashlight in the face of the lion, it growled but did not attack. Days later, when a local owner of a forty-pound chow-chow puppy came forth claiming his dog was the lion, Fontes said: "The puppy in no way resembled the 300- to 400-pound animal observed in the flood control channel."

The lion was last seen near Newark Boulevard and the Turk Island Dump at about 10 p.m., when the search was called off due to darkness. Charles Johnson, maintenance supervisor at Coyote Hills Regional Park, commented after the search that he thought the lion still lurked in the park.

"They didn't check that underbrush while I was here," Johnson observed. "They just flew the helicopter over it and turned on sirens to scare the lion."

No one saw the lion again. Fremont Police Identification Officer Karen Burhardt and an animal track expert from Marine World Africa USA labeled tracks found in the flood channel as those of "a large cat," but the lion seemed to have disappeared from the Fremont area.

America's Maned Lions

Compared to the African lion's 390 pounds, we are told that the American Lion, *Panthera atrox,* was a monster at 520 pounds. This massive cat lived on four different continents and some paleozoologists feel it was the widest ranging land mammal of all time. Does it still live today? Are they known to us in modern America as, yes, long-haired lions?

Large, maned mystery cats—looking like male African lions to witnesses—are nothing new in North America. Reports tick back over the years, from various parts of the United States and Canada. There appears to be a direct relationship between these "African lions" and the "black panthers" we have become so accustomed to hearing about, but more on

Panthera atrox: maned male and melanistic female

that later. First let's review a selection of modern cases of maned mystery felines.

Soon after the turn of the century, as mentioned in the last chapter, the famous "Nellie the Lion" incidents drew headlines in central Illinois. The furor started in July 1917 when Thomas Gullet, a butler at the Robert Allerton estate southwest of Monticello, was attacked while he was in the garden picking flowers.

Thomas Gullet had described "Nellie" as an "African lioness," as did Mrs. Shaw, the housekeeper for the Allerton Mansion. On the 15th of July, Mrs. Shaw spied "Nellie" as a 300-man posse searched for the lion on another part of the estate. Thus "Nellie" was very specifically described as an African lioness at the time (versus a cougar or mountain lion). But "Nellie" was not alone. Apparently, her male companion was nearby. Then, you will recall, on the 29th of July, a lion pounced on the automobile in which the families of Chester Osborn and Earl Hill were riding near Decatur.

Finally a view of the male occurred on the afternoon of July 31, 1917. James Rutherford, a farmhand, clearly saw a "large yellow, long-haired beast." A maned lion.

Throughout central Illinois during the summer of 1917, many witnesses viewed "Nellie" or her maned counterpart. In backtracking those stories and reviewing them, it is obvious that two cats were being seen, which were described as an "African lioness" and a maned "African lion." The lioness apparently was more aggressive, and seen more often, nevertheless, contemporary reports talk of two "lions" and not just the lonely "Nellie."

On March 1, 1941, according to the great panther chronicler Bruce S. Wright, a "large" panther in western New Brunswick stopped a team of horses by sitting in the middle of a log hauling road. The teamsters clearly saw the large cat, and said it was a yellow-gray-reddish color. Its "length of hair was such as to make the neck appear to be thicker than the head." The horses were terrified, but this seemingly maned "panther" merely strutted away into the woods.

Seven years later, we discover, thanks to the tedious newspaper archive research of Mark A. Hall, another fully maned lion reportedly was scurrying about. In the midst of a mystery cat flap (termed a "varmint scare" at the time) in which black panthers and tawny cats were being seen, a giant animal rushed a fishing party of four adults and two children in the Elkhorn Falls, Indiana region. The incident occurred in the early evening hours of the 5th of August, 1948.

According to Ivan Toney, who lived nearby: "About 7:30 p.m. a man came to the house and wanted to use the phone to call the sheriff. He said he and another man, along with their wives and two children, were fishing along the banks of the pool at the foot of the Elkhorn Falls. Their car was parked on the road near the gate leading to the falls. He said the animal came up the stream from the south. When they sighted it, they started running for the car. They reached it but the animal lunged at the car, then plowed through the fence into the sandy bar along the stream's edge."

The creature "looked like a lion with a long tail," the witnesses asserted, with bushy hair around the neck—the well-known trait of the male of the African lion, of course. Deputy Sheriff Jack Witherby examined the tracks and said they were like "nothing I have ever seen before." Witherby, after completing his investigations of the incident, issued a warning to persons in the area who fish along streams at night.

Two days after the Elkhorn Falls incident, the confusion in the reports was clarified somewhat. Two animals were being seen sometimes together. On August 7, two teenage farm boys, Arthur and Howard Turner, saw a strange beast near a plum tree not far from the gate leading into their Richmond, Indiana, barnyard. On a rise of ground to their right, another animal stood 200 feet away. Arthur raised his rifle to his shoulder and blasted away. The animals wheeled around, jumped a gate, and disappeared down a lane.

The Turner boys described one of the animals as "having the appearance of a lion." It was large-headed, shaggy, and brown in color. The other looked like a black panther. Tracks were found, but their dog "Shep" refused to help the Turners and the authorities search for the mystery cats.

The following afternoon, farmers northwest of Abington, Indiana, watched two animals identical to those the Turner boys had seen. And the next morning, the two beasts were sighted by others in Wayne County.

Later the cats were seen further to the east and north into Ohio in Drake County. Later still, in early September, 1948, unusual tracks were found to the south near Morning Sun, Ohio. Mark A. Hall comments:

"The reports suggest the movement of the pair from the south around the Ohio River to the north along the Whitewater River. Their path was a U-shaped journey, returning them southward toward the Ohio River."

Other "varmint" reports of black panthers continued coming out of Indiana in the late forties and early fifties, but we have not yet turned up any specifically mentioning the maned lions during that period.

One night in November 1950, researcher William Grimstad reports, an unseen creature or a pride of animals roared like an African lion, attacked, killed, and ate parts of forty-two pigs, twelve chickens, four calves, and four lambs in Peoria County, Illinois.

From 1951 through at least the mid-1950s, Nebraska was a hotbed of lion sightings. *The Omaha World Herald* for Monday, August 2, 1954, told of the latest sighting of what looked like an "African" lion to farmer Arnold Neujahr. "He reported he saw a lion as he topped a hill two miles west of Surprise," the newspaper informed. "The surprised lion, he said, dived into a ditch and disappeared into some trees. The lion had a mane, he said." (How else would one expect to find a lion seen near Surprise, Nebraska, but surprised?) One woman living in Surprise, the newspaper continued, said she saw a lion and mate running across her front yard. A similar incident took place in nearby Rising City, Nebraska. The Omaha paper ended by noting that these stories closely paralleled those which touched off a lengthy maned lion hunt near Ceresco, on November 12, 1951. Ceresco is 32 miles east of Surprise.

Bruce S. Wright's collection of New Brunswick sightings, of course, contains several black panther reports. It also holds a few intriguing reports of what he termed "roughed up" panthers, such as the "ragged coated" lion seen near a military base at Gagetown in 1954, and the "shaggy" lion seen a week before a "black panther" was sighted, also near Base Gagetown in 1958. The "black panther," interestingly, had a light spot on its chest and near the tip of its tail.

In January 1958, reports of a maned large cat again issued from Indiana, this time from Warrick County. Not surprisingly, this activity was followed by more sightings in neighboring Ohio. During the summer of 1959, in Lorain County, Ohio, eyewitnesses described a huge cat, which was killing and eating domestic livestock, dogs, and housecats. It was described as being somewhat like a miniature "African" lion.

In June of 1960, near Kapuskasing, Ontario, Leo Paul Dallaire had yet another experience. He reported seeing an animal resembling an African lion on his farm. Dallaire said it was light tan in color, had a mane, and was at least three feet tall and five feet long. The animal also had a four-foot-long tail with a bushy end. Orrie Lewis, an Ontario wildlife officer, commented, "Mr. Dallaire has been watching too much TV."

The next report comes from Cherokee country, in Craig County, Oklahoma, where an Ohio tourist saw an "African lion" in mid-March 1961. Around the same time, two nurses at Oklahoma's Eastern State Hospital in Vinta saw a lion going in and out of shrubbery there. Locals told the Craig and Rogers County authorities that the lion had been there for two months, and they had heard its roars. It, or they, had also been eating local chickens. Rogers County sheriff Amos Ward and Tulsa Zoo head Hugh Davis thought the mystery feline existed, but told the press they had heard rumors that the cat came from a circus truck's wreck some time earlier. They could not substantiate the wild story of the escape of any African lions, however. The media then lost interest and the story disappeared from the newspapers.

Other officials scratched their heads when black panthers and "hairy" lions showed up in the Joliet, Illinois area, in July 1963, and August 1964. The cats moved on after creating quite a stir.

Back in McGundy Stream, New Brunswick, it looked "exactly like an African lion," said guide M. McDonald of McAdam who saw a big, very dark brown cat with a long tail that 20th of October 1964.

In Illinois, again, Tom Terry and five other people called the Winnebago County Sheriff's Department after they saw a pair of cats along the Rock River in northern Illinois in May of 1970. Terry and his co-workers were loading sod on a truck two miles east of Roscoe when they saw a lion run off with a bag of meat put out for two stray dogs. Some of the people followed the cat in a car and got a better look. Terry recounted: "He must have been 8 feet long. He had a mane and a long tail. It looked...well...like a regular lion." The animal jumped a fence and vanished. Seeing these cats in pairs happens frequently.

Huge felid tracks were found in June 1970, on the eastside of the Rock River after several horses and calves were spooked. The pugmarks measured 5 inches long and 4.75 inches wide. The distance between each pawprint was 40 inches. Also found were tracks described as similar but smaller. Of the larger tracks, Winnebago County Sheriff Black noted: "It isn't a dog's; it's something else and we're going to find out what." Lyle Imig rounded up his livestock and returned them to his farm. He said once back the "very excited animals wouldn't leave the shed."

Late in August 1970, also along the east bank of the Rock River near Rockford, it seems the same "lion" was still exciting local animals. Dogs began to bark vigorously in the area after a "roar" was heard. Dorsey Hailey swears he was not kidding when he said he heard what sounded like an African lion roar in the vicinity of his home. "It sounded just like a lion," he said. "Like the lions they have in the Milwaukee Zoo." His wife, who was out hunting dewworms at the time, agreed. And of course so did the neighbors' dogs who were barking. Sheriffs deputies and neighbors with flashlights searched through the late August night, but found no trace of the beast.

Almost a year later, this time near Centralia in southern Illinois, Howard Baldridge encountered a small version of an "African lion," he said, at the start of March, 1971. He said it looked to be twice as big as a domestic cat, yellow, had a long tail, short legs, and a face like a lion "on television." Was it a feral domestic cat or the young of the American lion that looks like an "African" lion?

Another "African" lion was spotted in the vicinity of Croesbeck, Ohio, in 1971. Apparently, this animal disappeared as quickly as it came.

In 1976, a farmer near Alapaha, Georgia, watched a weird animal in his pasture. J. H. Holyoak was driving a pickup truck down to check on his cows in Berrien County that day. Suddenly, he saw this "thing" and thought it was a dog chasing his cattle. When he got within 50 to 100 feet of the animal, he noticed the "thing" resembled a half-panther, half-lion. Specifically, Holyoak said it looked like a panther all over its body except for the mane it had on its neck, which was just like an African lion. This maned cat was no cougar, he was sure. J. H. Holyoak's son, Ken, a farmer in his own right and a University of Georgia graduate, added these details in a 1979 interview: "The animal was big and was trying to catch a calf. He shot the animal with birdshot and saw blood running out of it, but it didn't do much damage. The animal crossed the fence and ran off into the woods."

Ken Holyoak noted the "lion" was seen in the forest and swampy woods between Alapaha and Enigma—an interesting name for a town considering the circumstances. He felt sure his father knew what he had seen because "it was daylight, and there was no mistake about it." His father, J. H. Holyoak was raised in the mountains of Arizona, killed mountain lions there, and knew the difference between them and this "African lion" in Georgia.

In 1977, in Arkansas, where people at Dierks were reporting panthers as "black as the ace of spades," a maned lion attacked two dogs at Dover.

In the autumn of 1977, a two-month-old lion cub was found in Muscatine, Iowa, by Lt. Ronald King. The police attempted to discover who had lost a cub, but the young lion's origins remained unknown. A lion cub turned up in August 1979, in West Chester, Ohio. An amusement park claimed it as theirs, and I am sure they were happy to have it in their collection. I have been sent reports, as well, from Nebraska, of the finding of "lion cubs," which were assumed to have been released in the wild. I spent years tracking down those cats to discover they have been traded from zoo to zoo, and attempts to breed them to lions had not been successful. Could these be examples of actual maned cryptid cubs that had fallen into the hands of humans who did not realize what they had found? Are these *atrox* cubs?

Loxahatchee, Florida, was the site of a January 23, 1978 account from a woman who saw a maned lion outside her window. She called the nearby Lion Country Safari to inform them that one of their lions must be missing; no African lions were gone. Patrol cars raced to the area, discovered no exotic cats were missing from two local lion owners either, and could not find the reported lion.

Authorities trying to account for all these maned mystery cats have had little success. These American lions continued to be seen in North America in the 1980s and 1990s, although hardly any systematic efforts have been in evidence to collect the data. Still, intriguing items have turned up.

Yes, pet lions may be responsible for some of these reports, but what we may be searching for may mirror the configuration of an African lion. Take, for example, an incident in 1982. Wildlife biologist Bob Downing, who was searching for evidence of cougars in the East, was shown a skeleton in a ditch near Rutherfordton, North Carolina. Downing sent the skull, which appeared to be from a young large felid, to C. O. Handley Jr., Curator of Mammals at the Smithsonian, who confirmed that it was an "African lion." The skeleton was not recovered, and probably decomposed in that ditch in the Carolinas, Downing told me. Downing also heard of a case in which two deer hunters had killed a young "African lion" in the Blue Ridge mountains of Georgia in the mid-1960s. Downing reports that a Malcolm Edwards owns the photograph of this kill, which at the time was rumored to be a pet.

And still the maned cats were seen as the century came to a close.

North Olmsted, apparently a very wild Cleveland suburb, was visited by one in July of 1984, and North Avondale, Ohio, by another, in November and December of 1984.

In February 1985, a maned giant cat was reported near the Fort Worth Zoo in Texas, perhaps attracted by the roars of the resident African lions. The zoo was checked, of course, but all lions were present and accounted for. Soon afterwards, two police officers sighted the animal themselves, and unquestionably said it was a maned lion. It was never caught and not seen again in those parts.

In June, 1992, several reports were phoned in to the Mentor, Ohio, police department. The accounts described a feline that was seven feet long, with a mane. The creature was seen crouching low to the ground on a number of occasions, by several witnesses who were quoted as saying the animal was definitely a lion. One individual who would only allow the press to use his first name, David, said the lion had big shoulders, and a mane like you would see on the animal programs on television. David confessed that he was genuinely afraid of it, and wondered how it got to where it was now. The police decided David and other witnesses had seen nothing but a "large golden retriever."

More often than not, as with the law enforcement officers in Mentor, the more urban-oriented police in America try to explain away the maned lion sightings as dogs—as in the Fremont case of 1979. Dog explanations buried the Cincinnati, Ohio's suburban Croesbeck lion report of April 1971, and the Tacoma, Washington, July, 1976, story. Indeed, the Tacoma lion was described by "all sorts of people" as having "a shaggy black mane, light brown body, and a black tuft at the end of a long tail." Police fanned out, fired their shotguns and revolvers, endangering mainly themselves, and did not catch or kill the lion, which was seen near Washington and South 56th. Instead, they caught a part-collie, part-shepherd dog named Jake at the city dump and labeled poor Jake the "lion."

The answers to the mystery felines are beyond the sphere of junkyard dogs, circus lions, and, as we shall see later, cougars.

Historical Searching

The search for, and discovery of, early evidence of large American cats different than the mountain lion or puma has been a difficult process. People do not "see" what may be there if they do not realize it is something that may be of interest. That maned felids could be of importance in zoology and cryptozoology remained a shocking idea in the mid-1980s. When in 1986 Bernard Heuvelmans mentioned what I said about these felids in his "Annotated Checklist of Apparently Unknown Animals with Which Cryptozoology Is Concerned" *(Cryptozoology 5),* many of my cryptozoological colleagues—who had ignored the maned American lions roaring in the midst of the closely studied pumas—were surprised. Critics immediately said, "Where are the pre-1930s accounts of these maned lions?"

"They are out there," Mark A. Hall and I have replied. Cautiously and carefully, the records are being revealed, hopefully before they disappear.

Take the case of environmental biologist Sunny Franson, who had studied mountain lions while a graduate student at the University of California at Davis. In 2000, Franson was working on some bibliographical research concerning the Middle Creek Watershed in northern Lake County, California. Franson's task was to read material about and by pioneers in this area and digest the memoirs of an early settler, Archie McMath, regarding Gravelly Valley (now Lake Pillsbury). Franson was interested in McMath's descriptions of the environment in the 1860s. Archie McMath and his brother George had trapped and hunted, especially bear, in the area extensively. Franson had read several pages of memoirs from each of them, and found the descriptions of the country and wildlife recounted in a straightforward manner. In doing so, the biologist came across the following remarkable puzzling passage, and forwarded it, for an opinion, to E. Lee Fitzhugh, Extension Wildlife Specialist, Department of Wildlife, Fish, and Conservation Biology at the University of California, Davis. Fitzhugh knew of my ongoing interest and research on maned felids and sent it on to me. He sensed it might be an important piece of data on the felines for my studies. Fitzhugh was certainly correct.

Sunny Franson had stumbled upon a remarkable record of an early maned cat incident. While doing the archival research, what caught Franson's curiosity was how this cat was clearly different from others in that era; the chroniclers would often speak of *Puma concolor* employing the term "panther." But this encounter was different; the specific word used was "lion." And there was more.

The passage Franson discovered concerned a "lion" killed in the spring of 1868, after it had killed several sheep and two young Clydesdales. From *The Memoirs of Archie McMath,* compiled by Marie and Ellery Sleeper for the Lake County Centennial, California (1961), here is McMath's intriguing account:

> As we were going along we found the ground all torn up under a tree and saw where a horse had run down hill. We followed the tracks and could see that something was wrong. We followed for about a quarter of a mile and found a dead horse. He had been killed by a California Lion. The horse was a large three-year [colt] and weighed about twelve hundred pounds. He was a Clidesdale and large for his age. Not far from there we found where the lion had killed a large two-year-old colt of the same stock. They had been opened and their entrails were cleaned out as nice as a butcher could have done with his knife.

Archie McMath, the memoirs continue, could not find the lion that day, but he did find him two days later:

> I came to several bunches of sheep that a lion had killed and carried together. There were ten or twelve in each bunch. I counted over forty that the lion had killed during the two nights that I had left the sheep alone.

He corralled the sheep that night, released them the next morning and heard them running back to him, apparently being chased by a lion. He set his dogs loose. His memoirs then noted:

> They treed the lion before they had run a half-mile. The lion had killed a half grown lamb and skinned it and taken the entrails out.
>
> When I was within seventy yards of the tree where the dogs had the lion treed, I was out of breath and tired so I stopped to rest and get my wind. The lion was in a large fir tree about fifty feet high. After I was rested, I worked around to the upper side of the tree; he had his legs around the trunk of the tree with his back to the limb and would look first to one side of the tree then to the other to see what was going on. When he saw me he got up to jump. He was too quick for me. I raised my gun to shoot just as he jumped so I missed him; but when he hit the ground the dogs did not give him time to climb another tree. The lion would reach out and grab a dog but the others would fight so hard he could not hurt the dog before he would have to let him up to fight off the others. I finally got up to a tree and waited until I had a chance to shoot and not hit a dog. I finally shot the lion in the head and killed him.
>
> He was the largest one ever killed in that country, weighing over three hundred pounds and measuring eleven feet from the tip of his nose to the tip of his tail. I had to get George to help me get the lion on a saddle horse and his feet touched the ground on both sides. I have killed many panthers and what they call California lions, but this was the only California lion that I have ever seen in those mountains. It was built entirely different from a panther, it was very heavy in front and light behind with black stripes along its shoulders and back and down the fore parts. The rest was of a yellow cast color. The black was on his back and shoulders and it resembled a mane. The hair was longer there.

Thanks to the questioning nature of biologist Franson, we now know a little bit more about this part of the puzzle from this case. A striped maned cat.

Striped American Lions?

The evidence of stripes has surfaced before. In Mark A. Hall's March 1994 *Wonders* overview on this topic, he writes:

> Also from western Mexico comes another indication of large cats with manes in 1940. Ivan T. Sanderson told me of his collecting a cat skin that he described as over 6 feet long from nose to tail. The tail, he recalled, was about 18 inches long. He continued: "The legs appeared to have been rather long compared to, say, a house-cat or a puma. The paws were very big and splayed and well furred. The claws were bright yellow. The fur was soft below and rather firm on top and basically was various browns throughout, plain on the head and shoulders but breaking up into light and dark sort of wavy stripes on the flanks and upper legs. The most singular feature of the skin was 'a large ruff around the neck' formed by hairs growing forward from behind the shoulders."
>
> This specimen was subsequently ruined in a hurricane that struck British Honduras (Belize) where his collection was stored. When in 1972 Ivan told me of this experience I asked him to write it down. A summary of this recollection was published posthumously.

Hall further points out that in 1992, Peter Hocking *(Cryptozoology 11)* recorded information of a "giant black panther" and a more seldom-seen striped cat of large size in the Peruvian forests. The *onza,* the mystery felid of Mexico, is frequently reported to be black with faint stripes over the shoulders. Could these other American cats have something to do with their kin from elsewhere in the New World?

Coming back to North America, what are we to deduce from the report of the famed explorer Jonathan Carver who saw the "tyger of America" in May-June 1767, in Pepin County, Wisconsin, on an island in the Chippewa River?

Still, another old record, from 1823, is clearer and worthy of noting at this point. While I briefly mentioned this case in my earlier *Creatures of the Outer Edge* (1978), perhaps it would be fitting to explore it here again. I first learned of the account from the Boston-based *New England Farmer* of 1 August 1823; Hall found the earliest version in the article "A Tiger in Kentucky" from the *Lexington* (Kentucky) *Gazette* for 17 July 1823. The report began:

> We learn from Russellville that a gentleman discovered an animal of alarming appearance a few miles from town, and hastened to the nearest house where he was joined by three men, two of whom were armed with guns, and attended by a dog. The strange monster was again discovered, and while bayed by the dog, the two guns continued to fire on him at a distance of about fifty yards without forcing him to move from his stand; a furious look and appaling brow frightened the two men without guns who fled to town. Experienced marksmen continued to fire, and on the twelfth shot the beast put off at full speed, marking his way by blood flowing from many wounds that it must have received. The dog was too much frighted to continue the pursuit, and the huntsmen dare not venture, although one of them was as fearless as Boone himself, and accustomed to the chase from early life.
>
> When the news reached Russellville about forty gentlemen repaired to the spot, and had a full view of the ground. The print which the paws of this animal made in the earth corresponds with the account given of his great bulk by those who had an opportunity of viewing him at a short distance for several minutes; he was of a brindle color with a most terrific front—his eyes are described as the largest ever seen in any animal. We are well acquainted with the party engaged in the attack, and give the fullest credit to the account we have received.

The Kentucky story fits with others coming from the eastern side of the Appalachians, from an area southeast of the Blue Ridge mountains.

The discoverer of these accounts was a teenager named Angelo Capparello III. In 2000, Capparello is a Ph.D. board member of the International
Society of Cryptozoology and zoology professor at Illinois State University, who has been involved in new bird species discoveries from the
Amazon. But back in the 1970s, Capparello was an eager youth sending
me old copies of some intriguing mystery cat reports from the last part of
the 19th century. He had searched the North Carolina newspaper files of
the Wilkesboro *Chronicle,* Salibury *Carolina Watchman,* and *Stateville
Landmark,* and found many articles on what the locals called the "Santer."
Sightings appeared in clumps down through the years. In August-Septem-
ber 1890, the Santer was seen throughout Iredell County, North Carolina,
with a sighting by Abe Harbin, among others, at Second Creek in September-October of that year. First near Roaring River in March-May 1897,
then around Elkin, in Yakin County, just north of Iredell County, in June
1897, the Santer was back. In October, 1897, at Piney Grove, Charlie
Smoot described the feline Santer as "striped from the end of its nose to
the end of its tail." The sightings, moving to Wilkes County, directly west
of Yakin County, were reported from around Wilkesboro in 1899. On May
27th of that year, a witness named Smoak said the Santer was gray. Capparello thought that the 1890s' Santer was a genuine large felid. He found
that a mystery beast, said to be the Santer, was seen around South Iredell
in May 1934, as well.

As with other old names for mystery cats, such as the Wampus, the
Santer, as a label, hides a deeper truth, a record of historical interactions
with giant American lions, maned and striped and some black. The maned
cat mystery gives clues that the occasional report of striping must be considered. Hall mentions that some recent black panther sightings also describe stripes. Bill Chambers noted streaks on the black panther he saw in
Illinois, and clearly the McMath's California report gives notice that the
maned lions appear to be striped upon closer inspection. Should we look
closer at what must be considered almost unbelievable striped cat reports
from America, too?

In the fall of 1967, in West Rock, Connecticut, of all places, witnesses reported seeing a "baby tiger" on the loose. Several police officers
searched but found nothing. Was it all a case of mistaken identification?

Jack Bowman of Kentucky shared with me his barnyard sightings of a large striped cat during the early 1970s. John Lutz has a report in his files of a large felid being seen with brown stripes near Marlington, West Virginia in 1977. It was spied by the crew of Train #62 of the Cass Scenic RR on their way to Spruce Knob in late June, 1977. Lutz interviewed the entire engine crew, railroad fireman, and engineer separately. Each had the same story. The great striped cat loped across the track, 30 feet ahead of the train at 1:45 p.m. There have been others, which can be drawn from my files. Here are some examples.

On July 27, 1986, near Nicholson, Pennsylvania, Carl Eastwood was walking along State Route 92 at 6:00 a.m., when he observed a large striped cat that looked similar to a tiger. It ran from some bushes about 50 feet from him, then turned around and ran back out-of-sight. Later in the afternoon, state police using a helicopter, spotted the tiger, but the officers lost it in the thick woods of Wyoming County. The next day, in Wyoming and Susquehanna Counties, Pennsylvania, state police continued the tiger hunt with a search of a ten-mile perimeter focusing on the two bordering counties. Authorities used a deer carcass to lure the cat, but to no avail. Police contacted the Bently Brothers Circus and Buk Young, who collected large felines. However, Young and circus officials maintained that their cats were not missing.

On July 29, 1986, a Newton Township, Pennsylvania schoolteacher, Gary Steier claimed that he and his family saw a large orange cat in high grass about 200 yards away from their porch. Steier reported that it was big, orange, long, and lopping. The following day, in Jackson, Pennsylvania, Cindy Belmont and her brother saw a huge long-tailed, beige "tiger" in a pasture. The Belmonts insisted the cat was running with a shaggy animal that looked like a "collie." Cindy Belmont, an amateur wildlife photographer, was sure of what she saw. Perhaps we should play a little reversal here on all of the quick dog explanations. What if this so-called "collie" was a misidentified American lion?

Meanwhile Pennsylvania State Police reported receiving ten calls per hour from the counties of Wyoming, Lackawanna, Pike, and Susquehanna. Switchboards were jammed with "cat" reports that July 1986. Things began to get a bit hysterical, as several sightings had different descriptions. One report was of a white tiger. The original report depicted an orange and black striped cat. No tiger was ever found by the police.

Miami Township, Ohio, police searched for a tiger on the loose on 26 May 1994 after receiving a call from Galen Emery, 43, of Centerville, of the animal on the prowl in a field near Washington Church and Spring Valley Pike around 9:25 a.m. Despite the fact police finally said the cat that Emery had videotaped was only a domestic cat, Emery remained adamant about what he saw. He said he worked in the office facing the empty field off Spring Valley Road for two years, and had seen and taped coyotes, deer and groundhogs from only a few hundred yards away. And he knew a thing or two about the size of objects in videos; he is a professional video producer.

Then on June 1, 1994, Clearcreek and Springboro, Ohio, police responded to a call of a possible tiger on the loose. The call, received at 14:16, was from Debbie Couch, a resident on North Ohio 741 near Pennyroyal Road. Couch claimed she saw a large, orange animal run from Ohio 741 into the wooded area behind the runways of the Dayton General South Airport, located just north of the Springboro city limits. She went on to describe what she had seen, which led police of both departments to believe that there could possibly be truth to the "rumor" (as the press was now calling Emery's May sighting) of a Bengal tiger.

Next we learn, according to police, that early in November 1994, three Hillsboro, Ohio, residents saw a lion running through Highland and Clinton counties. The lion was last reported on Turner Road in Clinton County, where police said they had found footprints.

"We haven't got anything that's substantiated," Sheriff Tom Horst said. "We're still looking." Horst had, however, a plaster cast of a pawprint that was 4 inches wide. The print shows no trace of claws.

Horst's office received the first telephone call reporting the mysterious creature just before sundown on November 10th from a woman on Murtland Road, at the northern edge of Salem Township. She had seen something walking across a nearby field. "She said it was tan and white," Horst said. "She originally called it a tiger. She thought it was striped."

Several minutes later, another woman spotted something chasing a deer across an open field about 2 miles north of the first caller. "I just know it was big and brown," said Chris Hawk, who reported that sighting from her home on Spilker Road just north of Rt. 50. About 5:30 p.m., just after sundown, "the dogs just went crazy," Hawk said. She was cooking supper when her 4-year-old son, Joshua, said, "There's a wolf out there." Hawk peered out the window and said, "No, it's too big to be a wolf."

"I was amazed," Hawk gasped.

Clara Stroop said she saw an animal sniffing around her mobile home on Turner Road later the same night. "It looked like a cougar or a female lion," she said. She lived two miles from Hawk, just across the Clinton County line. Stroop pointed to a small bush at the corner of her home to show where the animal stood. "It let out a great big roar, and then it went off running into the woods," she said. She watched the animal demolish her plastic trash cans, and showed a visitor the neatly sliced remains.

It came calling again a few days ago and, again, "It let out a great big roar," Stroop said.

"I don't let my kids go out at night."

A couple of hundred feet away, neighbor Kris Goad inspected a big fresh pawprint left in the mud just beneath her bedroom window. The print matched the plaster cast at the sheriff's office.

Lynchburg, Ohio, pharmacist Lance Lukas almost turned the mysterious animal into roadkill just before 9 a.m. on November 19th as he drove west along Anderson Road in Dodson Township, not far from the other sightings. "Just about hit it," Lukas said. "I saw a cat-like animal, 4 to 5 feet long, with a long tail, low to the ground and moving fast." Its tannish-yellow coat looked like that of a leopard without spots, maybe a little smaller, he said. Whatever it was, it left the pavement with a bound big enough to carry it straight into a cornfield and out of sight in a heartbeat, Lukas said.

Maned mystery cats and the "lionesses" with them may exhibit striping on the shoulders and elsewhere, perhaps as some echo back to the Ice Ages. So-called "black panthers" may too.

Pentz's Maned Lion and More

Hints of the concurrent existence of two large cats (the puma and the maned felids under discussion here) in the New World are the two "lions" seen in the Aztec zoo by Spanish explorers, and the two varieties of "lions" known to Friar Johann Jakob Baegaert when he was in Mexico in 1751-1768.

The oldest specific and detailed reference to maned cats comes from Henry Shoemaker, a prolific gatherer of data who today is merely remembered as a Pennsylvania folklorist interested in the wildlife of his state, especially the extinct species. This reference was first discovered by Hall in recent years. In Shoemaker's 1916 book *Juniata Memories,* he briefly described the big cats known in central Pennsylvania: "On very rare occasions panthers with manes were taken; one of the last such was killed in the Bald Eagle Mountains by the celebrated frontiersman, Peter Pentz, in 1797." Chad Arment reviewed the Shoemaker material in 2000, and published more details of Shoemaker's writings on this topic.

The following is almost the entire text of Shoemaker's 1912 summary of this matter, entitled "The Courage of Peter Pentz."

The best view of the big "bare place" on the Bald Eagle Mountain between McElhattan and Castanea is obtained from the new State Road on the opposite side of the river. The long, unbroken ridge stretches like a moss-green colored wall, and is so narrow in some places on the comb or summit that one can sit astride of the rocks with one leg in the West Branch Valley and the other in the Valley of the Kammerdiner.

There are two bare places on the long ridge; one, comparatively small directly above the village of McElhattan, and the other, a great lengthy space like the scalded flank of a backyard cat, and covering over fifty acres, stretching from the summit two-thirds of the way down the mountain, about midway between the small glen known as the "Little Gap" and the gap at Castanea.

* * *

The first settlers at the foot of the Bald Eagle Mountain, which contains the "bare places," attempted to raise cattle, sheep and hogs. This suited the panthers exactly, as calves, lambs and pigs were easier to capture, and gave up without the tussle common to the wild creatures. There was one panther which gave no end of trouble for six years. Those who saw him at close range, for he was very bold and would carry off a sheep out of a barnyard, stated that he had a tawney matted mane like a lion. If he were seen today he would be classed as an "escaped lion from a circus," but as there were no circuses in this country in those days he couldn't have been that.

Experimental zoologists would have ticketed him as a hybrid between a panther and a shepherd dog. But he was in most probability a particularly masculine panther, a veritable *Felis Couguar Rex*. A list of the settlers who had had a shot at or hunted the elusive monster would sound like a taxpayers' list from the Great Island to the Long Reach. The subject of destroying it had been discussed with the redoubtable Peter Pentz but he had been too busy fighting Indians to give much attention to the outlaws of the animal kingdom.

On one occasion when there was a lull in the hostilities with the Red Men he was paying a visit to Isaac Dougherty whose cabin was located where McElhattan Run empties into the Susquehanna. The evening of his arrival he was sitting with Dougherty on a bench under one of the giant linnwood trees on the river bank, discussing some of their expeditions against the Indians of ten years before, when they heard their dogs barking and a loud commotion in the barnyard. Seizing their guns with which they had been testing their old-time skill on a very alert loon in the river, they ran in the direction of the racket.

Five young steers were huddled in a mass in one corner, lowing pitifully. A full panel of the slab fence was down, and around it were several pools of blood. There was a bloody path three feet wide leading from the barn yard into the woods, looking as if every inch of the way had been contested in some fierce combat. The men were good runners and soon overtook the warring elements.

There was a level piece of ground covered with walnut trees that had been cleared of underbrush long ago by the herds of buffaloes. In the semi-darkness they made out the prostrate form of a red and white spotted steer; on it was crouched a huge yellowish animal with a long hood of matted hair like a lion.

Nearby lay the two hounds, panting and occasionally giving vent to howls of pain. *Felis Couguar Rex* was clearly master of the situation. When he saw the two hunters he gritted his teeth so audibly that they heard it plainly twenty yards away.

Then he buried his head in a hole he had ripped in the carcass of the steer, taking a last long drink of its blood, and turned and bounded off in the direction of the steep face of the mountain. Both men fired their muskets, but their shots went wide.

There was no time to put the suffering hounds out of their misery, so the men ran after the retreating monster, tracking him easily in the soft ground and by occasional drops of blood which dripped from his gorged mouth.

The climb up the mountain was steep and perilous after dark, but Peter Pentz and Isaac Dougherty had never turned back for man or beast, and this time they were thoroughly aroused. The panther was light of foot, but at times he would break a twig in his leaps, which kept his pursuers from losing him, as there was no tracking on the rocky, mountain slope, and it was too late at night to detect any drops of blood. "He's making for the bare place," whispered Pentz, who was a faster climber than Dougherty. He ran almost as fast as the animal, but stopped every few minutes to allow his companion to catch up with him.

At length they reached the lower end of the bare place just in time to see the tail of the panther disappearing into the great cavern near the middle of the stony desert. "We've got him!" shouted Peter Pentz in triumph. The two men climbed up to the mouth of the cave, which was so low that a human being could only enter by crawling on his belly. They lit a fire from a quantity of pine cones that had blown from the forest above, and soon had a brilliant blaze started. On it they threw a couple of logs which they found in a cranny in the rocks.

When the wind blew from the west the firelight illuminated the cavern, but disclosed no signs of the panther. "There must be a bend in the passage," remarked Dougherty. Peter Pentz took the two muzzle-loading rifles and primed them carefully. Then he got down on "all fours," dragging a gun under each arm and with a lighted pine torch in his mouth he crawled into the cave. "If I don't get him the first shot, I'll get him the second," was his cheerful au revoir.

Dougherty had seen his friend in a good many tight places in the past, but he could not help wonder what the panther would be doing if he dodged the first charge. The animal must have had his stronghold deep in the bowels of the earth, for it seemed a good ten minutes before the muffled report of the rifle was heard. "He's got him the first shot," murmured Dougherty in thankfulness.

But when, two minutes later, another report emanated from the cavern his worst fears were awakened. Drawing his hunting knife he crawled into the opening in search of his absent friend. When he came to the bend in the passage he called "Peter, Peter, are you alive?" Immediately came the cheery answer, "Yes, yes, Isaac, but I had to kill two of them."

Dougherty hurried his "snail's pace" as best he could, until by the wavering glare of his torch he could see the outlines of Peter Pentz and his victims. They lay one behind the other in the narrow gallery, but the foremost one was *Felis Couguar Rex* with a bullet hole through his mustard colored skull. The second was a female; she, too, had been shot through the head.

Death had been instantaneous in both cases and they lay with heads resting on their paws, like huge cats fallen asleep.

"When I got within three feet of the hairy one, he rushed at me, but my bullet was speedier and he dropped. The she one tried to do the same thing, but she was easy, as the roof was low, and I finished her before she could climb over the body of her mate." This was the modest way in which Peter Pentz described his wonderful "kill."

"Over yonder in that bowl in the rocks are three cubs, the cutest little things you ever saw," he continued. "We'll take them home as pets." With the enthusiasm of a child he crawled over the two carcasses and reached into the nest and drew out the young animals, which had slept through their parents' execution.

"We'll leave the dead ones here," said Dougherty, but

before they left Pentz scalped the male carcass, and hung the trophy, with its matted mane, to his belt.

The morning star was sole possessor of the heavens when they emerged from the gloomy labyrinth, but it appeared a trifle droopy as it dodged among the tops of the tall pines on the comb of the Bald Eagle Mountain. Carrying the three cubs they returned to the Dougherty cabin, and after a comfortable breakfast spent the morning building an enclosure for them. Peter Pentz rounded out the balance of his visit in peace, but when he left for "down country," he found the fame of his latest exploit had preceded him.

"We hear you killed the hairy panther in his cave," everyone would say. In reply the big red-haired frontiersman would smile modestly and point to the scalp with its long, matted brownish-yellow hair, which hung at his belt. "That's how a good many Indians would like to wear my scalp," he would add, and then turn the subject of the conversation into other channels.

This 1790s maned cat of Pennsylvania thus was seen with an unknown colored female and three cubs—certainly evidence of breeding and not merely an escaped African lion.

There are other comments from Shoemaker germane to our discussion. In 1917, Shoemaker wrote: "It is interesting to note that Peter Pentz, the famous Indian fighter, killed a maned male panther near McElhattan Run, Clinton County, in 1798 [yes, he says 1798 here and 1797 above— LC]. The Indians told the Dutch settlers on Manhattan Island that the hides of panthers they brought there to sell were from females, that the males had manes and were difficult to capture."

Early records of folklore for both maned and black cats have been found. John Lutz's eastern puma newsletter has a discussion regarding the fact that some American Indians termed the large black cats they observed in the wild as "black devils" or "devil cats." Lutz noted this terminology was different than the names that Native Americans would give to the tawny-colored panthers or pumas, referencing "Indian writings and legends" and the "elders of several nations [who] discussed the legends."

Chad Arment has commented on the confused linguistic history of the word *michichibi,* which was apparently a maned carnivore reported in the southeast USA in the late 1600s. The animal was said to have features similar to a wolf, but with the mane and claws of a lion. More on these legends should be documented. Who knows what results a search might reveal?

J. B. Tinsley in *The Puma: Legendary Lion of the Americas* (1987) writes: "In an early history of the state of Maine, William D. Williamson wrote that three species of cats were found in the forests, identifying them as the catamount, wild-cat, and black cat. He was quite explicit in his description of the last named: 'The Black Cat is much larger in size than the wild-cat, very ravenous and fierce, has shorter legs and a long tail, and is of a black colour; called by the natives Wooleneag.'" Perhaps, as some say, the wooleneag is the fisher or a wolverine, but something else seems to have been in the woods of Maine too.

Mark A. Hall found this item from my adopted state of Maine as reported in the *Bangor Courier* in 1836:

> The forests of Maine still abound in numerous species of wild animals, such as the moose, deer, caribou, *loupcervier, lunkasoose,* and many others—most of them valuable for food and for their skins. The *lunkasoose* (the orthography is arbitrary) is an animal of which we have only heard recently; but tradition says that a ferocious animal of huge size, with a mane like a lion, has actually been seen to come to the borders of the river, and the lumbermen say that they have heard him in the woods roaring most lustily. The Indians, too, talk about the *"lunkasoose,"* and they are conclusive authority in such matters.

An Answer from the Pleistocene

Mystery felines closely resembling and thus described as male "African lions" are not as familiar as the "black panthers" of cryptozoological literature, but they are just as elusive.

As the accounts demonstrate, these "African lions" have some unique traits. Indeed, the maned mystery cats seen in America have particular characteristics that separate them from the so-called "black panthers" in whose company they are often found. Besides being social, the mysterious maned lions appear to be more forthrightly venturesome, retreating less quickly than the black panthers, but then again not attacking as frequently either. Comparing them overall, the maned lions seem more even-tempered, less timid, and yet not as aggressive as the hauntingly hyperactive black phantom cats. Why?

There are many levels of reality in the shadowy investigative world of cryptozoology. I feel there may be a concrete, flesh and blood, if you will, answer to some accounts of mystery cats in America. I will here explore and develop an earlier suggestion made by Mark A. Hall that the "black panthers" and "maned lions" may be only two slices of the same pie, and that the answer seems to lie in the survival of relict populations of *Panthera atrox* (*Panthera leo atrox,* or *Felis atrox,* to some), the giant American lion of the Pleistocene.

For years, Mark A. Hall had talked of his theory that the survival of *Panthera atrox* might be related to some of the reports of mystery felids in North America. He discussed this with Ivan T. Sanderson's associate Dan Manning in 1969, and around the same time with me. I wrote about this concept first in the 1970s in my articles in *Fortean Times* and *Fate,* then into the 1980s through more articles in a variety of publications and the first edition of this book. I also gave a presentation on the relationship of "black panther" accounts to the *Panthera atrox* theory at the Eastern Cougar Conference, 1994, held at Gannon University, Erie, Pennsylvania. Karl Shuker, in his *Mystery Cats of the World* (1989), notes my contribution: "As with the panthers, the principal sources of information concerning these felids are the writings and researches of Loren Coleman, who has been instrumental in bringing these intriguing mystery cats to the attention of cryptozoologists." Shuker also mentions what he calls the "Coleman-Hall theory" for the survival of *Panthera atrox.*

There apparently was a small mention by Henry Shoemaker in his *Extinct Pennsylvania Animals* (1917) of those *atrox* thoughts. Chad Arment brought it to our attention in *BioFortean Review #3* (2000): "One suggested explanation for the occasional 'maned lion' reports in North America is a relict population of the American lion, *Panthera atrox.* This explanation has its roots in Shoemaker's writings," but Hall and I were unaware of it. Mark A. Hall's original suggestion, and the ensuing theory, was remarkably independently derived.

Nevertheless, Shoemaker's comment is intriguing: "Perhaps the earliest form of the panther possessed maned males. They may be a modification of the prehistoric lions which Prof. Leidy called *felis atrox,* and which ranged parts of the continent. The Indians may have repeated an old tradition, and not something made out of the whole cloth." *Felis atrox,* of course, is the former rendering of *Panthera atrox.*

When one begins to imagine the great felines of the American Ice Ages, thoughts usually run to images of the sabertoothed cats: the classic Rancho la Brea Tar Pit paintings of *Smilodon,* the lion-sized sabertooth, on the back of some grazing mammal, a camel perhaps, flashes to mind. The two prehistoric animals are stuck together in the tar pits, soon to be immortalized for thousands of years in the gooey mess. But a rarer (or maybe more intelligent?) visitor lurks in the background. There, larger by a third, is another cat. This cat is *Panthera atrox.*

Fossils of *atrox* have been found in forty sites, from Alaska to Peru, from California through Nebraska to northern Florida. This giant lion was killed by Paleo-Indians, and Dr. Bjorn Kurten has written of the evidence suggesting they were around until as recently as 10,370 years, plus or minus 160 years, before present. Do they persist in isolated pockets today? Why should we even consider such a notion?

Panthera atrox was closely related to the Eurasian cave lion, *Panthera spelaea* (also known as *Panthera leo spelaea*). An unbroken range of lions fringed the top of the world during the Pleistocene, with a distinct subspecies in each hemisphere. *Pantherea leo,* the so-called modern lion of Asia and Africa, is the reduced remainder of *P. spelaea.* But the cave lion seems to have actually persisted into historic Europe. Xerxes' expedition through Macedonia in 480 B.C. had to put up with such "annoyances" as the killing of some of his draft camels by lions. Some authors of ancient Greece—Herodotus, Aristotle, Xenophon, and others—wrote of their contemporary lions. Ralph Holinshed wrote during the 16th century: "Lions we have had very many in the north parts of Scotland, and those with manes of no less force than those of Mauretania; but how and when they were destroyed as yet I do not read." Pleistocene mammalia investigators such as W. Boyd Dawkins and W. A. Sanford see no difference between the cave lion and the modern lion. And Dawkins, Kurten, and others feel *spelaea* and *atrox* are identical.

Because men lived for so long with the cave lion, we can learn much about these lions from the prehistoric artists of Europe, for theorists and fossils do not tell us much about what the animals looked like. One reindeer shoulder-blade from France clearly shows a cave lion with a tufted tail. F. Ed Koby studied prehistoric drawings and sculptures of the large Ice Age cats and found two types. One was a heavily built feline without a mane; the other was a lion with mane and tufted tail. The art of Paleolithic man reinforces the idea that the prehistoric lions showed some quite clear differences between males and females. As C. A. W. Guggisberg wrote on the cave lion in art in his excellent overview, *Simba: Life of the Lion:* "Two lions in the *Grotte des Trois-Freres,* of which one is maned, turn their heads towards the viewer and stare at him with big eyes." Unfortunately, the color of the unmaned one in the pair shall remain unknown. But could this scene be a prehistoric reflection of what the Turner boys saw in Indiana in 1948?

The Ice Age's male and female lions were different. The giant American lion *P. atrox* reflected this sexual dimorphism, as would be expected, through the different limb sizes of the fossil finds, according to various discoveries. Furthermore, G. T. Jefferson, writing in *Current Research in the Pleistocene* in 1992, has found that the molar teeth, M1, are an indicator of sexual dimorphism in *Panthera atrox.* The sex-linked differences in the cats is the key to the lock that opens the mystery of the phantom feline question. Only lions are social. Only lions show wide physical differences between sexes.

Karl Shuker has not been silent in his criticism of the *Panthera atrox* theory. One point he notes in *Mystery Cats of the World* (1989) is "the total absence of sightings in modern America of mystery lion prides. As Coleman himself notes, lions are social…so if his *P. atrox* theory is true, why no records of prides?" (p. 171)

The simple answer to that question is while *Panthera atrox,* the Pleistocene American lion, may have been social, it did not exist in prides. The mystery lions show some evidence of being seen in pairs and alone. We now know that this is reflected in the analysis of *P. atrox* fossils. In the 1992 paper mentioned above, George Jefferson compares George Schaller's research findings that the modern African lion *(Panthera leo)* have a male:female:cub ratio of 74:100:48, with the Rancho la Brea dental

P. atrox finds showing 129:100:42 and *P. atrox* femoral (leg bones) analyses indicating a ratio of 127:100:272. Jefferson, seconded by separate research discoveries of W. A. Akersten and R. D. Guthrie, comments that it is "highly improbable that *P. l. atrox* lived in lion-like prides or cooperatively hunted in social groups…*P. l. atrox* may have hunted in pairs or alone."

The behaviors demonstrated by the mysterious maned cats of America are exactly what one would predict of a male *atrox*. The more aggressive huntress *atrox* perhaps would resemble the "black panther." The latter are more frequently seen, and definitely more aggressive than their maned male counterparts—following closely the pattern of the African and Asian (modern?) lions, *P. leo*. The "black panthers," making up part of the population of female *atrox,* are the mystery cats consistently reported with the cubs or young. They are downright nasty but intelligent. The strutting, careful maned male *atrox* are no dummies, either. Besides, it does not end with merely "black panthers" and "maned cats," as we shall see.

The fossil evidence of *atrox* supports the speculation that it was a bright cat. Thirty saber-toothed *Smilodons* ended up in the La Brea tar pits for every one *atrox*. Because of that amazing ratio, various authors have discussed the intellectual superiority of the lions of La Brea vs. the sabertooths. In B. Kurten and E. Anderson's *Pleistocene Mammals of North America* (1980), for example, they note that *atrox:* "…had a larger brain, relative to body size, than any of the Pleistocene or living lions of the Old World."

Added to its intellectual abilities are various natural selective processes that would have helped *atrox* adapt as the New World changed. A natural tendency towards melanism on the fringes of the lions' range appears to be one of these. One good example of this is the darkly colored (with black belly and head manes) Cape lions of South Africa and the Barbary lions of northern Africa. The reports of "black panthers" may be evidence that some females reflect a genetic drift to effectively use this melanistic adaptation. Then the stage would be set for what we find in Mysterious America today—large maned lions doing what males do (sleeping, mating, regally walking about), aggressive black cats doing what females do (hunting, killing, raising young), and their sister tawny, somewhat striped lionesses with tufted tails, all merging with the human's sense of what we should be seeing versus what we are really seeing.

The Tuft of the Tail

Sorting through the data, the mountain of reports, the stacks of sightings, and an entire two centuries of accounts, has taught mystery cat researchers many things. Several animals can be confused with our cryptid felids, of course, from fishers to black dogs, from wet pumas to escaped black leopards. Skeptical zoology is an important underpinning to our cryptozoological investigations. Mountain lions have black tips to their tails, which can be confusing, and a few African lions may escape from pet owners. Nevertheless, more appears to be happening than the mundane.

The information on *Panthera atrox* is only now slowly being revealed. While it appears that our theorized maned large cats of the American lion *(Panthera atrox)* do show up in the environment, though infrequently, the aligned "black panthers" are obviously more apparent recently but less so historically. However, all *atrox* females surely are not black.

Writing in the 1980s and 1990s, I contrasted the black panther accounts with the eastern *Puma concolor* reports. The sightings have long shown me, Hall, and a few others that the female *atrox* are hidden in the eastern cougar accounts. Indeed, there seems room enough for both, but officialdom would have us believe otherwise.

Historically, we have many hints of this. Shoemaker, writing in 1917, said: "The hide of a West Virginia pantheress killed on the Greenbriar River, Pocahontas County, in 1901, three-quarters grown, owned by Hon. C. K. Sober, of Lewisburg, has long white hair on chest and belly, a fluffy, dark brown tail, culminating in a large tuft of black hair, like the tip of the tail of an African lion." Shoemaker also mentioned a Florida specimen, sex not given, with a rich chocolate brown coat and a tuft on the tail. We have the record of the "African lioness" Nellie and her maned mate from Illinois in 1917, as well.

The *Puma concolor* has a black tip. But if *Panthera atrox* is reflective of its descendant, the African lion, why would it not have a very distinctive "tufted" tail, as shown in cave drawings of the cave lion?

Recent years have had such reports. Two examples separated by 37 years illustrate this point: Ed Moorman was attacked by what he and others said was an "African" lioness, as roaring occurred in the area around his farm in Monument City, Indiana, in June 1962. An "African" lioness was reportedly seen and heard roaring around Port Angeles, Washington in August 1999.

Some lessons on how these female tan *atrox* reports can be heard, then hidden, can be learned from looking at how the "African lioness" sightings from Sauk County, Wisconsin were handled in 1998. Richard Hendricks forwarded these investigations to me, and they give a good example of why it is no wonder that female *atrox* are being ignored.

It all began around mid-July 1998. A woman who had hunted big game out West was investigating the mauling of some calves at her place in the Lake Delton, Wisconsin, area. As she came upon a ditch, she noticed an animal in it. What she saw was, in her words, a "female African lion." Police tried to talk her out of this notion, but she said: "I know what I saw. I know it was a lion."

In the waning days of July, the Wisconsin Dells ranger station received reports of a lion roaring. Then on August 3, a man and his son saw a "big cat" cross their driveway at the Sauk-Juneau county line. More accounts of loud, disturbing roars were noted. By now, reports that a steer and a young pony had been killed were confirmed.

On August 3rd, an "African lion" was seen south of the Dells, near I-90/I-94, when it came out of a field, and went into the woods across from Rocky Arbor State Park. It was dark in color and had a long tail.

Officialdom began commenting on these occurrences. Some took the middle road and appeared open-minded. "We've been skeptical and remain skeptical, that it is an African lion, but the Sheriff's Department has requested assistance and we're going to provide it," said Greg Matthews, spokesman for the state Department of Natural Resources (DNR). The man asking for help, Sauk County Sheriff Virgil "Butch" Steinhorst, noted simply: "We are not lion hunters."

A woman who had kept quiet about her sighting decided to step forward. She told of how on July 29, she was driving on Highway 12 between Middleton and Sauk City when she clearly saw "a female African lion" cross the road in front of her car. Sauk County Sgt. Fred Coller, who knew the woman and kept her identity private, remarked that she was "very credible. She said it wasn't a puma or cougar because it was more muscular and it had a long tail with a puff on it."

On August 6th, talk centered on the possible presence of two lions.

Five separate encounters with the lioness had occurred, and the DNR and Sheriff's Department were no closer to a solution.

Law enforcement officers and the press were apparently growing tired of the "lion" problem. Business people were beginning to wonder if the reports of lions roaring near the tourist mecca, the Wisconsin Dells, might scare away visitors. And so the pushing of the "mountain lion" solution began. You can see the shift in the newspaper reports in the area starting around the 7th of August. By the 10th, it was in full swing when Madison's *State Journal* ran a story about the possibility all the reports might be something more mundane along with a "file photo" with this caption: "Although reports have been of an 'African' lion, a cougar, shown here, more likely would be found in the Wisconsin wilds."

A DNR spokesperson held a news conference and said it was awfully "tricky" to tell the difference between a cougar and an African lioness. He was sure people were seeing pumas. The reports disappeared from the press. The campaign of mundane explanations and ridicule had worked.

Or it did until September 16 and 21, 1998 anyway, when it was obvious the "lion" was still around but had crossed the Wisconsin River and was making its way east and north. Then on February 5 and 9, 1999, a lion was seen near the Devils Lake State Park, Sauk County, Wisconsin.

Tracks of the American Lion

If the American lion is among us, it has left its sign. People have reported the American lion, whether as black panther, maned cat, or African lioness, and sometimes have noted its very large tracks. I look forward to the continued collection of the evidence that is out there, the reports of something that should not exist, and the sightings of an animal that is supposed to be extinct. Meanwhile, an exciting discovery already made may have much to teach us about this cat.

Jerry Vineyard saw them first. In 1982, a cave survey team, led by James E. Vandike, from the Missouri Department of Natural Resources, found large cat footprints in the mud floor of a south-central Missouri cave, appropriately known today as Cat Track Cave. In 1996, a stunning analysis of these tracks was published by Russell W. Graham, James O. Farlow, and Vandike. These three men have now written in a formal, scientific fashion, that these footprints are of *Panthera atrox* ("Tracking Ice Age felids: Identification of tracks of *Panthera atrox* from a cave in southern Missouri, U.S.A.," in *Palaeoecology and Palaeoenvironments of Late Cenezoic Mammals,* University of Toronto Press).

Before the discovery of the *atrox* tracks, the only Ice Age cat tracks in Missouri and Tennessee caves were said to be made by the prehistoric jaguar *(Panthera onca augusta).* But the new tracks are larger than those of *P. o. augusta* and any other known felid. Measuring about 17 cm (6.69 inches) across, these extremely large *atrox* tracks are catlike without claws. But based on examples they have of living jaguars, the authors note that when the surface sediment is deep, cat tracks often do show claws.

Russ Graham, in a personal communication, confirms that the researchers were not able to actually date these tracks. Their published examination concludes: "The surfaces of the tracks and the clay banks were coated with black manganese. This demonstrated the antiquity of the tracks and the undisturbed nature of the cave floor" before the investigators' visits. "Finally, the preservation of these tracks on the surface of the unconsolidated clay deposits in a cave with an active stream documents long-stability of this cave-floor surface, because *P. atrox* has been extinct for at least 10,000 years." In others words, this has to be an old trackway because, as everyone knows (allegedly) *Panthera atrox* is extinct. It is a circular argument. I am not saying these tracks are "fresh" or even recent, but they may not be as old as 10,000 years in age. We just do not know how old they are, now do we?

This first finding of apparently ancient *P. atrox* tracks may, in the long run, have a direct impact on the matters discussed in this chapter.

The large mystery feline that leaves giant tracks apparently still roams that meadow or swamp near the forest or farmyard which lies just beyond your home. The mammoths, mastodons, and camels may be gone, but these great North American cats continue to put up with those fuzzy-headed little primates who make funny noises while searching for elusive answers.

We have today several records of more than one of these mystery cats being seen together; we have accounts of their roars floating across the landscape of North America. The gentle maned lions and their aggressive mates, some black, some showing tufted tails, some slightly striped, are there. The metaphor of the triad of visually disabled men feeling three separate segments of the elephant may be applied here. Hiding in plain sight, in the fields and in the file folders among all those eastern *Puma concolor* sightings, are sightings of very real "African" lionesses, "black pumas," and "maned cats." In other collections, records of "Santers," "Wampus cats," and maned "African lions" fill the three-ring binders of Fortean researchers. Elsewhere, certain cryptozoologists gather "black panther" sightings. The feline phantasmagoria jumbles the mind, but the solution may be a simple one. All may merely be different facets of the same mystery, that of *Panthera atrox,* the American lion in modern times.

Whether or not *Panthera atrox* is the final answer remains to be seen. But for now, for me at least, *P. atrox* seems an intriguing possibility worthy of further exploration.

Update: After sightings of mystery cats in Arkansas, in early September 2002, four 600- to 800-pound maned felines, identified as "African lions," were killed near Quitman, Arkansas. Were they *Panthera atrox*? No DNA analyses were done and the bodies were destroyed. Sheriff Dudley Lemon inspected Safari Unlimited and found the cats were not from there. Then on September 29, 2002, hundreds of miles away, Carter County, Tennessee, residents Troy Guy and Ashley Clawson saw a maned mystery cat on Poga Road. "It was standing on the bank looking at the cars," said Guy. "It was brown and big and had a thing around its neck." They saw it then take off up an embankment. Another eyewitness was Evelyn Cable, owner of Cable's Hampton Family Restaurant, who was driving on U.S. Highway 321 when she saw it. Cable said the "African lion" she saw had a mane around its neck. In October 2002, Maine cryptozoologist Christopher Gardner traveled to the Poga and Elk Mills areas of Carter County, and discovered the last sighting had happened earlier in that month.

CHAPTER 14

Mystery Kangaroos and Devil Monkeys

"It is difficult to determine just where a story of this sort has its beginning," *Hoosier Folklore* notes in a March 1946 article on "strange beast" legends. The journal then arbitrarily picks a story from Mt. Vernon, Illinois. It is here that I, too, shall begin.

During the summer of 1941 Reverend Marsh Harpole was hunting squirrels along the Gum Creek bottom near Mt. Vernon, a small city in the southeastern county of Jefferson, when "a large animal that looked something like a baboon" leaped out of a tree and walked upright toward the startled hunter. Harpole, in turn, struck the creature with his barrel and then frightened it away by firing a couple of shots into the air.

In the months that followed this incident, rural families would report hearing terrifying screams at night in the wooded bottom lands along the creeks. Hunters sometimes found mysterious tracks. By early spring of the next year, after the killing of a farm dog near Bonnie, large parties of volunteers—some with rifles and shotguns, others with nets and ropes—scoured the creek bottoms. But the creature easily evaded them—perhaps because of its reputed ability to leap from 20 to 40 feet in a single bound—and in fact appeared as much as 40 or 50 miles from the location of the original sighting, in Jackson and Okaw counties. Finally it disappeared and was not seen again—for a time, at any rate.

Hoosier Folklore concluded: "About 25 years ago, a 'coon hunter from Hecker one night heard a strange beast screaming up ahead on Prairie du Long Creek. Hunters chased this phantom from time to time all one winter. Their dogs would get the trail, then lose it, and they would hear it screaming down the creek in the opposite direction. It was that kind of creature: you'd hear it up creek, but when you set out in that direction you'd hear it a mile down creek."

The swampy land is a key. Native American folklore from Louisiana, as Mark A. Hall has pointed out, refers to swamp creatures known to the Choctaw as the *nalusa falaya,* meaning the Long Evil Being. Hall believes this being is probably the one referred to in this chapter, as its general description mentions the characteristic long, pointed ears.

Enfield, Illinois, less than 40 miles to the southeast of Mt. Vernon, is a sleepy little village of some 800 residents, which 31 years after the 1941-42 "monster" scare would play host to what must have been, if not the same animal, at least an awfully close relative.

About 9:30 p.m. on April 25, 1973, Mr. and Mrs. Henry McDaniel of Enfield returned to their home in the northwest section of town, where they were greeted by two of their children, Henry and Lil, with a fantastic story about how a "thing" had tried to get into the house by scratching on the door and the window air conditioner.

Not long afterwards the thing was back. Mr. McDaniel greeted it with a flashlight and a .22 pistol, firing at it four times as it sprinted across the yard and covered, so he would assert, 50 feet in three jumps. It ran north through brush along the L&N railroad tracks, which passed near McDaniel's residence, and vanished from sight.

"It had three legs on it," McDaniel reported, "a short body, two little short arms, and two pink eyes as big as flashlights. It stood four-and-a-half-feet tall and was grayish-colored…When I fired that first shot, I know I hit."

The creature had given out a hiss rather like a wildcat's.

McDaniel's sighting provided the impetus for a media-created "panic" that brought hordes of unwelcome visitors to Enfield, including curiosity seekers whom an angry White County Sheriff Roy Poshard, Jr., promptly jailed. But two of those incarcerated, Roger Tappy and Mike Mogle of Elwood, Indiana, swore they had seen a "gray monkey" moving faster than a man through some underbrush. Tappy, Mogle, and two companions opened fire on the animal with a .22 rifle and three shotguns, but it got away.

On Sunday, May 6th, Rick Rainbow, News Director of WWKI, Kokomo, Indiana, in the company of three friends from Kokomo, encoun-

Devil Monkey

tered the creature near an old abandoned house close to McDaniel's residence. The thing stood about five-and-a-half-feet tall and was gray and stooped over. When it saw the men, it fled. Since it had its back to the observers and was in the shadows, they were unable to get a very good look at the creature. However, as it ran, it uttered a high-pitched cry, which Rainbow recorded on his tape machine.

Just hours before, at 3:00 a.m., McDaniel had seen the creature again. Awakened by the howling of neighborhood dogs, he looked out the front door.

"I saw something moving out on the railroad track, and there it stood," he said later. "I didn't shoot at it or anything. It started on down the railroad track. It wasn't in a hurry or nothing."

About this time I visited Enfield, interviewed witnesses, and otherwise investigated the case. As Richard Crowe and I walked through a field near McDaniel's place, we heard a high-pitched loud screech that neither of us could identify.

Monkey-like and leaping about? Three back legs? What could these reports have to do with my files full of kangaroo reports? Let's have a look.

The 'Roos Take On the Cops

The place is Chicago's Northwest Side. It is early in the morning, nearly 3:30 a.m. The date is October 18, 1974; a normal day for most people, but for patrolmen Leonard Ciagi and Michael Byrne of the Chicago Police Force, a very strange drama is unfolding. Earlier, the patrolmen had responded to the call of an incredulous homeowner who claimed a kangaroo, of all things, had been on his porch. It was easy for the police officers to laugh about the report a couple of hours before, but now that Byrne and Ciagi had cornered the five-foot-tall marsupial at the end of a darkened alley the police had to come to grips with the situation.

And to make matters worse, the kangaroo was growling.

Byrne, understandably reluctant, attempted to handcuff the animal. It was at that point, as he later told reporters, that the kangaroo "started to scream and get vicious." The battle that followed was not soon to be forgotten by Chicago's finest.

"My partner got kicked pretty bad in the legs. He (the kangaroo) smacks pretty good, but we got in a few good punches to the head and he must have felt it."

Byrne then added, "Too bad we didn't have our nightsticks there, then we could have really hammered him."

The media had a field day. Newspapers from coast to coast blared with such headlines as "KANGAROO STAYS A JUMP AHEAD OF POLICE" and "KEYSTONE KOPS GO ON KANGAROO KAPER" in huge block letters the day following the encounter.

Short of using their guns, the men stood little chance of subduing the animal. Handcuffs were certainly of no use, so, lacking nightsticks and battered, the pair backed off. As additional squad cars began to arrive, the animal leaped over a fence and took off down the street "going 20 miles per hour," leaving only a mystery and sore shins in its wake.

And it is a mystery. Little known to the public-at-large, supposed "mystery kangaroos" have turned up all over the Midwest and continue to do so on a semi-regular basis. When these phantom creatures do make an appearance, they are never claimed. I am not describing escaped pets, or for that matter, animals that "got away" from the local zoo. What I am discussing, instead, is a very strange type of creature, animals, which for reasons unknown, see it fit to appear in areas that host the majority of "monsters" and cryptid activity. Animals, that for technical and other considerations, cannot, but *do,* exist.

In this report I shall examine the stuff that fantasies, dreams, and—perhaps more frequently—nightmares are made of.

A Short History of Hoppers

The legacy of mysterious marsupials of the Midwest has been an active one since the snarling kangaroo attacked the two Chicago policemen in 1974. But before I examine the bizarre events of more recent years, let me peer at some of America's earliest kangaroo sightings.

In a rather obscure book by Robert H. Gollmar, *My Father Owned a Circus,* I find the first modern record of an errant kangaroo. In his chapter on the tragedies affecting the Gollmar circus, he told of the day that a big tornado struck New Richmond, Wisconsin. The storm occurred on June 12, 1899, when the circus happened to be in town. According to a local historian, Ann P. Epley, writing in 1900, in the midst of the storm a Mrs. Glover saw a kangaroo run through the backyard of Mrs. Allen. Robert Gollmar takes issue with the claim the creature was an escaped circus animal. "I have no recollection of the circus owning a kangaroo; I particularly doubt it in 1899," Gollmar writes. Too often the escapee theory has been used without any basis in fact, and we run across it many times in the kangaroo stories.

Around 1900, near Mays Landing, New Jersey, something like a kangaroo was to add weight to that region's tales of the "Jersey Devil." Mrs. Amanda Sutts of Yardville recalled seeing and hearing the "Devil" in 1900 when she was a girl of ten.

"We heard a scream near the barn one night and ran out of our house," said Mrs. Sutts. "We saw this thing that looked like a kangaroo. It wasn't such a great big animal—it was about the size of a small calf and weighed about 150 pounds. But the noise is what scared us. It sounded like a woman screaming in an awful lot of agony."

The sound that resembles a woman screaming is nothing new to researchers of the unknown. This peculiar sound—also described like that of a baby crying—often spills out of haunted houses to bathe the locale in eerie vibration. Strangely, the awesome Bigfoot seem to emit this sound, as well as those elusive phantom panthers that prowl the landscape. And, of course, the legendary banshee is famous for its terrible scream. Often, a myriad of "unrelated" unexplained phenomena have the same element in common.

Mrs. Sutts reported that she saw the Devil's tracks many times, always around the family barn. She remembers the footprints were from eight to ten feet apart and led to a large cedar swamp at the rear of the farm.

The lore of the New Jersey Devil is a mixed bag of Bigfoot, panther, and thunderbird reports, as well as some obvious hoaxes, as we will see in a later chapter. Over the years, many eyewitnesses have reported seeing the thing. In general, the reports indicate that the Jersey Devil had the face of a horse, the body of a kangaroo, sometimes the wings of a bat, and often seemed half human and half animal. But the name is a catch-all, and each individual sighting should be treated separately, including this one.

Mrs. Sutts said her relatives would "pull my hair out when they find out I've been talking about the Jersey Devil. But I know there is such a creature. I'll never forget how frightened I was when I saw him. I was so scared, I thought I'd die."

Whether "it" was the Jersey Devil or not is really unimportant, for the kangaroos keep hopping down through history. Reports of the giant kangaroo of South Pittsburg, Tennessee, made it all the way to the pages of New York's daily newspapers. During mid-January of 1934, a kangaroo spread terror among the Tennessee hill farmers. This extremely atypical 'roo was reported to have killed and partially devoured several German police dogs, geese, and ducks. The Reverend W. J. Hancock saw the animal and described it as fast as lightning, and looking like a giant kangaroo as it ran and leapt across a field. Another witness, Frank Cobb quickly came upon more evidence of the kangaroo's activities. The head and shoulders of a large police dog were all that remained. A search party tracked the 'roo to a mountainside cave, where the prints disappeared.

In recent years, writers have tried to blame this Tennessee giant kangaroo story on the pen of the late Horace N. Minnis, a South Pittsburg correspondent of the *Chattanooga Times*. The only trouble with this "newspaper hoax" theory is that Minnis was not a newspaper correspondent for the area in 1934.

In 1949 the area surrounding Grove City, Ohio, experienced a monster flap. Perhaps it was coincidence, or perhaps it wasn't, but during the creature wave another type of "monster" decided to show up—this time a phantom kangaroo. Mr. Louis Staub, while driving a Greyhound bus near Grove City in January of that year, encountered a hopping marsupial-like beast when the vehicle's bright headlights illuminated it. He described it in the following terms:

> It's about 5½ feet high, hairy, and brownish in color. It has a long pointed head. It leaped a barbed wire fence and disappeared. It resembled a kangaroo, but it appeared to jump on all fours. I'm certain it wasn't a deer.

Sightings of kangaroos exploded all over the state of Nebraska in 1958. Not until researcher Ray Boeche passed along an aging newsclip did I learn that there was another person named Charles Wetzel that had seen something strange that year. (Read about the other Charles Wetzel in the Name Game chapter.) For years I had encouraged Boeche, as I had many others, to search their local newspaper libraries beyond the realm of lake monster and Bigfoot accounts, into the wide weird world of creatures that fill the cryptozoo surrounding us. I was thus happily amazed to discover that this Charles Wetzel was involved with one of my favorites—mystery kangaroos!

As soon as I tracked down this Charles Wetzel in the early 1980s, I interviewed him. The elements of his story were straightforward, as befits a true son of the plains. Charles Wetzel, born March 29, 1888, was at his Platte River cabin, near Grand Island, Nebraska, on the 28th of July, 1958, a Monday. Wetzel reported the thing he first took to be a deer was chasing some dogs, which in itself seemed a bit strange. Then he got within ten yards of it and saw what looked like a kangaroo bounding away with ten-foot leaps. To Wetzel, the animal, or whatever it was, appeared to be about six feet tall, brown, with large hind legs and small forelegs that barely touched the ground as it jumped. According to Wetzel, the kangaroo stayed around the cabin for several minutes but finally departed as Wetzel tried to get closer, first on foot, then in his car. The kangaroo finally disappeared into an alfalfa field.

Wetzel's report was no isolated event in Nebraska in 1958. Other sightings of kangaroos were reported from towns as distant as 100 miles from each other, Endicott, Stanton and Fairbury among them. Wetzel was operating a brewery in Grand Island at the time of his sighting. He was so obsessed with his bizarre experience, he named one of his brands "Wetzel Kangaroo Beer." With the advent of eBay, I've even talked to beer can collectors in Nebraska who have seen the Wetzel beer collectible, but it remains absent from my crypto-collection.

A year before Nebraska's flap, strangeness settled in Minnesota. From 1957 until about 1967, the woods around Coon Rapids, Minnesota, were frequently the site of kangaroo reports. Mrs. Barbara Battmer first brought these cases to my attention when I interviewed that area's residents. Her two sons were seven and nine, when in 1957 they were playing near a forested area of Coon Rapids off Highway 10. They claimed then, and have stuck to their story ever since, that they saw two kangaroos hopping together through the woods. The five-foot-tall animals hopped out of some trees, crossed a small clearing about fifty feet in front of the boys, and disappeared into another wooded area. With this clear view of the creatures, they were certain that the color of the kangaroos was a light tan to medium brown.

Because of Mrs. Battmer's efforts, more people came forth with their knowledge of Coon Rapids kangaroo stories. Linda Brodie is certain it was a kangaroo she saw in 1958. And Mrs. Gary Haider told me of her two brothers coming home in 1958 with reports of a "Big Rabbit." Mrs. Haider said the boys described the "enormous" rabbit as being as big as they were, and just hopping around. Mr. and Mrs. Willard L. Hays of Coon Rapids testify to the fact they saw two oversized "bunnies" on the evening of April 24, 1967. Hazel Hays told me that the kangaroos were in an open area approximately one mile west of Highway 47, near the Anoka County Fairgrounds.

During all this activity in Minnesota, kangaroos were making appearances elsewhere in the country. On July 26, 1965, Bert Radar spied a phantom 'roo east of Abilene, Kansas, on Interstate 70. Jerry L. Condray saw his mystery kangaroo on August 15, 1965, northeast of Wakefield, Kansas.

Sometime early in 1967, William Shearer encountered one of these critters in Puyallup, Washington, a town more well known for recurring reports of screaming Bigfoot than for hopping kangaroos.

Almost as if the kangaroos were again hopping their way across or around the Midwest, they turned up in Michigan and Ohio in 1968. On the last day of May, a motorist traveling along Ohio Route 63 reported to the Ohio State Patrol that he had seen a kangaroo hopping about near Monroe at 2:30 a.m. The radio dispatcher took the report lightly, but sent Patrolman James Patrick for a check. Patrick reported back within a matter of minutes. "The thing hopped right across the road in front of my cruiser," Patrick said. "It sure looked like a kangaroo to me." He said the animal leaped off in the direction of Lebanon, Ohio.

Meanwhile, the director of the Cincinnati Zoo, Ed Maruska, was telling the newspapers, "I doubt there's a kangaroo around here on the loose. We had a kangaroo story about two years ago. Never found one. Down the years we've chased after reported black leopards, panthers, and even a polar bear. Anyway, anyone seeing the kangaroo, which I doubt exists, should try to keep it in sight and call the zoo."

But to keep *it* in sight, you would have had to have been in Lansing, Michigan. There on the 3rd of August, a citizen reported to state police that he had seen a kangaroo hopping around the campus of Michigan State University, near College and Jolly roads.

November of 1971 was the month that "The Phenomenon" visited Kansas in two of its many guises; this time as kangaroos and as those darn UFOs. Mrs. Edward Johnson, who lives near Abilene, reported seeing a kangaroo not far from her home on the first of November.

Synchronistically, the next day *another* Johnson family encountered the unknown. The Dural Johnson Family of Delphos, Kansas reported that on November 2nd a donut-shaped flying object landed. (And this was not all. Two days later a Manhattan, Kansas retired Army dentist reported seeing a cigar-shaped flying object near Weida. Dr. Dean H. Stewart said he saw the object, which had an orange nose cone and a white body, as he was duck hunting on a lake.)

The Dural Johnson family of Ottawa County were quite puzzled by their November 2nd experiences. Ronnie Johnson, 13, was tending sheep when the blinding object landed in a field on the property, breaking several tree limbs. When Ronnie got his parents, the object made a rumble and a roar as it took off, leaving behind a classic landing spot for all to see. The Johnsons took a picture of the spot in the dark, and it revealed a fluorescent glow in the shape of the object where it had landed. Sheriff Ralph Enlow felt the Johnsons were quite sincere. Not only was Sheriff Enlow impressed, but a panel of ufological consultants were so intrigued by the physical and testimonial evidence that they awarded the incident their "Best Case of the Year" prize.

The fact that kangaroos and UFOs both were seen by Johnsons in the same state at the same time is interesting. The great German psychologist Carl G. Jung pioneered the study of synchronicity, which involves the non-causal "production" of meaningful coincidences. (Jung's thesis was presented in his *Synchronicity: An Acausal Connecting Principle.*) Are we dealing with a synchronicity, a meaningful coincidence? Synchronistically, did two unrelated Fortean phenomena, in this instance UFOs and kangaroos, manifest themselves in roughly the same time frame, and in the same state? Or are the laws of causality at play? We can't ignore the hints that the various phenomena are singular aspects of something larger.

And as if UFOs and the Jersey Devil were not enough to get involved with kangaroos, even the lake monsters of Ireland sometimes reflect the kangarooitis. There was Gay Denver, a 16-year-old student who in 1968 was quietly pushing his bike up the rise overlooking Glendarry Lake near Achill Sound. Denver came upon a "lake monster" climbing a turf bank into the woods. "It was moving in a jumpy way like a kangaroo," Denver breathlessly told the authorities. "It has a long head like a sheep and a long neck and tail. The hind legs were bigger than the front ones."

Back to Illinois and Indiana

The vast majority of Americans did not become aware of Kangaroo Mania until 1974. Needless to say, I had been following the reports for years. But the incident involving the Chicago police officers opened the floodgates and the Midwest experienced a kangaroo flap, a hectic period of increased activity that is, in turn, responsible for an increased public awareness.

Actually, the Chicago area had once before played host to the Unidentified Furry Objects, even before 1974. In 1971, during the month of July, a mystery 'roo apparently turned up in Evanston, Illinois. The animal made its appearance on the grounds of Northwestern University, where it was spotted by an unnamed campus policeman. The incident was reported to the Evanston police, who never caught up with the creature.

On October 18, 1974—the same day Chicago patrolmen Byrne and Ciagi encountered their screaming marsupial—another sighting occurred that set a standard for the days to follow. This time a four-and-a-half-foot-tall kangaroo was seen hopping around Belmont and Oak parks in the Windy City's Northwest Side.

The next day, Saturday, October 19, offered even more activity. It all began in the morning, around 7:00 a.m., when 13-year-old Kenneth Grieshamer was delivering newspapers. The boy, standing on the corner of Sunnyside and Mulligan streets, heard the screech of brakes and spun around. Instead of seeing a car, Grieshamer saw a kangaroo standing a few feet away. "He looked at me, I looked at him, and then away he hopped," the boy said.

That same day, about an hour later, two boys saw a kangaroo near Austin and Eastwood roads. And if two sightings weren't enough, an unidentified caller reported to the Chicago police that he had seen a kangaroo hopping around Belmont and Mango avenues at about 6:00 p.m. Apparently the kangaroo developed quite an appetite after making three appearances on Saturday because the next morning the Chicago police switchboard received calls from startled residents who claimed the creature was rummaging through their garbage cans.

On Wednesday, October 23, a kangaroo was seen roaming about Chicago's Schiller Woods, near Irving Park Road. This was to be the last kangaroo seen in Chicago until early November. From then on, things were pretty quiet all around until the marsupials started to pop up in other midwestern cities. On the first of November the epidemic spread to Plano, Illinois.

John Orr, an off-duty Plano, Illinois police officer spotted a kangaroo Friday evening while driving on Riverview Road, just outside the city limits. The animal leaped eight feet from a cornfield, landed in the middle of the road, and was caught in the bright lights of Orr's highbeams. "I'm positive I saw him," Orr said. "People don't believe you when you see things like that. I definitely know it was a kangaroo."

"If I hadn't slowed down, I would have hit him. My cousin was in the car behind me and when she saw him, she just plain ran off the road."

Orr told reporters that the kangaroo stood in the road for a few seconds and then hopped off into a wooded area.

Plano, Illinois is about 50 miles west of Chicago. Until Orr's sighting, the general assumption was that only one kangaroo was on the loose. But now a few folks began to have their doubts—either doubting the workings of the human mind or the assumption that there was only one kangaroo running around Illinois. However dramatic the Orr sighting might have been, it only served as a taste of things to come because the day after *kangaroos were seen in Chicago and Plano at approximately the same time.*

Jerry Wagner, Steve Morton, and Shawne Clark—all 17—were driving along Plano's Shafer Road, around 9 p.m. on the night of November 2, 1974. Suddenly, the car's headlights picked up something in the middle of the road. The something turned out to be—you guessed it—a creature that looked remarkably like a full-grown kangaroo!

"We almost ran over it. It jumped onto the road about 20 feet ahead of us," Jerry Wagner said. "I was on the passenger side in the front seat and I pointed it out to Shawne and Steve and all three of us saw it."

"It landed on the road near the intersection with the main road, and there was no traffic. It sat up on its haunches as kangaroos do and then jumped over a fence about five feet high and disappeared into the woods."

Wagner continued, telling reporters, "I never really believed those stories about people seeing a kangaroo around here, but I do now."

After the sighting the three youths reported the incident to the Kendall County Sheriff's Office. And while they were doing that, a similar scenario unfolded in Chicago, some fifty miles away.

Cathy Battaglia, 17, and her boyfriend, Len Zeglicz, 19, were out for a walk around 9:30 p.m. when they encountered a strange creature in the 5600 block of South New England Avenue. At first they thought it was a dog. But when the animal looked at the couple, turned, and hopped away down the street, the two knew for a fact they had seen a kangaroo.

If the two reports of November 2nd are accurate, it is obvious that more than one kangaroo was hopping around the Midwest in 1974. The possibility that one kangaroo—capable of doing 25 miles per hour, and then only for a short while—had traversed a distance of 50 or so miles in 30 minutes is simply too difficult to accept. The other sightings of November 1974 provide excellent evidence to confirm the general suspicion that more than one 'roo was on the loose.

On the morning of November 3rd, Frank Kocherver, 21, saw a kangaroo near a forest preserve on Chicago's Northwest Side. Kocherver reported that the animal leaped from a two-legged position into the woods.

Then on Monday, November 4th, a truck driver saw a deer and what he thought to be a kangaroo near Plano, Illinois. The driver pulled his rig over to the side of the road and tracked the deer and "another animal that definitely is not a deer—its prints in the mud of the field are different and I think it is a kangaroo."

And then the kangaroos *really* started to get around. And their publicity leapt to the national level.

According to the *Wall Street Journal,* on November 6th near Lansing, Illinois, a truck driver was forced to swerve off the road in order to avoid hitting one of our maverick marsupials.

Six days after the Lansing encounter, Rensselaer, Indiana experienced a mini-flap of kangaroo sightings. It started when Alfred Hentschel, an employee of St. Joseph's College, saw one of the bounding phantoms come out of a cornfield bordering a drugstore on Rensselaer's south edge around 8:30 a.m. From there, the kangaroo hopped down Charles Street, and then crossed over into another cornfield. When last seen by Hentschel, the animal was hopping west toward some trees on the distant edge of another cornfield. The sighting touched off a massive search, but not a trace of the animal was found.

"I hope some farmer or somebody else sees it, or everybody'll think I'm a nut," said Hentschel. "But it was a kangaroo…I know it was." Hentschel really didn't have long to wait because, later that day, two more sightings occurred.

Around noon Charles James of Rensselaer saw what he thought was a kangaroo. He saw the animal bounding out of some woods near St. Joseph's College, after which it hopped over a hill about 1,000 feet from the witness. Following this sighting, seven law enforcement units sped into the area only to find…no kangaroo.

Then about 5 p.m. that day, Bill Babcock reported that he, too, had seen the animal. The kangaroo, he reported, was hopping around near a gravel pit located near his construction company office. Babcock stated he last saw the creature heading west.

Three days later on November 15, 1974, the kangaroo—or a kangaroo—was back in Chicago. Joe Bernotus was taking a train to work that Friday morning when he saw the creature through the vehicle's window: "I'm sure that somebody else must have seen it because I was in an eight-car train. But when people see something like that they don't always want to say anything."

Bernotus reported that the animal was five feet tall and "black all over, except for the stomach and face, which were brown." He went on to say that the kangaroo was just standing in a vacant lot near Damen and Montrose streets.

On Sunday, November 17th, a mystery kangaroo was seen in Carmel, Indiana, which is located several miles north of Indianapolis. Amos Miller, his wife, and another couple spotted the animal while driving to church that Sunday morning. Those four people reported that the kangaroo was sitting on its haunches near the Cool Creek Bridge at Indiana 234 and Keystone. Later that afternoon police received a call from a woman who saw the marsupial hop off into some woods.

The police believed the kangaroo reports. "We don't doubt the story one bit," said a police spokesman. But officials never did catch up with the creature.

Actually, no one caught up with the kangaroo, or kangaroos, that were hopping around the countryside in 1974. The last sighting that year occurred on the 25th of November and came from Sheridan, Indiana.

Donald Johnson, a Sheridan farmer, was driving his pickup truck down a deserted rural road when he encountered the creature. Johnson slowed down at the intersection and, looking to his right, saw a kangaroo "running on all four feet down the middle of the road." The animal spotted Johnson, jumped over a four-foot-tall barbed wire fence, and bounded across a field where he was lost to sight. I think we begin to see in this report a hint that the mystery kangaroo phenomena goes deeper than mere sightings of regular kangaroos; more about that soon.

But even this was not to be the end of the kangaroo sightings. The mysterious marsupials, although fewer in number, decided to stage a few appearances in these same hopping grounds, in both 1975 and 1976.

It was a Monday morning, about 7 a.m. on the 14th of July 1975. Mrs. Rosemary Hopwood was winding her way along Illinois Route 128.

South of Dalton City, near Decatur, she was startled to see an animal she first took to be a dog. Getting closer, she saw it was a kangaroo walking on all fours at the side of the road. Then, as she told me, the kangaroo moved across the road and lifted itself up on its back legs. She described the animal as light beige in color, about five-and-a-half-feet long when it traveled on all fours, and about two and a half feet in height sitting upright. The thing had pointed ears and a long, thick tail. It hopped away into an Illinois cornfield.

Three days later, a couple of other people saw a kangaroo in the same general area.

Rosemary Hopwood was the recipient of much "ribbing," as she put it, because of her experience. A more positive side effect was that other people with weird tales to tell felt comfortable sharing them with Mrs. Hopwood. For example, one St. Elmo farmer told her about the time a black panther had paced his car. But still, all these stories, and her frequent feeling that she was seeing strange lights in the area, did not make Rosemary Hopwood think it was any less weird to say she saw a kangaroo in Illinois.

DuQuoin, Illinois, was the site of another July, 1975, 'roo encounter. Kevin Luthi was one of several people who saw a five-foot kangaroo-like animal bound through some cornfields. Luthi was not quick to report his sighting, as he felt "everyone would think" he was "crazy."

In 1976 Illinois was once again the site of kangaroo activity. Harry Masterson of Rock Island spotted one of the animals near his home on Tuesday, April 6th. Masterson, 25, was out walking his dog at 6:30 a.m. when he encountered the animal.

"I looked across the street and there it was. A kangaroo. It was a big one. It came hopping through the yard. The kangaroo and I stood there looking at each other for about a minute. Then it turned around and went hopping away off to the north."

Masterson was sure the animal he had seen was a kangaroo. He told me that he had been to the Milwaukee Zoo and knew what a kangaroo looked like. More witnesses also chimed in with their testimony.

When the animal began its exit, Harry ran into the house and persuaded his wife, Barbara, and his mother-in-law to come outside and see the creature. By the time the others had made it outside the kangaroo was already on its way, hopping "faster than a dog" according to Barbara. With no alternatives, the trio just stood incredulously on the front lawn and watched the marsupial disappear into the rapidly rising sun.

Mrs. Masterson said that exactly one month to the day after their sighting an unnamed woman saw a kangaroo in Rock Island.

Monkey-like Kangaroos and Waukesha Wonders

Then in 1975, Oklahoma erupted in a wave of sightings of a creature described as "a hairy monster that looks like a huge monkey and hops like a kangaroo." Strange hairy creatures were seen in two locations in Oklahoma, and these accounts soon jumped to the national media. The Noxie Monster of September 1975 might be something different than what we are talking about here, but it made people pay attention to later reports from around Indianacola. In that series of encounters, in October 1975, witnesses Anthony and Steve Ketchum and their friend, Allen Herrin, heard and then saw something strange in a fenced farm lot, where horses and hogs were kept. The thing jumped out of some bushes, then appeared in front of their car's lights. "It was big, taller than a man," Anthony said. "It had hair all over it. It looked like a big monkey and it made a grunting noise. It started chasing us, hopping like a kangaroo."

The Indianacola sightings included sightings of one of these creatures on top of a two-story building, and a terrified woman telling police one looked in her bedroom window.

On August 17, 1976, a kangaroo was seen by a citizen's band radio operator near Golden, Colorado at 2:10 a.m. The radio operator's report was forwarded to the police and five law enforcement officers had some success tracking the marsupial. At 4:15 a.m. one of the group, Patrolman Donald Douglas, saw the kangaroo near some clay pits. He said the kangaroo was full grown and hopped away when he approached it.

The kangaroos seemed to have literally leapt over 1977, or at least, I didn't hear about any reports for that year. The next big outbreak of sightings took place in Wisconsin in 1978. The most startling result of the Wisconsin drama was the first alleged photograph of a phantom kangaroo. But prior to the photograph, a series of kangaroo close encounters occurred.

The 5th of April, 1978, is the first recorded date of a sighting in the area of Waukesha, Wisconsin. On that day, at 6:45 a.m. on East Moreland Blvd., east of Highway A, witnesses Wilcox and Kroske saw a kangaroo. This was followed by the April 12th sighting by members of the Haeselich family of nearby Pewaukee Township. "It was going pretty quick. It was hopping. We knew it had to be a kangaroo," Jill Haeselich said at the time.

Jill, her husband, Peter, and his mother, Esther, were sitting in the dining room eating supper about 6:15 p.m. when they spotted the kangaroo in their backyard. It disappeared over a hill as Peter tried to pursue it. "It was so fast," Jill recalled.

The next day, at 4:45 p.m., William J. Busch was returning home from his job as a social worker at a Waukesha County residential school when he saw his kangaroo. Busch was driving on Highway 83, when about 15 feet in front of him, a three-foot-tall creature with a "slightly odd-shaped" head, little front legs, and long back feet scampered across the road.

Three days later at 3 a.m. on April 16, Greg and Janet Napientek saw a kangaroo as they were driving home along Highway A, east of Waukesha.

"I've seen deer before. I know what a deer looks like. I know it was a kangaroo," Janet Napientek observed.

Up in their hilltop home on Sierra Drive in Brookfield Township, near Waukesha, the Nero family has a good view of the nearby wooded terrain. On the 23rd of April, around 10:45 a.m., Lance Nero was having toast and coffee when he glanced outside to see two kangaroos hop out of the woods, across a road, through part of a field, and across another road. Lance and Loretta Nero, along with members of the Waukesha County Sheriff's Department, discovered tracks left behind by the animals. Some deputies tried to quickly debunk the tracks by saying they were made by deer or cows, in spite of their appearance.

Veteran cryptozoologist Mark A. Hall interviewed the Neros and found them to be intelligent and sincere people. They showed Hall five casts, and he described the tracks to me: "Generally the tracks have a two-pronged fork appearance with two knobs at the rear of the 'fork handle.' The tracks were impressed into mud at a new housing development, which accounts somewhat for their depth."

Measuring two of the casts, Mark Hall found this range in length, 5.75 inches to 6.0 inches; and width, 2.75 inches to 3.125 inches. The animal appeared to have three toes.

As if the tracks of a mystery kangaroo were not enough, on the 24th of April, 1978, a good photograph of one of the elusive beasts was taken. At 5:20 p.m. on that Monday, two 23-year-old Menomonee Falls men spotted a kangaroo in the bush near Highway SS and Highway M. They took two Polaroid SX-70 color photographs. One photograph is blurry, but the other clearly shows a kangaroo-like animal. The two men refused to give their identity to a reporter in 1978, fearing public ridicule.

As with most photographs that appear in this shadowy world of cryptids, a story surfaced, 30 years after they were taken, of the pictures being a hoax. Kim Del Rio, an International Fortean Organization member, told me a strange story about this. In 1988, she met a taxidermist who works at the Milwaukee Public Museum. They got to talking about zoology and then cryptozoology, and she showed him a copy of the photograph in the 1983 edition of *Mysterious America*. This gentleman, Del Rio tells me, then started laughing. When she asked what was so funny, he claimed to have taken the photo himself after seeing the newscast of a kangaroo sighting in Brookfield and Waukeesha. He said that he and a fellow worker took a stuffed wallaby, put it in some bushes, and took a picture of it. Then another friend of theirs sent it to the newspapers. Or so his story goes.

Del Rio says she wrote all this up for the *INFO Journal,* but they apparently lost the article in the administrative shifts that have rocked the organization over the years. She could not use the real name of the museum man and did not get far in her request to take a photograph of the actual wallaby for comparison. The museum man was very rude to her and said she was silly for believing in anything that "didn't already exist." Nothing more has come of this debunking, as certainly anyone can claim to be the source of a hoax, anonymously and without proof.

The clear color Polaroid picture shows a tan animal with lighter brown front limbs, hints of a lighter brown hind limb, and dark brown or black patches around the eyes, inside the two upright ears, and possibly surrounding the nose and upper mouth area. The animal compares favorably with Bennett's wallaby or brush kangaroo, a native of Tasmania, found from snowy summits to lower valleys. The Waukeska photographed animal also looks like the black-tailed or swamp wallaby, a marsupial inhabiting the dense wet gullies from Queensland to SE South Australia. Or, of course, it could be some undiscovered form of mammal we have as yet not imagined. Or the photo could be a hoax.

Still, whatever the actual mystery kangaroos are, they continued to be seen in Wisconsin in 1978. At 2:30 a.m., on the 24th of April, Tom Frank saw one near Highway C in Merton Township. On the 9th of May, at the Camelot Forest housing development, Waukesha County's last kangaroo of 1978 was seen.

Later in the month of May, some 185 miles northeast of Waukesha, in Eau Claire County, Wisconsin, another kangaroo was spied. On the 21st, a Sunday night, an Eau Claire woman was returning home, on Highway 12 between Augusta and Fall Creek, when she saw a creature the size of a man hopping across the road.

So ended the 1978 Wisconsin kangaroo accounts.

North of the Border, All Over the Map, and Escapees

During the warm months of 1979 Canada was the site of some more mystery kangaroo visitations. Early on the morning of the 31st of May, a police officer radioed the station to report he had sighted a kangaroo in the Markham Road-Finch Avenue area of Scarboro, a section of Toronto, Ontario. A Metro Toronto Zoo official, when asked for his opinion, said: "We're definitely not missing any wallabies or any other kind of creature, and we haven't sent anyone out to look for anything. It's likely just a rabbit with long ears."

A few days later and several hundred miles to the northeast, another kangaroo popped up. Roy Hanley, a guard at the Acadia Forest Products, Ltd. mill in Nelson-Miramichi, New Brunswick, saw a kangaroo at 3 a.m. on the 5th of June, 1979. Hanley was on duty at the time when he came upon the creature. "I was standing no more than 10 feet from him. As far as I'm concerned it was a baby kangaroo," Hanley told reporters. "It was about three to three-and-a-half-feet in height, had large powerful looking hind legs, small front paws, a long large tail, big droopy ears, and a greyish-brown coat."

A taxi driver and her passenger had also seen a kangaroo near the mill, and other encounters were reported from Millton and Douglasville, New Brunswick, near the Maine border.

The Hanley sighting stimulated interest in the folk collection of the

"Songs of the Miramichi." Folksong No. 47 is entitled, "The Wild Cat Back on the Pipe Line," and tells of the many people who saw a strange animal on the pipeline. One passage goes:

> The next one that saw it, his name was LeClair.
> He said 'twas no monkey, nor neither a bear,
> For he came from Australia and knows it is true,
> For he saw many like it, 'twas a big kangaroo.

This song, written by Jared MacLean, is dated 1948, and gives a good deal of historical backdrop to the recent kangaroo reports out of New Brunswick. As the title of the song demonstrates, the kangaroo and phantom panther accounts often merge. Along with the reported encounter between Herman Belyea and an erect panther in 1951 in New Brunswick, strange, upright, kangaroo-like animals appear to have a lengthy history in this part of Canada, separate from the eastern Bigfoot/Windigo lore.

In September, 1979, the action was back in the United States. A dark-colored leaping kangaroo was seen near Delaware's tiny village of Concord. Police found a six-inch lock of hair and four-by-four-and-a-half-inch tracks.

The year 1980 was uneventful in terms of mystery kangaroos. Ed Barker of KGO radio, San Francisco, told me that a crew of his searched Golden Gate Park, probably in 1980, after some San Franciscans reported they spotted a kangaroo there. But the following year, 1981, produced a bumper crop of kangaroo stories. Beginning in June, they stretched into October, and ranged from the Rockies to Appalachia.

Ray Ault saw the year's first 'roo early in June. Rancher Ault was out with his sheep near Cedar Fort, Utah County, Utah, when he was spooked by an animal jumping six feet straight in the air. "I was checking the sheep up the canyon and off to the side of them I saw something jump straight up. I thought that was a little strange. I got closer to the animal that jumped and it looked me right in the eye. Then jump, jump, jump, off it went," Ault said.

Ray Ault was certain it was a kangaroo, and commented, "I've seen kangaroos in the movies and on TV and there was no mistaking it. It looked like a big kangaroo rat, kind of yellowish with some dark on the ears. Who knows where the thing came from?"

The Utah rancher was frightened at first, but then began to worry about what his friends would think. "Of course they all thought I was crazy and they said I'd been hanging around in the sheep pen too long. But after I described everything they finally believed me," Ault said later.

From Tulsa, Oklahoma, a new twist was added to the usual mystery kangaroo tales. On Monday, the 31st of August 1981, a blond bearded man went into a Tulsa cafe, ordered a coffee, and told the waitress, Marilyn Hollenback, he had just hit a kangaroo. She laughed, off and on, for twenty minutes, she later said. The unidentified man also told Tulsa Police officers, patrolman Ed Compos and his partner Sgt. Lynn Jones. The officers and the waitress then went outside, and looked in the back of the man's truck. They were surprised to see what looked like a 3½ foot kangaroo. The skeptical cafe patrons were convinced. But there is more. The man told them there were two kangaroos because he swerved and missed one. The man and his dead kangaroo drove away in his truck, never to be seen again. Officer Ed Compos told reporters, "I wish I had taken a picture of it. I told the whole squad and they are laughing about it. There was a dead kangaroo! Everyone [at the cafe] saw it."

An Owasso, Oklahoma family came forth later in the week insisting they frequently had to dodge three-foot-tall kangaroos while making early morning rounds delivering newspapers.

Finally late in September 1981, something happened which frequently occurs in the midst of a mystery animal flap. Namely an exotic animal, which could not realistically be confused for the reported creature, is captured, and officials and the media then use the alien animal to "explain away" the mystery beast sighting. Just such an event occurred on the 27th of September, 1981, a Sunday, when a 25-pound Patagonian cavy or mara was caught. What this particular South American rodent was doing in Tulsa, Oklahoma, no one could guess, but it fits well into the pattern of such Fortean events.

Reflecting historically for a moment, we only have to go back to 1974 to find two other such examples. During the Chicago kangaroo flap, a kinkajou was seized. This wee South American procyonid was exploited by the skeptics, and immediately utilized as a convenient candidate to debunk the widespread series of kangaroo reports. During the same year, an incredible something attacked and killed dogs, cats, and rabbits in Arlington County, Virginia. This mystery beast flap was detoured by the capture of a palm civet. I have observed more and more exotics appearing in the middle of monster sighting waves. It's not too surprising, then, that a Patagonian cavy should turn up in Oklahoma when the news began to emerge of kangaroo capers.

From Oklahoma, the kangaroos next made an appearance in North Carolina. Near Asheville, home of the famed Brown Mountain Lights, a kangaroo was seen on Friday, the 9th of October 1981, near a Biltmore, North Carolina motel. Police and reporters gave chase.

"I was afraid someone might shoot it!" exclaimed motel desk clerk Jeff Greene.

The kangaroo was neither shot nor caught. It, like the scores before it, disappeared into the morning dew, and this one was not seen again around the motel.

On Sunday, 23 September 1984, a woman motorist said she saw a kangaroo hopping across I-94 near the Detroit, Michigan, Metropolitan Airport. The next morning, sheriff deputies reported the same thing. But nothing more was heard of this creature.

A Sidetrek in Search of Kangaroos

Back across the border, the Canadian island of Nova Scotia was again the site of some reports. Spying a "strange" animal in 1984, George Messinger of Bridgetown described the beast as about two and a half feet tall, with short front paws, tight to the body, with large back legs and a deer-like head. "Actually, it looked like a small kangaroo at the time, but I thought that was ridiculous being in this country," Messinger commented at the time. My two contacts in Nova Scotia—Bob Bancroft, a wildlife biologist, and John Sansom, a folklorist—keep me updated on the latest kangaroo sighting.

During August of 1995, I was finally able to travel to Nova Scotia to conduct an on-site review of this "mystery kangaroo" series. Once there, I found myself the recipient of one of those wonderful "on-the-road" experiences that often befalls those who chase after these wild beasts. I had heard that the sightings were centered around a lake in Antigonish County named Lochaber. That certainly sounded like a good place for an unknown animal and I was surprised the tourist conscious Nova Scotia media had not headlined the stories something like "The Lochaber Monster Makes Another Appearance." But they had not, and it had been rather quiet there lately, so I figured I could poke around without making too many waves.

As I was traveling back from Cape Breton Island (the site of some sea and lake monsters accounts but that's another story), my map clearly showed that a quick side trip off Rt. 104 would put me within easy reach of Lochaber Lake. I was driving my new sports utility vehicle, which I later learned had been built in the mystically named location of Lafayette ("little enchantment"/ "little fairy"), Indiana. I had felt lucky that in the few months I had been paying off the loan to own this rugged little truck, nothing had gone wrong. That was until I headed for Lochaber. I was tooling around, watching the road, glancing at the map, cheerfully talking to my boys Malcolm and Caleb who were along for this investigative trip, when all of a sudden, the dashboard went wild. One thing of immediate concern was that the gauge for oil pressure started bouncing up and down like, yes, a kangaroo. I had never seen anything like it in all the cars and small trucks I had owned. But there it was. I was a mere ten or so miles from Lochaber and my vehicle was having a fit. I was on this little hilly and winding road (#7) and I had just passed an auto body shop. Perhaps if I turned around right now, I thought, I could make it back and they could sell me some oil. So I hightailed it back to Stewart's Auto Body Shop.

I went in and was calmly buying some oil to try to fill it up and see if I could get on my way when a man with a friendly manner walked in. It turned out to be Mr. Hugh Stewart, the owner. He asked me what the problem seemed to be and we chatted for a while about the state of my vehicle. Then he casually asked me about the reason for my being in these parts, and I carefully mentioned my interest in "animal folklore" (since most people don't understand cryptozoology, right off the mark) and I explained that I was on my way to Lochaber Lake where a kangaroo-like animal had been seen.

Mr. Stewart immediately told me that I was looking too far south as, indeed, the animal had been seen by a friend of his (they had been schoolmates thirty years ago) right down the road from the auto shop, near

Gaspereaux Lake. Hugh Stewart told me that he had been with his friend Hugh MacLean and biologist Bob Bancroft when they all had found tracks after returning to the location of the encounter. Mr. Stewart did not know I knew about Bancroft's involvement or that I was aware of many details of MacLean's sighting, so it was obvious to me that my vehicle problems had led me to an unnamed participant in the events of almost a decade earlier. In his gravel driveway Hugh Stewart outlined the shape of the footprint (which, I realized, matched that of the three-toed track that others had photographed and described in October, 1986). He also told me of the frozen ground in the days that followed, frustrating all efforts to search for the beast. I spent some pleasant moments with Mr. Stewart who very matter-of-factly told me of his experiences and pointed me in the right direction to the spot where the kangaroo had been seen. I went on and looked at those places. But for me, the highlight of the day had already occurred. The peak, of course, was the chance meeting with this unassuming man who had been there and who had taken his time to make the event live again for me. Hugh Stewart may only be a footnote in the events regarding the kangaroo reports of Nova Scotia, but it is brushing an individual such as him that makes the journey worthwhile.

And, by the way, Mr. Stewart, an extraordinary mechanic, could find nothing wrong with my truck and could not understand why it acted up just as I was passing Gaspereaux Lake, sending me back to his door.

On to the End of the Century

During the 1990s, reports of mystery kangaroos kept coming my way. Richard Hendricks, an active Wisconsin anomalist, passed along one of the latest sightings.

Lois Eckhardt, 68, of Wellman, Iowa, said she was checking cattle on her farm on August 4, 1999, when she saw a "kangaroo."

"I noticed this tan thing standing on the hill, looking at me," she said. "It looked like a deer, but it had a bigger belly and a boxy nose. The tail was too long for a deer."

Eckhardt believes she surprised the animal because she had approached it quietly on a motorized electric cart. "Those are pretty quiet," she said. "After a few seconds, this thing took off with sort of a long, low hop."

Like many other witnesses, she didn't even think of reporting it until she read newspaper reports about another witness, a Mary Stangl, having seen a kangaroo in the countryside south of Ottumwa.

"When I saw that story in the paper, it just sort of clicked," Eckhardt said. "I want that woman to know she wasn't seeing things."

"Honestly, I tell you it was a kangaroo" was the headline for the August 26, 1999, story of the Mary Stangl sighting. The Ottumwa woman said she and her husband, Pat, spotted a kangaroo—definitely not a usual sight in Iowa—while driving in the countryside the afternoon of August 19, 1999, about 16 miles south of town.

"It was bouncing from the west side of the highway toward the east side," Mary Stangl said. "Pat turned around to make sure he saw what he thought he saw, and watched it slowly bound across the road."

Davis County sheriff's officials say they have not had any reports of a runaway kangaroo. And Keiko Sampson, who works at the Wilderness Kingdom Zoo south of Ottumwa, said it's "definitely not" the zoo's kangaroo.

As many people have done before her, and many will in the future, despite skeptical authorities who tried to convince her that she had not seen what she knows she saw, Mary Stangl stuck to her story.

Seed catalogues of sightings like the above are sometimes tiresome. But readers interested in this phenomena will understand why I have listed so many reports of these creatures. The mounting nature of the data is brought to bear and speaks for itself. Something like kangaroos are being seen in America. Some may be misidentifications of deer and other common animals. A few may be escaped exotic pets. In a light-hearted Fortean vein, perhaps, we might even view a few as teleported examples of Australian or Tasmanian kangaroos. But perchance, could there be something else out there? Something that merges, in some people's minds, with stories too often filed under "Bigfoot" sightings?

Devil Monkeys

Some researchers like Mark A. Hall, Chad Arment, and myself have begun calling North America's mystery kangaroos "Devil Monkeys."

In 1969 Bigfoot researchers John Green and Rene Dahinden investigated reports of a large monkey-like animal with a long tail, seen near

Mamquam, British Columbia. I investigated the 1973 case of livestock killings at Albany, Kentucky, caused by three giant monkeys, each with a long, black bushy tail. In both the Kentucky and British Columbia cases the animals left distinctive three-toed tracks.

In 2000, Chad Arment examined the Boyd family's and friends' sightings spanning the years 1959 to the 1990s, in the mountains around Saltville, Virginia of just such "devil monkeys."

The parents of ghost investigator Pauline Boyd and James Boyd had experienced a 1959 attack on their automobile by a creature that had "light, taffy colored hair, with a white blaze down its neck and underbelly. It stood on two large, well-muscled back legs, and had shorter front legs or arms." It left three scratch marks on the car, apparently put there by its front limbs. Arment quotes Pauline as saying: "Several days after this incident, two nurses in the Saltville area were driving home from work early one morning, and were attacked by an unknown creature who ripped the convertible top from their car before they escaped."

One evening in 1973, James Boyd's friend observed one of these animals on the mountain road between Marion and Tazewell, Virigina. The animal had rushed his car and tried to grab his arm.

Two friends of Pauline recorded a recent encounter, also from a car, of a similar creature near Saltville. The beast crossed the road in front of them, jumped a ditch line, went over a fence, and then moved through high weeds lining the road only to disappear into ground cover. Pauline Boyd said: "According to all witnesses, this animal was unlike any they had seen before. Walking on all four legs, it stood around three feet high. Covered in shaggy, rough, graying brown fur, it had a long muzzle and small, pointed ears. The legs of the creature were short, with the hind legs much larger than the front, and sporting long, kangaroo-like rear feet. Claws were evident on both the hind, and smaller front feet. If this creature had stood on these powerful looking hind legs, they stated, it would have been at least five and a half to six feet tall. It also sported a long, hairless (opossum-like was the term they used) tail. Though moving quickly, it gave the appearance in its gait and gray mottled fur of being an older animal. They watched in amazement as it quickly disappeared from sight."

You see here the merging of the descriptions between these monkey-like creatures and the kangaroo accounts.

On June 26, 1997, near Dunkinsville, Ohio, another ordinary person found herself encountering one of these extraordinary critters.

Debbie Cross lives on a wooded ridge, near Peach Mountain, at the foothills of the Appalachian Mountains. To the east lies the Shawnee State Forest. Between the hours of midnight and 1:00 a.m. on the night in question, Cross was watching television when she heard her dogs barking outside. When she turned on the porch light, she observed a strange animal about 30 feet away, near the pond in her front yard.

"It was about three to four feet tall and gray in color," she told researchers Ron Schaffner and Kenny Young. "It had large, dark eyes and rounded ears extended above the head. It had real long arms and a short tail. It made a gurgling sound. From the available light, the animal appeared to have hair or fur all over its body about 1½ inches long."

The animal looked at Cross for a few seconds then headed towards a tent on the southern part of the pond. It kind of "skipped" when it moved, Cross noted, and appeared to walk on its hind legs while using the "knuckles" of its front arms on the ground one at a time. When her two dogs then started to chase it, she called them back. The animal then headed along a barbed wire fence and went out of view. Cross heard a screeching sound shortly afterwards.

These Devil Monkeys, at four to six feet tall, are relatively short, with the smaller juveniles often resembling wallabies or "baby kangaroos." Their leaping mode of locomotion is one of the major reasons that they have been confused with kangaroos. They have a barrel chest, thick arms, powerful legs, and a tail. Their faces are baboon- or dog-like, with dark, "mean" eyes and pointed ears. They have short to shaggy hair, varying in color from gray to red to black. Devil Monkeys have large flat feet that tend to narrow somewhat as they lengthen in adulthood. Their footprints are usually about 12 inches long, but tracks up to 15 inches have been found. Their foot bears three rounded toes, usually of the same size and length, with regular spacing between each one. You would know them immediately if you saw them.

The animals can be obstinate toward dogs and humans, causing eyewitnesses to sometimes comment on the creatures' aggressive looks. Though generally thought to be vegetarians, they may kill livestock and small game. Devil Monkeys exhibit a wide range of primate hoots, calls, screeches, whistles, and "blood-chilling screams." Their smell has compounded the identification problem, as some are labeled as Skunk Apes or Napes.

Mark A. Hall, in decades-long discussions with me, developed the concept of the Devil Monkey. We have chronicled reports of this kind for over 35 years. Today it appears rather clear that we may be dealing with a kind of giant baboon that moves by saltation, leaping as do kangaroos— and thus have filled my files full of "mystery kangaroo" reports. *The Field Guide to Bigfoot, Yeti, and Other Mystery Primates Worldwide* discussed this group of reports under the label "Giant Monkeys," but they do seem to have made a *devil* of a mess in our attempts to sort them out.

Oh, and by the way, if anyone finds an extra old, empty can of Wetzel Kangaroo Beer, please send it my way.

CHAPTER 15

Eastern Bigfoot: Momo and Marked Hominids

Reports of hairy human-like creatures comparable to the legends of the Yeti of the Himalayas are older than American history. In a study published in *The INFO Journal* in 1970, Mark Hall and I noted: "A vast folklore and a belief in a race of very primitive people with revolting habits is found from northern California up into the Arctic lands themselves. This tradition covers not only the whole stretch of the Pacific coast, but much of the rugged territory to the east, even into Greenland. Generally, these subhominids are described as very tall, fully haired and retiring. Sometimes they are described as carnivorous."

Wendigo and Wildmen

First Nations' folklore and cultural artifacts (such as masks, totem poles, and carvings) exist in abundance, demonstrating a prehistoric knowledge of these creatures. Native American, Native Canadian, and Inuit accounts discuss these half-men with words special for each linguistic and tribal group. In the East, the Algonquian have their Wendigo, Windigo, Wetiko, Wittiko, and other variant names for the giants of the bush covered in hair. Among EuroAmericans, the early sightings talk of these beings with words such as "wildmen."

European and EuroAmerican notices of hairy upright creatures from the eastern fringes of the New World are very old. Leif Erickson wrote in A.D. 986 of encountering monsters who were ugly, hairy, and swarthy with great black eyes. In 1603, on Samuel de Champlain's first voyage to eastern Canada, he reportedly was informed by the local natives of the

Gougou, a giant hairy beast that lived in the northern forests and was much feared by the Micmac. During the late 1700s, the Delaware of Ohio, as mentioned in *The History of Newcomerstown,* described to the new settlers their encounters with the hairy hominids and that "...they had to leave out foods for the wild ones of the woods to keep the peace." A *London Times* article of 1784 records the capture of hair-covered hominids by local natives, near Lake of the Woods, in south-central Canada.

In the *Boston Gazette* of July 1793, the following dispatch appeared from Charleston, South Carolina, May 17, 1793, concerning a creature seen in North Carolina:

> A Gentleman on the South Fork of the Saluda river in a letter of the 23rd sends his correspondent in this city the following description on the Bald Mountains in the Western Territories. This animal is between twelve and fifteen feet high, and in shape resembling a human being, except the head, which is in equal proportion to its body and drawn in somewhat like a tarapin; its feet are like those of a negroe, and about two feet long, and hairy, which is of a dark dun colour; its eyes are exceedingly large, and open and shut up and down its face; the hair of its head is about six inches long, stands straight like a negroe's; its nose is what is called Roman. These animals are bold, and have lately attempted to kill several persons—in which attempt some of them have been shot. Their principal resort is on the Bald Mountain, where they lay in wait for travellers—but some have been seen in this part of the country. The inhabitants call it Yahoo; the Indians, however, give it the name of Chickly Cudly.

Investigator Scott McNabb notes the term Chickly Cudly could be an English variant on a Cherokee name, "ke-cleah" (Chick Lay), which means hair in Cherokee, and/or "kud-leah" (Cooed Lay), which means either man or thing. The term "kud-leah" in Cherokee can also mean a man bear or a bear thing, and thus Chickly Cudly = ke-cleah kud-leah = hairy man/thing.

Another old eastern North American newspaper account appeared in the *Exeter Watchman* of New York on September 22, 1818. The item told of a sighting of a Wild Man of the Woods near Ellisburgh, New York, on August 30, 1818. The hairy creature was said to bend forward when running and left footprints showing a narrow heel with spreading toes. Mark A. Hall has found a good 1829 account of the killing of a 13-foot-tall "wildman" in a Georgia swamp. Such accounts were followed by reports of hairy child-sized creatures seen in Indiana and Pennsylvania, in the 1830s. Then, beginning in 1834, in Arkansas, a giant wild man was seen by many people in the Ozarks. *The Memphis Enquirer* of May 9, 1851, reported on the Arkansas sightings of the previous March, noting, "This singular creature has long been known traditionally in St. Francis, Greene and Poinsett counties. Arkansas sportsmen and hunters having described him so long as 17 years since." The wildman was said to be of gigantic stature, hairy, and with long shoulder-length hair on its head. The man-like beast reportedly stared at those in pursuit, ran away very quickly, and leapt fourteen feet at a time. Footprints found measured fourteen inches long.

Sightings of these hirsute hominoids have continued up to the present day. Researchers have attempted to standardize the names used. Specifically Ivan Sanderson, Mark A. Hall, and I like to call those from the West the Neo-Giant, which includes the Pacific Northwest's Sasquatch, a name coined by Canadian journalist J. W. Burns in the 1920s, and the now ever-popular Bigfoot, a moniker used by Bluff Creek construction workers and widely disseminated by California newspaperman Andrew Genzoli in 1958. These Neo-Giants are best known from the famous Roger Patterson–Bob Gimlin film taken October 20, 1967, at Bluff Creek, California. This footage is to the Bigfoot branch (hominology) of cryptozoology what the Zapruder film is to the JFK assassination. The Patterson film is the most sterling piece of evidence in existence of what a Neo-Giant looks like and what kind of footprints this specific PNW Bigfoot leaves behind. But today, something else appears to be haunting the East.

At the dawn of this new century, in 2000, practically every state and province in North America has logged its share of so-called "Bigfoot" reports. In the past several years sightings have increased dramatically and probably will continue to grow. Throughout the 1960s through the 1990s, an increase in the number of sightings of "Bigfoot" occurred in many parts of the continent, but the ones in the eastern USA and Canada are some of the most problematic in mysterious America. Something different than the classic or traditional Neo-Giant is being seen. Could a different regional subspecies or even varied species be responsible for these Eastern sightings?

The Missouri Monster: Momo

Let's begin with a detailed case example.

Northeastern Missouri has had its share of mysteries. "Momo," as the monster of July-August 1972 was called, is only the most famous. Along River Road, which stretches north from Highway 54 along the Mississippi River and past the mouth of the Salt River, there is a longstanding tradition about a phantom man who walks across the road and vanishes. In the 1940s travelers and residents repeatedly heard what sounded like a woman's screams emanating from the general vicinity of an abandoned lime kiln. The screams always came around midnight; they were never explained.

In addition to recurring reports of fireballs or spook lights, there have been a number of mysterious deaths in the area. The strangest of all occurred during the winter of 1954, when a man and a woman were found dead in a car along the roadside. The woman sat on the passenger side and seemed to be asleep. The man lay crouched under the steering wheel completely nude, his clothing piled neatly 20 feet behind the car. The coroner listed the deaths as caused by "asphyxiation," even though the window on the driver's side was open all the way, and this in ten-degree-below-zero weather no less.

Joan Mills and Mary Ryan were not on River Road that day in July 1971, but they were not far from it. Highway 79 is a backwoods road which runs north of Louisiana, Missouri, a place that a year later would achieve a measure of immortality in Fortean annals. Mills and Ryan had taken the highway on their way back to St. Louis because they were looking for a picturesque spot for a picnic. When they found a promising site, they turned off on a dirt road, put out a blanket and brought out the food. "We were eating lunch," Mary Ryan recalled, "when we both wrinkled up our noses at the same time. I never smelled anything as bad in my life."

Momo

Her friend suggested they were smelling a whole family of skunks. Suddenly her jaw dropped and she pointed toward a brushy thicket behind her companion.

"I turned around and this thing was standing there in the thicket," Joan Mills said. "The weeds were pretty high and I just saw the top part of this creature. It was staring down at us."

Ryan added, "It was half-ape and half-man. I've been reading up on the abominable snowman since then, and from stories and articles, you get the idea that these things are more like gorillas. This thing was not like that at all. It had hair over the body as if it was an ape. Yet, the face was definitely human. It was more like a hairy human."

"Then it made a little gurgling sound like someone trying to whistle underwater," according to Mills.

The hairy creature stepped out of the brush and proceeded to walk toward the young women, who dashed for their Volkswagen and locked the doors. The beast, continuing to gurgle, caressed the hood of the car and then, in a clear demonstration of intelligent behavior, tried to open the doors.

"It walked upright on two feet and its arms dangled way down," Ryan stated. "The arms were partially covered with hair but the hands and the palms were hairless. We had plenty of time to see this…."

The women were terrified, all the more so because Mills had left her car keys in her purse, which she had abandoned outside in the flight to the safety of the automobile. "Finally," said Mills, "my arm hit the horn ring and the thing jumped straight in the air and moved back." So what would you do in this situation? Mills decided to just keep on beeping the horn.

"It stayed at a safe distance, then seemed to realize that the noise was not dangerous," Mary Ryan said. "It stopped where we had been eating, picked up my peanut butter sandwich, smelled it, then devoured it in one gulp. It started to pick up Joan's purse, dropped it and then disappeared back into the woods."

Joan Mills ran out of the car to retrieve her purse, started her car, and roared down the highway at 90 miles per hour. Once back in St. Louis, the two women submitted a report to the Missouri State Patrol.

"We'd have difficulty proving that the experience occurred," Mills noted, "but all you have to do is go into those hills to realize that an army of those things could live there undetected."

This was a dramatic introduction to the events that erupted exactly a year later. Joan Mills and Mary Ryan were to have their story confirmed in startling fashion.

The "Momo," after the newspapers' abbreviations for "Missouri monster," scare began on Tuesday, July 11, 1972, at 3:30 p.m. on the outskirts of the city of Louisiana (pop. 4600). Terry Harrison, 8, and his brother Wally, 5, were playing in their yard, which sits at the foot of Marzolf Hill. The two boys had gone off by some old rabbit pens in the woods next to the Harrison property. Suddenly an older sister, Doris, who was inside, heard them scream. When she looked out the bathroom window, she saw something "six or seven feet tall, black and hairy" standing by a tree. "It stood like a man but it didn't look like one to me."

The thing was flecked with blood, probably from the dead dog it carried under its arm. Its face was not visible under the mass of hair that covered it, and it seemed to be without a neck.

The Harrisons' dog got very sick shortly after the incident. Its eyes grew red and it vomited for hours afterwards, finally recovering after a meal of bread and milk.

That same afternoon Mrs. Clarence Lee, who lives half a block away, heard animal sounds, growling, and "carrying on something terrible." Not long afterwards she talked with a farmer whose dog, a recent gift, had disappeared. He wondered if the "monster" had taken it.

Three days later, on July 14, Edgar Harrison, Terry's and Doris' father and a deacon in the Pentecostal Church, conducted the regular Friday evening prayer meeting at his house. About forty-five minutes after the meeting broke up, around 9:15, Harrison heard ringing noises such as might be caused by the throwing of stones onto the metal water reservoir at the top of Marzolf Hill. The reservoir, which holds a million and a half gallons of water, is in an area where neighborhood children often play. After one especially loud ring, "I heard something that sounded like a loud growl. It got louder and louder and kept coming closer. At that time my family came running from the house. They began urging me to drive off. I wanted to wait and see what it was that was making this noise. My family insisted that I drive away and so I drove down Allen Street across the Town Branch. I stopped the car and my wife and family told the congregation, 'Here it comes!' And those forty people turned and ran. . . ."

Police officers Jerry Floyd and John Whitaker went to the Harrison home, searched the residence, but found nothing.

Late that evening, Harrison, along with several others, explored Marzolf Hill and came to an old building from which a pungent, unpleasant odor emanated. Harrison subsequently described it as "a moldy, horse smell or a strong garbage smell." This was not to be the only time he encountered the odor. In the days ahead he would find it whenever he approached an area that emanated the strange noises.

Around 5:00 the following morning Pat Howard of Louisiana saw "a dark object" walking like a man cross the road near the hill.

On the 19th Police Chief Shelby Ward led a search through Marzolf Hill, accompanied by Harrison, State Conservation officer Gus Artus, and seventeen others. They uncovered nothing.

But the next day Richard Crowe, a reporter for Chicago's *Irish Times* and for *Fate* magazine, and Loren Smith went up the hill with Harrison for another look. Near the tree where Doris had seen the monster, Crowe found "a circular spot in the brush where leaves and twigs had been stripped from the branches." Further along Crowe found evidence that someone or something had been digging in an old garbage dump, and not far away Harrison showed him two disinterred dog graves with the bones scattered about. Higher up the hill they came upon two tracks some distance from each other. The first, over ten inches long and five inches wide, appeared to be a footprint; the other, five inches long and curved, was evidently the print of a hand. The prints had been made in hard soil (there had been no rain for ten days), and Crowe estimated that it would take a minimum of two hundred pounds of pressure to create such impressions.

Harrison led Crowe to an abandoned shack, which Harrison thought might serve as a resting place for the monster. While they were there, Harrison's dog Chubby suddenly ran away. "Then," Crowe wrote, "we smelled an overwhelming stench that could only be described as resembling rotten flesh or foul, stagnant water."

"That's him, boys!" Harrison exclaimed. "He's around here somewhere." They shone their flashlights through the surrounding trees but saw nothing. In the distance they could hear dogs barking furiously.

(While the monster was about, dogs would refuse to go up the hill but would run up and down the street in an agitated state.) Within five minutes the odor had subsided.

Harrison, Smith and Crowe smelled it twice more before the night was over. On Friday, July 21, Ellis Minor, who lives along River Road, was sitting home alone around 10:00 or 10:30 p.m. when he heard his bird dog start to growl. At first Minor thought the stimulus was another dog passing through the yard, but when the dog growled again, Minor snapped on a powerful flashlight and stepped outside—where he saw a six-foot-tall creature with long black hair standing erect. As soon as the light hit it, the thing turned around and dashed across the road, past the railroad tracks and into the woods.

By now Edgar Harrison had become obsessed with finding the solution to the monster mystery. His family had refused to come home again after the howling incident on the night of the 14th; they had taken up residence in the restaurant the family runs in the downtown section of the city. Harrison took a leave of absence from his job at the waterworks to devote his full attention to the monster; in the company of assorted friends, reporters and curiosity seekers he camped out at the foot of the hill for twenty-one straight nights. Nothing could shake Harrison's firm conviction that something very strange was taking place. Not even the negative report of Oklahoma City's zoo director Lawrence Curtis on the plaster casts of the prints. "It does not seem to be an actual print made by a natural living animal," Curtis said on the 25th. "It appears to have been made by one of those rubber-type gloves women use to wash dishes with—either that or a snow mitten."

Though he never saw the monster himself, Harrison felt he succeeded in making a discovery that added a whole new dimension to the riddle. The timing of the notorious odor led him to believe the odor was really a stink gas used to distract the searchers' attention.

Late in July mysterious three-toed tracks made by something with an oval foot appeared on the Freddie Robbins farm eight miles south of Louisiana. On August 3rd, just before dawn, Mr. and Mrs. Bill Suddarth, who farmed northwest of the town, heard a high-pitched howl in their yard, grabbed flashlights, and headed outside. In the middle of the garden mud they observed four tracks of a three-toed creature.

Suddarth quickly phoned Clyd Penrod, a hunting buddy, who drove over to make a plaster cast of the best print. Penrod was puzzled by the whole affair.

"It was 20 to 25 feet from the tracks to anything else," he said. "I can't understand how they were made." They began nowhere and ended nowhere, and no other tracks were found anywhere else on the property.

The Suddarth prints were different from the ones discovered at the Robbins farm; these second prints were narrower, longer, and more perfectly formed. But both clearly showed three toes, not five.

Momo Kin

Momo was not the only monster to frighten Middle America that summer of 1972. In the extreme northwestern part of Arkansas, a state which borders Missouri from the south, the summer brought several reports of an imperfectly-observed, vaguely described "creature." It first appeared, according to an article in Fayetteville's *Northwest Arkansas Times,* sometime in January, when on two occasions Mrs. C. W. Humphrey of Springdale heard dogs barking loudly, looked out the door of her trailer home and saw a "creature" strolling on by. In the following months, several other persons in the neighborhood caught a glimpse of the thing, but only in the dark, and so they did not get a good look at it. Early in July, Pete Ragland shot at the creature with a .22 pistol.

Then, starting at 10:15 on the evening of July 20th, the climactic events took place. Mrs. Humphrey, her three sons and a daughter-in-law were sleeping when they were awakened by pounding on the trailer. Mrs. Humphrey quieted one of the children and went outside to find the cause. There she encountered the "biggest looking thing I ever saw"—something that alternately walked upright and crawled on all fours.

Shortly afterwards Bill Hurst, who lives just south of the Humphrey residence, sighted the creature in his garden. It was staring at him with "two great big eyes." He was sure it was some sort of animal (others had thought it might be a huge man). When he yelled at it, it took off running. The night of September 6th, Barbara Robinson of Springdale called police to report that a prowler had peered through a bedroom window of her house. The policeman who investigated remarked that the prowler "had to be at least seven feet tall" since the window was that high and there was nothing in the immediate area on which he could have stood.

The *Peoria* (Illinois) *Journal-Star* for July 26th told of Randy Emert, 18, who reportedly saw a monster two different times over the previous two months. Emert said the thing resembled the Missouri beast in most particulars although its height was between 8 and 12 feet, and it was "kind of white and moves quick." When it appeared, it brought with it Momo's rancid odor and it also seemed to scare the animals living in the woods near Cole Hollow Road. Emert said, "It lets out a long screech, like an old steam-engine whistle, only more human."

Emert asserted that a number of friends had seen either the creature or its footprints (unfortunately undescribed). "I'm kind of a spokesman for the group," he said. "The only one who has guts, I guess."

Mrs. Ann Kammerer of Peoria corroborated Emert's story, stating that all of her children, friends of Emert's, had seen the thing. "It sounds kind of weird," she admitted. "At first I didn't believe it, but then my daughter-in-law saw it."

According to Emert, there was an old abandoned house in the woods with large footprints all around it and a hole dug under the basement. Readers will recall the empty shack in Louisiana where Edgar Harrison thought Momo might be staying.

Two days later, on July 25th, the *Pekin* (Illinois) *Daily Times* announced that "Creve Coeur authorities said a witness reported seeing 'something big' swimming in the Illinois River." The Illinois River flows through Peoria. On the night of the 27th "two reliable citizens" told police they had seen a ten-foot-tall something that "looked like a cross between an ape and a cave man." A United Press International account described it (with perhaps more details than seems possible) as having "a face with long gray U-shaped ears, a red mouth with sharp teeth, [and] thumbs with long second joints....It smelled, said a witness, like a "musky wet down dog." The East Peoria Police Department reported it had received more than 200 calls about the monster the following evening.

Leroy Summers of Cairo, Illinois, saw a 10-foot, white, hairy creature standing erect near the Ohio River levee during the evening hours of July 25th. The Cairo police found nothing when they came to investigate and Police Commissioner James Dale warned that henceforth anyone making a monster report would have his breath tested for alcoholic content.

A series of "monster" sightings reported by a group of excitable teenagers in the Vineland, New Jersey, area were apparently caused by the sight of a 6-foot, 5-inch bearded swimmer. Or so the local police would have us believe. By the fourth week of July 1972, "monstermania" evidently had taken a grip on the consciousness of many Americans.

Interestingly, Momo and these events have much to show us about what is still afield in the Midwest. One of the best ways to analyze the relative reality and nature of these cryptids is to look to similar creature descriptions given before the massive publicity experienced from "Bigfoot" sightings at the end of the last century. Beginning slowly after the Patterson-Gimlin Bigfoot footage was taken in 1967, and rapidly increasing with the commercial release in 1987 of *Harry and the Hendersons,* most people developed a set idea of what a Bigfoot looked like. Reexamining the cases from the 1960s and 1970s is a good exercise in clarification of what may really be out there.

A few examples will serve our purposes. In the decade before the Momo sightings, people were being visited by creatures that looked like the Missouri monster, huge, hulky, and with hair in their eyes. One series was from Sister Lakes, Michigan. The Cass County events of 1964 were labeled quickly as the "Monster of Sister Lakes" by the papers. They involved sightings by migrant strawberry workers, the strawberry farm's owners, and, very soon, local residents. First seen in 1962 but kept mostly quiet, the Sister Lakes creature was described much like Momo with little facial detail, a huge hairy bulk, and shoulders disappearing into its neck. Finally in May 1964, the Sister Lakes "monster" caused terrified fruit pickers to leave the fields. Then on June 9, one of the workers, Gordon Brown, and his brother clearly saw the thing in their car headlights—it looked like a nine-foot-tall, rigidly upright cross between a bear and a gorilla. The farmers, Evelyn and John Utrup, also reported several encounters. On June 11, Joyce Smith fainted, and Gail and Patsy Clayton froze in fear when these three 13-year-old girls saw it on a lonely road in Silver Creek Township. It merely turned and took off into the woods.

On August 13, 1965, a similar huge, dark creature with hair all over its body and face placed its arm in the car Christine Van Acker was sitting in with her mother near Monroe, Michigan. Due to panic, they took off, and the image of the black eye that Van Acker received from the encounter was sent around the world by the wire services. The animal she drew was almost a mirror reflection of what was seen less than a decade later in Louisiana, Missouri. Van Acker's drawing showed a bulky, hairy, bipedal beast with hair in its eyes. The image of Harry created by Rick Baker for the movies was not part of the equation yet, and these sightings clearly were showing something other than the Patterson Bigfoot.

An Ohio Hotbed of Activity

In recent years, one of the most active areas in the East for "Bigfoot" reports has been Ohio. Maybe it is because Ohio has so many people to "see" the creatures, or there are more of the hairy hominids there. After I moved from Illinois in the mid-1970s, I noted an explosion of activity occurred in Ohio. The state's place in "Bigfoot" studies became very prominent, due in large part to the early work there of Thomas Archer, Jim Rastetter, Earl Jones, Charles Wilhelm, and especially Ron Schaffner who remains active today. Maybe it has something to do with the large number of researchers who have been involved in field research in Ohio. Outside of California, I don't know of another state that has as many "Bigfoot" investigators. The roster of past and present members include Robert W. Morgan, Dennis Pilichis, Don Worley, Don Keating, Betty Parks, Leon Parks, Blake Mathys, Mark Swift, Chung-Min Chen, Dawn DeWerth, Marc A. DeWerth, Jeff DeWerth, Barbara Balinovich, Todd Hogarth, Jack Elbin, Laurie Fascina, Linda Wygle, Bob Gardiner, Mike Claar, Jim Davis, Chuck Storrie, Chris Kraska, Rich LaMonica, Bob Daigle, Peter Massaro, John McGhee, Frank Poirier, Bruce Rutkoski, George Clappison, Joedy Cook, Mark Francis, Hawk Spearman, Karen Spearman, Art Caruso, Steve Jones, John Mathia, George Wagner, and Matt Moneymaker. I have investigated sightings in the state many times, but I'm just an interloper. These residents are committed Ohio hairy hominid hunters; they are the reason we have heard about so many "Eastern Bigfoot" reports from this one location.

One of the best cases from the 1970s issued from Minerva, Ohio, and was chronicled in some detail by researcher Ron Schaffner. What did the Bigfoot from Minerva look like? Like Momo. Schaffner calls the Minerva case "by far, the most complex and interesting one" in his Ohio files.

The rumors of activity east of Minerva actually began surfacing in early July and early August, 1978. It was around this date that Evelyn and Howe Cayton's grandchildren and their friends came running into their Minerva house crying in a frightened state. They claimed to have seen a large hairy monster in a nearby gravel pit. Vickit Keck and the Caytons went outside to see what had scared them. They saw a creature that was covered with dark matted hair. They estimated it to be about 300 pounds and seven feet tall. "It just stood there," said Evelyn Cayton. "It didn't move, but I almost broke my neck running back down the hill." She later observed the creature in the daylight. It was sitting in the pit picking at the garbage. She could not make out any facial features due to the amount of long hair covering its face. She remembered that the creature had no visible neck.

The Minerva sightings then began in earnest on August 21, 1978, at 10:30 p.m. Here are Schaffner's case notes, reprinted here with his permission:

> Evelyn Cayton's family and friends were out on the front porch when they heard noises in the direction of an old chicken coop just to the right of the house. They saw two pairs of yellow eyes that seemed to be reflecting a porch light. Scott Patterson went to his car and turned the headlights on in hopes of getting a better look. The eyes were on what appeared to be two "cougar-type" felines. Then, the party saw what looked like a large bipedal hairy creature step in front of the large cats as if to protect them. This creature then proceeded to lurch towards Patterson's car.
>
> The witnesses fled to the house and called the Stark County Sheriff's Department. While waiting for the deputies, the bipedal creature appeared at the kitchen window—about four yards from the kitchen table. Patterson pointed a .22 caliber pistol at it, while Evelyn Cayton loaded a .22 caliber rifle. The creature stood outside the window for close to ten minutes. They all could clearly see the creature because of the back porch light. They decided they would not shoot at it unless the creature made any advances toward them. The biped suddenly left without harming anyone.

"It doesn't seem to want to bother anyone," said Mary Ackerman. "It was just curious. We all felt that it wanted to be friends."

Deputy Sheriff James Shannon arrived about 15 minutes after the call was made and about five minutes after the creature left the scene. A strong stench was still lingering in the area when Deputy Shannon began to interview the witnesses. Shannon later told reporters that it smelled like "ammonia-sulfur." Extra deputies were brought in and they searched the entire area on horseback and in jeeps. (The land behind the Caytons' was an old abandoned strip mine and beyond that were dense woods going up a gradual hill.) Unusual, but unsubstantiated footprints were discovered.

August 22 at 9:00 p.m.:

Mrs. Mary Ackerman of Minerva drove to the Cayton residence to pick up her daughter and a friend. (Mrs. Ackerman is Evelyn Cayton's daughter.) As she turned into the driveway, she saw the same creature standing on top of the hill next to the strip mine. She watched it until it walked out of her view.

August 23 at 11:00 p.m.:

The creature appeared again at the Cayton residence. Howe Cayton was not sure if it was the same thing. He fired a gunshot into the air and the figure departed.

September 8 at 6:00 p.m.:

During the late daylight hours, Mrs. Ackerman observed two ape-like animals across the strip mine. She stated that she thought the creatures were standing in a tree but was not sure because of the distance. Again, she watched them for a while, until they were no longer visible in the thick weeds.

September 9 in the evening:

Investigator Jim Rastetter interviewed Henry Colt who lives about five miles east of Minerva on U.S. 30. He told Jim that he was walking through some woods by his house when he caught a glimpse of an unknown furry animal. Mr. Colt said that the animal was squatting next to a tree and let out a sound similar to a loud cough.

Canine Activity:

Prior to the August 21 sightings, one of the Caytons' German shepherds was found dead with a broken neck. The dog had been chained up by the collar to the dog house. The collar was found next to the dead animal still attached to the chain.

The other shepherd, Missey, was still in a schizophrenic state during our investigations. At times, she was extremely calm and affectionate and on other occasions, she was scared and vicious. Missey spent a lot of time digging, which is not uncharacteristic of a canine. However, she dug a tunnel about eight feet into the ground. This hole is almost large enough to contain two medium-sized dogs.

Evaluation:

According to the Caytons and Barbara Mudrack (*Akron Beacon-Journal* reporter), the sheriff's department (our contact was James Shannon, Stark County Deputy Sheriff) did an excellent investigation. However, there are some conflicting reports. The deputies stayed with the family until the early morning hours. They studied alleged prints and hair, but came up with no monster. They covered up the incidents to discourage hunters. They supposedly took the soft evidence to a local college in Canton for analysis. When we tried to obtain this evidence, Mallone College told us they did not receive anything.

Many investigators have since talked to the Cayton family. I believe that they are sincere people who would receive no real benefit from a hoax. Evelyn had just been released from the hospital due to an ulcer and a thyroid tumor. Her doctors told her to avoid emotional stress, so why would she fabricate a story like this? She did not need this type of publicity. One must not forget that this is a multiple witness incident. With this many witnesses, (interviewed separately, then as a group) it could be easy for one to slip up, but all stuck to the same story.

One cannot forget about the deputies' investigation and other phenomena surrounding these incidents. The witnesses were unfamiliar with the term Bigfoot, until the press caught wind of the story. Mudrack gave an excellent character reference of the witnesses. She really believed that the Caytons were telling the truth about their visitor.

Earl Jones and Ron Schaffner interviewed the Caytons on two separate occasions (September 9 and 30, 1978). During their second visit, they backpacked and spent the night in the upper woods looking for physical evidence. They came up with no evidence, nor did they witness anything unusual. For Schaffner, one of the most bizarre elements of the sighting has always been the sighting of the phantom panthers along with the hairy hominid. He still is perplexed by that detail. Perhaps they were dogs—or juvenile Bigfoot?

Marked Hominids and More?

Over the last forty years, I have reflected on the descriptions I had obtained from interviewing people and chasing down these stories of the 1960s and 1970s. I became aware of a remarkable feature that cropped up in one group of these hair-in-the-eyes, half-ape-like, large creatures. They seemed often to exhibit—more frequently than the Napes and the Devil Monkeys—either a two-toned, multicolored hair pattern, a lighter-haired mane, a near albino appearance, or a white patch in the midst of a field of darker hair. Some like "Yellow Top" in Ontario even wore their coloring in their name. The Siberians called one such individual "Mecheny," meaning the Marked One, and since that seemed a fitting name, I decided for the first time, in 1999, as a new classification name in my *Field Guide to Bigfoot, Yeti, and Other Mystery Primates Worldwide,* to call these beings the Marked Hominids. Additionally, I saw this as a fitting tribute to my fellow researcher Mark A. Hall, who had noted how markedly different they were from Bigfoot and first identified these beings as "Taller-hominids."

Though often mistaken for the Pacific Northwest's Bigfoot, Marked Hominids are actually more human-looking and somewhat shorter than the classic Neo-Giant. Essentially neckless, the face of male Marked Hominid has hair, or a beard, from the eyes down, giving the impression of a mask. The hair is short, brown, or dark, and slightly longer on the head. As noted, they have a tendency to piebald, showing lighter patches amongst the darker colors. Some are albino or lightly maned.

The cases from this era, before the corrupting influence of the mass media Bigfoot, gives cryptozoologists much to ponder. Momo and his friends, for now, seem definable as Marked Hominids, a name I like to use instead of "Eastern Bigfoot." But there are a lot of things mixed under the cases labeled "Momo" in 1972. The troubling matter of those three-toed so-called "Momo" footprints, however, will have to wait for a more in-depth discussion in a forthcoming book. There are still a lot of mysteries out there.

CHAPTER 16

The North American Ape

Stretching all through the Mississippi Valley and the valleys of its tributaries is a vast network of closed-canopy deciduous and mixed forests. The gallery forests of the Mississippi Waterweb consist mainly of oak, gum, and cypress trees in the southern portions, and elm, ash and cottonwood in the northern branches. These *bottomlands,* as they are technically termed, cover a good deal of the southern United States. They are more or less unexplored and ignored most unfortunately, for hidden deep in the bottomlands could be a remarkable zoological mystery waiting for discovery.

"Gorillas" in Early America

The record begins, so far as written accounts go, in 1869 with two news accounts uncovered by Mark A. Hall. The first concerns the reports from Gallipolis, Ohio, on the Ohio River. The account appeared on 23 January 1869, in an article headlined "A Gorilla in Ohio." It told of a hairy creature haunting the woods near the town that had jumped on a man riding in a carriage. The man's daughter, who was also in the carriage, threw a stone at the animal as it struggled with her father. The rock hit the animal's ear and the "gorilla" departed.

The second incident occurred on the western fringes of the bottomlands, along the Osage River of Missouri and Kansas. During the summer of 1869, in the Arcadia Valley, Crawford County, Kansas, people started seeing a "wild man or a gorilla, or 'what is it?'" Called "Old Sheff" by the locals, it was seen by more than 60 people. "It cannot be caught and nobody is willing to shoot it," reported the *Osage City Journal Free Press* of 6 August 1869. The debate of the day was whether it was of the "human family or not." The writer of the piece noted that "probably it will be found to be a gorilla or large orangutan that has escaped from some menagerie in the settlements east of here." The item, signed "M. S. Trimble," was reprinted in the Missouri and Minnesota newspapers. The creature allegedly had a stooping gait, very long arms, and immense hands. It walked on its hind legs but sometimes went on all fours. The gorilla escapee theory, upon closer examination, hardly holds any water.

The first historical mention of the gorilla in the Old World was in 500 B.C. However, the modern era of the "gorilla" has a very American flavor to it. In 1844, in the *Boston Journal of Natural History,* American Dr. Thomas Savage gave the first scientific description of the gorilla. Only when a skull was obtained by another American, Dr. Leighton Wilson, in 1846 and the animal described in 1847 by Wilson and Savage, both West African missionaries, did the popularity of the "gorilla" really start skyrocketing. Sir Richard Owen, thanks to Savage and Wilson, was the first to "formally" describe the gorilla.

In 1851 Captain Harris brought the first gorilla skeleton to England. That same year a skeleton was sent to Philadelphia. Also in 1851, French naturalist Saint-Hillaire first gave the animal its own genus. This was quickly followed by a good deal of media attention about gorillas, whipped up by Paul du Chaillu's sensationalistic travels in Africa and his book that came out in 1861. Indeed, primatologist Vernon Reynolds mentions, "After (du Chaillu's) trip, which lasted from 1856 to 1859, du Chaillu returned to the United States, where he received widespread acclaim." In 1863, another famous gorilla travel book was published; it was written by American explorer Winwood Reade, after he spent five months in gorilla country.

It appears logical that any American witness seeing a hairy unknown ape-like creature would have used the gorilla as a frame of reference in describing their encounter. We do know that chimpanzees and monkeys in American traveling circuses were sometimes labeled "gorillas." Despite the European framework of the gorilla discoveries, the media storm was really being generated out of America. The "lost from a circus" explanation, groundless as usual, could have been used without any gorillas even being in America.

The first four gorillas to be brought from the wild into captivity arrived in 1855, 1883, and 1897 at Liverpool, and in 1883 at Berlin. The first gorilla in Liverpool was thought to be a chimpanzee. The first two gorillas in the United States did not arrive until 1897, at Boston, and 1911, at New York. The Ringling Brothers Circus exhibited the gorilla "John Daniel" in the 1920s. The combined Ringling Brothers/Barnum circus owed and exhibited the famed "Gargantua" from 1937, until he died in 1949.

Mystery "Gorillas" Precede Bigfoot

Nevertheless, reports of "gorillas" in America span over a century, before things were labeled Bigfoot on the West Coast or Abominable Snowmen in the Himalayas.

The Pennsylvania naturalist and folklorist Henry W. Shoemaker once wrote a short essay called "The Gorilla," about the sightings of such an animal in Pennsylvania late in 1920 and early in 1921. Thanks to research by Chad Arment, we hear again of the escaped animal explanation in Shoemaker's writings. Shoemaker pondered: "The papers have told us how a gigantic man-ape escaped from a carnival train near Williamsport, and seeking the South, fled over the mountains to Snyder County, where it attacked a small boy, breaking his arm, held up automobiles, rifled smoke houses and the like, and then appeared in Snyder Township, Blair County, still further south, his nocturnal ramblings in that region proving an effective curfew for the young folks of a half-dozen rural communities. This story sounds thrillingly interesting, but as gorillas live on fruit, and do not eat flesh, the animal in question would have starved or frozen to death at the outset of his career in the Alleghenies, and there the unknown quantity of the real story begins. The newspapers have only printed the most popular versions of the gorilla mystery, only a fraction of the romance and folklore that sprang up mushroom-like around the presence of such an alien monster in our highlands. Already enough has been whispered about to fill a good-sized volume, most of it absolutely untrue, yet some of the tales, if they have not hit the real facts, have come dangerously close to it."

Conveniently, crashed circus and carnival trains must have dotted the horizon in early America to explain all the "escaped animals" being reported. However, the fact is that upon double-checking such debunking, the truth is that very few train wrecks resulted in wild animals roaming the countryside. But gorillas, nevertheless, were seen. And continue to be.

The word "gorilla" crops up often in more recent accounts of beasts observed in creek bottoms. In Boone County, Indiana, in 1949, fishermen Charles Jones and George Coffman were chased from the banks of Sugar Creek by a brown "gorilla." In 1962 farmer Owen Powell of Trimble County, Kentucky, spotted what he called a "gorilla," about six feet tall, black, walking on its hind legs, and having front legs or arms hanging down to its knees. A boy was snatched up in the backyard of his home in Kinloch, Missouri, in 1968, by what he would call a "gorilla." The screaming of his aunt and the barking of the family dog encouraged the "gorilla" to drop the boy. At Hamburg, Arkansas, also in 1968, the *Arkansas Gazette* noted stories of a prowling "gorilla."

In the 1970s, the gorilla-like reports of "Knobby" seen in North Carolina, some of the Fouke Monsters in Arkansas, the "manimals" of the Red River, and the Lake Worth Monster of Texas all describe similar creatures.

At least one bottomlands resident believes the animal he saw was a "chimpanzee." Over a three-year period, from 1967-70, Howard Dreeson of Calumet, Oklahoma, left out bananas and oranges for the animal, which he had hoped to capture.

Apes in North America?

Now, what we must remember, obviously, is that all these things are "impossible" according to virtually unanimous zoological opinion. Apes, the primates most closely related to man, exist only in Southern Asia and tropical Africa. Specifically, gibbons and orangutans are Asian and chimpanzees, bonobos, and gorillas are African.

But quite aside from this highly important consideration, our North American apes—which for purposes of convenience I shall call Napes hereafter—are "impossible" for another reason: they usually walk and run upright.

It is true, as we all know, that most monkeys and all apes are *capable* of assuming an erect posture. But that is not quite the point. Monkeys such as the rhesus or the baboon stand erect only as a means of looking about or as a threatening gesture. Apes occasionally walk or run bipedally to free the hands for fighting or to carry food or offspring. Clearly, however, these are unusual situations. Napes, though able to move quadrupedally, are *habitually* bipedal as part of their natural mode.

In general the American apes *appear* to be chimpanzees, or, during the 1800s, "gorillas." Ape-like, hairy and tailless, they range in height from four to six feet, though now and then some very scared person reports a seven-footer. ("A creature covered with long hair always looks bigger than it really is," zoologist Bernard Heuvelmans writes in *Personality, South Africa*, June 5, 1969, in reference to reports of seven-foot-tall creatures with 10-inch footprints.) The hair color seems to be brown to black, but there are reports of gray or white individuals. This color variation in pelage may be the result of age differences. Certainly a 1971 report from Broward County, Florida, involving a small brown-black "skunk ape" (so called because of its foul smell) seen with a larger gray one with splotches and sores all over it suggests this. The foul odor (sometimes called "musky") is a fairly common feature of Napes reports. The eyes are often said to be green.

Napes appear so radically out of place that those rare individuals who encounter them never forget the experience. Sometimes sightings even leave a lasting impression on the geography of an area. One such place is in Allen County, Kentucky, where, according to folklorist Harold Holland: "The name 'Monkey Cave Hollow' apparently was given to one locality about four miles northeast of [Scottsville, Kentucky] by the earliest settlers for the simple reason a forested valley was inhabited by a tribe of what the pioneers identified as some sort of monkeys. These creatures foraged in the woods and took refuge in small caves."

Holland mentions that he once talked with an old-timer who, when a boy of seven or eight, saw the carcass of the last "monkey." He stated that a hunter came by his father's house and displayed the dead beast. He said that he could not recall exactly what it looked like (after all, it had been 80 years or thereabouts) but the creature had hands and feet "like a person," was about the same size as he was, had no tail, and was covered with brown hair.

The Swimming Ape

As I have already mentioned, travelling circuses and carnivals play an important role in the story of the North American ape. The "gorilla sideshows" of the circus and carnival lots are, says former circus man and animal trainer Robert Barbour Johnson, all populated by old chimpanzees. Inevitably the question arises: Are escaped old chimps the source of the Napes population in America's bottomlands? The answer very probably is no, for reasons I shall explain later. What in fact may be happening is the reverse: Perhaps in days past clever circus managers might have added to their exhibits members of this American species and claimed they were theirs all along!

Take, for example, an incident from the Hannibal, Missouri, region. One day around 1900, mainland residents noticed a mysterious animal moving about on a large wooded island in the Mississippi River near that city. The locals notified the sheriff, who subsequently saw it and thought it might be a hyena, except that it was eating grass. When the sheriff and others managed to capture it, it turned out to be "the man from Borneo," allegedly escaped from a circus. Said circus was most happy to get him "back."

Fine. Unfortunately we must once again complicate things by pointing out that the orangutan of Borneo and Sumatra is constitutionally incapable of swimming the Mississippi or any other river, while our primate friends from the bottomlands seem to be able to do so without inordinate difficulty.

Which leads us to another more complex capture report:

On August 16, 1926, according to the *New York Times* of the next day, one J. Blanchard, a watchman at the New Jersey Power and Light Company, at Booton, caught an ape by knocking it off a power line with a pole. A *Times* story on August 18th reports some apparently contradictory details: it alleges that a chimpanzee was recovered at Booton after it escaped from a travelling zoo at Rockaway. The chimp, the article says, slipped from its cage and *swam* the Rockaway River. An attendant pursued it into a grove of trees but it evaded him. On August 17th Francis Murphy, proprietor of the zoo, found the animal in the woods, called to it, and received it into his open arms.

Is this a case of two different apes being caught in the space of as many days near Booton, New Jersey? What are we to surmise from the travelling zoo's claim that their chimpanzee escaped by *swimming* the Rockaway River? Was this "swimming chimpanzee" instead one of the North American variety? What are we to deduce from such reports of swimming "chimpanzees" and island-stranded "orangutans"?

Most primates swim remarkably well, but authorities agree that anthropoid apes avoid water and cannot swim. For example:

The famous gorilla Mokoko of the Bronx Zoo, the first male of its species ever to reach sexual maturity in captivity, was tragically drowned in a water-filled barrier in 1951. (Heini Hediger, *Man and Animal in the Zoo*.)

A chimpanzee drowned quickly in the moat of the new ape-house of the Antwerp Zoo, and a gibbon in the London Zoo drowned even in very shallow water at the bottom of its large cage. (Adolph H. Schultz, *The Life of the Primates*.)

During the summer that we had Bobby and the little female chimpanzee Jenera on an island in the lake in front of the house of Emory's president, they would go into the water, on many occasions up about waist high, but they never made any attempt to go any deeper or to swim away from the island. (Geoffrey Bourne, *The Ape People*.)

Cyclone fencing was placed in the moat (at the Chimpanzee Consortium at Holloman Air Force Base in New Mexico) as a protective device to prevent drownings....The drowning of a female chimpanzee in 1966 might have been prevented if the fence had extended to the point where she slipped into the moat. (Wendell and Carolyn Wilson, Aeromedical Research Laboratory, New Mexico.)

Only in one rather vague case has any evidence for swimming ability among known apes been suggested. Vernon Reynolds, the British primatologist, examined that case, writing in *The Apes:*

A report from Spanish Guinea states that four chimpanzees were observed swimming across the 60 to 65-meter-wide Benito River. They made swimming motions like dogs ... I am inclined to think that the "chimpanzees" seen swimming in the above report were some other species. The general response of chimpanzees is universally agreed to be one of avoidance and even fear. I have myself on two occasions helped to pull chimpanzees out of a water-filled moat in which they were quite clearly drowning, and I am convinced they cannot swim.

Plainly, then, known species of apes do not swim. But from all indications, Napes do. Their range up and down the Mississippi Waterweb implies water dispersal as well as the use of the gallery forests bordering the river systems. Even a cursory examination of Napes accounts, taking place in locations with such revealing names as Sugar Creek (Indiana), Walnut Creek (Alabama) and the Anclote River (Florida), reveals a high percentage of sightings along the creek bottoms of rural America. The docudrama (mostly factual in the details but melodramatic in the re-creations) about Fouke, Arkansas's, ape-like "monster," *The Legend of Boggy Creek,* notes several times that "he always travels the creeks."

The sighting of a swimming ape by Charles Buchanan serves as an illustration. On November 7, 1969, Buchanan, camped out on the shore of Lake Worth, Texas, awoke about 2:00 a.m. to find a hairy creature that looked "like a cross between a human being and a gorilla or an ape" towering above him. Buchanan had been sleeping in the bed of his pickup truck when the thing had suddenly jerked him to the ground, sleeping bag and all. Gagging from the stench of the beast, the camper did the only thing he could think of: he grabbed a bag of leftover chicken and shoved it into the long-armed beast's face. The beast took the sack in its mouth, made some guttural sounds, and then loped off through the trees, first splashing in the water then swimming with powerful strokes toward Greer Island.

Bears are good swimmers and no doubt a few accounts of the North American apes may arise from misidentifications of bears. But from the overall descriptions, as well as the evidence of footprints, there are some powerful reasons to question the across-the-board bear explanations sometimes used in attempts to debunk appearances of wild apes in America.

Then There's That Hallux!

The evidence of footprints, more than anything else right now, strongly supports the notion that an undiscovered species of apes exists on our continent.

All primates are pentadactyl—five-toed. Among the higher primates, hominids (men) and pongids (apes) have a foot that is plantigrade. Both hominids and ursids (bears) leave behind a footprint clearly showing the foot is plantigrade and has an opposable big toe. One of the great differences between the foot (and thus the footprints) of men and apes is the existence in humans of a great toe, the hallux, that lies alongside and points in the same direction as the other toes.

Among the apes the first or great toe is opposed to the other toes. Because of this easily discernible feature in the track of a pongid, the record of an ape in America is quite certain.

As far back as pre-Columbian times, America's native inhabitants were apparently noting appearances of tracks of this type. The Indians often made stone carvings of items common in their environment, and an ape track was likely one such item. According to John W. Allen's *Legends and Lore of Southern Illinois,* in Jackson County there are "carvings...in the bed of Rock Creek....Here are *the footprints with the great toes turned at right angles,* arms, hands, face profiles, snakes lizards, and chiseled trenches." (Author's emphasis.)

Curiously, as our survey of footprints moves into historic times, we again find ourselves in southern Illinois. In the spring of 1962, I along with my brothers William and Jerry came upon an ape-like footprint in a dry creek bed near Decatur, Illinois. The print was about 10 inches long, with a clearly visible large opposed toe, the hallux, sticking out to the right of a left foot impression. About 13 inches in front of this print was another partial footprint. The complete track is very much like ones found throughout the South. This Illinois track seems to record the most northern of the Napes' recent appearance.

Moving from the fringes of the apes' range, let us consider the footprint evidence from the deep South.

An ape observed near Clanton, Alabama, in 1960 left a track, preserved in a cement cast, which was "about the size of a person's foot but looking more like a hand," according to what Clanton *Union-Banner* edi-

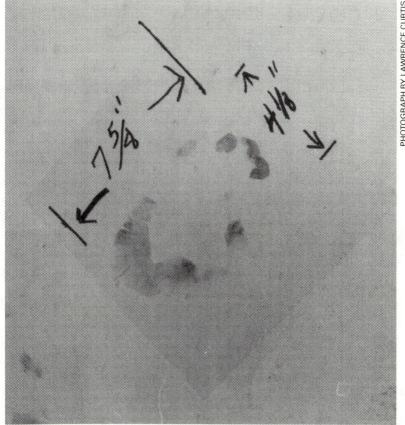

Dermal evidence of the El Reno Nape

tor T. E. Wyatt told me. Of course, the pongid foot does resemble a hominid hand more than a hominid foot.

Farther south, in Florida, the ichnological finds are overwhelming. In 1965, following the late-night visit of a stooping figure in Hernando County, investigators discovered rounded tracks with "one big toe stuck out to the side like a thumb on the hand."

In 1971, a "skunk ape" prowled through the Big Cypress Swamp, producing footprints from which casts were made. These casts show a footprint about nine inches in length, with an opposed great toe. Arguing most convincingly for the pongid nature of the "skunk ape," however, is the existence of knuckle prints.

Broward County (Florida) Rabies Control Officer Henry Ring, investigating sightings of two apes by the residents of the King's Manor Estates Trailer Court during August 1971, reported that he had "found nothing but a bunch of strange tracks, like someone was walking around on his knuckles." What Ring discovered was hardly "nothing"—to the contrary, it was striking evidence of the presence of anthropoid apes in Florida. Whereas most quadruped mammals, as well as monkeys, "walk" on the flats of the hands, the gorilla, chimpanzee, and orangutan use the backs of the fingers to "knuckle-walk." Officer Ring's finding of knuckle prints is a vital clue in any effort to piece together the Napes puzzle.

Handprints resembling those of a gorilla-like man or man-like gorilla are also part of the puzzle. Near El Reno, Oklahoma, in December 1970, something which moved on all fours raided a chicken coop, leaving a handprint on the door. The door and the 7"x5" handprint were taken to Lawrence Curtis, Director of the Oklahoma City Zoo, for an opinion. Curtis was frankly baffled. He found the thumb of the print quite unusual—it was crooked as if deformed or injured. Curtis thought it was from a primate but was uncertain of what kind. (Howard Dreson, it will be recalled, said he had fed a "chimpanzee" in the same area from 1967 to 1970.)

An examination of the photograph of the handprint left on the chicken coop door shows not so much a deformed hand as a typical anthropoid footprint. And in a good quality reprint of the photograph dermal ridges are slightly visible.

Similar tracks were reported at the Skunk River near Lockridge, Iowa, in 1975, and in Humboldt County, Iowa, in 1978, as chronicled by Mark A. Hall in *The Minnesota Archaeologist* (1979). These mystery anthropoids are still around, but do not command the attention of most "Bigfoot" hunters because the Napes' footprints are not as dramatic. Nevertheless, as Hall nicely put it to me in 2000, the Napes are "in hiding as always," as we enter this new century.

What Is It?

So what kind of primates do we have living in the wilds of North America?

In the 1970s, I conducted a survey of all information relating to feral or introduced primates in the United States and Canada. I contacted every continental state fish and game agency, all primate research centers, various humane societies and select zoological garden and wildlife authorities. From this research, I can make some brief observations about apes in America and their origin.

Some pet monkeys do escape and usually are recaptured, or die in the wild. A few have gone entirely feral. Examples from Indiana, where a rhesus lived for 10 years in the wild, or from Nova Scotia, where hunter Ralph Marr shot at a monkey and later collected hair, skin, and blood samples, illustrate the point that scattered escapees are successful. However, breeding feral populations are rare. To date there are only two "official" and one "questionable" feral monkey populations of importance to the Napes question. One is a squirrel monkey group near Coral Gables/Miami, Florida (Monkey Jungle). Another collection of about two hundred rhesus monkeys once lived along the Silver River near Ocala, Florida; they were escapees from a 1930s Tarzan movie but fear of AIDS in recent years has caused their demise. In Texas, in the 1980s, a band of baboons was supposedly sighted along the Trinity River; maybe they were just cryptid "devil monkeys" and not a feral band, after all.

All of the known feral monkey populations in America are the result of probable introductions by human beings within the last fifty years. Other evidence of such introductions and their resulting feral populations may be found in the Ozarks, Appalachia, and perhaps Mississippi, the latter due to hurricane dispersal.

It is clear, though, that these feral monkeys are not the large apes seen in the bottomlands. What then of anthropoid ape escapees?

Escapes of higher primates from zoological gardens are very rare. In October, 1970 one gorilla and five chimpanzees escaped from the Los Angeles Zoo but were recaptured within a very few minutes with tranquilizer guns. On the 29th August 2000, a 30-year-old male orangutan named Junior made a brief escape from the National Zoo's Great Ape House. He was captured 22 minutes after his escape. Marvin Jones, the foremost compiler of zoological park longevity records, observes, "Few zoos have had escapes that I know of, and having looked closely at many zoo files, I am sure that they would have been noted. In most cases these were caught."

The deliberate release of four chimpanzees on the uninhabited Bear

Island off the coast of Georgia in the 1960s is apparently the first attempt at establishing a free-ranging North American chimpanzee population.

From Where Cometh the Napes?

A rather free-ranging, swimming, nocturnal ape already exists in many parts of the southern United States. The American Indians seem to have known it, giving it in the name *memegwicio* in their folktales. If we consider only the historical written records, however, the appearance of the ape in these sources may be significant in the context of their possible introduction from Africa.

While slave-trading between Africa and the United States began in the early 1600s, it did not become routine until after the invention of the cotton gin in the 1790s. It is possible that some chimpanzees, or a subspecies, might have been brought over then, since slave ship captains often kept chimps as pets. In fact, the first chimpanzee to reach a zoo in England was brought to Bristol in the autumn of 1834 by a Captain Wood, who had picked it up on the Gambia Coast. But for many reasons, particularly the behavioral differences I have described, I think it unlikely that the source of the American apes might have been chimpanzees or gorillas brought over on slave ships.

Much confusion, however, exists about just what kinds of apes live in Africa. In 1967, for example, the Basle Zoo received an alleged Koolokamba or gorilla-like chimpanzee *(Pan troglodytes koolokamba),* which turned out to be a red-backed female gorilla.

The problem of "Ufiti" is also worth noting. "Ufiti" was first seen near Lake Nyasa in 1959. The Nyasaland Information Department recounts that first sighting in melodramatic fashion: "The first white man to see the strange monster opened fire with a revolver as it slunk eerily along the road in the misty moonlight."

When Ufiti was finally photographed, experts could see that she was a chimpanzee, though a very out-of-place one. But then she was no typical chimpanzee: she was almost six feet tall and had a gray lumbar saddle that's found among mature male gorillas, but was unknown in chimpanzees until Ufiti. Ufiti was finally captured and sent to the Chester Zoo in March 1964; there she lived for a little over a month before being euthanized due to her deteriorating health.

Other than the Ufiti affair, there is some slight evidence that something like the Napes have been reported in Africa. The Swiss professional animal collector Charles Cordier found in the Congo in January 1961 three footprints which compare favorably with the Napes footprints found in southern America.

My own belief is that a wide-ranging, supposedly prehistoric subfamily of the pongids, the dryopithecines, which paleontologists tell us existed in Africa, China and Europe, may be the source of the swimming apes of Africa and the bottomlands of the United States. This idea, I realize, is heretical enough, since the generalized pongids of the Dryopithecinae are supposed to have lived only from the Miocene to Pleistocene times.

Gigantopithecus, anthropologist Grover Krantz's candidate for the Bigfoot/Sasquatch of the Pacific Northwest, is at one end of an evolved giant end of dryopithecines; Mark A. Hall senses the *Gigantopithecus* are evidenced in the True Giants. Nevertheless, dryopithecines appear to be important in the mystery primate picture in North America—from the chimp-sized small Napes of the South to the *Gigantopithecus*-related giants of the West.

The obvious immediate objection is that the geological evidence for New World monkeys is "very scanty," in Le Gros Clark's words, and is represented by only a few genera from the Miocene in the tropic Americas. But if the dryopithecines appeared in the Nearctic in recent times in conjunction with the appearance of prehistoric man, the lack of fossil finds is not startling. The gap in fossils in forest environs is found for many species of mammals. In addition to the probably low numbers of dryopithecine specimens, the swampy bottomlands of the Nearctic are likely just as unfossiliferous as the forests of South America.

The dryopithecines seem to be the perfect candidates to explain the North American apes. Napier writes that they were "a highly successful family living in both temperate and subtropical woodlands." Theodosius Dobzhansky remarks that it is not surprising that fossil apes have been found in Europe "since that continent, together with North America, enjoyed warm temperate to tropical climates during the Tertiary period."

Even the name *Dryopithecus* furnishes a clue. It means "oak ape," and was so called, Alfred Sherwood Romer wrote in *Man and the Vertebrates,* "because of the presence of oak leaves in the deposits from which the first remains of this form were obtained." *Dryopithecus fontani* was found on the continent of Europe and occurred during the middle Miocene. The holotype of this species was discovered by naturalist M. Fontan near the village of St. Gaudens, France, in 1856.

All evidence points to the occurrence of "oak apes" in North American marshy habitats and temperate bottomland hollows. I do not know whether they are recent arrivals brought over from Africa or Pleistocene immigrants from Asia. But however they got here, they are here—wild apes which have adapted to the American environment, habitually bipedal, nocturnal, and able to swim. They now await the attention of zoologists, and are yet another important part of the countryside's unusual wildlife to be found in America's swampy backyard.

CHAPTER 17

Minnesota Iceman

During 2000, the newly published book entitled *My Quest for the Yeti* by famed mountain climber Reinhold Messner got lots of press attention. The book chronicles Messner's climbing feats, his spotty thoughts on bears as Yetis, and the worst rehashing of Abominable Snowmen history that I have seen since the hastily written Bigfoot paperbacks of the 1970s.

Then to top off things, Messner includes the Minnesota Iceman in his book with this statement: "Another practical joke involved a yeti found in 1968 in a freezer in Minnesota. It was, said reports, a humanlike corpse covered with hair, supposedly discovered in rural Minnesota, in a trailer of an actor by the name of Hansen. The corpse was displayed in an enormous block of ice. Hansen claimed it came from Asia. Russian seal hunters had found it floating in the Bering Sea. After a wild odyssey, the corpse somehow ended up in the actor's trailer—nobody knows how. Zoologists drew pictures of this iceman and described his features as being those of a hominid. No one thought to crack the ice and remove tissue samples. And then one day the corpse simply disappeared. Unbelievers asserted it had been made of latex."

Interestingly, Messner is so sloppy with his facts that this simple paragraph comes across as silly. No one has ever claimed that the Minnesota Iceman is a Yeti or even looks like one. Indeed, the Minnesota Iceman resembles the smaller hominoids seen in dry areas of south-central Asia, not the Himalayas. Frank Hansen is no actor. Zoologists may have later drawn pictures of the Iceman, but at the time Ivan Sanderson and Bernard Heuvelmans took photographs and made scientific sketches.

Down through the years, many people have asked me about the Minnesota Iceman, and it is obvious that this 1960s episode still holds a fascinating grip on people. This story belongs in *Mysterious America* because it occurred in the same era as many of this book's other investigations.

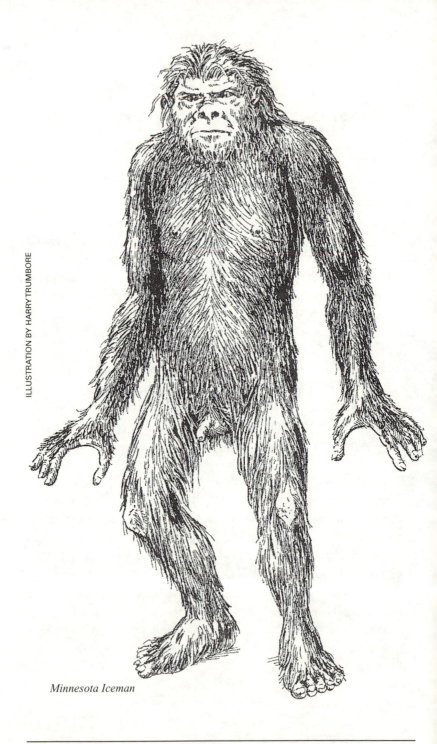

ILLUSTRATION BY HARRY TRUMBORE

Minnesota Iceman

What is the story behind the Minnesota Iceman?

During the autumn of 1967, college zoology major Terry Cullen spotted an extraordinary exhibit in Milwaukee—a fresh, apparently authentic corpse of a hairy man-like animal. For twenty-five cents people could see the "man left over from the Ice Age" that exhibitor Frank Hansen kept frozen in a block of ice inside a refrigerated glass coffin.

After trying unsuccessfully to interest mainstream academic anthropologists, Cullen alerted Ivan T. Sanderson, a naturalist and author of the successful book on Abominable Snowmen. Sanderson's house guest in New Jersey at the time happened to be none other than the Belgian cryptozoologist Bernard Heuvelmans, author of *On the Track of Unknown Animals.*

What everyone wanted to know was: Why hadn't anyone noticed this thing before? After all, the body had been on public exhibit for almost two years in Minnesota, Illinois, Wisconsin, Texas, Oklahoma, and other states. Why didn't anybody spot what Cullen saw in Chicago? Sanderson answered such questions this way: "Just how many people with proper training in any of the biological sciences (including medical practitioners and students) go to such shows? If any do, how many are trained physical anthropologists or primatologists? How many have ever heard of the ABSM search? The answer is: practically nobody who attended the exhibit."

After hearing from Cullen, however, Sanderson responded to that instinct that he used to discover new animals when he was a teenager, invited Heuvelmans, and the two immediately traveled to see firsthand what Hansen was showing at fairs and shopping centers across the American Midwest.

For three days, Sanderson and Heuvelmans examined the creature in Hansen's cramped trailer. The specimen was an adult male with large hands and feet. Its skin was covered with very dark brown hair three to four inches long. The creature had apparently been shot through one eye, which dangled on its face, but it also had a gaping wound and open fracture on its left arm. Smelling putrefaction where some of the flesh had been exposed because of melting ice, the two concluded that the creature was authentic. Through the ice, they could hardly believe what they saw. Heuvelmans described it this way in the *Bulletin of the Royal Institute of Natural Sciences of Belgium:*

The specimen at first looks like a man, or, if you prefer, an adult human being of the male sex, of rather normal height (six feet) and proportions but excessively hairy. It is entirely covered with very dark brown hair three to four inches long. Its skin appears waxlike, similar in color to the cadavers of white men not tanned by the sun...The specimen is lying on its back...the left arm is twisted behind the head with the palm of the hand upward. The arm makes a strange curve, as if it were that of a sawdust doll, but this curvature is due to an open fracture midway between the wrist and the elbow where one can distinguish the broken ulna in a gaping wound. The right arm is twisted and held tightly against the flank, with the hand spread palm down over the right side of the abdomen. Between the right finger and the medius the penis is visible, lying obliquely on the groin. The testicles are vaguely distinguishable at the juncture of the thighs.

Sanderson and Heuvelmans nicknamed the thing "Bozo." Later Sanderson would write in "Missing Link" (*Argosy,* May 1969):

Bozo's face is his most startling feature, both to anthropologists and anyone else—and for several reasons. Unfortunately, both eyeballs have been "blown out" of their sockets. One appears to be missing, but the other seems (to some, at least) to be just visible under the ice. This gives Bozo a gruesome appearance, which is enhanced by a considerable amount of blood diffused from the sockets through the ice. The most arresting feature of the face is the nose. This is large but only fairly wide, and is distinctly "pugged," rather like that of a Pekinese dog—but not like that of a gorilla, which actually doesn't have a nose, per se. The nostrils are large, circular and point straight forward, which is very odd. The mouth is only fairly wide and there is no eversion of the lips; in fact, the average person would say he had no lips at all. His "muzzle" is no more bulging, prominent, or pushed forward than is our own; not at all prognathous like that of a chimp. One side of the mouth is slightly agape and two small teeth can be seen. These should be the right upper canine and the first premolar. The canine or eye-tooth is very small and in no way exaggerated into a tusk, or similar to that of a gorilla or a chimp. But—to me, at least—the most interesting features of all are some folds and wrinkle lines around the mouth just below the cheeks. These are absolutely human, and are like those seen in a heavy-jowled, older white man.

Hansen wanted the discovery kept quiet, but both Heuvelmans and Sanderson wrote scientific papers on the creature within the year. Heuvelmans named it *Homo pongoides*. Sanderson, who was a well-known nature personality on TV, mentioned the Iceman on the "Tonight Show with Johnny Carson" during Christmas week of 1968. Bozo was out of the bag.

Soon the original body disappeared under mysterious circumstances. A model, said by some to have been made in California, then replaced it, with various Hollywood makeup artists claiming to have created the Iceman. When the Smithsonian Institution and the FBI got involved, Hansen explained that the creature was owned by a millionaire and declined to have it examined further.

The Mystery Continues

The Minnesota Iceman has been shelved by some skeptics as a joke, a carnival display to fool people. But the Iceman was never a "carnival" exhibit. Throughout the Midwest, in the 1960s and 1970s, the Minnesota Iceman was shown at stock fairs, state fairs, and shopping malls. It may seem unimportant to those that continue, in a somewhat demeaning way, to call this a "carnival exhibit," but the connotation of such a linguistic choice is significant. Carnivals have a certain reputation, personnel, and level of exhibitions. The exhibition milieu in which the Minnesota Iceman was shown was not that of a carnival. Hansen had, for example, also shown antique tractors. He was not a "carnie." The elitist practice of labeling the Minnesota Iceman a "carnival exhibit" is a way to immediately diminish the possible significance of this evidence even before another word is spoken.

How do we know that a model replaced the original body? Thanks to photographs of the travelling exhibit that Mark A. Hall and I took, Sanderson and Heuvelmans would later be able to enumerate at least fifteen technical differences between the original and the replacement. They held these in secret in order to differentiate a model from the real thing. These were differences on such a seemingly minor zoological level that a manufacturer would not know that these changes would be "seen" by a biologist.

I saw the "exhibit" at the Illinois State Fair in 1969. I wondered at the time whether this was the real thing or the copy. I photographed it extensively and sent copies of those photos to Ivan T. Sanderson and Mark A. Hall. From those photos, Sanderson told me I had seen a copy. I have been saying, in a humble fashion, that I only saw a copy. That's what Sanderson said I had seen. But with the frost differences and changed lighting, maybe it *was* the original. I assumed Heuvelmans and Sanderson knew what they were talking about. Researcher Jean Roche tells me today, however, that Heuvelmans knows that sometimes the real one was still being seen in the late 1960s, and because of the configuration of the spreading toes, I may have seen the original. Who knows?

Mark A. Hall in Minnesota had a similar experience in 1969, photographing Hansen's exhibit as it travelled around the upper Midwest, and exchanging those photos with me and Sanderson. Hall would later go on to be director of Sanderson's Society for the Investigation of the Unexplained, and become the main chronicler of the Minnesota Iceman mystery. In 1994, when I became consultant to NBC's "Unsolved Mysteries" for the Minnesota Iceman segment, I worked with the show's producers to assemble some of the major players in the Iceman drama. I thought it would be important to get some of the testimony on film before it was too late. Indeed, it was the first time that any television documentary segment had interviewed Cullen, Hansen, and Hall regarding the Minnesota Iceman. Unfortunately, Heuvelmans was too ill to fly to the United States to be interviewed for the segment. With Sanderson's death, Heuvelmans and Hansen are the only living links to that icy photo session of 1967.

Early in 2000, French researchers Jean Roche and Michel Raynal reminded the cryptozoology world that Bernard Heuvelmans' detailed color slides of the Minnesota Iceman have never been scientifically or popularly published. From what I have heard of Heuvelmans' many problems getting his book translated, and the comments of those who find the Minnesota Iceman unworthy of further examination, why should any of us be surprised to learn that high-quality color photos have not been widely circulated? But then remarkably, much of Heuvelmans' work on the Iceman remains outside of an English language readership as well.

Bernard Heuvelmans and Boris F. Porchnev, in *L'Homme de Neanderthal est toujours vivant* (Paris: Librairie Plon, 1974), wrote a single-spaced, 500-page technical overview of the Minnesota Iceman that should have been translated into English years ago. It has not. Translator trouble, then the death of a translator, a publisher's unwillingness to pursue the project, and other rumored factors, have all contributed to more than a quarter-century wait for this book to appear in English.

L'Homme de Neanderthal est toujours vivant has a dozen black and white photographic plates from Heuvelmans' session with the Minnesota Iceman. Most of these have not been seen by the English-speaking public either. Interestingly, the cover of the book has a color photograph made from the composite layout, per the photographic series Heuvelmans took of the entire length of the body. What might some of these color photographs show? Only time will tell, but Terry Cullen gave us a hint long ago. Cullen, who today is a professional herpetologist, was the first to show an awareness that the Minnesota Iceman was something special in 1967.

Mark A. Hall reminds us in his *Living Fossils* (1999, page 71): "Some of the reasons for Cullen's avid interest in the Iceman exhibit were that he could see: plant matter in the teeth, shed skin of ekto-parasites (lice) on the skin, and unique dentition showing in the mouth where a lip was curled back."

The Smell of a Mystery

One of the pieces of evidence that many who support the reality of the Minnesota Iceman point to is the smell of rotting flesh that Heuvelmans and Sanderson mentioned in their discussions of the Iceman. Here's how Sanderson noted it: "Let me say, simply, that one look was actually enough to convince us that this was—from our point of view, at least—'the genuine article.' This was no phony Chinese trick, or 'art' work. If nothing else confirmed this, the appalling stench of rotting flesh exuding from a point in the insulation of the coffin would have been enough."

Debunkers have said this is an old "carnie" illusion, wherein one puts a piece of old meat underneath the exhibit, discouraging people from staying long, so that more people will pay to get in. But it's not such a simple matter with the Minnesota Iceman. As to the putrefaction smell, let's look at the record.

Terry Cullen noted "that he had a much better look at the mouth and other parts of the body because the ice would melt down close to the body surface and Hansen would periodically replenish the ice cover" (Hall, *Living Fossils,* page 76).

Heuvelmans and Sanderson observed that some discoloration of the toes on the right foot suggested decomposition, that some downright rotting was occurring.

Few have stopped to note the exact situation that has caused all of the widely reported "smell of putrefaction" speculations concerning the Minnesota Iceman. It was not some "carnie" trick that followed the exhibition around. I saw the model in exhibition in 1969, and there was no smell manufactured to distract or fool people. The Minnesota Iceman was exhibited in a glass coffin, as was the original, with no smell coming from the exhibit. If this was a faked model, which was supposed to reek with reality, more than ever, a manufactured smell would have been called for in such a showing.

The whole putrefaction episode is well summarized in Hall's book (page 81): "In the course of the inspection Heuvelmans touched a hot lamp to the top pane of glass, causing cracks in it. The result was the smell of putrefaction came through the cracks." The smell was the result of an accident during Bernard Heuvelmans' close quarters examination, not the result of something that Frank Hansen could have ever foreseen.

We may never know what became of the Minnesota Iceman. Until one of these mystery primates is discovered, we may not understand the true role it should play in the history of hairy hominoids studies. But for now, we must accept that the enigma of the Minnesota Iceman remains as one of the most hotly debated episodes in hominology.

What Is the Minnesota Iceman?

Ivan T. Sanderson and Bernard Heuvelmans were in disagreement about what the Iceman was and to what fossil candidate it should be assigned. Four years before his death, Sanderson wrote that he had not fully "formulated" his feelings on the matter. Mark A. Hall set down his thoughts on the subject in one fashion in 1994, and after reexamining the evidence felt differently about it in 1999. Most hominologists in France and Russia have followed Heuvelmans. And Heuvelmans has never wavered. Zoologist, Father of Cryptozoology, Dr. Bernard Heuvelmans wrote in 1969: "For the first time in history, a fresh corpse of Neanderthal-like man has been found. It means that this form of Hominid, thought to be extinct since prehistoric times, is still living today. The long search for rumored live 'ape-men' or 'missing links' has at last been successful. This was not accomplished by expeditions to far away places and at great expense, but by the accidental discovery, in this country, of a corpse preserved in ice...this specimen is a contemporary representative of an unknown form of Hominid, most probably a relic of the Neanderthal type. The belief, based on strong testimonial evidence, that small, scattered populations of Neanderthals survive, has been held for years by some scientists, mostly Russian and Mongolian."

Heuvelmans' scientific paper of his description of this new form of living Neandertaler, which he named *Homo pongoides* (i.e., "Apelike Man"), was published in February, 1969, in the *Bulletin of the Royal Institute of Natural Sciences of Belgium* (Vol. 45 No. 4). Few anthropologists today have read it, of course.

Sanderson's paper was written in 1969, for the Italian scientific journal *Genus,* and there he wrote that the Minnesota Iceman "most certainly should not be assigned to the Neanderthals race or complex." Several notable Heuvelmans followers disagree with Sanderson, of course. One is Jordi Magraner, a French-Spanish zoologist who did fieldwork in North Pakistan during the 1990s in search of the local wildman, the *Barmanu.* He collected more than fifty firsthand sighting accounts, and all eyewitnesses recognized the reconstruction of Heuvelmans' *Homo pongoides.* They picked out *Homo pongoides* as their match to Barmanu from Magraner's id-kit of the drawings of apes, fossil men, aboriginals, monkeys, and the Minnesota Iceman. Magraner agrees this may be a Neandertal. Of course, this only proves the Barmanu looks like *Homo pongoides*, not that it is a Neandertal.

Helmut Loofs-Wissowa, an anthropologist at Australian National University, also thinks Heuvelmans was correct. He, too, points to the Neandertals, represented by the Minnesota Iceman, as the source of surviving relict populations of wildmen he has studied in Vietnam. Loofs-Wissowa's creative work links the semi-erect penis of *Homo pongoides* with what he sees as paleolithic cave art and other evidence he connects to Neandertals. His scholarly considerations are worthy of a close reading by all interested in this question.

Mark A. Hall, after being close to the investigation for the last quarter century, is not bothered by the assignment of *Homo pongoides* to the Asian examples that these scholars have focused on. He merely thinks they have the wrong fossil ancestor linked to the accidental American, the Minnesota Iceman. Hall considers the more proper prehistoric candidate may be *Homo erectus.*

The Iceman appears to be an *accidental,* in other words, not of local origin. Heuvelmans theorized the Iceman was a Neandertal that had been murdered in Vietnam during the war and smuggled into the U.S. in a "body bag." Its erectus-like features, however, match quite well some of the reports coming out of Central Asia, within and just north of Pakistan. Hall questions the Iceman's supposed Vietnamese origin and alleged Neandertal affinity and today feels the original Minnesota Iceman was of south-central Asian *Homo erectus* origin, perhaps even a Barmanu.

The behavior of the Barmanu and other wildmen that Patrick Huyghe and I call "Erectus Hominid" in our field guide suggests a unique sleeping position that is characteristic of these beings. They sleep with their knees and elbows drawn up under them and their hands wrapped around the back of their neck. They lie down on all fours, in other words, using the knees, hands, and elbows to rest slightly off the ground. Ivan T. Sanderson and Mark A. Hall have noted that this special sleeping position produces a prominent pad on the heel of the hand, as well as on the knees and elbows. These "pads" are found in the Central Asian varieties of the Erectus Hominid, but apparently not in the subtropical ones. The Minnesota Iceman has some diagnostic pads on the heel of the hands that, to Mark A. Hall, are a key feature that associates *Homo pongoides* with a *Homo erectus* origin.

Of course, how the Asian wildman we call the Minnesota Iceman got to America and where his remains are today must remain unsolved questions—perhaps forever.

Phantoms Afield...

ILLUSTRATION BY PHIL HEMSTREET/BETH FIDELER

Kelly Creature

CHAPTER 18

The Jersey Devil

One January night in 1909, E. P. Weeden of the Trenton, New Jersey, City Council bolted upright in bed when he heard someone trying to break down his door. It was a most unusual "someone," apparently, because Weeden also heard distinctly the sound of flapping wings. Councilman Weeden rushed to his second-floor window and looked outside. He did not see the intruder, but the sight that greeted his eyes chilled him far more than the icy temperature ever could: In the snow on the roof of his house something had left a line of tracks. And whatever that "something" was, it had hoofs.

On the same night, "it" left hoofprints in the snow at the State Arsenal in Trenton. And shortly afterward John Hartman of Centre Street caught a full view of it as it circled his yard and then vanished into the night. Trenton residents living near the Delaware River were shaken by loud screeching sounds, like the cries of a giant cat, and stayed in their homes that night too frightened to venture out.

"It" reappeared in Bristol during the early morning hours of January 17th. The first person to observe it, a police officer named Sackville, was patrolling along Buckley Street around 2:00 a.m. Officer Sackville was alerted by the barking of dogs in the neighborhood that something was amiss. Feeling increasingly uneasy, he reached the race bridge when a sudden movement from the path below caught his eye. Carefully he turned his head. When he saw it, he was so stunned that, for a moment, he could not move.

Gathering his wits, Sackville drew his revolver and plunged toward "it." It let out an eerie cry and hopped rapidly away, with the officer in hot pursuit. Suddenly it raised its wings and flew above the path, and Sackville, afraid that it would get away, fired his gun. He missed. By the time he got off a second shot, the thing was gone.

Major recorded sightings of the Jersey Devil

The second witness was Bristol postmaster E. W. Minster, who the next day told this story to reporters:

"I awoke about two in the morning ... and finding myself unable to sleep, I arose and wet my head with cold water as a cure for insomnia.

"As I got up I heard an eerie, almost supernatural sound from the direction of the river...I looked out upon the Delaware and saw flying diagonally across what appeared to be a large crane but which was emitting a glow like a firefly.

"Its head resembled that of a ram, with curled horns, and its long thin neck was thrust forward in flight. It had long thin wings and short legs, the front legs shorter than the hind. Again, it uttered its mournful and awful call—a combination of a squawk and a whistle, the beginning very high and piercing and ending very low and hoarse...."

John McOwen, a liquor dealer who lived on Bath Street with the back of his house facing the Delaware Division Canal, heard his infant daughter crying and went into her room to see what was wrong. It was about 2:00 a.m. A "strange noise" brought him to the window, which overlooked the canal.

"It sounded like the scratching of a phonograph before the music begins," he said later, "and yet it also had something of a whistle to it. You know how the factory whistle sounds? Well, it was something like that. I looked from the window and was astonished to see a large creature standing on the banks of the canal. It looked something like an eagle...and it hopped along the tow path."

The next day Mrs. Thomas Holland discovered hoofmarks in her snow-covered yard, as did other residents of Buckley and Bath streets.

And Trenton and Bristol were not the only places where the creature was seen. At Camden twelve men at work in the Hilltown clay bank took one glance at the thing as it descended toward them, and then, as one account wryly notes, they "were off to set an unofficial record for the three-mile run in working clothes."

Other New Jersey towns and cities reporting visitations were Wycombe, Swedesboro, Huffville, Mantua, Woodbury, Mount Ephraim, Haddonfield, and Mount Holly. Said a contemporary news story, "Hoofprints have been noticed in hundreds of places over a strip of country at least 16 miles long and three miles wide."

What was it? It was the "Jersey Devil." Whatever the Jersey Devil is.

The Jersey Devil is one of those localized names that residents and written histories have applied to any supposed strange beast, entity, or phantom seen in the state of New Jersey. The legendary creature, in fact, is the state's "official demon," an unofficial regional mascot, and now the name of the state's National Hockey League team. The Jersey Devil, as a feral human initially identified as a Bigfoot, was featured in the third episode of *The X-Files* as that series' first ever "monster of the week." A Sony PlayStation game has turned the savage beast into a likable 1990s video game character. But the history of the "beast" is much older.

The Jersey Devil, sometimes called the Leeds Devil, has been seen since the 1930s, but long before that a great body of folklore had grown up around the elusive beast. Some versions of the legend—folklorists claim there are over thirty variants of the tale in circulation—list the creature's alleged birth as having taken place in 1887. However, the Gloucester Historical Society has traced the tale back as far as 1790, and there is every reason to believe it was around even earlier.

The most frequently related account of the Devil's origins goes like this: In 1735 a Mrs. Leeds of Estellville, New Jersey, upon finding she was pregnant for the thirteenth time and less than exhilarated about it, snorted that if she was going to have another child it might just as well be a devil—and it was. It was born with an animal's head, a bird's body, and cloven hoofs instead of feet. Cursing its mother (it could speak at birth), it promptly flew up the chimney and took up residence in the swamps and pine barrens of southern New Jersey, where it has lived ever since. (American folklore is filled with similar stories about a pregnant mother's careless words backfiring on her. As late as 1908 a tale circulating through rural Alabama had it that a Birmingham baby was born "with horns like a devil." During her pregnancy the mother had remarked, "I'd as soon have a devil in the house as a baby!")

Over the years the story, like all good stories, grew in the telling. Eventually the Devil was held responsible for every major calamity that befell the state, and some people even maintained that its appearance presaged the coming of war. On a less cosmic scale it was said that its breath could sour milk, kill fish, and dry up cornfields.

The late Rev. Henry Carlton Beck recounted another part of the myth in his *Jersey Genesis:*

> Accompanied, as it usually is, by the howling of dogs and the hooting of owls, there can be no surer forerunner of disaster. Where the barrens line the shore it flits from one desolate grass-grown dune to another and is especially watchful upon those wild heights when coasting schooners, driving their prows into the sand, pound to splinters upon the bars and distribute upon the waves their freight of good and human lives.
>
> Upon such occasions Leeds' Devil is seen in the companionship of a beautiful golden-haired woman in white, or yet of some fierce-eyed, cutlass-bearing disembodied spirit of a buccaneer whose galleon, centuries ago, was wrecked upon the shore of Cape May County.

How seriously anyone took these yarns is hard to say, though some Jerseyites must have at least half-believed them. Most people probably treasured the story for its quaint and amusing character and kept it alive chiefly as a story to entertain their children with on Halloween.

Certainly Jersey citizens and others as well have had their share of fun with the beastie. In 1906 huckster Norman Jefferies, publicity manager for C.A. Brandenburgh's Arch Street Museum in Philadelphia, came upon an old book which mentioned Mrs. Leeds' curious offspring, and it gave him an idea. With attendance at his shows declining, Jefferies had been on the lookout for a stunt to bring the crowds back. Unfortunately for him, the Philadelphia papers, having been taken in by earlier Jefferies tricks, were not about to offer him any cooperation. So he planted this story in a South Jersey small-town weekly:

> The "Jersey Devil," which has not been seen in these parts for nearly a hundred years, has again put in its appearance. Mrs. J. H. Hopkins, wife of a worthy farmer of our county, distinctly saw the creature near the barn on Saturday last and afterwards examined its tracks in the snow.

The report created a sensation. All over the state men and women started glancing over their shoulders and bolting doors and windows. While always taking care publicly to profess skepticism, Jerseyites steadfastly refused to take any chances. What if the monster was real after all? Had not an "expert" from the Smithsonian Institution said that it "bore out his long cherished theory that there still existed in hidden caverns and caves, deep in the interior of the earth, survivors of those prehistoric animals and fossilized remains..."? The expert was sure the Devil was a pterodactyl.

Shortly thereafter the animal was captured by a group of farmers. After making sure every paper around got the news, Jefferies took the "Devil" with him to Philadelphia and placed it on exhibition in the Arch Street Museum. The crowds, huge and mostly uncritical, gazed in wonder at the thing—actually a kangaroo with bronze wings fastened to its back and green stripes painted the length of its body.

Jefferies confessed in 1929 that he had bought the animal from a dealer in Buffalo, New York, and let it loose in a wooded area of South Jersey where it was certain to be caught without difficulty.

The *Woodbury Daily Times* got into the act, too, reporting in its December 15, 1925, issue that farmer "William Hyman" had killed an unknown animal after it raided his chicken coop. "Hyman describes the beast," the paper said, "as being as big as a grown Airedale with black fur resembling Astrakhan; having a kangaroo fashioned hop; forequarters higher than its rear, which were always crouched; and hind feet of four webbed toes."

Fine, except that "William Hyman" never existed. And neither, needless to say, did his specimen of the Jersey Devil.

But is there more to the Jersey Devil than mere folklore and fabrication? The question is certainly heretical enough. Even Charles Fort drew the line here, writing in *Lo!* that "though I should not like to be so dogmatic as to say there are no 'Jersey Devils,' I have had no encouragement investigating them." But Fort's knowledge of the phenomenon may have been confined to the Jefferies and "Hyman" hoaxes only.

The problem is complicated by the virtually absolute refusal of journalists to take the Devil at all seriously, even though some commentators have admitted rather uneasily that there are portions of the legend that are, well, odd. Like, for example, the sterling characters of some of those individuals who insist they saw a mysterious thing with wings hopping and/or flying through the pine barrens. Like the persistent discoveries of unusual tracks and the unexplained disappearances of livestock. Like the haunting cries sometimes heard emanating from the woods.

But reporters, perhaps understandably, would rather have the Devil be a charming, harmless piece of Halloween lore than an annoying puzzle for which there may be no ready answers. As a consequence, their treatment of even apparently authentic reports of unknown animals in New Jersey is almost invariably flippant, dotted with references to such obvious nonsense as Mrs. Leeds' baby, and ultimately confusing to anyone who endeavors to separate fact from fiction.

If the Jersey Devil is no more than a creation of the folk imagination, then what was it that a city councilman, a policeman, a postmaster, and many other reputable people encountered in January 1909? What made the tracks on Weeden's roof and all along the Delaware River? Perhaps it was the same thing Mrs. Amanda Sutts saw on her family's farm in 1900. She recalled the incident for the *Trenton Evening Times* sixty years later, still convinced that the creature was the Jersey Devil. At the time of the incident she was ten years old and living on a farm near Mays Landing in the heart of Devil country.

"We heard a scream near the barn one night and ran out of our house," she said. "We saw this thing that looked like a kangaroo. It wasn't such a great big animal—it was about the size of a small calf and weighed about 150 pounds. But the noise it made is what scared us. It sounded like a woman screaming in an awful lot of agony."

Mrs. Sutts said that was the only time she ever actually viewed the creature, but her family often heard it and would follow its tracks, which were 8 to 10 feet apart and led to a large cedar swamp at the rear of the farm. Her father had seen the thing once before, when he was sixteen years old.

"When the horses heard the Devil scream," she observed, "they would carry on so you'd think they were going to tear the barn down. You could hear the Devil scream a long way off when the horses would quiet down. People may say there's nothing to it but I know darned well there is. Some might say I'm an old crank but when you know a thing you know it."

So you begin to see the peculiar problem here. Perhaps this was a real cryptid, a mystery kangaroo, a devil monkey, a Bigfoot? The screen of time influences the report on one level, but the location and overall lore of the Jersey Devil does even more so. Folklorists feel this is their domain, which surely it is, but my question has to be, are there any real animals underneath some of these stories from Jersey?

The first persons to note the presence of a peculiar animal in the area were the Indians, who said it originally appeared in what is now Bucks County (where many alleged sightings of the Devil have been made in recent years), near the boundary line of Philadelphia. In fact they named the creek there *Popuessing,* meaning "place of the dragon." In 1677 Swedish explorers examined some weird footprints in the rocks near the same creek and renamed it "Drake Kill," which also refers to the dragon.

The legend claims that by the mid-1700s the Devil had become such a nuisance that a clergyman was called in to exorcise it. A century later, in 1840, a strange animal went on a rampage, slaughtering livestock, attempting to seize children, and generally terrorizing the area. In the course of one foray it supposedly killed two large dogs, three geese, four cats, and 31 ducks. (If that sounds incredible to you, consider the case of an enigmatic marauder that destroyed 51 sheep in a single night on a farm near Guildford, England, in March 1906.)

During the winter of 1873-74 the Devil was seen prowling in the vicinity of Bridgeton; in 1894-95 a trail of unidentifiable footprints around Leeds Point excited speculation that the beastie had returned to the place of its birth. Near Vincentown in 1899 farmers reported losing livestock to some kind of mystery animal.

After the 1909 flap the Devil went back into hiding and did not reappear until June 1926, when two 10-year-old boys in West Orange reportedly saw what news accounts refer to vaguely as a "flying lion." A large posse scoured the area in search of the creature but found nothing.

About August 1st of the following year huckleberry pickers near Bridgeport startled an animal resting in a cedar swamp and chased it until it outdistanced them, hooting angrily all the while. A *New York Times* dispatch describes the animal "as large and as speedy as a fox and with four legs, but also having feathers and a cry that is partly bark and partly the hoot of an owl."

Almost exactly a year later berry pickers at Mays Landing and Leeds Point allegedly encountered a similar creature. Another witness was Mrs. William Sutton, a farmer's wife, who said she saw it in her cornfield. An unidentified man flagged down a car driven by Charles Mathis and pleaded to be taken from the scene of his meeting with "a horrible monster." A thirteen-year-old boy said he had seen the Devil gazing at him through his bedroom window.

A badly shaken John McCandless reported a terrifying experience, which he said occurred on January 21, 1932, while he was passing through an area five miles north of Downington, Pennsylvania. Hearing a moaning sound in the brush, McCandless spotted "a hideous form, half-man, half-beast, on all fours, and covered with dirt or hair." After others told of seeing the figure, McCandless and a group of friends armed with rifles and shotguns plowed through the trees and fields every day for a week, but by this time the thing had disappeared.

In 1935 Philip Smith, "a sober gentleman of honest reputation," claimed he saw the Devil walking down a Woodstown street and the next year, following an outbreak of alleged sightings, a posse of farmers searched neighboring forests and swamps without success.

It may be no more than a part of the legend that has the Devil popping up on December 7, 1941 (for those that have the same memory lapses as President Bush, this is "Pearl Harbor Day"), but perhaps I should take a bit more seriously a report of its appearance in Mount Holly in 1948. In 1949 a "green male monster" supposedly was seen at Somerville; unfortunately that is the extent of my information. In 1952 something killed large numbers of chickens on Atlantic County farms. Since Atlantic County is in Devil territory, locals held the beast responsible.

Let me catch my breath here. The list is endless. Thank goodness we are only looking at a small state under the file created for one name.

On October 31, 1957, state newspapers asked in the headlines of front-page stories: "Is Jersey's 'Devil' Dead? Skeleton Baffles Experts." Said the stories, "The Jersey Devil may have met his final end this summer in the depths of the Wharton Tract down in the pine barrens of central South Jersey. Foresters and other members of the New Jersey Department of Conservation and Economic Development at work on the state-owned property report the finding of a partial skeleton, half-bird and half-beast, and impossible of conventional identifications." It was a Halloween gag, of course.

But five students from the Spring Garden Institute at Philadelphia were not amused when "unearthly screams" kept them awake one night in 1960 as they camped near Lake Atsion in Burlington County, New Jersey. "We were pretty much on edge," said Bert Schwed, one of the group, "after finding four large tracks earlier in the underbrush near our camp. They were about 11 inches long and they looked something like a large bird print with the heel dug in and the toes spread out."

Over in Dorothy, near Mays Landing, in October of the same year, residents complained to Game Warden Joseph Gallo that they were hearing weird cries in the night and discovering unusual tracks in the ground in the morning. After a brief investigation, Gallo and State Game Trapper Carlton Adams concluded that the tracks were caused by a large hopping rabbit whose feet touched the ground together to form one print, and that the noises were made by owls. Not terribly impressed by this official conclusion, locals said they know an owl's screech when they hear it. Shortly afterwards, the Broadway Improvement Association of Camden offered a $10,000 reward to anyone who could catch the Devil alive. "They do not seem worried about the prospect of having to pay up," the *Trenton Times* noted sardonically.

Toward dusk on May 21, 1966, a creature "at least seven feet tall" ambled through the Morristown, New Jersey, National Historical Park and left in its wake four hysterical witnesses who had viewed it from a parked car. They said the creature was "faceless," covered with long black hair, and had scaly skin. It had broad shoulders and walked on two legs with a stiff, rocking movement.

The four drove to the park entrance and stopped approaching cars to warn people that a "monster" lurked inside. Raymond Todd, one of the witnesses, caught a ride with a young lady who took him to the Municipal Hall in Morristown, where he blurted out his story to the police. Oddly enough, the girl had seen a similar entity a year before. She told police that she and several friends were in the park one night when a huge, broad-shouldered something had loomed up in their rear window and thumped on the back of the car. Her mother had asked her not to report the incident, she said.

Is there a Jersey Devil?

Well, there is *something*. Or perhaps a number of somethings. Underneath all the myth, all the nonsense, all the fabrication, is a small core of truth from which the legends have grown. There are just too many loose ends—like tracks and sightings by reliable witnesses—that can no longer be glossed over.

But it is difficult to move beyond these simple (and by now, fairly obvious) conclusions. To start with, nothing *precisely* like a "Jersey Devil" has ever been reported elsewhere. But then the same is true of those entities called "Mothman," whose activities seem confined generally to certain southeastern states.

Mothman and the Jersey Devil share other traits as well. For one thing both supposedly possess wings; they also sometimes "glow" or "flicker" in the dark. The differences, however, are greater. Witnesses have reported three Mothman types; one a winged quasi-humanoid, another an enormous bird, and the last a mechanical contrivance. None bears much resemblance to the ram-headed Jersey Devil. Moreover, Mothman glides through the air with the greatest of ease; the Devil on the other hand flies clumsily and close to ground level and can negotiate only short distances at a time.

Of course, there is no shortage of winged weirdies of all sizes and varieties around the world, so we should not hold the Devil's distinctive shape against the poor fellow. But just what is that distinctive shape?

Assuming for the moment the Devil exists at all, one would assume the creature probably most resembles what was observed in January 1909. These reports are more detailed than most others and for once the press treated them with reasonable objectivity.

But the 1909 reports are very suspect. Nearly two centuries after the creature's reputed birth, this rash of bizarre reports erupted in the first decade of the 20th century. The episode has been dubbed the Jersey Devil's "finest hour." In the course of five January days, more than 100 persons across eastern Pennsylvania and southern New Jersey swore they had seen the beast. All over the region, accounts of such a creature or creatures were heard, as well as the discoveries of bizarre, unidentifiable hoofprints in the snow. Schools and businesses closed. Newspaper articles were written and read.

A climax to the events took place on January 21, in West Collingswood, when the town's fire department supposedly confronted the monster and sprayed it with fire hoses as it swooped menacingly overhead. The next morning, a Camden woman said the Jersey Devil attacked her pet dog. This report marked the end of the 1909 flap, although another solo sighting occurred in February.

But years later, information provided to me by Ivan T. Sanderson offered a likely explanation for the scare: apparently an elaborate real estate hoax. Sanderson even found the fake feet used to make the footprints in the snow. Hoofprints and other evidence were faked or misidentified. The stories of sightings seem to have been a combination of planted stories, hoaxes, and imaginations fueled by fear.

Despite the hoaxes of the past, however, we must ponder that perhaps *several* Jersey Devils do haunt the pine barrens region, including "flying lions" and "kangaroos," or in any case creatures that looked like that to flustered individuals seeing them in less than ideal light conditions. Most of the folklore, though, clearly takes its inspiration from those alleged run-ins with a beastie of the 1909 variety.

Not everything that gets shoved under the "Jersey Devil" banner really belongs there. Like other states, New Jersey harbors more than one mystery animal, but whenever one appears, inevitably it gets hailed, usually for purposes of ridicule, as the latest manifestation of the Devil and so joins the great body of myth, legend, and lore.

The Morristown creature might be more closely related to Bigfoot than to the Jersey Devil, but its scaly skin is not characteristic of Bigfoot creatures sighted in other parts of the country. When Sasquatch researcher John Green came to the state in the 1970s, he was struck by how Bigfoot-type reports were being called Jersey Devil sightings.

Possibly pumas or phantom panthers deserve blame for at least some of the stock kills. The last year of normal *Felis concolor* abundance in New Jersey was 1840, but the behavior of the rampaging creature of that year suggests that it could have been a phantom panther.

More modern sightings, if taken seriously, remind us that a diverse number of creatures have been lumped under the Jersey Devil rubric. In one recent sighting from December 1993, a witness named John Irwin, a summer park ranger in the Wharton State Forest of New Jersey and a respected figure in the community, was patrolling at night when he noticed a large, dark figure emerging from the woods. It stood like a human, over six feet tall, and it had black fur, which looked wet and matted. The Forest Service report of the incident went on to state: "John sat in his car only a few feet away from the monster. His initial shock soon turned to fear when the creature turned its deer-like head and stared through the windshield. But instead of gazing into the bright yellow glow of a deer's eyes, John found himself the subject of a deep glare from two piercing red eyes." Some New Jersey researchers compared what Irwin saw to the Australian Bunyip.

Is there a Jersey Devil?

I remain open-mindedly skeptical and hope that in the future someone will make a discovery or report a sighting that will settle the question once and for all.

Mystery cryptids of many kinds, from little otter-shaped animals to hairy bipeds, from strange birds to unknown panthers, seen in New Jersey are always called Jersey Devils, though surely none really is.

In the meantime I am convinced of this much: The Jersey Devil is more than just a legend, more than a centuries-old folktale, more than a convenient gimmick for hucksters to use in fooling the unsuspecting. It is all these things, true, but it is also one thing more: a mystery.

CHAPTER 19

Kelly's Little Men

Some UFO investigators call this event the "granddaddy" of all flying saucer occupant accounts. Today it would be labeled an alien attack story. This incident, which occurred in Kentucky, is one of the most thoroughly investigated and documented in the annals of modern mysteries. The individuals who extensively looked into the accounts within the first few hours included local police and sheriff officials, state police, Air Force and Army personnel, radio station and newspaper reporters and photographers, and various civilian investigators from as far away as New York City. The in-depth examination of the reportedly unsophisticated witnesses, the mid-1950s date of the sightings, and the fantastic details of this truly close encounter have made this event one of the few "classics" in ufological literature.

In the popular mind, Hopkinsville, Kentucky, is the site of this 1955 happening, but actually, it occurred in the small community of Kelly (population 150), located seven miles north of Hopkinsville. At the time, the specific location of the "invasion" was the Kentucky farmhouse of the Sutton family, a modest one-story frame structure with a corrugated iron roof. The house had electricity, but did not have a telephone, television, or radio. The farmhouse was occupied by eight adults and three children, who maintained a rural and limited lifestyle. The residents were members of the Sutton/Lankford family, and Elmer "Lucky" Sutton's friend Billy Ray Taylor and his wife.

Billy Ray Taylor was the first to have a strange experience that hot, mosquito-filled night of August 21, 1955. The new moon was out and the sky was clear. As darkness fell, Billy Ray went to the backyard well for a drink of water. He quickly ran inside, telling everyone about having seen a silver flying saucer that was shooting out flames "all the colors of the rainbow." Billy Ray said it had passed overhead, stopped dead in the air, and dropped straight down into a gully about three hundred feet behind the Sutton farm. No one in the house took Billy Ray seriously; they all thought he was pulling their collective leg, or had merely seen a shooting star. No one gave it much thought; no one even bothered to even venture out into the backyard to look around.

An hour later, at about eight o'clock, the family dog started barking violently. Lucky Sutton, Mrs. Lankford's oldest son from a previous marriage and the no-nonsense head of the household, noticed a strange glowing globe moving towards the house. The dog yelped, apparently quite scared by the apparition. Soon Lucky Sutton and Billy Ray Taylor saw that the glow was from a little man who was holding both of its extremely thin arms up over its head. The little man was about three and a half feet tall, had huge eyes with no pupils or eyelids, and large pointed, crinkly ears. In the glare of the outside electric light bulb, its skin was silvery and metallic, but its body seemed to glow when in a darker area near the house. And they noted it liked to stay in the shadows. As the features of the little man grew clearer, they saw its body was very thin and the arms ended in talon-like claws. The thing was bald, appeared to have a straight slit from ear to ear for its mouth, and completely lacked a nose. It was the most frightening and strangest creature the two men had ever seen.

Confronted with this terrifying situation, the men reacted quickly and decisively. They both reached for their guns—a .22 rifle for Billy Ray and a twenty-gauge shotgun for Lucky—and blasted away at the little man who was then less than twenty feet from the house. What occurred when the visitor was hit surprised the two men. As they described it, the little man was apparently not hurt but "flipped over" backwards and scurried off into the shadows. Lucky and Billy Ray went inside and soon another (or the same?) little man appeared at a side window. The men again shot right through a screen at the entity. Again it flipped over and vanished into the night. Since the women were beginning to scream, and things were getting rather frightening, the men decided to go outside to see if they had actually killed one of the little men.

Cautiously and quietly, Billy Ray moved through the darkened house towards the screen door that faced the backyard. He was followed closely by Lucky Sutton and the rest of the adults and children. As Billy Ray went through the door and stood under the small roof over the step, Lucky Sutton and the others saw a claw-like hand grab Billy Ray Taylor's hair. Instantly, Alene Sutton pulled Billy Ray back into the farmhouse, and Lucky ran into the yard, blasting at the thing on the roof. The little man was knocked off the roof but floated to the ground. Before they knew where it had actually landed, the group saw another little man in a tree near the house. Billy Ray rushed back outside and joined Lucky in firing on this one. This creature, too, floated to the earth. And every time one of them was shot at, or shouted at, they glowed brighter. As the little man in the tree hightailed it from the scene, another one came from around a corner of the house and dashed in front of Lucky.

In all, the residents of the Sutton farmhouse said they had to fight off six separate advances. By eleven o'clock, after several harrowing hours of claws scratching on the roof, shotgun blasts, creature faces at the windows, and crying children, the Suttons decided to abandon the farm. All eight adults and three children piled into two automobiles, and sped down U.S. Route 41, to Hopkinsville. Once in town, the Suttons, Lankfords, and Taylors went straight to the police station.

Police Chief Russell Greenwell would later describe the Kelly witnesses as genuinely terrified. "Something scared those people," said Chief Greenwell to one investigator. "Something beyond reason—nothing ordinary."

The police were struck by the sincerity of these frightened folks. Soon a caravan of local and state police cars roared off at high speed towards Kelly. Before long, the farm was flooded with authorities and investigators—including the local police, the military police from Fort Campbell, a big-city news photographer, and a local radio station newsman. It was about 11:30 p.m. by now, and tension filled the air as the various investigators attempted to assess the situation. At one point, with everyone probing around (possibly destroying evidence of the encounter), someone stepped on a cat's tail; it let out a screech that had everybody's nerves jumping. The skeptics looked for evidence of drinking and found none. No one saw the little men. Nothing unusual was found. Well, almost nothing. Police Chief Greenwell and a group of other men reported they saw a luminous patch in some grass near the house, but as they went closer to it, it seemed to disappear.

Slowly, one by one, the investigators left. By about 2:30 a.m., having found little and promising to come back after dawn, the crowd was gone. The only people remaining at the farmhouse were the Suttons, Lankfords and Taylors. And the little men! As soon as the residents of the farmhouse had settled down, turned all the lights out, and gone to bed, one of the creatures' clawed hands reached up on the screen. Noticing a glow at the window, Mrs. Glennie Lankford, 50, was the first to see it. She alerted the rest of the family. Lucky, as he had done before, grabbed his shotgun and fired at the little man. Although the creatures were seen off and on until just before dawn, the events of the second visitation were not as dramatic as those of the first.

As the sun rose, the "invasion" of the little men at Kelly, Kentucky, was over, but the onslaught of investigators and media had just begun. Despite the efforts of many skeptics, the testimony of the Suttons, the Taylors, and the Lankfords was never contradicted, or proven false. In one of those twilight language tricks that happens in cases like this, "Sutton" means "south." For people reading about this case, it "felt" very "southern." In the politically incorrect times of the 1950s, a few would call the witnesses "hillbillies," in an illogical and biased way to try to discount the series of incidents that befell the Suttons.

Down through the years, I have talked to two people who were on site and interviewed many of the participants—Isabel Davis, author of the informative *Close Encounters at Kelly and Others of 1955* (1978) and Bud Ledwith, the announcer-engineer at the Hopkinsville radio station. The contemporary interviewers came away from Kelly convinced these people had had a very real experience. What the true nature of that experience was, and *who* the little men were, is one of the deepest mysteries in Forteana.

CHAPTER 20

The Mad Gasser of Mattoon and His Kin

Some very strange entities haunt some rural towns in America. Following the Civil War and for the next seventy years, a strange something
dubbed the "Ghost of Paris" frequently terrorized Paris, Missouri.
In October 1934, a wave of sightings of the "Ghost of Paris" occurred.
Local residents were frantically telephoning the City Marshal and de-
manding he drive the ghost away. The poor marshal was at his wits' end as
to how to handle the situation. The phantom was described as tall, dressed
in black, and carrying some sort of wand in "her" hand. According to
local tradition, "she" appeared in Paris, Missouri, every year about October, and then was seen sporadically until spring. The "Ghost of Paris" was
said to frighten children, and cause grown men to run down the middle of
the main street, yelling for help. Whatever "she" was, the "Ghost" certainly seems to be the Midwest's precursor to, and female relative of, the
Mad Gasser of Mattoon.

Until the late summer of 1944, Mattoon, Illinois, had nothing in
its history to distinguish itself beyond the fact that in 1861 General
Ulysses S. Grant had arrived there to muster the 21st Illinois Infantry
into state service. Other than that, Mattoon was a typical, peaceful little Midwestern city (population 15,827 in the 1940 census), depend-
ing for its livelihood on the railroads and the prosperous farm lands
that surround it.

Then one night the first of a series of events would occur that would
shake Mattoon out of its complacent anonymity and draw to it the attention of the entire nation. And within two weeks its citizens would be the
objects of ridicule for falling victim, so it was said, to classic mass hysteria because they insisted something was happening to them that authori-

ties said could not be taking place. In the end Mattoon, and perhaps the truth as well, would lose.

During the early morning hours of August 31st, a resident of the city woke up feeling ill. He tottered out of bed, stumbled into the bathroom, and vomited. Then he roused his wife to ask her if she had left on the gas.

"I don't think so," she said, "but I'll check." When she tried to get up, she discovered that she was paralyzed.

Shortly after, a housewife in another part of town awoke when she heard her daughter coughing. She got up to find she could barely walk.

The next evening, about 11:00 p.m., Mrs. Bert Kearney, asleep in a bedroom shared with her three-year-old daughter Dorothy, was stirred from slumber at the sudden appearance of a peculiar smell. "I first noticed a sickening sweet odor in the bedroom," she later told a reporter for the local newspaper, "but at the time I thought that it might be from flowers outside the window. But the odor grew stronger and I began to feel a paralysis of my legs and lower body. I got frightened and screamed."

Mrs. Kearney's neighbors searched the yard and the rest of the neighborhood without finding any clues to the origin of the mysterious gas. Police investigation proved similarly unproductive. But at 12:30 a.m., as he arrived home from work, Mr. Kearney caught a glimpse of someone who matched the later descriptions of the "mad gasser of Mattoon," as the newspapers would call him.

The stranger who stood at the window was, said Kearney, "tall, dressed in dark clothing and wearing a tight-fitting cap." When Kearney approached, he fled. Kearney pursued, but could not catch him.

The next day Mrs. Kearney complained of having burned lips and a parched mouth and throat.

It was the Kearney report that brought the *Mattoon Journal-Gazette* into the picture. By handling the events in an extremely sensationalistic manner (its initial story refers to Mrs. Kearney as the "first victim," strongly implying that there "would be more victims"), the *Journal-Gazette* would open itself to controversy and severe criticism. Several years later a writer for the *Journal of Abnormal and Social Psychology* would blame the paper for in effect "manufacturing" the scare and frightening citizens to the extent that they took leave of their senses enough to spend the next fourteen days imagining that a "mad gasser" was prowling the streets. That particular approach to the Mattoon affair has become the standard one, but as we shall see, it does not quite explain everything.

By September 5th the police had received four more reports of "gas attacks." Each time the individuals concerned said they first had sniffed a "sickly sweet odor," then become nauseated and partially paralyzed for 30 to 90 minutes. During the afternoon of September 5th, according to a news account, police "checked what they thought might be a hideout for the anesthetic prowler but found nothing to bear out the theory." That same evening a woman named Mrs. Beulah Cordes handed over to police the first concrete physical traces of the gasser's existence.

Mrs. Cordes and her husband Carl had returned home, entering their house through the back door, about 10:30 that night. Mrs. Cordes proceeded to the front door and while unlocking it, she spotted a white cloth on the porch. Curious, she picked it up and noticed that it had been soaked in some kind of liquid.

"When I inhaled the fumes from the cloth," she related subsequently, "I had a sensation similar to coming in contact with a strong electric current. The feeling raced down my body to my feet and then seemed to settle in my knees. It was a feeling of paralysis."

She suddenly vomited. Several minutes later her lips and face swelled and burned, her mouth began to bleed and she lost her ability to speak. Two hours later the condition was gone.

Police found a skeleton key and an empty lipstick tube on the porch where Mrs. Cordes had seen the cloth. These two items led them to suggest that a prowler had been trying to break into the house when he heard the couple approaching.

That same night a Mattoon housewife heard someone at the bedroom window, but before she could act gas had seeped into the room and she was partially paralyzed for several minutes.

Spurred in part by the *Journal-Gazette*'s lurid accounts of the "fiendish prowler," who in fact had neither robbed nor molested anyone, public alarm mounted. Police Chief E. C. Cole ordered the ten men on the force on twenty-four-hour duty, and Thomas V. Wright, City Commissioner of Public Health, appealed to the State Department of Public Safety to dispatch investigators to the city. Mrs. Cordes' cloth was passed on to chemists at the University of Illinois for analysis.

"This is one of the strangest cases I have ever encountered in many years of police work," Richard T. Piper, a crime specialist with the State Department of Public Safety, told reporters. His mystification is not hard to understand. The weird attacks, which were rising in intensity, seemed senseless and random. The only "pattern," a pretty dubious one, was that most of the victims were women; this was not necessarily significant since a large percentage of the city's male population was in uniform and fighting overseas. The lack of any obvious "motive" would prove a major factor in dismissing the attacks as hysterical imaginings.

On Wednesday night, the 6th, the gasser struck three times. At 10:00 Mrs. Ardell Spangler smelled a sickly sweet odor, felt a peculiar dryness in her throat and lips, and suffered from nausea. Mrs. Laura Junken reported a similar experience shortly after midnight and Fred Goble told of one at 1:00 a.m. Robert Daniels, a neighbor of Goble, saw a "tall man" fleeing from the house.

The *Decatur Herald* for September 8th summarized the events of the preceding several days:

"Twelve persons in the last week have been visited by the nocturnal prowler who shoots an unidentified chemical into bed chambers through open windows. Cases have been reported in all sections of Mattoon.

"Victims report that the first symptom is an electric shock, which passes completely through the body. Later nausea develops, followed by partial paralysis. They also suffer burned mouths and throats and their faces become swollen.

"Mattoon police advanced the theory yesterday that the marauder was a young person experimenting with a chemistry set....

"Mayor E. E. Richardson said he planned to call a meeting of the city council to authorize a reward for the capture of the prowler if he is not found soon."

Other victims, whose stories were not released until Friday, included Mrs. Cordie Taylor and Glenda Hendershott, an 11-year-old girl who was discovered unconscious in her bedroom.

Thursday night was relatively calm in Mattoon, the first breathing spell for the community since the beginning of the month. Police took calls from three people who said they had seen a strange man in their neighborhoods, but these reports may have been anxious citizens jumping to conclusions. Mrs. Mae Williams' story may have been more than that, however. Mrs. Williams notified police that at midnight a tall, dark man answering the gasser's description had attempted to force open her door but her screams had driven him away.

The *Journal-Gazette,* while taking note of the reduced number of attacks, still managed to strike a note of alarm. "Mattoon's 'Mad Anesthetist' apparently took a respite from his maniacal forays Thursday night," John Miller observed in the Friday issue, "and while many terror-stricken people were somewhat relieved, they were inclined to hold their breath and wonder when and where he might strike again."

And the citizenry were not taking any chances. If the police could not catch the elusive prowler, they would do it themselves, they decided—and they took to the streets with rifles and shotguns looking for suspects. For their part, the police, recipients of considerable public abuse for their failure to stop the attacks, succeeded only in collaring one lowly suspect whom they were forced to release after he passed a lie-detector test. All the while anti-police and anti–city hall feelings grew by leaps and bounds as the helplessness of officialdom became increasingly clear.

Businessmen announced that on Saturday afternoon they would lead a mass protest rally to put additional pressure on the already-harried Mattoon force, who, it must be said in fairness, were doing the best they could under impossible circumstances. To local officials the gasser now was more than a menace to public safety, he was rapidly evolving into a political liability as well.

That night the gasser resumed his attacks, hitting first the residence of Mrs. Violet Driskell. Mrs. Driskell and her daughter Romona, 11, awoke late in the evening to the sounds of someone trying to remove the storm sash from their bedroom window. They dashed outside to the porch to call for help, but fumes overcame Romona and she vomited. At the same moment her mother sighted a man sprinting away.

Shortly afterwards, at 1:45 a.m., the prowler sprayed gas through a partly-open window into a bedroom where Mrs. Russell Bailey, Katherine Tuzzo, and Mrs. Genevieve Haskell and her seven-year-old son lay sleeping. Elsewhere, Miss Frances Smith, principal of the Columbian Grade School, and her sister Maxine sniffed the mysterious gas and fell ill. The *Journal-Gazette* put it this way:

"The first infiltration of gas caught them in their beds. Gasping and choking they awoke and soon felt partial paralysis grip their legs and arms. Later, while awake, the other attacks came and they saw a thin, blue, smoke-like vapor spreading throughout the room.

"Just before the gas with its flower-like odor came pouring into the room they heard a strange 'buzzing' sound outside the house and expressed the belief that the sound was made by the 'madman's spraying apparatus' in operation."

By now the town was beside itself with fear. At the last moment state authorities succeeded in talking organizers of the protest out of having their meeting, arguing that it would serve no purpose but to increase the hysteria. They promised to bring in a large force of state police. Already two FBI agents from Springfield had slipped quietly into Mattoon. Their chief interest, according to rumor, was in trying to identify the type of gas the prowler was using; presumably, once the identification had been made, it could be traced to its source. (As I have pointed out in an article in *Fortean Times,* this incident seems to be a true-life example of the FBI having an X-Files unit in operation as early as 1944.) Mrs. Cordes' cloth had been of no help in that respect, for the State Crime Bureau's analysis had revealed nothing. In the meantime authorities worked with only limited success to keep the vigilante bands off the streets.

While solid evidence was lacking, there was no shortage of guesses to explain the event. Most theories, taking cognizance of the apparent senselessness of the whole affair, centered on the possibility that the gasser was a lunatic. State's Attorney W. K. Kidwell even checked with Illinois mental hospitals for information on individuals they had released recently. Police Commissioner Wright opined that the anesthetist might be an "eccentric inventor" who had devised a new weapon that he was testing on local people. The wildest story of all, whose origins are unfortunately obscure, contended that the culprit was really an "apeman"...a most interesting idea in view of the tradition and history of anthropoid and Bigfoot-type reports in central and southern Illinois.

Then on Saturday night, dozens of armed farmers from the surrounding area joined citizens and police in patrolling Mattoon. Still, at least six alleged attacks took place. One of these was reported by the Smith sisters, who had been victimized just the night before. Another couple, Mr. and

Mrs. Stewart B. Scott, returned late in the evening to their farm on the southern edge of Mattoon to find it filled with the sickly sweet gas.

The next morning Commissioner Wright issued a statement urging residents to get a grip on themselves:

"There is no doubt but [sic] that a gas maniac exists and has made a number of attacks," he said. "But many of the reported attacks are nothing more than hysteria. Fear of the gas man is entirely out of proportion to the menace of the relatively harmless gas he is spraying. The whole town is sick with hysteria and last night it spread out into the country."

Wright's remarks were aimed obliquely at discouraging further reports, the only way city officials could see out of a situation that was at once dangerous to the public and embarrassing to the city politically. The police commissioner's directive ordering those making reports to submit to examination at Mattoon Memorial Hospital was even more to the point. Since analysis of the Cordes cloth already had shown that the "gas" left no traces, its victims risked looking like fools.

The city fathers had carefully shifted the burden of responsibility from themselves to those whose safety they had failed to protect. And now the victims, in a dilemma worthy of Kafka, had to answer for their own victimization.

Most of the gasser's activities took place on the northwest side of town, one of the city's better residential districts, and Sunday night he struck there again, spraying gas into the kitchen of the Kenneth Fitzpatrick residence. Mrs. Fitzpatrick nearly collapsed, and when her husband came to her rescue he was almost overcome himself.

A short time later three sisters, two of them young girls aged twelve and eight, smelled a sickly sweet gas in their living room. The oldest, Mrs. Richard Daniels, was affected seriously enough for a physician to order her to bed.

That night was the climax of Mattoon's mad gasser scare and after that events moved rapidly to denouement. Newspaper accounts affected increasingly skeptical tones and the police now openly suggested to those who reported being attacked that they were imagining things. To those who had not smelled the gas, seen the gasser or chased him through their neighborhoods, the possibility that he might exist at all seemed more and more remote After all, how could anyone have so completely escaped detection when all the resources of the city and the state were mobilized against him? And besides, none of it made any sense.

On the evening of the eleventh police received numerous calls, but with only the most perfunctory investigation, dismissed them all as false alarms. But in one case a physician who appeared on the scene shortly after an attack, while finding no evidence of gas on the victim's person, conceded that there was a "peculiar odor" in the room.

Officialdom was not impressed. Anxious to wrap everything up as quickly as possible, Police Chief Cole called a press conference the next day and said that he and his men had cracked the case. "It was a mistake from beginning to end," he asserted. "Local police, in cooperation with state officers, have checked and rechecked all reported cases," he said, "and we find absolutely no evidence to support stories that have been told. Hysteria must be blamed for such seemingly accurate accounts of supposed victims.

"However, we have found that large quantities of carbon tetrachloride are used in war work done at the Atlas Imperial Diesel Engine Company plant and that it is an odor which can be carried to all parts of the city as the wind shifts. It also leaves stains on cloth such as those found on a rag at a Mattoon home."

A spokesman for the plant was quick to reply. W. J. Webster, works manager, said, "We use tetrachloride at the Atlas plant only in fire extinguishers. Trichlorethylene gas is used in our work and it is odorless and produces no ill effects in the air."

The *Decatur Review* added its own objections to the police claims: "There was no explanation of why several screens had been cut prior to reported gassing by several persons....Many persons wondered why the odor from the Atlas Diesel plant hadn't caused illness among the towns-people before...."

Nor, of course, did the official explanation account for the sightings of the man believed to be the gasser, the same one who was seen fleeing from houses shortly after attacks, sometimes by those who did not know that an attack was taking place at the moment. One such witness, who chased the stranger several blocks, sticks to his story even today. So do the gas victims I was able to interview in preparing this chapter. And there is still the concrete testimony of Mrs. Cordes' cloth.

The last recorded attack was made on September 13th, when a "woman dressed in man's clothing" sprayed gas into Mrs. Bertha Bench's bedroom. The next morning she and her son Orville, 20, found imprints of high-heeled shoes on the ground by the bedroom window.

And so, as the saying goes, the mad gasser of Mattoon passed into history.

The truth about Mattoon probably will never be known. First and most obvious, the genuine hysteria of the period helped to create a confusion of its own and it is likely that some of the reports, especially those made in the last few days, may have described occurrences real only in the minds of the persons involved. Second, most of the principals are either dead or impossible to locate, and in any case memories of the event have dimmed over the years, though they have not faded altogether. At best we can only guess what really happened, and point to parallel phenomena of which the Mattoon citizens could not have been aware.

It is noteworthy, for example, that on February 1, 1944, three people living in a house in Coatesville, Pa., died after inhaling a mysterious "sweet-smelling gas" of unknown origin. Neighbors fell ill and had to seek medical attention.

And in December 1961, at a Baptist church in Houston, Tex., a "sickening sweet gas" disrupted a Christmas program, sending a hundred persons reeling outside into the fresh air. The victims complained of nausea, headaches, vomiting and sweating, and eight individuals, mostly children, were admitted to the hospital for oxygen treatment. Firemen could find no cause. Perhaps someone suggested "mass hysteria."

Gasser's Cousin: Springheel Jack

The mad gasser of Mattoon was not the first of his kind either. Victorian England knew a peculiar character dubbed "Springheel Jack." In the 1961 article "The Mystery of Springheel Jack," J. Vyner wrote:

"The intruder was tall, thin and powerful. He had a prominent nose, and bony fingers of immense power which resembled claws. He was incredibly agile. He wore a long, flowing cloak, of the sort affected by opera-goers, soldiers and strolling actors. On his head was a tall, metallic-seeming helmet. Beneath the cloak were close-fitting garments of some glittering material like oil-skin or metallic mesh. There was a lamp strapped to his chest. Oddest of all: the creature's ears were cropped or pointed like those of an animal."

His name was "Springheel Jack," or at least that is what people called him. On the heels of his boots he supposedly wore springs, hence his name. Those springs enabled him to jump great distances, clearing roads and eight-foot walls without difficulty. (One hundred years later, when German parachutists tried to ease the shock of landing with sprung boots, they discovered that it didn't work; all they got for their troubles were broken ankles.)

When the *London Times* called him an "unmanly brute," the newspaper was referring to his conduct, not his biological composition. But there is something decidedly unearthly about this Victorian denizen who, from his first appearance in the dark lanes of Middlesex, England, in November 1837 to his last 40 years later, behaved in a manner so bizarre and so without apparent motivation that the only parallel events seem to be the weird incidents that took place in Illinois a century later.

Like the Illinois mad gasser whose depredations have been examined herein, Jack was vicious but not deadly. His victims suffered fear and discomfort but they survived, never understanding exactly what happened to them or why. His operation, whatever it was, began in Middlesex where he frightened and sometimes assaulted lone nocturnal wayfarers, some of them public officials who complained to the Lord Mayor of London, who in turn set up horse patrols to scour the suburban areas of the city. That did not stop Jack. He moved from village to village and for a time he took up residence on the grounds of Kensington Palace, where he was seen climbing over the park wall at midnight and bouncing across the lawns. He seemed to prefer private parks where he rested before setting out to commit fresh outrages.

The *Times* for February 22, 1838, details one such "outrage." Two days before, at 8:45 in the evening, a violent ringing of the bell summoned Jane Alsop, 18, to the front door of her home in the village of Old Ford. When she saw a man standing outside, she asked him what he wanted. "For God's sake bring me a light," he snapped, "for we have caught Springheel Jack here in the lane!" Immediately Miss Alsop left to find a candle; when she returned, she handed it to the stranger. In the words of the *Times:*

The instant she had done so…he threw off his outer garment [a large cloak], and applying the lighted candle to his breast, presented a most hideous and frightful appearance, and vomited forth a quantity of blue and white flame from his mouth, and his eyes resembled red balls of fire. From the hasty glance which her fright enabled her to get at his person, she observed that he wore a large helmet, and his dress, which appeared to fit him very tight, seemed to her to resemble white oil skin. Without uttering a sentence he darted at her, and catching her partly by her dress and the back part of her neck, placed her head under one of his arms, and commenced tearing her dress with his claws, which she was certain were of some metallic substance, and by considerable exertion got away from him and ran towards the house to get in. Her assailant, however, followed her, and caught her on the steps leading to the hall door, when he again used considerable violence, tore her neck and arms with his claws, as well as a quantity of hair from her head; but she was at length rescued from his grasp by one of her sisters. Miss Alsop added that she had suffered considerably all night from the shock she had sustained, and was then in extreme pain, both from the injury done to her arm, and the wounds and scratches inflicted by the miscreant about her shoulders and neck with his claws or hands.

Within a day or two of the Old Ford incident, according to the 1838 Annual *Register,* two sisters named Scales, while passing along Green Dragon-alley in Limehouse, spotted a strange-looking man lurking nearby. He suddenly stepped up to one of them, "spurted a quantity of blue flame right in her face" and walked away. Lucy Scales dropped to the ground, unable to see, and fell into a violent fit which did not subside until several hours later.

Their brother, whose house they had left just prior to the attack, heard his sisters screaming and rushed to the scene. His other sister described the assailant as "tall, thin and of gentlemanly appearance," covered with a cloak and carrying in front of him a small lamp. He had remained silent during the entire incident.

Theories about Springheel Jack's identity were legion. One had it that he was a dressed-up kangaroo that had escaped from a circus act. Another held the Marquis of Waterford, a deranged peer whose activities had led to his arrest on several occasions, responsible for the scare.

There was no accounting, however, for Jack's apparent return in 1872, this time in the Peckham area of southeast London. Said the *News of the World* for November 17, 1872: "We can hardly be expected to credit that the figure is eight feet in height, springs over stone walls and lofty hedges, and on nearing a victim changes from grim blackness to luminous white." But the reports, some of them involving several witnesses, were hard to dismiss. The *News* recounted an incident that allegedly occurred to two teenaged daughters of the headmaster of Dulwich College and their governess, who had seen "a figure enveloped in white and with arms extended" moving toward them from across the road. Their screams frightened it away.

But in 1877 Jack was back. On April 28, 1877, the *Illustrated Police News* stated: "A curious story comes from Aldershot. For some time past, the sentries on two outlying posts have been frightened by the appearance at night of two spectral figures. The figures, glowing with phosphorous, are in the habit of suddenly manifesting themselves, making tremendous springs of 10 or 12 yards at a time and upsetting the sentry before he had been able to collect himself sufficiently to oppose earthly arms to his ghostly visitants. The latter do him no bodily injury, contenting themselves with upsetting the poor man, after which they mysteriously disappear. So great has been the alarm that it has been found necessary to post double sentries."

Later, sentries did, indeed, fire on Jack.

And the *News,* in its November 3rd issue, lists this curious item: "For some time Newport, near Lincoln, has been disturbed by a man dressed in a sheepskin or something of the kind. The man has springs on his boots and can jump a height of 15 feet. The other night he jumped on a college, got into a window by the roof and so frightened the ladies that one has not yet recovered."

Other Kin: Houston Bat Man

All of this is unlikely enough, but not nearly so unlikely—or so discomforting—as the affair of the "Houston Bat Man," which carries the activities of Springheel Jack, or someone much like him, into our own time and links them with the great 20th century riddle of the flying saucers. The "Houston Bat Man" also discourages us from treating the legend of Springheel Jack as no more than a bit of Victorian folklore.

According to witness testimony, at 2:30 a.m. on June 18, 1953, Mrs. Hilda Walker, Judy Meyers and Howard Phillips were sitting on the front porch of an apartment building, seeking relief from the summer heat, which was robbing them of sleep, when suddenly Mrs. Walker glanced up.

"About 25 feet away I saw a huge shadow cross the lawn," she said. "I thought at first it was the magnified reflection of a big moth caught in the nearby street light. Then the shadow seemed to bounce upward into a pecan tree. We all looked up.

"That's when we saw it. It was the figure of a man with wings like a bat. He was dressed in gray or black tight-fitting clothes. He stood there for about 30 seconds, swaying on the branch of the old pecan tree. Suddenly the light began to fade slowly. Little Judy screamed as the light died out and the figure disappeared.

"Immediately afterwards we heard a loud swoosh over the housetops across the street. It was like a white flash of a torpedo-shaped object."

Phillips told the *Houston Chronicle* that the figure "was encased in a halo of light" and dressed in what looked like a paratrooper uniform. He stood about six-and-a-half-feet tall and was framed in a dim gray light.

Was this "Springheel Jack" one hundred years later? The details are compelling—the "bouncing" motion, the luminosity, even the "wings," which could have been a cloak imperfectly observed in the half-light—except one, and that is the peculiar gas-like substance Jack allegedly sprayed in the faces of his victims. It would take the mad gasser of Mattoon to supply that last dangerous item.

Illinois' Blue Phantom

Meanwhile, back in Illinois, by 1952 Mattoon's mad gasser was only a memory. Chief Cole had officially disposed of his presence, and in a 1954 issue of the *Journal of Abnormal and Social Psychology*, Donald M. Johnson—arguing that even the supposed gas existed only in the minds of hapless hysterics scared out of their senses by the *Journal-Gazette*'s sensationalistic reporting—did it scientifically. No one betrayed any willingness to consider the disquieting alternative: that the mad gasser might have been a real, if shadowy, manifestation of some unimaginable Unknown. If his motives were incomprehensible, if he inexplicably evaded capture, if he did not behave as some good earth-bound criminal should, then why could he not have existed? And so neither, as it turned out, could the "blue phantom" of 1952.

The blue phantom first showed up, it is said, on U.S. 66 near Joliet, Illinois, late in May. Two drivers independently reported that someone had fired at them from a moving blue car. One of them was wounded, though not seriously. Later the same day another driver said a man in a blue automobile had taken a shot at him, this time three miles south of Lincoln on U.S. 66.

On the afternoon of June 2nd the phantom chose a new tactic: ambush. Edward Smith of St. Louis, Illinois, was driving just south of the Sangamon River when something hit his car. He slowed down and glanced back just in time to see a man jump from bushes beside the road, hop into a big blue car, and speed north on Route 48. Police interviewed an eleven-year-old girl who had watched the sniper make his escape in what she thought was either a Ford or Buick sedan. Highway patrolmen speculated that a .38 caliber bullet had caused the crease in Smith's back window.

By June 8th there had been ten reported shootings along central Illinois highways, including one in which the sniper's bullet shattered a windshield. State police and sheriff's deputies set up roadblocks along a 70-mile area and even employed the services of a low-flying airplane in an attempt to nab the gunman—but to no avail. On June 10th the phantom, as if to thumb his nose at those so desperately trying to stop him, chose as his fifteenth target a Marengo squad car. Police officer Lawrence Brown, who had been patrolling the streets at dawn when the incident occurred, chased his assailant's car at speeds up to 90 m.p.h. but could not overtake it.

The same day, State Police Chief Thomas J. O'Donnell was telling reporters, "We have not relaxed our search and we are investigating every case but we are not convinced there is a phantom gunman or that any shots were fired in most of the 'shooting incidents' reported.

"We have yet to find anyone who saw a gun or who could give anything definite about the description of the sniper. On the other hand, we have a maze of vague and conflicting information that does not add up to the conclusion that one gunman is causing all these reports."

Perhaps not. On June 9th, on Route 66 east of Springfield, William Moffit's car window was struck by a bullet fired from a *dark green* automobile speeding by in the opposite direction. But it is unlikely that Moffit took seriously O'Donnell's theory that nearly all the "sniping" incidents resulted from stones hitting cars or from the setting off of "torpedo" firecrackers. Neither, one suspects, did a truck driver in the Clinton area who early in the morning of June 17th saw two bullets penetrate his windshield. Police officers who inspected the holes concluded they were made by .22 caliber slugs fired from an automatic rifle. Nothing was said about stones or firecrackers.

The previous evening, in fact just a matter of hours before the Clinton incident, D. L. Weatherford had observed someone standing on a bridge on Route 121 north of Mount Pulaski. The "someone," a man who wore khaki shirt and trousers, held a revolver and stood close to a parked blue Chrysler sedan. Weatherford did not stop to ask questions.

It was a *blue* Ford, however, which a Decatur couple pursued through the city the evening of June 19th after its occupant ungraciously took a potshot at them. And at Mattoon (of all places) the same night police investigated a report from Fred Manley who said a man in a *yellow* Chevrolet panel truck had fired at him with a shotgun about 7:30 p.m. as he was driving on Route 16 between Charleston and Ashmore.

Near Champaign on June 24th, in what seems to have been the last appearance of the phantom sniper—or at least a phantom sniper—a man in a *black* sedan pulled up alongside a car driven by L. J. Wiles and let loose a volley of four shots, one of which crashed through Wiles' right window. Wiles, understandably shaken, still managed to collect his wits enough to chase the gunman's car into Champaign, but lost it in the city traffic.

The phantom was lost to history as well apparently, for that was the last anyone saw of him, or them, or whomever—unless we count the epidemic of cracked windshields in Bellingham, Washington, during the spring of 1954, which really is something else altogether.

Conceivably some "phantom snipings" were not that at all, but the work of demented individuals taking advantage of the publicity in order to commit vicious "practical jokes" of their own. Fred Wanley's attacker may have been one of those.

But the real phantom comes out of the same eerie mold as Mattoon's Mad Gasser (and probably England's Springheel Jack, too), a weird entity that leaves traces but remains curiously untraceable. The bullets the sniper shoots into windows do not pass through the car and out the windows on the other side, yet they cannot be found inside the vehicle; and he escapes a police dragnet sufficiently extensive to snare a more mundane law-breaker. But we have physical evidence—wounds and shattered glass—that he, or at any rate *something,* does exist, Chief O'Donnell to the contrary.

Like the other phenomena in Mysterious America, the Mad Gasser and his kin are tangible but intangible, real but unreal. Certainly nothing the conventional mind, given the choice, would wish to deal with. But when forced to, it will opt inevitably for the easy, irrelevant answer.

Charles Fort summed it all up in his inimitable way when he wrote, "In hosts of minds, today, are impressions that the word 'eerie' means nothing except convenience to makers of crossword puzzles. There are gulfs of the unaccountable but they are bridged by terminology.... Probably vast holes of ignorance always will be bridged by very slender pedantries."

Today, Mattoon hardly remembers its Gasser history. During 2000, Mattoon was the first town in America to host the Cal Ripken Baseball World Series for 11-12 year olds. But in 1944, something more sinister was visiting the streets of this all-American city.

CHAPTER 21

The Phantom Clowns

The new multicolored clothing on the stranger made people feel slightly uneasy. The man's name, Bunting, was a reflection of his attire, the residents of the small Westphalian town were soon to learn. The tall, thin newcomer offered his services to the town council, and they readily accepted. Pest control was a serious problem in 1284 and this fellow Bunting said he could get rid of all the rats in town. Thus the beginning of the legend of the Pied Piper of Hamelin was born. Bunting did lure the rats with his mystical music into drowning in the Weser River, but the townspeople refused to pay him. The Pied Piper decided to collect in another fashion. On St. John's Day, June 24th, Bunting returned to Hamelin and piped his haunting tune. Soon all one hundred and thirty children were enchanted into following him out of the town and into a cave in the Koppenberg Mountain. The entrance was sealed and the children were trapped forever.

The legend of the Pied Piper of Hamelin is said by some scholars to be based on truth. Others feel the story grew out of the Children's Crusade of 1212 in which 20,000 young crusaders marched towards the East and were never seen again. Whatever its origin, the tale is a well known one, having been retold in many ways at various times. Robert Browning's poem, for example, was written in the 1800s, and places the events of the Piper's last visit to Hamelin on July 22, 1376. The town of Hamelin does exist, and perhaps the sinister character and deeds of Bunting did as well.

In the spring of 1981, Boston, Massachusetts appears to have been the port of entry for a new version of the Pied Piper story. During the first week of May some individuals in multicolored clothes just like Bunting's began trying to entice schoolchildren into coming along with them. The reports of clowns in vans bothering children were openly discussed in the newspapers, by the School Committee, the area police, and scores of parents and children.

On May 6, 1981, the Boston police, responding to persistent complaints, warned that men in clown suits were harassing elementary school children. One of the men was seen wearing a clown suit only from the waist up; from the waist down he was naked. According to reports, the clown had driven a black van near the recreational-horseshoe site of Franklin Park in the Roxbury area of Boston between 4:00 and 6:00 p.m. He also appeared in the Jamaica Plain neighborhood of Boston near the Mary F. Curley School.

A day earlier, in the adjoining city of Brookline, two clown men reportedly had tried to lure children into their van with offers of candy. The Brookline police had a good description of the van: older model, black, with ladders on the side, a broken front headlight and no hubcaps. After the clown men and van had been seen near the Lawrence Elementary School on Longwood Avenue in Brookline, the police told school administrators to be "extra cautious."

The previous week Investigative Counselor Daniel O'Connell of the Boston Public School District had sent a memo to the district's elementary and middle school principals. He wrote, "It has been brought to the attention of the police department and the district office that adults dressed as clowns have been bothering children to and from school.

ILLUSTRATION BY PHIL HEMSTREET/BETH FIDELER

Phantom Clown

Please advise all students that they must stay away from strangers, especially ones dressed as clowns."

By May 8th reports of clown men in vans harassing children had come in from East Boston, Charlestown, Cambridge, Canton, Randolph, and other cities near Boston. Police were stopping pickup trucks and vans with clowns delivering birthday greetings and "clown-a-grams," but no child molesters were arrested.

Frustrated policemen pointed out that virtually all of the reported sightings originated with children aged five to seven. The headlines in the May 9th issue of the *Boston Globe* told the story: "Police discount reports of clowns bothering kids." The public had been calmed and that was the end of the story. Or so the papers would have had us believe.

However, 50 miles south, in Providence, Rhode Island, reports of clown men disturbing children were coming to the attention of psychiatric social workers counseling the city's youth. Perhaps these sightings can be explained as spillovers from Boston. But the reports since Providence are more difficult to dismiss.

The focus of activity shifted 1000 miles west to Kansas City, Kansas, and Kansas City, Missouri. On the afternoon of May 22nd police cruisers on the Missouri side crisscrossed the city chasing a knife-wielding clown in a yellow van that had been reported at six different elementary schools. Earlier in the day, at 8:30, a mother had watched a yellow van approach her children as they walked to a school bus stop. The van stopped and someone inside spoke to her two girls who then screamed and fled; the vehicle sped away. The children told their mother that a man dressed as a clown and carrying a knife had ordered them inside. By noon the police had received dozens of similar reports—of a clown in a yellow van. The calls did not taper off until five o'clock that afternoon.

The previous week in Kansas, schoolchildren said a clown had chased them home from school and threatened them if they didn't get into his van. Some reports claimed the clown brandished a sword instead of a knife.

Residents of the two Kansas Cities called it the "Killer Clown" affair. Some parents in Kansas were even keeping their children out of school.

Before long "group hysteria" was touted as the explanation for the reports. But still firsthand accounts continued to be reported. LaTanya Johnson, a sixth-grade student at Fairfax Elementary School, said she saw the clown near the school. "He was by the fence and ran down through the big yard when some of the kids ran over there. He ran toward a yellow van. He was dressed in a black shirt with a devil on the front. He had two candy canes down each side of his pants. The pants were black too, I think; I don't remember much about his face," she told a *Kansas City Star* reporter.

"These kids are terrified," one school principal remarked.

And Kansas City, Missouri, and Kansas City, Kansas, were not the only midwestern cities in which children were terrified. Omaha also had reports of clowns bothering children, as did Denver.

In Pennsylvania during the first week of June 1981, children in the Hill District of Pittsburgh said two men dressed in clown suits and driving in a van had bothered them. These were the first of a series of peculiar reports of costumed figures in the Pittsburgh area.

In the Garfield neighborhood of the city someone wearing a pink and white rabbit costume reportedly frightened children and eluded capture by hopping from his blue van and scampering into an East Liberty bar. Later in the week police got a report of a "rabbit" in Allegheny Cemetery.

Some of the other weird stories involving costumed persons included accounts of "Spider-Man" joining forces with a "gorilla" and a "clown" in Arlington Heights, Pa., and trying to entice a boy into a vehicle. During the last week in May, Police Inspector William Moore said the department was getting 15 such reports every day. After a sighting of a clown on Bentley Drive in Terrace Village, police conducted a search with the help of two canine patrols and 100 kids with clubs. The police and volunteers never were able to capture any clowns but witnesses insisted the costumed figures they had seen were real and not imaginary.

The story of the phantom clowns went unnoticed on a national scale until I began getting a hint we were in the midst of a major flap of a new phenomenon. Slowly, after contacting fellow researchers by phone and mail, I discovered the phantom clown enigma went beyond Boston, Kansas City, and Omaha. Indeed, the reports filtering into me demonstrated that a far-reaching mystery was developing. In the individual cities, the local media were not aware they were living through a series of puzzling events that were occurring nationwide. Only through the Fortean underground was I able to ascertain the depth and breadth of the phantom clown drama. The national media was not spreading word of this. Something quite unusual was happening in America in the spring of 1981.

But what is going on here? Group hysteria, as one newsman would have us believe? Or more? Phantom clowns in at least six major cities, spanning over a thousand miles of America in the space of one month is quite a mystery. Were the "clowns in vans" being sighted elsewhere in the United States? Are they still being seen? Only time will tell, but something strange happened earlier in the year in Mineral Point, Wisconsin, which served as a precursor.

During the last week in March, 1981, the small village of Mineral Point was swamped with sightings of a strange entity which terrorized teenagers. This phantom was labeled a "vampire" and seemed to haunt the Graceland Cemetery.

One police officer actually saw the "vampire." Officer Jon Pepper described the being as a "huge person with a white-painted face" wearing a dark cape. (Strangely, the Mineral Point Vampire's white-face seems to be almost derisively related to the greasepaint of clowns!) As the events unfolded in Wisconsin, an incident in Washington, D.C., would distract the media's attention from the vampire's terror. The sightings quickly faded from the press's and public's consciousness when President Ronald Reagan was nearly assassinated on March 30th.

The Mineral Point Vampire seems to have a host of deadringers in the Fortean and occult literature. Springheel Jack of Victorian England had pointed ears, was tall and thin, and wore a long, flowing cloak. Springheel Jack terrorized women of his day with a mysterious blue light he shone from his chest, and the weird mist that issued from this "lantern." Closely allied to the Mineral Point Vampire, also, is the Mad Gasser of Mattoon who sent fear into the heart of that Illinois community in 1944. And then there is the strange story of the dark-coated, tall "grinning man" that stepped out of a UFO on a rainy night in 1966, and into the life of Woody Derenberger of Mineral Wells, West Virginia. Woody Derenberger's encounter propelled him into the world of contactees. From Mineral Point, Wisconsin to Mineral Wells, West Virginia, a connectiveness between these mysterious beings seems to exist.

Since 1981, the world has become a much different place for children. Phantom social workers, so well chronicled in the pages of *Fortean Times* during the 1990s, attempted to come take the children away in the United Kingdom. But in North America, the very real school shootings and satanic scares of the last decade have taken a toll on innocence here. Phantom clowns were sinister enough in 1981; in 2000, they are downright scary.

Sometimes, knowledge of my research on phantom clowns from the 1983 edition of this book made life uncomfortably humorous for some. James Boyd, a Maine Fortean, wrote me in 2000: "I was lunching with a local Chief of Detectives, and he mentioned a bizarre case from the recent past. It was a 'Clown' flap picture perfect. When I stopped him and continued his story for him he became convinced that I knew 'Too Much' of what the police held back from publication. I had to bring him my copy of [your] book to be removed as a suspect! He was so impressed that he gave me the class notes from the seminars on 'Occult Based Crime' that he had attended. They implicated all Forteans as potential Satan Worshipers and general Lowlifes. Fort would be rolling in his grave!"

Stephen King's *It*, a novel about a scary clown that tries to abduct and take children into a sewer, wasn't even a book when the wave occurred. But today people try to kindly inform me that the phantom clown sightings of 1981 were just mass hysteria caused by King's book—even though the first editions of King's book were not published in New York by Viking, and London by Hodder & Stoughton until 1986.

Michael Goss considers the above phantom clown events in his "The Lessons of Folklore" (*Magonia 38,* January 1991). Goss gives insights into why reports like the phantom clowns, which to him are a subform of satanic child abuse allegations, "feel," and are treated, like they are just Urban Legends. He feels that they are "folkloric." Goss writes:

> "Folkloric": a slightly gawky adjective and perhaps one that exudes too much an aroma of musty libraries and still mustier academics who browse in them. But, a convenient adjective for all that. Can mean more or less what you want it to mean.
>
> What I want it to mean when I'm writing on satanic child abuse—and what I don't want it to mean—goes like this.

When we refer to something as "folkloric" we do not wish to imply that the thing in question has no literal reality, that it's "just a story"—we don't mean that necessarily, though that may turn out to be a true assessment. To call a thing "folkloric" means that it displays aspects familiar to us from the study of folklore. The narrative(s) contained in it show certain similarities, perhaps structural or conceptual, with those found in the folklore canon; there may be types, motifs and subdivisions of either. Even more important, the audience's response to the narrative(s) may fall into a category wherein general rules relating to conviction and perception apply after models we have encountered in contemporary folklore—in which case this response too can be called "folkloric."

* * *

I believe that satanic child abuse allegations are, in these generic senses, folkloric. I do not say they are "entirely folklore" or "only rumours." But in the broadest meaning of the adjective, they are folkloric.

And still they keep popping up in the real world—with names and places attached to the reports. Fortean researcher Richard Hendricks discovered one recently in his home state. The *Wisconsin State Journal* of Madison reported on June 20, 2000: "A man dressed in a complete clown costume and holding three helium balloons tried to lure children into woods near the King James Court Apartments at about 12:30 p.m. Monday, Fitchburg police said."

Then two days later, the *Wisconsin State Journal* ran this article:

Suspicious Clown Had Unique Face Paint

Fitchburg police, investigating a man in clown costume who tried to lure children into woods on Monday, have concluded he's not a "legitimate" clown.

Detective Todd Stetzer, who said he's learned a lot about clowning since the man appeared near the King James Court

Apartments, said the man's black face paint set him apart from any of three mainstream styles of clown costumery.

"That's extremely, extremely unique," he said. "It isn't in the legitimate style of clowning, which kind of leads us to believe the person was using it as a costume only for this purpose (enticement)."

Police have ruled out several clowns who were in the Fitchburg area on legitimate business, such as a clown at a Boy Scouts picnic, he said. "We've been tracking tips down as they come in, but we have nothing definite yet."

Children reported that the man, who was holding three helium balloons, tried to call them over to woods where he stood. His hair or wig was white. He had a round, red nose, a black face, huge red shoes and yellow overalls.

Perhaps the phantom clowns have something to tell us. Certainly the shadowy monk-like figures and checker-shirted characters mentioned so often in the occult and contactee literature have become almost too commonplace and familiar. Even reports from the 1970s told of plaid-shirted Bigfoots being seen. The denizens of the netherworld have apparently dreamed up a new nightmare to shock us. The scores of Fortean, ufological, and flying saucer "people," thus, have now been joined by leagues of phantom clowns in vans. The Men in Black terrorizing UFO witnesses from their Black Cadillacs may be too obviously sinister compared to this new chapter of the story. The cosmic joker is alive and well, and living in a clown suit. The masquerade of the elementals is taking on a new multicolored phase. After all, can you think of anything more frightening than "Ronald McDonald," a modern Pied Piper, with a mission?

Fireside
Thinking...

Wetzel's "It"

CHAPTER 22

The Name Game

As you travel about in this Mysterious America, be it on your way to work or play, or to some vacation destination, you pass many streets, or transit many towns with names we all have come to take for granted. How often have we paused to think about the meaning behind the names? Was the word of some special significance? Was this location named for a person, another place or an event? And if it was named for a person, what did their name originally mean? And who and why was it tacked on to this place? Are there some harmonic insights we can gain from looking a little deeper? Why do some places or even people seem to be the focus of inexplicable events while others are the host of more mundane incidents?

Earlier I discussed devils' names and Fortean places. The fact that some areas had strange and weird vibrations or events connected to them gave Native Americans and later settlers enough evidence to actually label these locales after the Ruler of Hell. In America, the use of the name "devil" regarding certain geographical fixtures, therefore, gives some indication of a history of mystery surrounding these spots.

An interesting English science fiction film illustrates this process—the hidden meanings behind names. In the 1967 movie *Five Million Years to Earth,* a new subway excavation in the Hobbs End section of London unearths an apparent extraterrestrial craft. The scientists involved in the unraveling of this drama soon discover this part of London on Hobbs Lane has a long history of poltergeist, haunting and apparition activities. One keen young researcher discovers an old street sign near the diggings, and she notes the spelling is "Hob's Lane," not "Hobbs Lane." "Hob," it turns out, is another name for "devil," or the "Devil," if you prefer.

Some words do not appear to be what they so calmly convey. "Hob," for example, is an alteration of Robin or Robert, as in Robin Goodfellow, a rustic, a clown (lest we get too far from the phantom clowns). Robin

Goodfellow, sometimes called Puck, was/is a tricksy house sprite or elf in popular English fairy lore. And Puck is sometimes called hobgoblin. Even the descriptive verb "hobble" refers to the word's origins, as the classic view of the Devil shows cloven hooves.

In the United States, consequently, Hobbs, New Mexico, and Hobbs, Indiana, have "devil's names." Although the local folks know a great deal about the strange things happening thereabouts, most probably do not know that the etymological origins of their towns' names flash back to a demonic past. In Indiana, Hobbs had been the location of UFO sightings in the 1950s and 1960s. Hobbs, New Mexico, near the 33-degree latitude (another power point), has experienced a never-ending stream of UFO encounters since Bill Watson's April 1955 sighting became known in ufology as the "Hobbs Incident." Indeed, this southwest corner of New Mexico is a hotbed of so-called flying saucer activity with the most famous event being the "Roswell Incident." Allegedly, as is well-known today, a UFO crashed in nearby Roswell, New Mexico, on July 8, 1947, and the U.S. Air Force recovered small bodies from the craft, according to numerous ufological researchers. The whole use of the term "little green men" appears to have been added to American slang by way of the incidents taking place in the Hobbs-Roswell area in 1947. Considering the background to the name "Hobbs," such events are not too surprising.

But then, the name of the game is name selectivity. According to that profound student of American place names, George R. Stewart, approximately 3,500,000 named places—about one to the square mile—exist in the United States of America, with another million recorded but no longer in use. As I have plied the byways of this country, opened my ears to witnesses' stories, blackened my hands on newsprint, and weakened my eyes on computer screens, I have been struck by how over and over again, the same town or ones with similar names appear to get all the mysterious action. Or that same-named witnesses continually pop up in the Fortean reports. Against the percentages, the name game is a reality.

Fortean author "Jim Brandon" (William Grimstad) has done considerable thinking and writing about the correlation of place names and weird phenomena. He has come forth with some rather interesting findings. Brandon, writing in the thoroughly enjoyable *The Rebirth of Pan,* chooses, as his peculiar candidate for this game, the name Fayette and its variants Lafayette and Fayetteville, which appear in 18 counties and 28 towns or cities across the U.S.A. He gives scores of examples, and I refer the reader to his book for the details of the weird stories Brandon weaves. I shall give a few illustrations of this "Fayette" pattern from my files.

Near Mt. Diablo, California, site of the Black Mountain Lion of Devil's Hole are the haunts of the "Beast of Lafayette Lake." The search was on for this creature from boats, helicopters and horseback during October of 1975. James Lattie of the East Bay Regional Park District told the news media at the time: "You won't believe this but our men reported a most unusual occurrence. That is, an alligator, you know, the kind with jaws and long teeth well, you won't believe it. Well, here goes our image, but two of our patrolmen were sitting on the dam; they were looking in the water. Now they noticed this long shape moving along the water, sort of like a log and slow-like. And one of these patrolmen, he hails from Florida, says to his buddy: 'Hey, you know, if I wasn't in California, I'd swear that that's a 'gator trying to make the other side. Matter of fact, that *is* an alligator.'"

The patrolmen could not locate the eight-foot alligator, the Regional Park district closed the lake, and the search parties were sent in. As with some errant 'gators, at last word, this Lafayette croc was never found.

Mark A. Hall has passed on old clipping about the "Headless Horseman" of Fayette County, Ohio's "Haunted Hill." Apparently in June, 1953, diggings at Cherry Hill, known thereabouts as "Haunted Hill," revealed a headless skeleton. Fayette County legend tells of a man on horseback coming to the hill. His saddlebags were filled with gold. The man was murdered but his body was never found, although his horse was recovered. Folklore then developed about the "Headless Horseman of Haunted Hill." The 1953 skeleton was quickly reburied as Fayette County officialdom said the bones were Amerindian in origin.

My 1977 black panther investigations in Ohio concentrated around the northeastern town of La Fayette. Fayette County, Pennsylvania, has some peculiar petroglyphs, lots of Bigfoot reports, and was visited by UFO occupants in 1973. Lafayette Hill, Pennsylvania, had a UFO swing by there in August 1975. Fayetteville, New York, experienced a strange skyquake on April 17, 1968. Lafayette, Wisconsin, was visited by a phantom panther in November, 1977. Fayette, Indiana, had a UFO encounter in

October, 1966. Fayette, Maine, is five miles from the haunted location of Devil's Den. Fayetteville, Arkansas, near Decatur, is a hotspot of oddities, according to Jim Brandon. And to his list of UFOs, water monsters, and mad gasser-types from there, I can add a fall of metal, a mystery skyquake, Bigfoot sightings, phantom panthers, bizarre electromagnetic effects to cars, and frequent train derailings.

With amazing regularity the newspapers carry offbeat stories originating from a town or county with the Fayette root. On Friday, August 8, 1980, you could read the Associated Press wire stories about the escape and recapture of two elephants along the highway near Lafayette, Oregon. Exactly a year later, you could do a double take with UPI's Friday, August 7th accounts of the escape and recapture of an elephant on a road near La Fayette, Ohio. It's not a stretch to see where episode 2.18, "Fearful Symmetry" of *The X-Files,* about the teleporting appearance of zoo elephants, might have its Fortean origins.

The Fayette stories continue into this century, but you get the idea. Jim Brandon feels the triggering element in Fayette, Lafayette, and Fayetteville is the root word "fay/fey." The literal meaning of "fayette" is "little enchantment" or "little fairy" from the Old French *feer,* "to enchant" plus the feminine diminutive, *ette.* Brandon believes the locations may be enchanted by the use of the "fayette" name, the mere titling giving it some name power.

In parallel research, I have found the use of "fay" intermingled in a significant way with a location important in the Joan of Arc stories. Another meaning, from the French, for "fay" is "beech." Near the home of Joan of Arc was a large old beech tree (French: *fay;* Latin: *fagus*). It was under this tree that the "voices" spoke to Joan. By the 1400s, the tree was considered holy to Our Lady of Domremy, but many people felt it had once been a sacred place during the times of the old pagan religion. Near the beech was a spring where locals came to be cured of disease. At night, fairies were said to dance around the tree.

As T. Douglas Murray noted in *Jeanne d'Arc,* during her trials, Joan of Arc mentioned her involvement with this tree: "Not far from Domremy there is a tree that they call 'The Ladies Tree.' Others call it 'The Fairies Tree'....It is a beautiful tree, a beech, from which comes the 'beau mai' (maypole)...I have sometimes been to play with young girls, to make garlands for Our Lady of Domremy. Often I have heard the old folk…say that the fairies haunt this tree."

The Joan of Arc incident quite clearly points to the "fay," the beech tree being an enchanted spot involved and influenced by mysterious forces quite beyond mortal understanding. What we appear to be seeing in America at all of the present "fayette" sites is merely the threading of this magical web into the modern world.

Has the labeling of certain locations given them some form of occult power or energy magnetism on a level not yet fathomed? The evidence with the "fayette" places, and others, seems to hint at this.

For there are other special places. Speaking of maypoles, let's look at Rowan County, North Carolina. During the last week in April, and the first in May, 1982, Rowan County was hit with a wave of "wampus cat" (i.e., phantom panther) sightings. Now, interestingly enough, the rowan tree is an extremely important and magical tree in Old England, used in Wicker Man sacrifices and as a maypole. What are we to make of the "co-incidence" of something mysterious happening in Rowan County, on May the 1st, May Day, the day of the maypole?

"Logan" is another one of those words. Rocking logan stones are a part of ancient megalithic research. My brother and I interviewed the Lowe family (Chapter 2) about the big birds' attempted abduction of Marlon from their front yard, in Logan County, Illinois. Another Logan County, this one in Colorado, has had an unusually high number of cattle mutilations and one 1975 mystery helicopter report. Logan County, Colorado, also has had an 1897 airship account, as has Logan, Ohio. Loganville, Wisconsin, sits but a stone's throw from the woods around Baraboo, said to be haunted by ghost elephants. A lake monster supposedly made an 1835 appearance in Logansport, Indiana. Logan Peak, near Huntsville, Alabama, the location of UFO, Bigfoot and mystery explosion reports, is a short distance north of Hobbs Island. Logan, Kansas, saw some unexplained bird deaths in 1978. Logan, Utah, was frequented by UFOs during the late 1940s and early 1950s. A May 1, 1954, flash of light was followed by an explosion and huge crater in Logan, Utah. In the 1980s, women were disappearing from Boston's Logan Airport and thus ending this list unended.

Decatur is another "hot" name, as you already know from its long history of panther accounts. During the spring of 1982, my brother Jerry Coleman investigated black panther sightings between two well-named locales, Decaturville and Devil's Knee, Missouri. Growing up in Decatur, Illinois, I noted all types of phenomena—erratic 'gators, UFOs, panthers, (by the way, Decatur means "dweller at the sign of the cat") hairy apes, falls, mutilations, skyquakes, airships—centered on the town. Years later, when attempting to make some sense of the name game, my attention was drawn to the fall of frogs in Decatur, Indiana, in 1937. Charles Fort once wrote that we might gain some insight, we might know an existence by its frogs. In a humorous sort of way, I figured the ole boy was trying to tell me something. But the game has sinister tones, too. In February, 1981, the town of Decatur, Tennessee, was hit with a month of mutilations. As with the classic pattern of cattle mutilations, which peaked in middle America in the 1970s, the Tennessee incident included the surgically skilled removal of one calf's sexual organs—in Decatur.

The point is made. Cities with certain names appear to have more than their share of strange events taking place in their boundaries. But some cities' "power names" might come from something connected to the individual for whom they were named. Take, for example, Decatur, Illinois. This city and the others were named after Stephen Decatur, naval hero. Not too amazingly, the man seems to be linked to matters occult.

The Stephen Decatur House in Washington, D.C., is haunted. The Decatur House is located on Lafayette Square! Perhaps more amazingly, the Jersey Devil legend involves Stephen Decatur. In about 1804, at the Hanover Iron Works, Brown's Mills, New Jersey, Decatur is said to have observed a bizarre creature flapping its wings as it flew across the cannon firing range. Decatur, the story goes, took aim and shot at "it," but the creature continued on its way. This almost folkloric account adds yet another piece to the puzzle of the name game. And it raises more questions.

Are particular names attached to specific people then the focus of mysterious activity, weird wonders, and strange sightings, akin to the name magic of special places? Surely something is occurring.

Late in 1973, John Keel, anomaly expert extraordinaire, was pondering reports I had sent him. These were the Enfield, Illinois critter stories of Henry McDaniel (mentioned earlier in this book). Keel noted the name

McDaniel had crossed his path before. He pointed to the family of that name who were at the center of the West Virginia Mothman series he had investigated. Mabel McDaniel had seen Mothman on January 11, 1967, near Tony's Restaurant in Point Pleasant; then later during March, had a run-in with one of those Mad Gasser/Springheel Jack-type fellows, the Men-In-Black. Parke McDaniel had likewise been frightened by the Men-In-Black on December 23, 1967. Keel felt the name McDaniel had a far greater recurrence in these matters than random. He had also uncovered an 1870s story of an individual named McDaniel who had met up with the Devil in New York State's Catskill Mountains.

Keel himself has raised the question of name selectivity in his writings: "Hundreds of thousands of phenomenal events have been described in newspapers, magazines and books, and hundreds of thousands of witnesses have been named in print. When dealing with such a large body of evidence—or population—certain laws of probability should surface. We might expect that more Smiths would see UFOs than anyone else, simply because there are more Smiths around. But, in actuality, the name Smith rarely appears in a UFO report."

What Keel found was that unusual names were the point of convergence for the phenomena. He saw McDaniel, Reeves/Reaves, Maddox, Heflin, Allen, Hill, and others, as being selected for UFO and related experiences. The Smiths, Browns, Williams, and Johnsons—the four top surnames in America—are not the most frequent precipitant names to crop up. I would add that the most unusually named witnesses seem to have the more bizarre encounters.

A good example of such a situation took place in 1958, in the strange case of the two Charlie Wetzels.

In the midst of the Bigfoot craze hitting America in 1958, an eerie encounter was to occur in Southern California which soon took an aberrant but classic place in the Bigfoot literature. This was the Charlie Wetzel sighting. The details of the story are familiar through the writings of Janet and Colin Bord, John Green, Ivan T. Sanderson, and others, but during 1982, I was able to interview Wetzel and his family personally, coming up with some interesting new information.

Charles Wetzel, born July 8, 1934, was driving his green, two-door 1952 Buick Super near Riverside, California, when he saw "it." Saturday,

November 8, 1958, is a night Charlie told me he would not soon forget. He even remembers which radio station (KFI in Los Angeles), he had tuned in. Wetzel neared that part of North Main Street where the Santa Ana River infrequently overflows its banks, and sure enough, at a spot where the road dips, water was rushing across the pavement. So Charles slowed down.

Within moments he was struck by two sensory events which caught him off guard. First, his car radio started to transmit lots of static. He changed stations, he told me, but to no avail. Next, he saw what he thought was a temporary danger sign near the flooded site. Before he could think twice about any of this, Charles Wetzel saw a six-foot-tall creature bound across his field of vision and stop in front of his Buick. The creature had a "round, scarecrowish head like something out of Halloween," Wetzel told reporters at the time. He described it then, and to me later, as having no ears; no nose; a beak-like, protuberant mouth; and fluorescent, shining eyes. The skin was "scaly, like leaves, but definitely not feathers," Wetzel recalled during our 1982 talk.

The creature was waving "sort of funny" with its incredibly long arms, and seemed to be walking from the hips, almost as if it had no knees. Wetzel then remembered another detail not noted at the time: the legs stuck out from the sides of the torso, not from the bottom. The gurgling sounds it made were mixed with high-pitched screams. When it saw Wetzel it reached across the hood and began clawing at the windshield. Terrified, Wetzel grabbed the .22 High Standard pistol he kept in the car because he was often on the road at night. Clutching the gun, but not wanting to break the one barrier he saw between himself and the beast, the frightened Californian stomped on the gas. "Screeching like a f——r," as Wetzel graphically put it, the creature tumbled forward off the hood and was run over by the car. Wetzel could hear it scrape the pan under the engine, and later police lab tests revealed that something had indeed scrubbed the grease from the Buick's underside.

The police used bloodhounds to search the area, but the dogs found nothing and the officers were left with only the sweeping claw marks on Wetzel's windshield to ponder. Then, the very next night, a black something jumped out of the underbrush near the same site and frightened another motorist.

In recent years, sightings of the strange three-toed Bigfoot have been reported from surrounding areas of Southern California, notably the Buena Park smelly eight-footer seen emerging from a drainage ditch in May, 1982. But the Wetzel sighting near Riverside has won near-classic status among Southern California cases, having been widely discussed and debated by Bigfooters since 1958.

As I mentioned in the mystery kangaroo chapter, that same year, another Charles Wetzel was involved in a sighting of something that looked like a kangaroo near Grand Island, Nebraska. I interviewed this other Wetzel, also in the 1980s.

In talking with California's Charles Wetzel and Nebraska's Charles Wetzel, I discovered that both had sons named Charles, but neither family knew of the other. What are we to make of this bit of synchronicity of Wetzels, both named Charles, both having encountered creatures beyond the norm, in the year 1958? After much head-scratching, I thought it might be useful to look for some kind of underlying pattern via the name "Wetzel." Now, monsters do not seem to be seen by people with the most common names, but why would a couple of Charlie Wetzels be picked? "Wetzel" is a German name, a corrupted form of "little Varin," from "Warin," meaning "protector." Should we therefore assume some elemental insight from a name that literally means "little protector or guardian"?

Next, I went on a search to determine whether the name "Wetzel" is used geographically. On a map of the United States I discovered but only one "Wetzel"—the name of a very rural county in northern West Virginia. I was not too surprised to find that the folklore of Wetzel County is a repository of historic ghost stories. No surprise, either, to find some curious Fortean items in surrounding areas. Nearby Sisterville, West Virginia, is well known as one of the few eastern American cities to have been visited by the phantom airships of the 1890s. Moundsville, just north of Wetzel, is the site of a significant earthen mound built by ancient unknown people. Other mounds are still being discovered in the area; one was recently exposed when a hill was cut away to provide a building site for a glass factory. Bordering counties in Pennsylvania, Greene and Fayette are the sites of many strange accounts of hominoid and UFO visitations in the last few years. All in all, Wetzel County probably feels very at home in the state of the Flatwoods Monster and Mothman.

Wetzel County, West Virginia, was named after Lewis Wetzel, whom Teddy Roosevelt called a "one-man army, the greatest scout, woodsman, and Indian fighter in America's history." Wetzel was credited with killing hundreds of Native Americans. He was so feared by the Shawnee, they called him the "Dark Destroyer"; the Delawares referred to him as "Deathwind" because of the eerie, hollow cry he let out when he killed. His massacre of Indians continued after the signing of the peace treaties. This led to his capture and escape to Spanish Louisiana, where he was arrested as an American spy. Not exactly someone you'd want as your neighbor, I suppose. Wetzel died a broken man in 1808 at the age of 45, soon after his release some four years after his imprisonment.

What kind of influence did his name carry with it to the county in West Virginia? The strange events there appear to have started soon after he died. In 1845, a mysterious "Frenchman" showed up in the area, and remained awhile without any means of support. He was soon arrested under the vagrancy law, and quickly produced papers stating he was an agent of France, searching for $87,000 buried below a Wetzel County creek. The money was never found. Shortly thereafter, stories circulated that a Mr. Watkins had buried 960 silver dollars, weighing over sixty pounds, sixty steps from the river, under a pawpaw bush.

What I found of interest in the two buried treasure incidents is their connectedness to patterns running through dozens of mysterious sites in America. Buried treasure stories are common fixtures of spook light and Devil's Den sites. Strangers appearing in towns, giving out "disinformation," and leaving a wake of questions in their path occur all too frequently. It happened in the midst of the 1890s airship wave, during the 1960s Mothman episodes, and then again during the Men-In-Black encounters of more recent years. Wetzel's 1845 "Frenchman" falls right into this category.

And what of a Mr. Watkins showing up in the tales of Wetzel County? The name is a familiar one in the name game. Alfred Watkins, the English intellectual who formulated the notion of ley lines, comes to mind when thoughts of hidden power points are mentioned. And Watkins Glen, New York, is the site of reoccurring disappearances.

Cryptologic or coincidence?

Jim Brandon should be credited with calling attention to the name

Watts/Watkins/Watson, and its entanglement with inexplicable things. Some other names involved in mysterious events pinpointed by Brandon are Bell, Mason, Parsons, Pike, Vernon and Warren. The influence of such names as Mason, Pike, Warren, and Lafayette, for example, issues, in some cryptopolitical and occult way, from their ties to the Masonic tradition. Jim Brandon's *The Rebirth of Pan* discusses this thesis in detail. Clearly, however, a massive name game is being played out across Mysterious America, and the proof of such a hypothesis goes beyond mere chance.

In *Wild Talents,* Charles Fort thought about some of these same things when he wrote: "My liveliest interest is not so much in things, as in relations of things. I have spent much time thinking about the alleged pseudorelations that are called coincidences. What if some of them should not be coincidences?"

Noting that the vanishing act of Ambrose Bierce was followed by the vanishing of Ambrose Small some six years later, Fort continued: "But what could the disappearance of one Ambrose, in Texas, have to do with the disappearance of another Ambrose, in Canada? There was in these questions an appearance of childishness that attracted my respectful attention."

Charles Fort, thus, engaged in the name game, and attempted to understand the quick explanation given for it, coincidence. "In the explanation of coincidence," Fort emphasized in *Wild Talents,* "there is much of laziness, and helplessness, and response to an instinctive fear that a scientific dogma will be endangered. It is a tag, or a label: but of course every tag, or label, fits well enough at times."

So, in the midst of all the Fayettevilles, Wetzels, Decaturs and Devils, someone must feel comfortable in knowing they believe they are merely coincidences.

But ponders Fort: "There is a view by which it can be shown, or more or less demonstrated, that there never has been a coincidence. That is, in anything like a final sense. By a coincidence is meant a false appearance, or suggestion, of relations among circumstances. But anybody who accepts that there is an underlying oneness of all things, accepts that there are no utter absences of relations among circumstances."

And what of any one of our own name games? To look personally closer at your name or the place you live, is instructive. For me, one who has examined deeply the pattern in names and things, I was struck by some insights pointed out to me, personally, by Jim Brandon concerning "Coleman." Alfred Watkins, mentioned above, wrote in his *The Old Straight Track,* the "Coleman, who gave his name to all kinds of points and places on the tracks, was a head-man in making them, and probably worked from the Colehills, using beacon fires for making out the ley."

In a similar vein, I. Shah's *The Sufis* demonstrates the origin of my name via Coalman, the charcoal burners, the Perceivers, the Carbonari, and their links with the occult.

Perhaps, then, the name game has played a special trick on me. I seem predisposed to try to scrutinize names of people and places for the purpose of perceiving the possible hidden meanings and patterns behind them. The lay of the land, and the sighters of the strange, then, truly hold many secrets as we hobnob about America.

CHAPTER 23

Some Concluding Thoughts After Some Years "On the Trail"

I have never been able to understand why all things serious have to be taken seriously; and especially, all the time. —Ivan T. Sanderson

In the 1960s and 1970s, up until his death, Ivan T. Sanderson and I exchanged some interesting letters on the various creature and phantom reports sweeping Mysterious America. Sanderson, a well-known investigator of the unexplained and successful Fortean author, had been corresponding with me for over a decade. Trained as a zoologist, as indeed I was, we shared a great deal of similar insights and droll intuitions with regard to the state of mysterious phenomena research of the time.

For example, in 1962, I suggested to Sanderson that an organization be created to deal with an examination of the worldwide abominable snowmen reports, be they termed Yeti, Bigfoot, or North American Ape. He thought that was a good idea, but jokingly said, "The only trouble is that it would probably be full of Russians." Five years later, the Ivan T. Sanderson Foundation was a reality, soon to be followed by his Society for the Investigation of the Unexplained. Sanderson apparently had to build a formal organization in response to the incredible numbers of creature reports flooding the countryside of America.

Since the early 1960s I had fed reams of case investigations of eastern USA creature accounts to Sanderson, then of Columbia, New Jersey, and John Green of British Columbia, and they were beginning to wonder what was going on. In 1967, Sanderson finally wrote, "Yes....Please...any reports you have...Little Red Men of the... or Giant Hairys in the suburbs. The whole bit is getting hotter and hairier by the month; and now we have the damned UFOs mixed up in it."

The lines between cryptozoology, parapsychology, and ufology were merging again in the late 1960s and 1970s, after the writers in the 1940s and 1950s had forced artificial boundaries between creatures, UFOs, and phantoms. As Charles Fort had noted after the turn of the century, there is a oneness to it all. During the 1970s this admixture seems to have been re-discovered by authors examining the mysterious.

I am a product of this era. I wrote my first article of note in the March 1971 issue of *Fate*. Living in Illinois at the time, I discussed in the *Fate* article my field investigations into local bipedal hairy creature and black mystery feline reports. I invented the concept of phantom panthers.

After reading my article, Sanderson wrote me a long letter detailing the dilemma such reports raised for him: "Dammit. I don't like this sort of 'paraphysical' stuff, and I have kept strictly off it for 20 years now, despite ever increasing volumes of evidence (so called). But, in view of Jacques Vallee's ponderings on UFOs, and holograms, and solid (matter) projections; meaning, one can only assume, teleportation, I begin to wonder if the time has not come to take the proverbial ox by its frontal excrescences, and tackle the issue frontally also. However, it might do more harm than good, because it might put all of us serious minded and sane Forteans right back into the kook-klass in the eyes of both the genuine scientists and the newsmen. Quandary!"

Within two years, Sanderson was dead. It was left for Vallee, John Keel, Jerome Clark, D. Scott Rogo, myself, and others to take the bull by its horns and attempt to answer some of the questions posed by the events breaking out all over Mysterious America. Not coincidentally, when Ivan Sanderson died in 1973, part of the void he left was quickly filled by *Fortean Times* (first called *The News* back then). Since the 1970s, the pages of *Fortean Times, INFO, Fate, The Anomalist,* and for a while *Pursuit* and *Strange,* have all served as the windows into the minds of weird wonders investigators.

Looking back demonstrates an intriguing evolution in the thinking of those examining the accounts of strange creatures, foggy phantoms, and mysterious locations. When Jerry Clark and I wrote our first two books in the mid-1970s, we suggested that UFOs and monsters were psychic projections of a collective unconscious, literal thought forms which took on a solid state existence, be they footprints where a ufonaut stepped, or the knocking out of witnesses by a mad gasser.

As we observed, "Extraterrestrial spaceships simply could not be touring the earth in the massive numbers UFO sightings suggest. Neither could massive numbers of large unknown animals be roaming country-side and city streets without long ago having been officially recognized and catalogued (and probably driven into extinction as well).

"Moreover, they could not have done all this in such numbers without providing us with more conclusive physical evidence than they have given us so far. The 'physical evidence' is always just enough to suggest that the reported manifestation was not purely hallucinatory; it is never enough to prove that it was objectively real."

Through the 1970s, the idea that UFOs, monsters, and poltergeist activity may be part of the same phenomenon, or as Janet and Colin Bord noted, at least triggered by the same stimulus, gained favor. For example, tales of creatures and phantoms with tattered, checkered shirts were compared to early occult literature by John Keel, Clark and myself. Such events continue to be reported.

The flesh and blood answers of cryptozoologists such as Bernard Heuvelmans and Ray Mackal, or the nuts and bolts solutions of ufologists like Stan Friedman, were eclipsed by the paranormal thoughts abounding in the 1970s. *Fortean Times'* Robert J. M. Rickard and his colleague John Michell's interesting and intelligent notion that monsters might be time-travelers, that is animals teleporting on a temporal plane, added a new twist to the para-whatever school in a novel attempt to account for the tangible intangibility of the creatures. In 1982, Rickard and Michell presented their "theory of revivals" in *Living Wonders,* proposing that animals return from extinction. In 1983, Jim Brandon in *The Rebirth of Pan* detailed his belief that the pagan, earthy energy termed "Pan" in folklore manifests itself from spook lights to sea serpents.

It's interesting and enjoyable to hop from one theory to another to explain phenomena as elusive as this. In the 1980s, D. Scott Rogo and Jerome Clark made an almost wholesale retreat from their earlier planetary poltergeist positions to embrace their "intermediate reality" or parallel universe positions.

After *Creatures of the Outer Edge* was published, I was aghast to be labeled an occultist, a paranormalist, or somesuch. The paraphysical answer was articulated as an exercise in providing yet another possible explanation to the mysterious wonders surrounding us, but what became clearly apparent to me was that theorists are quickly pigeonholed.

This is unfortunate, as I and many other pursuers of the unknown, Forteans all, believe in nonbelief. An open-minded attitude to the many unexplained situations is the stock and trade of the Fortean. I and the membership of the International Society of Cryptozoology can accept concrete answers, actual flesh and blood critters as the foundation to monster accounts. But then again, a psychological answer may be at work with some of these accounts, and the rational, conventional, undiscovered animal answer may not be viable for all reports.

There is room enough to consider many possibilities. But please don't tell me that as a cryptozoologist I "believe" in monsters! Cryptozoology builds its database on many forms of evidence. Eyewitness accounts by credible, down-to-earth folks do form a solid foundation of our investigations. But cryptozoology is not about "belief." Believing is the realm of religion; cryptozoology, like all sciences, is about gathering the data and evidence to develop trends, patterns, and evidence which lead to hard facts and discoveries.

Lest we lose our sense of humor about this business, I refer you to the words of Rickard and Michell where they note their theories should be taken "with the customary Fortean promise that it will sit lightly on our shoulders, and that we will gladly give it up as soon as someone finds us something better to wear."

Indeed, I sense some monsters in America are chimpanzee-like dryopithecines, that some mystery cats and maned lions are relict populations of *atrox,* and some lake monsters are unknown long-necked seals. However, I also have room in my cosmic jokebox for teleporting 'gators, Dover Demons, and phantom clowns that imitate UFOs in all aspects but flight. Some spook lights in America, those ghostly globes of illumination that seem glued to specific locations, may be related to discharges of electric energy produced by geological fault stresses, some to various kinds of parapsychological disturbances akin to ghosts, or others to a form of geophysical phenomenon as yet not understood. I also am not afraid to say "I don't know."

Simply stated then, I "believe" in nothing and the possibility of everything. Ivan T. Sanderson once telegraphed me this message: "Forteanism is not an organized anything." Orderly chaos, an openness to the incomprehensible and unthinkable, and a jolly good sense of humor best describe how I have dealt with America's remarkable array of creatures, phantoms and strange events since 1960. And yet in search of the answers, my youthful passion for this field has never waned.

Fortean reality has many levels of satisfaction, and these become more and more apparent to me every day. The procession of the damned, those wonderful things excluded by science, schools and governments, continues daily. In some sense, in some ways, these things, chased and seen, exist.

We are like viewers of a grand cinema in an unknown foreign language. The pictures are forming images in our heads, which at once are familiar and yet uncomfortable and alien. We know it looks serious sometimes, but at other times we feel we are witness to a great comedy with tragic overtones. All too often, however, the movie becomes three dimensional, and then there is no escaping the fact that this experience is personal and real, or very nearly so. Our mind brings up more rational explanations to make it all fit, but again we come away frustrated and unsatisfied. All the pieces—be they glowing red eyes, silvery balls of light, or rays of blue gas, falling frogs, impish figures, or screeches in the night—don't fit the answers proposed. We try to sit back and grasp once again what is going on. Sometimes we succeed—partially. More often than not we fail, and want to agree very quickly with those around us saying this film is an illusion, a false picture, a pseudoscientific fiction, or at worst, a hoax. It is a struggle, but we remain tied to the idea that the flickering image is something only mildly reflected and understandable in the context of *Homo sapiens* of the 21st century. There is nothing wrong with not having all of the answers at this stage of the game. Quandary, indeed.

The Lists...

There is no money-back guarantee that anyone going to these places will see a spook, will-o'-the-wisp, flying saucer, or tumbling geode within the first 10 minutes of arrival. But perhaps there is a certain aura or spirit of place—obviously there is something special about these sites—on which we should concentrate our long-dormant powers of total perception.

Jim Brandon, *Weird America,* 1978

The American Lion *(Panthera atrox)*: Cryptid Black Panthers, Maned Cats, and Striped Felines / Selected Sightings

The first edition of *Mysterious America* (1983) detailed decades of large mystery felid sightings. This edition updates that work, gathering old records, as well as new ones. This revised volume also adds, for the first time, this appendix to support the added details in Chapters 12 and 13.

In 1994, Mark A. Hall published a list of seventy specific cases to illustrate the black panther and maned cat data in his article, "The American Lion (*Panthera atrox*)," *Wonders* 3(1): 3-20, in conjunction with his theory that *Panthera atrox* may be a Pleistocene survivor. The following list of more than 140 events doubles Hall's original, which is reprinted here with permission, and expanded with other material from my files; any mistakes are mine and not his. While there are literally hundreds of cases, the following chart contains a selection to demonstrate the diversity and chronological nature of the reports, as well as specific hints of geographic distribution.

Please note, several sightings may be grouped under one entry, as mystery cat reports often occur in a concentrated series. Some effort has been made to highlight incidents involving more than one feline, demonstrating the social nature of these cats, but several melanistic records may include multiple sightings not referenced as such.

Eastern Reports of Black Panthers, Maned Cats, and Striped Felines

Ref. # / Date / Location / Source / Remarks
1. 1700s / New York Co. NY / H. Shoemaker, see Chapter 13 / **maned**
2. 1767 / Pepin Co. WI / H. Shoemaker, see Chapter 13 / **"tyger," striped?**
3. 1797 or 1798 / Clinton Co. PA/ H. Shoemaker, see Chapter 13 / **maned + female + 3 cubs = 5**
4. 1823 / Logan Co. KY/ See Chapter 13 / **striped**
5. 1836 / Penobscot Co. WV / see Chapter 13 / **maned, roaring**
6. 1869 / Tolland Co. CT / G. Mangiacopra, D. Smith "Connecticut's Mystery Felines: The Glastonbury Glawackus 1939-1967" in *The Anomalist*, 1995 3: 90-123 / **black**
7. 1877 / Rising Sun IN / J. Clark, L. Coleman *Creatures of the Outer Edge*, 1978: 123-5 / **dark, six inch tracks**

8. 1890 / Second Creek NC / *Salisbury Carolina Watchman* 9 Oct 1890 / **striped?**
9. 1890 / Iredell Co. NC / *Stateville Landmark* 28 Aug 1890; *Salisbury Carolina Watchman* 11 Sep 1890 / **striped?**
10. 1895 / Lamartine OH / G. Eberhart *Pursuit*, 1977 10: 2-8 / **black?**
11. 1897 / Wilkes, Yakin Cos. NC / *Wilkersboro Chronicle* 17 Mar, 5 May, 9 Jun, 20 Oct 1897 / **striped**
12. 1899 / Wilkes Co. NC / *Wilkersboro Chronicle* 31 May 1899 / **striped?, black**
13. 1901 / Pocahontas Co. ME / see Chapter 13 / **long chest & belly hair, tufted tail**
14. 1917 / Piatt-Macon Cos. IL / see Chapter 12 / **"African lioness" + maned = 2**
15. 1929 / Dade Co. FL / "Florida Mammals," *Nature*, Dec 1929 / **black**
16. 1934 / Iredell Co. NC / A. Capparella III, "The Santer," *Shadows*, 1977, 4:1-3 / **striped?, black?**
17. 1939 / Hartford Co. CT / G. Mangiacopra, D. Smith *The Anomalist*, 1995 3: 90-123 / **black + tawny**
18. 1941 / New Brunswick / B. Wright, *The Eastern Panther*, 1972: 24 / **possible maned**
19. 1945 / St. Mary-Terrbonne Parishes LA / J. Clark, *Unexplained!*, 1999: 223 / **black**
20. 1946 / Oquawka IL / *Doubt*, 1947, 17: 206 / **black + black = 2**
21. 1948 / New Brunswick / B. Wright, *The Eastern Panther*, 1972: 40 / **black**
22. 1948 / Wilton NH / C. B. Colby, *Mysterious New England*, 1971 / **black**
23. 1948 / Pittsfield MA / C. B. Colby, *Mysterious New England*, 1971 / **black**
24. 1948 / Indiana-Ohio / *Richmond* (IN) *Palladium-Item* 3 Aug-5 Sep1948 / **black + maned + tawny = 3+**
25. 1948 / Owen Co. IN / *Richmond* (IN) *Palladium-Item* 17 Aug 1948 / **black**
26. 1949 / Jasper Co. IL / *Richmond* (IN) *Palladium-Item* 1 Sep 1949 / **black**
27. 1950 / Peoria Co. IL / W. Grimstad, *Weird America*, 1978: 82 / **roaring**
28. 1951 / Hamilton Co. IN / *Richmond* (IN) *Palladium-Item* 8 Jan 1951 / **black**
29. 1951 / New Brunswick / B. Wright, *The Eastern Panther*, 1972: 57ff / **black**
30. 1952 / Oakland Co. MI / *Detroit News* 15 Jul 1986 / **black**
31. 1953 / New Brunswick / B. Wright, *The Eastern Panther*, 1972: 43 / **two "African lionesses" + black = 3+**
32. 1953-54 / Bladenboro NC / *North Carolina Folklore*, Aug 1976 / **black**
33. 1954-55 / New Brunswick / B. Wright, *The Eastern Panther*, 1972: 33, 123 / **black, "ragged coated"**
34. 1954+ / Chippewa Co. MI / *Detroit News* 23 Nov 1972 / **black**
35. 1955 / Somerset Co. ME / See Chapter 12 / **black**
36. 1955 / Macon Co. IL / See Chapter 12 / **black**
37. 1955 / Champaign Co. OH / See Chapter 12 / **black**
38. 1956 / Oakland Co. MI / *Detroit News,* 15 Jul 1986 / **black**
39. 1957 / Mountainside NJ / *NY Journal-American*, 17 Jan 1957 / **black**
40. 1957 / Chillicothe MO / *Kansas City* (MO) *Times*, 23 July 1957 / **black**
41. 1957-1959 / CT / G. Mangiacopra, D. Smith *The Anomalist*, 1995 3: 90-123 / **black**
42. 1958 / Cedartown GA / *Atlanta Constitution* 15, 18 Apr 1958 / **black**
43. 1958 / Warrick Co. IN / *Indianapolis News* 25-29 Jan 1958 / **black, maned**
44. 1958 / New Brunswick / B. Wright, *The Eastern Panther*, 1972: 34 / **black, "shaggy"**

45. 1959-60 / New Brunswick / B. Wright, *The Eastern Panther*, 1972: 29 / **black**
46. 1959 / Lorain OH / See Chapter 13 / **maned**
47. 1959 / Sudbury ONT / *Toronto Star* 21 Aug 1959 / **black**
48. 1960 / Kapuskasing ONT / *Toronto Telegram* 28 Jun 1960 / **maned**
49. 1960 / Macon Co. IL / See Chapter 12 / **black with white spot on chest**
50. 1960 / Southfield MI / *Detroit News* 15 Jul 1986 / **black**
51. 1961-62 / New Brunswick / B. Wright, *The Eastern Panther*, 1972: 34ff; 123 / **black**
52. 1962 / Huntington Co. IN / *Huntington Herald-Press* 27-29 Jun 1972 / **"African lioness" + roaring = 2?**
53. 1962 / Montgomery, Clark Cos. OH / *Springfield News,* 27 Jun 1973 / **black**
54. 1962 / Champaign Co. OH / See Chapter 12 / **black**
55. 1962 / Delhi NY / *Walton Reporter* 28 July 1982 / **black**
56. 1962-1963 / CT / G. Mangiacopra, D. Smith *The Anomalist*, 1995 3: 90-123 / **black**
57. 1962 / Hancock Co. IN / *Indianapolis News* 2 Oct 1962 / **black**
58. 1963 / Champaign Co. IL / *Champaign-Urbana Courier* 4 Jan 1963 / **black with stripes**
59. 1963 / Dupage-Will Co. line IL / *Joliet Herald News* 24 Apr 1963 / **black**
60. 1964 / Will Co. IL / See Chapter 13 / **black + maned = 2**
61. 1964 / Chippewa Co. MI / *Detroit News* 23 Nov 1972 / **black**
62. 1964 / Blue Ridge GA / R. Downing, *Cryptozoology*, 1984 3: 31-49 / **"African lion" killed**
63. 1964 / New Brunswick / B. Wright, *The Eastern Panther*, 1972: 30 / **dark, like an "African lion"**
64. 1965 / Macon Co. IL / *Decatur Review* 25 Jun, 1 Jul 1965 / **black**
65. 1966 / Alexander Co. IL / *Carbondale Egyptian* 22 Apr 1966 / **black**
66. 1967 / York Co. New Brunswick / B. Wright, *The Eastern Panther*, 1972: 31 / **black**
67. 1967 / CT / G. Mangiacopra, D. Smith *The Anomalist*, 1995 3: 90-123 / **"lion"? + roaring + striped = at least 2**
68. 1968 / Greene Co. AR / *Arkansas Democrat* 25 Sep 1968 / **black**
69. 1970s / Bemidji MN / See Chapter 12 / **black**
70. 1970 / Fredericton NB / B. Wright, *The Eastern Panther*, 1972: 122, 158 / **black**
71. 1970 / Macon Co. IL / *Decatur Review* 10 Jan 1970 and interview / **black + cub = 2**
72. 1970 / Jasper Co. IL / *Newton Press* 19 Feb 1970 / **black**
73. 1970 / Winnebago Co. IL / *Rockford Star* 30 May, 2 Jun, 25 Aug 1970 / **maned, roaring**
74. 1970 / Randolph, Union Cos. IL/ *Southern Illinoisan* 11 Jun 1970 / **black**
75. 1970s / Rockcastle Co. KY / See Chapter 13 / **striped**
76. pre-1971 / Flintstone MD / *Washington Post* 26 Aug 1971 / **black**
77. 1971 / Fairfax Co. MD / *Washington Daily News* 8 Feb 1971 / **black**
78. 1971 / Eaton Corners NY / *Knickerbocker News* (Schenectady) 29 Mar 1971 / **black**
79. 1971 / North Brunswick NJ / *S.Woodbridge News Trib* 11 Sep 1971 / **maned**
80. 1971 / Croesbeck OH / See Chapter 13 / **maned**
81. 1972 / Fayetteville AR / *Northwest Arkansas Times* 16 Dec 1972 / **black**

82. 1972 / Chippewa Co. MI / *Detroit News* 23 Nov 1972 / **black**
83. 1974 / Monroe MI / *Detroit News* 15 Jul 1986 / **black**
84. 1974 / Southfield MI / *Detroit News* 11, 12 Oct 1974 / **black**
85. 1975 / Stockbridge GA / *Atlanta Constitution* 18 Sep 1975 / **black**
86. 1975 / Geauga Co. OH / *Cleveland Plain Dealer* 5 Sep 1975 / **maned**
87. 1976 / St. Clair Co. IL / *Millstadt Enterprise* 21 Apr 1976 / **black**
88. 1976 / Little Rock AR / *Arkansas Gazette* 17 Nov 1976 / **black**
89. 1976 / Alapaha GA / *Atlanta Journal* 2 Aug 1979 / **maned**
90. 1976 / Macon Co. IL / See Chapter 12 / **black**
91. 1977 / Allen Co. OH / L. Coleman, *Fate Magazine* Nov 1977 / **black**
92. 1977 / Van Etten NY / *Elmira Daily Telegram* 21, 25, 28 Jul, 18 Aug 1977, *Sunday Telegram* 8 Jan 1978 / **black**
93. 1977 / Marlington WV / See Chapter 13 / **striped**
94. 1978 / Loxahatachee FL / *Palm Beach Post* 24 Jan, *Fortean Times* 28: 49 / **maned**
95. 1978 / Council Bluffs IA / *Nonpareil* 23-30 Jun 1978 / **black**
96. 1978 / Pt. Pleasant WV / *Pt. Pleasant Register* 18, 20, 21 Sep 1978 / **black**
97. pre-1979 / Cleveland Co. NC / *Shelby Star* 15 Jan 1979 / **black**
98. 1979 / West Chester OH / *Res Bureaux Bulletin*, 1979, 50: 4 / **"lion" cub found**
99. 1980 / Russellville AR / *Courier Democrat* 24-25 Jan 1980 / **black**
100. 1980 / Lone Jack MO / *Kansas City Star* 4 Feb 1980 / **black**
101. 1981 / Piscataquis Co. ME / Augusta *Kennebec Journal* 6 May 1981 / **black**
102. 1982 / Rutherfordton NC / R. Downing, pers. comm. 2000 / **"African lion" skeleton found**
103. 1984 / North Olmstead OH / See Chapter 13 / **maned**
104. 1984 to 1987 / Oakland, Washtenaw, Livingston Cos. MI / *Detroit Free Press* 13 Sep 1984 +, *Detroit News* 12 Jul 1986 + / **black**
105. 1984 / Flint MI / *Flint Journal* 14 Aug 1984, 4 Dec 1984 / **black**
106. 1984 / Logan Co. IL / See Chapter 12 / **black**
107. 1986 / Wyoming, Susquehanna, Lackawanna, Pike Cos. PA / See Chapter 13/**striped + maned = 2**
108. 1986 / St. Clair Co. IL / See Chapter 12 / **black with white on chest**
109. 1987 / St. Clair Co. IL/ See Chapter 12 / **black**
110. 1987 / Nauvoo AL / *Tuscaloosa News* 27 May 1967 / **black**
111. 1987 / Salem, Cumberland Cos. NJ / K. Shuker, *Mystery Cats of the World* 1989: 159 / **black**
112. 1991-1993 / WI / M. A. Hall, *Wonders*, 1994, 11: 89 / **black**
113. 1992 / North Avondale OH / See Chapter 13 / **maned**
114. 1994 / Highland, Clinton Cos. OH /See Chapter 13 / **striped + roaring + "African lioness" = 2+**
115. 1995 / Macon Co. IL / See Chapter 12 / **black**
116. 1999 / Christian Co. IL / See Chapter 12 / **black**
117. 1998-99 / Sauk, Juneau Cos. WI / See Chapter 13 / **"African lioness" + roaring = 2**

Western Reports of Black Panthers, Maned Cats, and Striped Felines

Ref. # / Date/Location/Source/Remarks
1. 1519 / Montezuma's Menagerie, Tenochtitlan, Mexico / R. Marshall, *Onza*, 1961: 82-88 / **one of "two kinds of lions"**
2. 1750s / lower California / R. Marshall, *Onza*, 1961: 92-95 / **other kind of "lion"**
3. 1868 / Lake Co. CA / See Chapter 13 / **maned with stripes**
4. 1897 / Fairmont NE / *Omaha Daily News* 18 Feb 1897: 2 / **black**
5. 1940 / w. Mexico / See Chapter 13 / **maned with stripes**
6. 1951 / Waterloo NE / *New York Times* 29 Nov 1951 / **maned**
7. 1954 / Surprise, Rising City NE / *Omaha World Herald* 2 Aug 1954 / **maned + mate = 2**
8. 1960 / Fort Worth TX / interview with Sallie Ann Clarke, April 1970 / **black**
9. 1961 / Craig and Rogers Cos. OK / *Newsweek* 27 Mar 1961: 31-34 / **maned, roaring**
10. 1964 / Marin Co. CA / *San Rafael Independent-Journal* 14 Sep 1964 / **black**
11. 1964 / Ventura Co. CA / See Chapter 12 / **black + black = 2**
12. 1967 / Ventura Co. CA / *Ventura Star-Free Press* 13 Dec 1967 / **black**
13. 1968 / Thousand Oaks CA / *Ventura Star-Free Press* 9 Jan 1968 / **black**
14. 1972 / Contra Costa Co. CA / See Chapter 12 / **black + tawny = 2**
15. 1973 / Concord to Danville CA / *Vallejo Times-Herald* 5 Mar 1973 / **black**
16. 1973 / Alum Rock (east of San Jose) CA / AP, 16 Dec 1973 / **black**
17. 1975 / Nobility TX / *Sherman Democrat* 22 May 1975 / **black**
18. pre-1976 Big Thicket TX / *Corpus Christi Caller* 8 Feb 1976 / **black**
19. 1976 / Tucson AZ / *Tucson Citizen* 17 Sep-27 Oct 1976 / **black**
20. 1976 / Tacoma WA / See Chapter 13 / **maned**
21. 1977 / Talihina OK / *Talihina American* 20 Jan 1977 / **black**
22. 1977 / Oklahoma City OK / *Oklahoma Times* 25-26 Oct 1977 / *Oklahoman* 26-27 Oct 1977 / **black**
23. 1977 / Dierks, Dover AR / See Chapter 13 / **black + maned = 2**
24. 1977 / Muscatine IA / *Res Bureaux Bulletin*, 1977, 27: 6 / **"lion" cub found**
25. 1979 / Fremont CA / *Fremont Argus* 11-17 Nov 1979, *San Francisco Chronicle* 13 Nov 1979 / **maned, roaring**
26. 1983 / El Toro CA / UPI 9 Oct 1983 / **maned**
27. 1984 / San Dimas CA / *San Gabriel Valley Tribune* 21 May 1984 / **black**
28. 1985 / Fort Worth TX / *F. W. Star Telegram* 21-22 Feb 1985, UPI 21-22 Feb 1985 / **maned, roaring**
29. 1988 / Fairfield CA / UPI 10 Apr 1988 / **black**
30. 1999 / Port Angeles WA / See Chapter 13 / **"African lioness" + roaring = 2**

APPENDIX II

Thirty-five Reoccurring "Spook Lights" in America

by Mark A. Hall

Mysterious, usually mobile globes of illumination seemingly attached to, and appearing periodically at, specific locations are referred to as "spook lights." This phenomenon has fascinated the public for decades. Although their exact origin is still shrouded in mystery, their existence is hardly in doubt.

State, Province	Location	Number	Movement
Alabama, Lamar Co.	10 miles west of Vernon, road	one	?
Alaska	mountains rimming Lake Iliamna	multi	?
California, San Diego Co.	above Oriflamme Mts., near Julian	multi	yes
Colorado, Custer Co.	a cemetery at Silver Cliff	multi	yes
Florida, Seminole Co.	State Road 13 near Oviedo	multi	yes
Hawaii, Hawaii Co.	Parker Ranch	multi	yes
Iowa, Warren Co.	a farm near St. Mary's	one	?
Louisiana, Ascension Co.	near Gonzales	one	?
Maryland, Wicomico Co.	one mile west of Hebron	one	yes
Missouri, Cedar Co.	10 miles east of El Dorado Springs	one	yes
Missouri, Newton Co.	12 miles south-west of Joplin	multi	yes
Nevada, Humboldt Co.	Oregon Canyon Ranch near McDermitt	multi	yes
New Jersey, Passaic Co.	hills west of Lake Wanaque	multi	yes
New Mexico, Taos Co.	river near Llano	multi	yes

State, Province	Location	Number	Movement
North Carolina Brunswick Co.	trestle near Maco	1 or 2	yes
North Carolina Burke Co.	Brown Mtn. and Catawba Valley	multi	yes
North Carolina, Watauga Co.	Big Laurel	2 or 3	yes
North Dakota, Cass Co.	road between Fargo and Kindred	one	yes
Ohio, Ashland Co.	open field and woods near Loudonville	one	yes
Oklahoma, Cimarron Co.	8 miles east of Kenton	one	?
Oklahoma, Cimarron Co.	15 miles south-west of Kenton	one	yes
Oklahoma, Tulsa Co.	2 miles west of Sand Springs	one	yes
Oregon, Union or Umatilla Co. to Elgin	road from Weston	one	yes
South Carolina, Dorchester Co. near Summerville	Sheep Island Road	one	yes
Texas, Angelina Co.	RR track near Lufkin	one	yes
Texas, Bell Co.	bank of the Leon River	one	yes
Texas, Brazoria Co.	5 miles west of Angleton	one	yes
Texas, Hardin Co.	Bragg Road north or Saratoga	multi	yes
Texas, La Salle and McMullen Creek Cos.	along Esperanza	one	yes
Texas, Presidio Co.	Chinati Mountain	one	yes
Virginia, Nansemond Co.	Jackson Road south of Suffolk	one	yes
Washington, Franklin Co.	near Pasco	one	yes
Manitoba	forest area near Woodridge	one	?
Ontario	shore of Lake Simcoe near Brechin	one	yes
Saskatchewan	Buffalo Basin district near Beechy	one	yes

Erratic Crocodilians and Teleporting 'Gators

Many Forteans have been intrigued by the deep involvement of crocodilians in various mysteries. A survey of the mysterious appearances of alligators and crocodiles, therefore, may be helpful to those interested in finding some more pieces to the puzzle.

As the following list, created in 1983, shows, crocodilians fall from the sky and materialize inside cotton bins from South Carolina to Texas. To the horror of humans, they slither and slink from basement drains and sewers from Kansas to New York City. Unlike some mystery animals, alligators are caught, killed, and placed in museums. Although actual alligators seem to appear and persist in northern winters (e.g., sightings and finds for Oakland County, Michigan, 1953–1957) to the dismay of herpetologists, random out-of-place finds seem to be the rule.

Pet escapee explanations cannot deal adequately with these accounts of alligators in northern waters, when it is caimans that are being sold as pets.

It should be noted that "found" is used in this list when that is the only word given in the account and proper disposition is not apparent. "Found" may refer to an actual seizure or to a mere noticing of the specimen. Often "found" specimens may be dead or alive and in incidents where one or the other is clear, it has been noted.

Explanation of "remarks" symbols: s = sighted only; c = caught; f = found; k = killed

Ref. No.	Date	Location and Source	Length (inches)	Remarks
1.	1843, July 2	Anson St., Charleston, S.C. WAND-TV, Decatur, Ill., Weather Almanac Feature, July 2, 1971; *Charleston Evening Post,* Charleston, S.C., Aug. 11, 1971.		fell from thunder storm
2.	1877, Dec.	turpentine farm, Aiken Co., S.C. *New York Times,* Dec. 26, 1877.	all about 12	6 fell
3.	1892, Feb.	bank, Rock River, Janesville, Wis. *The Books of Charles Fort* (henceforth BCF), page 598. *Chicago Citizen,* Chicago, Ill., Feb. 27, 1892, page 3.	66	f-frozen

Ref. No.	Date	Location and Source	Length (inches)	Remarks
4.	1901, Nov.	South Canadian River, Norman, Okla. Lane, H.H., "Alligator mississippiensis in Oklahoma," *Science,* Dec. 24, 1909, pp. 923-924.	54	k
5.	1922	Dismal Swamp, Ware, Mass. MacDougall, Curtis D., *Hoaxes,* Dover, 1958, pp. 31-32.	72-96, 24	s c
6.	1926	Potomac River, Md. "'Baby' Alligators Astray in Northern Rivers," *Literary Digest,* Dec. 11, 1926, pp. 68-72.	36	s
7.	1926	creek, Philadelphia, Pa. ibid		c
8.	1927, Sept. 3	stream, Middleton, N.Y. *New York Times,* Sept. 4, 1927.	"good-sized"	c
9.	1927, Nov.	Mumford River, Mass. *New York Times,* Nov. 13, 1927.	- one was 34	6 s 2 k
10.	1929, Jun. 17	Galt, Ontario *New York Times,* Jun. 19, 1929.	36	c
11,	1929, Jun. 18	Toronto, Ontario, *ibid*	60 12	s c
12.	1929, Jul. 2	Matamoras, Port Jervis, N.Y. *New York Times,* Jul. 3, 1929.	24	
13.	1929, Sept.	Hackensack Meadows, N.J. *BCF,* p. 591; *New York American,* Sept. 19, 1929.	31	
14.	1929, Sept.	creek, Wolcott, N.Y. *BCF,* p. 591; *New York Sun,* Sept. 23, 1929.	28	c
15.	1929, Oct. 2	Collender's Point, Darien, Conn. *New York Times,* Oct. 3, 1929.	3	f
16.	1930, Summer	Tulare Lake Basin, Corcoran, Cal. *Sacramento Union,* Sacramento, Cal., May 17, 1971.	72	s
17.	1931, Mar. 22	bushes on estate, Pleasantville, N.Y. *New York Times,* May 22, 1931.	24	c
18,	1932, Jun. 28	Bronx River, Westchester Co., N.Y. *New York Times,* Jun. 30, 1932.	- 36	2-3 s 1 f dead
19.	1932, Jul. 1	Crestwood Lake, Westchester Co., N.Y. *New York Times,* Jul. 2, 1932.		
20.	1932, Jul. 7	Shrewsbury River, Wharf St., Red Bank, N.J. *New York Sun,* Jul. 7 or 8, 1932.	14	

Ref. No.	Date	Location and Source	Length (inches)	Remarks
21.	1933, Sept. 11	Passaic River, N.J. *New York Times,* Sept. 12, 1933.	36 30	2 s k
22.	1933, Dec. 4	sandbar, Riverdale, Md. *Times-Herald,* Washington, D.C., Dec. 5, 1933.	46	c
23	1935, Feb.	sewer, East 123rd St., N.Y., N.Y. (See text.)	90	k
24.	1935, Mar. 7	Northern Yonkers, N.Y. *New York Times,* Mar. 8, 1935.	36	
25.	1935, Mar.	Grass Sprain, Westchester Co., N.Y. *ibid.*	72	f dead
26.	1935, Jul. 6	Huffman Pond, Xenia, Ohio *New York Times,* Jul. 7, 1935.	36	c
27.	1937, Jun. 1	Pier 9, East River, N.Y., N.Y. *New York Times,* Jun. 7, 1937.	49	c
28.	1937, Jun. 6	Brooklyn Museum subway station, N.Y., N.Y. *New York Times,* Jun. 7, 1937.	24	c
29.	1937, Jul. 18	brook, Franconia Golf Course, Palmer, Mass. *New York Times,* Jul. 18, 1937.	15 18	c c
30.	1937, Aug. 30	bayou, Lake Decatur, Decatur, Ill. *Decatur Herald,* Decatur, Ill., Sept. 1, 1937, p. 3.	-	s
31.	1938	Huron River, Mich. *Detroit News,* Detroit, Mich., Jul. 7, 1955.	22	
32.	1938, Aug. 11	Huguenot Lake, New Rochelle, N.Y. *New York Times,* Aug. 16, 1938, and Aug. 20, 1938.	longest was 19	5 c
33.	1939, Aug. 7	Honeoye Creek, Staunton, Va. *New York Times,* Aug. 7, 1939.	24	c
34.	1941, Jun.	stream, Lakefield, Minn. Minneapolis *Sunday Tribune and Star Journal,* Minneapolis, Minn., Jun. 22, 1941, p.12.	-	shot but untaken
35.	1942, Aug. 16	Lake Mindowaskin, Westfield, N.Y. *New York Times,* Aug. 17, 1942.	48	k
36.	1942, Nov. 18	Herring Creek, lower Potomac River, Md. *Washington Post,* Washington, D.C., Nov. 19, 1942.	2 86	s k
37.	1943, Jun.	Colorado River, Lost Lake, Ariz. *Copeia,* No. 3, 1954, pp. 222-223.	120	k
38.	1946, Dec.	Mariah Creek, Vincennes, Ind. *Indianapolis Star,* Indianapolis, Ind., Dec. 31, 1946.		

Ref. No.	Date	Location and Source	Length (inches)	Remarks
39.	1949, Jul.	Rock Creek, Eagletown, Okla. *Copeia,* No. 1, Mar. 30, 1950, p. 57.	102	k
	1949, Aug. 9-16	Lake Bradford, Princess Anne Co., Va. *Herpetologia,* Vol. 9, No. 2, pp. 71-72.	48 36	s c
41.	1949, Fall	irrigation ditch, Ariz. *Copeia,* No. 3, 1954, pp. 222-223.	15	
42.	1950, Spring	tourist court, Tucson, Ariz. *ibid.*	60	c
43.	1950?- 1953?	La Paz Slough, Parker, Ariz. *ibid.*	large	s
44.	1953	Elizabeth Lake, Oakland Co., Mich. *Detroit News,* Detroit, Mich., Jul. 10, 1955.	24	c
45.	1955, Jul. 9	Island Lake, Oakland Co., Mich. *Detroit News,* Detroit, Mich., Jul. 7, 1955.	60-72	c
46.	1955, Jun-Jul.	Lower Long Lake, Oakland Co., Mich. *Detroit News,* Detroit, Mich., Jul 7, 1955.	36-72	s (also tracks found)
47.	1956, Jun.	Harris Lake, Oakland Co., Mich. *Detroit News,* Detroit, Mich., Jun. 25, 1956.	17	c
48.	1956, Jun.	Susan Lake, Oakland Co., Mich. *ibid*	-	rumors
49.	1957, Jul. 10	Lower Long Lake, Oakland Co., Mich. *Detroit News,* Detroit, Mich., Jul. 10, 1957.	57	
50.	1957, Aug. 4	Susan Lake, Oakland Co., Mich. *Detroit News,* Detroit, Mich., Aug. 5, 1957.	42	k
51.	1957, Sept. -1958, Jun.	Folsom Lake, Calif. Personal communication from Patricia Masterson of the *Folsom Telegraph,* and from Jim McClarin. *Sacramento Union,* Sacramento, Calif., May 17, 1971.	-	s (of several)
52.	1958, Oct.	Mount Clemens, Mich. *Detroit News,* Detroit, Mich., Oct. 18,1958.	14	
53.	1959, Sept.	Fall Creek, Indianapolis, Ind. *Indianapolis Star,* Sept. 10, 1959, p.51.	18	
54.	1960, Nov. 18	Hines Park, Detroit, Mich. *Detroit News,* Detroit, Mich., Nov. 20,1960.	36	
55.	1962, Dec.	Pennsylvania Avenue, Washington, D.C. *Washington Post,* Dec. 23, 1962.	12	c

Ref. No.	Date	Location and Source	Length (inches)	Remarks
56.	1966, Oct. 24	hot water ditch, Lake Decatur, Decatur, Ill. *Decatur Review,* Oct. 26, 1966.	48-72 all were 12	s 13 c
57.	1967, May 31	horticulture pond, MSU, Lansing, Mich. *State Journal,* Lansing, Mich., Jun. 1, 1967.	16	c
58.	1967, Jun. 26	895 West Eldorado, Decatur, Ill. *Decatur Review,* Jun. 27, 1967, p. 22.	10	c
59.	1968, Jun. 6	Capitol Building, Lansing, Mich. *State Journal,* Lansing, Mich., Jun. 7, 1968.	18	c
60.	1970, Jul.	basement drain, Newton, Kans. *Newton Kansan,* Newton, Kans., Jul. 16, 1970.	10	k
61.	1970, Jul. 30	shore of man-made lake, Lombard, Ill. *Chicago Tribune,* Jul. 31, 1970, p. 3.	18	
62.	1970, Aug. 4	pond, Red Hook, N.Y. *Denver Post,* Denver, Colo., Aug. 5, 1970. *Daily Freeman,* Kingston, N.Y., Aug. 5 & 6, 1970. *Gazette-Advertiser,* Rhinebeck, N.Y., Aug. 6, 1970.	48	k
63.	1970, Sept. 20	Wyandotte St. West, Windsor, Ont. *Windsor Star,* Windsor, Ont., Sept. 21, 1970.	36	
64.	1970, Sept. 21	cotton bin, Brownsville, Tex. *Brownsville Herald,* Brownsville, Tex., Sept. 21, 1970	18	c
65.	1970, Sept.	neatly clipped lawn, Metaire, La. *New York Times,* Sept. 25, 1970.	48	c
66.	1971, Jul. 9	Pewaukee Lake, Pewaukee, Wis. *Milwaukee Journal,* Milwaukee, Wis., Jul. 10, 1971, p. 1.	30	c
67.	1971, Aug.	Sangamon River, Oakley, Ill. *Decatur Herald,* Decatur, Ill., Aug. 9, 1971.		
68.	1972, Sept. 22	US 66, Chenoa, Ill. *Courier,* Champaign-Urbana, Ill., Sept. 22, 1972, p. 6.	36	
69.	1973, Jul. 28	vacant lot, Montreal, Que. *Toronto Star,* Toronto, Ont., Jul. 30, 1973.	10.5	
70.	1973, late summer	upper Morris and lower Sussex Cos., N.J. *The Monster Times,* N.Y., N.Y., Nov. 1973, p. 25.	"giant"	

Ref. No.	Date	Location and Source	Length (inches)	Remarks
71.	1975, Oct. 23	Lafayette Lake, Lafayette, California *Lebanon* (PA) *Daily News* 24 Oct., 1975	96	
72.	1978, Summer	Interstate 70, Olathe, *Kansas Daily News,* Olathe, Kansas 10 Mar. 1979	?	
73.	1978, Jun. 30-Jul. 7	Little Arkansas River, Wichita, Kansas *Wichita Eagle Beacon,* 8 July 1978	120	
74.	1978, July 2	13th Street Creek, Wichita, Kansas *Wichita Eagle Beacon,* 8 July 1978	18	
75.	1978, Nov.	Linden, New Jersey *The Patriot,* Harrisburg, Pennsylvania 25 November 1978	36	
76.	1979, Mar.	small creek, Stilwell, Kansas *Daily News,* Olathe, Kansas 9 Mar. 1979	36	
77.	1980, Aug. 24	Edison Board Basin, Edison, New Jersey *News Tribune,* Woodbridge, NJ 27 Aug. 1980	60	
78.	1980, Sept. 20	backyard, Windsor, Ontario *Windsor Star* 33 Sept. 1980	24	c
79.	1981, Jun. 23	Kings River, Fresno, California *San Francisco Chronicle* 24 June 1981	48	s
80.	1981, Aug. 5	Feather River, Yuba City, California *San Francisco Examiner,* 13 Aug. 1981	82	s claw prints
81.	1982, Apr. 1	Dover, Delaware *The Sun,* San Bernardino, California 2 Apr. 80	57	c
82.	1982, Aug. 7	drainage pipe, Hampton, Virginia *Boston Globe,* 8 Aug. 1982	30	c
83.	1982, Aug. 9	Kensico Reservoir, Valhalla, New York *New York Post,* 12 Aug. 1982	26	
84.	1983, Jun. 18	lake shore, Berne, New York *Schenectady* (New York) *Gazette,* 22 June 1983	28	c

Phantom Ships

by Mark A. Hall and Loren Coleman

Ref. No.	Location	Descriptions	When Seen
1.	Tombigee River, Alabama	spectre vessel	?
2.	near Farallon Islands, Calif.	phantom ship	autumn
3.	San Diego Bay, Calif.	phantom ship	spring
4.	off San Francisco Bay, Calif.	clipper ship, Tennessee	in fog
5.	New Haven Harbor, Conn.	sailing ship, against wind	June
6.	sea sw of Cortez, Florida	spectre ship	summer
7.	Casco Bay, Maine	the Dash with crew and always in fog; full sails	August
8.	near Foggs Point, Smith Island, Maryland	British man-of-war; sounds, voices, music	moonlit nights
9.	off Cape Cod, Mass.	spectre ship with a phantom light	after a storm
10.	Lake Michigan, Michigan	phantom ship	?
11.	Lake Saint Clair, Michigan	phantom ship	?
12.	near Raccourci Island, Miss.	phantom ship	?
13.	near Isles of Shoals, N.H.	the schooner *White River*	summer twilight; noonday mists
14.	Gravesend Bay, New York Harbor, New York	phantom vessel	spring
15.	Hudson River, New York	clipper ship	before, after, or during a storm
16.	Tappan Zee, New York	"America's Flying Dutchman"	summer twilight; calm sea
17.	Albemarle Sound to Cape Hatteras, North Carolina	phantom ship	?
18.	Devil's Lake, North Dakota	phantom steamboat; lights; sounds	moonless nights
19.	over Lake Erie, near Erie, Pennsylvania	burning object 200 or more feet in length	during or after storm
20.	off Block Island, Rhode Island	sometimes small; a burning ship; emits luminous rays	late December; sometimes before storms
21.	Galveston Bay, Texas, and coast of Mexico	a schooner and two feluccas	?
22.	Lake Morey, Vermont	Aunt Sally, phantom steamship	moonlit, still, foggy nights; August
23.	Dismal Swamp and Lake Drummond, Virginia	phantom canoe; spectre ship	?
24.	Rappahannock River, Virginia	phantom ship	?

Ref. No.	Location	Descriptions	When Seen
25.	Devil's Lake, Wisconsin	phantom canoe	still, cold nights; mists
26.	Platte River, Wyoming	phantom ship	autumn
27.	near Vancouver Island, British Columbia	phantom vessel	?
28.	Askins Point, Ontario	phantom ship	?
29.	Etobicoke Creek, Ontario	phantom vessel	summer
30.	near Manitoulin Islands, Lake Huron, Quebec	sailing vessel	during storms
31.	off Cape D'Espoir in Gaspe Bay, Quebec		
32.	Chaleur Bay, seen between Dalhousie and Perce Rock, Quebec and New Brunswick	a flame, a burning ship, a great bonfire	before a storm
33.	Bay of Fundy, off St. Martins, New Brunswick	burning ship	September or October
34.	Northumberland Strait off Richibucto, New Brunswick	burning ship; burns for one hour	before a storm; seen every seven years
35.	Northumberland Strait off Cape John, Nova Scotia	burning ship	early December
36.	Northumberland Strait off Merigomish, Nova Scotia	burning ship	before or after the autumnal equinox
37.	Mahone Bay, Nova Scotia	called the "Teazer Light"	?
38.	Gulf of St. Lawrence near Prince Edward Island	called "Packet Light"; a firebird; a ball of fire; a burning ship	before a storm, after a storm

A Few Bedeviled Places

Name of Location	State/County	Phenomena
Devil's Hole Cave	Arkansas/Boone	monster lizard
Canon Diablo	Arizona/Coconino	anomalous meteoritic activity
Devil's Knoll	California/Santa Barbara	mystery deaths
Devil's Gate Reservoir	California/Los Angeles	children's disappearances
Mt. Diablo/Devil's Hole	California/Contra Costa	see Chapter 3
Seven Devils Canyon	Idaho/Adams	cattle mutilations
Devil's Kitchen	Illinois/Williamson	see Chapter 3
Devil's Bake Oven & Backbone	Illinois/Jackson	see Chapter 3
Devil's Backbone	Indiana/Lawrence	hauntings; woman's scream
Devil Swamp	Louisiana/West Baton Rouge	bubbling unexplained chemicals
Devil's Den	Maine/Kennebec	hauntings
Devil's Den	Massachusetts/Middlesex	buried treasure; Ghost
Devil's Pulpit	Massachusetts/Berkshire	lover's leap lore
Devil's Lake	Michigan/Lenawee	mystery plane crash
Devil's Track Lake	Minnesota/Cook	evil spirits
Devil's Elbow	Missouri/Pulaski	phantom panthers (see Chapter 21)
Devil's Hole	Nevada/Nye	Charles Manson's "hole in the world"; strange deaths and disappearances
Devil's Den	New Hampshire/Grafton	see Chapter 3
Devil's Highway	New Mexico/Dona Ana	evil spirits; Trinity A-bomb site
Devil's Tramping Ground	North Carolina/Chatham	curious cleared circle; Bigfoot hauntings
Devil's Lake	North Dakota/Ramsey	lake monster; phantom steamboat; mystery drownings
Devil's Promenade	Oklahoma/Ottawa	spook lights; UFOs
Devil's Den	Pennsylvania/Adams	giant snake/river monsters
Devil's Race Course	Pennsylvania/Bucks	ringing rocks; thunderbird lore
Devil's Foot Rock	Rhode Island/Washington	devil lore; opposite Lafayette House
Hill of the Little Devils	South Dakota/Clay	little evil spirits or elves
Devil's Lake	Wisconsin/Columbia	see Chapter 3

Name of Location	State/County	Phenomena
Devil's Tower	Wyoming/Crook	giant phantom bear; CE III movie fame
Devil's Outpost	Labrador	enormous phantom black dogs; horned imps; the devil
Devil's Hole Cave	Ontario/Welland	cold air blasts; evil spirits; misfortune; strange deaths
Le Champ du Diable (Devil's Field)	Quebec	misfortune; bad luck; transformations

Lake and River Monsters of North America

Alaska
Big Lake
Crosswind Lake
Lake Iliamna
Kalooluk Lake
Lake Minchurnina
Nonvianuk Lake

Arkansas
Bedias Creek
Lake Conway
Illinois River
Mud Lake
White River

California
Elizabeth Lake
Lake Elsinore
Lake Folsom
Homer Lake
Lafayette Lake
Lake Tahoe

Colorado
Lake Como

Connecticut
Basile Lake
Connecticut River

Florida
Lake Clinch
Lake Monroe
North Fork St. Lucie River
St. John's River
Suwanee River

Georgia
Chattahoochie River
No Man's Friend Pond
Savannah River
Smith Lake

Idaho
Lake Coeur d'Alene
Lake Payette
Pend Oreille Lake
Snake River
Tautphaus Park Lake

Illinois
Four Lakes Village Lake
Lake Michigan
Stump Pond
Thompson's Lake

Indiana
Bass Lake
Big Chapman's Lake
Eagle Creek
Hollow Block Lake
Huntington's Lake
Lake Manitou (Devil's Lake)
Lake Maxinkuckee
Wabash River

Iowa
Spirit Lake

Kansas
Kingman County Lake

Kentucky
Herrington Lake
Ohio River
Reynolds Lake

Louisiana
Calcasieu River

Maine
Boyden Lake
Chain Lakes
Machias Lake
Moosehead Lake
Rangeley Lake
Sysladobsis Lake

Massachusetts
Silver Lake
Twin Lakes

Michigan
Au Train Lake
Basswood Lake
Lake Huron
Lake Michigan
Narrow Lake
Paint River
Lake Superior
Swan Lake

Minnesota
Big (or Great) Sandy Lake

Mississippi
Mississippi River
Pascagoula River

Missouri
Lake Creve Coeur
Kansas River
Mississippi River
Missouri River
Lake of the Ozarks

Montana
Flathead Lake
Missouri River
Waterton Lake

Nebraska
Alkali Lake
(Renamed Walgren Lake)
Missouri River

Nevada
Lake Mead
Pegrand Lake
Pyramid Lake
Lake Walker

New Jersey
North Shrewsbury River
Passaic Falls

New York
Baldwinsville Mill Pond
Black River
Canandaigua Lake
Lake Champlain
Lake George
Hudson River
McGuire's Pond
Lake Onondaga
Lake Ontario
Silver Lake
Spirit Lake
Wading River
Lake of the Woods

North Carolina
Little Tennessee River
Valley River

North Dakota
Devil's Lake

Ohio
Lake Erie
Olentangy River
Slaven's Pond

Oregon
Crater Lake
Crescent Lake
Forked Mountain Lake
Hollow Block Lake
Upper Klamath Lake
Wallowa Lake

Pennsylvania
Wolf Pond

South Carolina
Goose Creek Lagoon

South Dakota
Campbell Lake

Texas
Brazos River
Klamath Lake

Utah
Bear Lake
Great Salt Lake

Mud Lake
Sevier Lake
Utah Lake

Vermont
Lake Champlain
Connecticut River
Dead Creek
Lake Memphremagog
Winooski River

Washington
Chelan Lake
Omak Lake
Quinault Lake
Rock Lake
Lake Washington

Wisconsin
Brown's Lake
Chippewa Lake
Devil's Lake
Elkhart Lake
Fowlei Lake
Lake Geneva
Madison Four Lakes
Mendota Lake
Mississippi River
Lake Monova
Pewaukee Lake
Red Cedar Lake and River
Rock Lake
Lake Superior
Lake Waubeau
Lake Winnebago
Yellow River

Wyoming
Lake DeSmet
Hutton Lake
Lake Katherine
Lake La Metrie

Alberta
Battle River
North Saskatchewan River

British Columbia
Campbell River
Lake Cowichan

Harrison Lake
Lake Okanagan
Seton Lake
Sushwap Lake
Lake Tagai
Thetis Lake

Manitoba
Cedar Lake
Lake Dauphin
Dirty Water Lake
Lake Manitoba
Lake Winnipeg
Lake Winnipegosis

New Brunswick
Skiff Lake
Lake Utopia

Ontario
Lake of Bays
Berens Lake
Deschenes Lake
Mazinaw Lake
Muskrat Lake
Lake Ontario
Ottawa River
Lake Sirncoe

Quebec
Lac Aylmer
Lac Baskatong
Blue Sea Lake
Lake Champlain
Reservoir Gouin
Lac Massawippi
Lac Mekinac
Lac Memphremagog
Mocking Lake
Moffat Lake
Lac-des-Piles
Lac Pohengamok
Lac Remi
Lac St. Clair
Lac St. Francois
Lac St. Jean
Lac-a-la-Tor-tue
Les-Trois-Lac
Lake Williams

Mysterious America:
A Regional Bibliography

The charting of a journey, be it on the road or through the library, can begin in many ways. As investigators of Mysterious America, you may be in pursuit of a specific unknown creature or phenomenon, or in quest of all inexplicable events for a specific area. For those who wish to explore the unexplained happenings of a particular location, I have assembled this bibliography of books, which I find the most helpful for regional inquiries. This bibliography was created in 1983, before instant searches of databases could be done via the Internet. For that reason, I am preserving it in mostly its original state, a document that will be helpful for those in search of volumes and resources that hold the treasures of a quieter, slower era of hunting down books in libraries and old bookstores. Today, you can go to various Internet search engines and type in a location and then do a sub-search for a specific anomaly. Look to the following books for a more in-depth overview of a collection or a location. Some of the dozen or so newer titles have been added because they have extensive resources and detailed location lists.

North America

Bord, Janet and Colin. *The Bigfoot Casebook.* Harrisburg: Stackpole, 1982.

Clark, Jerome. *The Unidentified!* Detroit: Visible Ink, 1999.

Clark, Jerome and Loren Coleman. *Creatures of the Outer Edge.* New York: Warner, 1978.

Coleman, Loren and Jerome Clark. *Cryptozoology A to Z.* New York: Fireside/Simon and Schuster, 1999.

Coleman, Loren and Patrick Huyghe. *The Field Guide to Bigfoot, Yeti, and Other Mystery Primates Worldwide.* New York: Avon, 1999.

Corliss, William R. Lightning, *Auroras, Nocturnal Lights and Related Luminous Phenomena.* Glen Arm, MD: Sourcebook Project, 1983.

Costello, Peter. *In Search of Lake Monsters.* New York: Coward, McCann & Georghegan, 1974.

Eberhart, George M. *A Geo-Bibliography of Anomalies.* Westport, Conn.: Greenwood, 1980.

Eberhart, George M. *Monsters: A Guide to Information on Unaccounted-for Creatures, Including Bigfoot, Many Water Monsters, and Other Irregular Animals.* New York: Garland, 1983.

Evans, Hillary and Patrick Huyghe. *The Field Guide to Ghosts and Other Apparitions.* New York: Quill/HarperCollins, 2000.

Fort, Charles. *The Books of Charles Fort.* New York: Dover Publications, 1974.

Green, John. *Sasquatch: The Apes Among Us.* Seattle: Hancock House, 1976.

Hall, Mark A. *Living Fossils.* Minneapolis: MAHP, 1999.

Hall, Mark A. *The Yeti, Bigfoot, and True Giants.* Minneapolis: MAHP, 1997.

Hall, Mark A. *Thunderbirds—The Living Legend!* Minneapolis: MAHP, 1994.

Heuvelmans, Bernard. *In the Wake of the Sea-Serpents.* New York: Hill & Wang, 1968.

Hitching, Francis. *The Mysterious World: An Atlas of the Unexplained.* New York: Holt, Rinehart & Winston, 1979.

Huyghe, Patrick. *The Field Guide to Extraterrestrials.* New York: Avon, 1996.

Kirk, John. *In the Domain of the Lake Monsters.* Toronto: Key Porter, 1998.

Michell, John and Robert J. M. Rickard. *Living Wonders.* London: Thames & Hudson, 1982.

Peterson, Natasha. *Sacred Sites: A Traveler's Guide to North America's Most Powerful, Mystical Landmarks.* Chicago: Contemporary, 1988.

Phillips, Ted. *Physical Traces Associated with UFO Sightings.* Evanston: Center for UFO Studies, 1975.

Roth, John E. *American Elves: An Encyclopedia of Little People from the Lore of 380 Ethnic Groups of the Western Hemisphere,* Jefferson, North Carolina: McFarland, 1997.

Sanderson, Ivan T. *The Continent We Live On.* New York: Random House, 1961.

Stacy, Dennis and Patrick Huyghe. *The Field Guide to UFOs.* New York: Quill/HarperCollins, 2000.

Trento, Salvatore M. *Field Guide to the Mysterious Places of Eastern North America.* New York: Henry Holt, 1997.

Trento, Salvatore M. *Field Guide to the Mysterious Places of the West.* Boulder: Pruett, 1994.

United States of America

Barth, Jack, Doug Kirby, Ken Smith, and Mike Wilkins. *Roadside America.* New York: Fireside/Simon and Schuster, 1986.

Bolte, Mary. *Haunted New England.* Riverside, Conn.: Chatham, 1972.

Botkin, B. A. *A Treasury of New England Folklore.* New York: Crown, 1965.

Botkin, B. A. *A Treasury of Western Folklore.* New York: Crown, 1975.

Brandon, Jim. *Rebirth of Pan: Hidden Faces of the American Earth Spirit.* Dunlap, IL: Firebird, 1983.

Brandon, Jim. *Weird America.* New York: Dutton, 1978.

Carey, George. *A Faraway Time and Place: Lore of the Eastern Shore,* New York: R. B. Luce, 1971.

Davidson, James Dale. *An Eccentric Guide to the United States.* New York: Berkley, 1977.

Fawcett, George D. *Quarter Century of Studies of UFOs in Florida, North Carolina and Tennessee Mount Airy:* Pioneer, 1975.

Federal Writers' Program. Each state's edition. Produced during the 1930s–1950s.

Fell, Barry. *America B.C.* New York: Quadrangle, 1976.

Folsom, Franklin. *America's Ancient Treasures.* New York: Rand McNally, 1974.

Goodwin, John. *Occult America.* Garden City: Doubleday, 1972.

Holzer, Hans. *Haunted Houses.* New York: Crown, 1971.

Holzer, Hans. *Yankee Ghosts.* New York: Ace, 1966.

Joseph, Frank. *Sacred Sites.* St. Paul: Llewellyn, 1992.

Life Editors. *The Life Treasury of American Folklore.* New York: Time, 1961.

Miller, Tom. *On the Border.* New York: Harper and Row, 1981.

O'Neill, J. P. *The Great New England Sea Serpent.* Camden, Maine: Down East Books, 1999.

Reynolds, James. *Ghosts in American Houses.* New York: Paperback Library, 1967.

Skinner, Charles. *American Myths and Legends.* (2 volumes) Detroit: Gale Research (reprint), 1974.

Skinner, Charles. *Myths and Legends of Our Own Land.* (2 volumes) Philadelphia: Lippincott, 1896.

Squier, E. G. and E. H. Davis. *Ancient Monuments of the Mississippi Valley.* Washington, D.C.: Smithsonian, 1848.

Stern, Jane and Michael. *Amazing America.* New York: Random House/Obst Books, 1978.

Trento, Salvatore Michael. *The Search for Lost America.* Chicago: Contemporary, 1978.

Webb, Richard. *Great Ghosts of the West.* Los Angeles: Nash, 1971.

Williams, Brad and Choral Pepper. *Lost Treasures of the West.* New York: Holt, Rinehart & Winston, 1975.

Williams, Brad and Choral Pepper. *The Mysterious West.* New York. World, 1967.

Yankee Editors. *Mysterious New England.* Dublin, NH: Yankee, 1971.

Alabama

Windham, Kathryn Tucker and Margaret Gillis Figh. *13 Alabama Ghosts and Jeffrey.* Huntsville: Strode, 1969.

Alaska

Badlam, Alexander. *The Wonders of Alaska.* San Francisco: The Author, 1891.

Carrighar, Sally. *Wild Voice of the North.* New York: Garden City, 1959.

Colp, Harry D. *The Strangest Story Ever Told.* New York: Exposition, 1953.

Higginson, Ella. *Alaska: The Great Country.* New York: Macmillan, 1917.

Marshall, Robert. *Arctic Village.* New York: Literary Guild, 1933.

Arizona

Barry, Bill. *The Ultimate Encounter.* New York: Pocket Books, 1978.

Gentry, Curt. *The Killer Mountains.* New York: New American Library, 1968.

Jennings, Gary. *Treasure of the Superstition Mountains.* New York: Norton, 1973.

Kluckholn, Clyde. *Navaho Witchcraft.* Boston: Beacon, 1962.

Walton, Travis. *The Walton Encounter.* New York: Berkley, 1978.

Waters, Frank. *Book of the Hopi.* New York: Viking, 1963.

Arkansas

Allsop, Fred. *Folklore of Romantic Arkansas.* New York: Grolier, 1931.

Crabtree, Smokey. *Smokey and the Fouke Monster.* Fouke: Days Creek Production, 1974.

Randolph, Vance. *Ozark Superstitions.* New York: Columbia University Press, 1947.

Randolph, Vance. *We Always Lie to Strangers.* New York: Columbia University Press, 1951.

California

Andrews, Richard. *The Truth Behind the Legends of Mt. Shasta.* New York: Carleton, 1976.

Bailey, Philip A. *Golden Mirages.* New York: Macmillan, 1940.

Bell, Horace. *On the Old West Coast.* New York: William Morrow, 1930.

Druffel, Ann and D. Scott Rogo. *The Tujunga Canyon Contacts.* Englewood Cliffs: Prentice-Hall, 1980.

Eichorn, A. F. *The Mt. Shasta Story. Mt. Shasta: The Herald,* 1957.

Gross, Loren E. *The UFO Wave of 1896.* Fremont: The Author, 1974.

Holzer, Hans. *Ghosts of the Golden West.* New York: Ace, 1968.

Marinacci, Mike. *Mysterious California: Strange Places and Eerie Phenomena in the Golden State.* Los Angeles: Panpipe Press, 1987. (Marinacci notes this book is a direct result of *Mysterious America, 1983.*)

Reinstadt, Randall A. *Ghosts, Bandits and Legends of Old Monterey.* Carmel: Ghost Town Publications, 1972.

St. Clair, David. *The Psychic World of California.* New York: Bantam, 1973.

Colorado

Davidson, Lavette J. and Forrester Blake. *Rocky Mountain Tales.* Norman: University of Oklahoma, 1947.

Eberhart, Perry. *Treasure Tales of the Rockies.* Chicago: Swallow, 1968.

O'Brien, Christopher. *Enter the Valley,* New York: St. Martins, 1999.

O'Brien, Christopher. *The Mysterious Valley,* New York: St. Martins, 1996.

Orr, Cathy M. and Michael J. Preston. *Urban Folklore from Colorado.* Ann Arbor, MI: Xerox, 1976.

Smith, Frederick W. *Cattle Mutilation: The Unthinkable Truth.* Cedaredge: Freedland, 1976.

Connecticut

Taylor, John M. *The Witchcraft Delusion in Colonial Connecticut.* New York: Grafton, 1908.

Delaware

Baker, Denise. *Delaware Folklore.* Sussex County: Delaware Arts Council, 1978.

District of Columbia

Alexander, John. *Ghosts: Washington's Most Famous Ghost Stories.* Washington, D.C.: Washingtonian Books, 1975.

INFO Editors. *Weird Washington Guidebook.* Arlington, VA: International Fortean Organization, 1976.

Florida

Fuller, Elizabeth. *My Search for the Ghost of Flight 401.* New York: Berkley, 1978.

Fuller, John. *The Ghost of Flight 401.* New York: Berkley, 1976.

Tinsley, Jim Bob. *The Florida Panther.* St. Petersburg: Great Outdoors, 1970.

Georgia

Fancher, Betsy. *The Lost Legacy of Georgia's Golden Isles.* Garden City: Doubleday, 1971.

McQueen, A. S. and H. Mizell. *History of the Okefenokee Swamp.* Folkston: The Authors, 1949.

Hawaii
Armitage, George T. and Henry Judd. *Ghost Dog and Other Hawaiian Legends.* Honolulu: Advertiser, 1944.
Beckwith, Martha. *Hawaiian Mythology.* New Haven: Yale University, 1940.
Cox, Halley. *Hawaiian Petroglyphs.* Honolulu: Bishop Museum, 1970.
Kalakaua, David. *The Legends and Myths of Hawaii.* Rutland, VT: Tuttle, 1972.
Rice, William H. *Hawaiian Legends.* Honolulu: Bishop Museum, 1977.
Thrum, Thomas. *Hawaiian Folk Tales.* Chicago: McClurg, 1917.
Westervelt, W. D. *Hawaiian Legends of Volcanoes.* Boston: George Ellis, 1916.
Westervelt, W. D. *Legends of Old Honolulu.* Boston: George Ellis, 1915.

Idaho
Bird, Annie L. Boise: *The Peace Valley.* Boise: Canyon County Historical Society, 1975.
Erwin, Richard. *Indian Rock Writing in Idaho.* Boise: Idaho Historical Society, 1930.
Fisher, Vardis. *Idaho Lore.* Caldwell: Caxton, 1939.

Illinois
Allen, John W. *Legends and Lore of Southern Illinois.* Carbondale: Southern Illinois University, 1963.
Angle, Paul M., ed. *The Great Chicago Fire.* Chicago: Chicago Historical Society, 1946.
Hyatt, Harry Middleton. *Folklore from Adams County,* Illinois. Hannibal, MO: Hyatt Foundation, 1965.
Means, Ruth. *The Piasa.* Alton: Alton-Godfrey Rotary Club, n.d.
Rath, Jay. *The I-Files: True Reports of Unexplained Phenomena in Illinois.* Madison, Wisconsin: Trailside, 1999.
St. Clair, David. *Watseka.* Chicago: Playboy, 1977.
Steiger, Brad. *Psychic City: Chicago.* Garden City: Doubleday, 1976.
Taylor, Troy. *Haunted Decatur Revisited.* Alton, Illinois: Whitechapel, 2000.
Taylor, Troy. *Haunted Illinois.* Alton, Illinois: Whitechapel, 1999. (Taylor has written more than a dozen books on Illinois wonders, phantoms, and haunts.)

Indiana
Black, Glenn. *Angel Site.* Indianapolis: Indiana Historical Society, 1967.
Hartle, Orvil R. *A Carbon Experiment?* LaPorte: The Author, 1963.
Kellar, James. *An Introduction to the Prehistory of Indiana.* Indianapolis: Indiana Historical Society, 1973.

Iowa
McKusick, Marshall. *The Davenport Conspiracy.* Iowa City: University of Iowa, 1970.
McKusick, Marshall. *Men of Ancient Iowa.* Ames: Iowa State University, 1964.
Steiger, Brad. *Irene Hughes on Psychic Safari.* New York: Warner, 1972.
Steiger, Brad. *Mysteries of Time and Space.* New York: Dell, 1972. (Steiger, who used to live in Iowa, is a prolific writer and often discusses Iowa phenomena.)

Kansas

Koch, William E., ed. *Folklore from Kansas: Customs, Beliefs and Superstitions.* Lawrence: Regent Press of Kansas, 1980.

Sackett, Samuel and William E. Koch. *Kansas Folklore.* Lincoln: University of Nebraska, 1961.

Kentucky

Atkinson, Paul Lewis. *Kentucky: Land of Legend and Lore.* Fort Thomas: Northern Kentucky Historical Society, 1962.

Davis, Isabel and Ted Bloecher. *Close Encounter at Kelly and Others of 1955.* Evanston: Center for UFO Studies, 1978.

Meloy, Harold. *Mummies of Mammoth Cave.* Shelbyville, Indiana: Micron, 1973.

Montell, William Lynwood. *Ghosts Along the Cumberland: Deathlore in the Kentucky Foothills.* Knoxville: University of Tennessee, 1975.

Louisiana

de Lavigne, Jeanne. *Ghost Stories of Old New Orleans.* New York: Rinehart, 1946.

Kane, Harnett T. *The Bayous of Louisiana.* New York: William Morrow, 1943.

Saxon, Lyle. *Gumbo Ya-Ya.* New York: Houghton-Mifflin, 1945.

Saxon, Lyle. *Fabulous New Orleans.* New York: Appleton-Century, 1935.

Tallant, Robert. *Voodoo in New Orleans.* New York: Macmillan, 1946.

Maine

Beck, Horace. *The Folklore of Maine.* Philadelphia: Lippincott, 1957.

Reich, Wilhelm. *Contact with Space.* Rangeley: Core Pilot, 1957.

Snow, Edward Rowe. *Romance of Casco Bay.* New York: Dodd, Mead, 1975.

Snow, Edward Rowe. *Mysterious Tales of the New England Coast.* New York: Dodd, Mead, 1961. (Snow has written several books on the lore of Maine and the sea nearby.)

Verrill, A. Hyatt. *Romantic and Historic Maine.* New York: Dodd, Mead, 1938.

Maryland

Carey, George C. *Maryland Folk Legends and Folk Songs.* Cambridge, MO: Tidewater, 1971.

Parke, Francis Neal. *Witchcraft in Maryland Baltimore:* Maryland Historical Society, 1937.

Massachusetts

Allen, Joseph. *Tales and Trails of Martha's Vineyard.* Boston: Little Brown, 1938.

Delabarre, Edmund Burke. *Dighton Rock.* New York: Walter Neale, 1928.

Fowler, Raymond E. *The Andreasson Affair.* Englewood Cliffs: Prentice-Hall, 1979.

Fowler, Raymond E. *UFOs: Interplanetary Visitors.* Jericho, NY: Exposition, 1974.

Hansen, Chadwick. *Witchcraft at Salem.* New York: George Braziller, 1969.

Snow, Edward Rowe. *Boston Bay Mysteries and Other Tales.* New York: Dodd, Mead, 1977.

Snow, Edward Rowe. *The Islands of Boston Harbor.* New York: Dodd, Mead, 1971.

Summers, Montague. *The Geography of Witchcraft.* Secaucus, NJ: Citadel, 1965.

Michigan

Boyer, Dwight. *Ghost Ships of the Great Lakes.* New York: Dodd, Mead, 1968.

Boyer, Dwight. *Ghost Stories of the Great Lakes.* New York: Dodd, Mead, 1966.

Boyer, Dwight. *Strange Adventures of the Great Lakes.* New York: Dodd, Mead, 1974.

Boyer, Dwight. *True Tales of the Great Lakes.* New York: Dodd, Mead, 1971.

Dorson, Richard M. *Bloodstoppers and Bearwalkers: Folk Traditions of the Upper Peninsula.* Cambridge: Harvard University, 1952.

Dorson, Richard M. *Negro Folktales in Michigan.* Cambridge: Harvard University, 1956.

Gourley, Jay. *The Great Lakes Triangle.* Greenwich, CT: Fawcett, 1977.

Minnesota

Blegen, Theodore C. *The Kensington Rune Stone: New Light on an Old Riddle.* St. Paul: Minnesota Historical Society, 1968.

Festinger, Leon and Henry W. Riecken, Stanley Schachter. *When Prophecy Fails.* Minneapolis: University of Minnesota, 1956.

Holland, Hjalmar. *The Kensington Stone.* Ephraim, WI: The Author, 1932.

Rath, Jay. *The M-Files: True Reports of Unexplained Phenomena in Minnesota.* Madison, Wisconsin: Trailside, 1998.

Mississippi

Claiborne, J. F. H. *Mississippi: As a Province, Territory and State.* Baton Rouge: Louisiana State University, 1964.

Missouri

Collins, Earl. *Folktales of Missouri.* Boston: Christopher, 1935.

Collins, Earl. *Legends and Lore of Missouri.* San Antonio: Naylor, 1951.

Loftin, Bob. *Spookvilles Ghost Lights.* Tulsa: The Author, 1967.

Moore, Tom. *Mysterious Tales and Legends of the Ozarks.* Philadelphia: Dorrance, 1938.

Randolph, Vance. *Ozark Ghost Stories.* Girard, Kansas: Haldeman-Julius, 1944.

Randolph, Vance. *Tall Tales from the Ozarks.* Girard, Kansas: Haldeman-Julius, 1944.

Randolph, Vance. *Wild Stories from the Ozarks.* Girard, KS: Haldeman-Julius, 1943.

Rayburn, Otto. *Ozark Country.* New York: Duell, Sloan & Pearce, 1941.

Montana

Donovan, Roberta and Keith Wolverton. *Mystery Stalks the Prairie.* Raynesford: THAR, 1976.

Nebraska

Pound, Louise. *Nebraska Folklore.* Lincoln: University of Nebraska, 1959.

Welsch, Roger L. *A Treasury of Nebraska Pioneer Folklore.* Lincoln: University of Nebraska, 1966.

Nevada

Chalfant, Willy. *Gold Guns and Ghost Towns.* Palo Alto: Stanford University, 1947.

Greenway, John. *Folklore of the Great West.* Palo Alto: Western Folkways, 1969.

Heizer R. F. and M. A. Baumhoff. *Prehistoric Rock Paintings of Nevada and Eastern California.* Berkeley: University of California, 1962.

New Hampshire

Glynn, Frank. *Report of Excavations at North Salem.* Harrisburg, PA: Eastern States Archaeological Federation, 1959.

Goodwin, William B. *The Ruins of Great Ireland in New England.* Boston: Meador, 1946.

Gore, M. P. and Eva Speare. *New Hampshire Folktales.* Plymouth: NH Federation of Women's Clubs, 1932.

Feldman, Mark. *The Mystery Hill Story.* Derry: Mystery Hill Press, 1977.

Fuller, John. *The Incident at Exeter.* New York: Putnam, 1966.

Fuller, John. *The Interrupted Journey.* New York: Dial Press, 1966.

Speare, Eva. *New Hampshire Folk Tales.* Plymouth: The Author, 1964.

New Jersey

McCloy, James F. and Ray Miller, Jr. *The Jersey Devil.* Wallingford, PA: Middle Atlantic Press, 1976.

McMahon, William H. *Pine Barren Legends, Lore and Lies.* Wallingford, PA: Middle Atlantic Press, 1980.

United States Naval Research Laboratory. *NRL Investigations of East Coast Acoustics Events.* Washington, DC: Government Printing Office, 1978.

New Mexico

Berlitz, Charles and William L. Moore. *The Roswell Incident.* New York: Grosset & Dunlap, 1980. (Roswell books are plentiful, of course.)

Bullock, Alice. *Living Legends of Santa Fe Country.* Santa Fe: Sunstone, 1972.

Cushing, Frank. *My Adventures in Zuni Country.* Palo Alto: American West, 1970.

Fry, Daniel. *The White Sands Incident.* Los Angeles: New Age, 1954.

James, George Wharton. *New Mexico: The Land of Delight Makers.* Boston: Page, 1920.

Simmons, Marc. *Witchcraft in the Southwest.* Flagstaff: Northland, 1974.

New York

Jones, Louis C. *Spooks of the Valley.* Boston: Houghton-Mifflin, 1948.

Jones, Louis C. *Things That Go Bump in the Night.* New York: Hill & Wang, 1959.

Merrill, Auch. *The White Woman and Her Valley.* Rochester: Creek Books, n.d.

Thomas, Howard. *Folklore from the Adirondack Foothills.* Prospect: Prospect Books, 1958.

Thompson, Harold W. *Body, Boots and Britches.* Philadelphia: Lippincott, 1940.

North Carolina

Harden, John. *The Devil's Tramping Ground.* Chapel Hill: University of North Carolina, 1949.

Harden, John. *Tar Heel Ghosts.* Chapel Hill: University of North Carolina, 1954.

Howe, C. K. *Solving the Riddle of the Lost Colony.* Beaufort: Skarren, 1947.

Lael, Ralph L. *The Brown Mountain Lights.* Morgantown: The Author, 1965.

Mansfield, George Rogers. *Origin of the "Brown Mountain Light" in North Carolina.* Washington, DC: US Geological Survey, 1971.

Morgan, Fred T. *Ghost Tales of the Uwharries.* Winston-Salem: John T. Blair, 1968.

Roberts, Nancy. *An Illustrated Guide to Ghosts and Mysterious Occurrences in the Old North State.* Charlotte: Heritage House, 1959.

Robinson, Melvin. *Riddle of the Lost Colony.* New Bern: Owen G. Dunn, 1946.

Whedbee, Charles. *The Flaming Ship of Ocracoke.* Winston-Salem: John T. Blair, 1971.

Whedbee, Charles. *Legends of the Outer Banks.* Winston-Salem: John T. Blair, 1966.

North Dakota

Bicentennial Committee. *Devil's Lake Bicentennial History.* Devil's Lake: Bicentennial Committee, 1976.

Devil's Lake Diamond Jubilee Committee. *Devil's Lake: 75 Years.* Devil's Lake: Ness Press, 1957.

Pioneers' Society. *Devil's Lake Region.* Devil's Lake: *Daily Journal,* circa 1923.

Ohio

Greenman, Emerson F. *Serpent Mound,* Columbus: Ohio Historic Society, 1970.

Page Research Editors. *Bigfoot: Tales of Unexplained Creatures.* Rome, OH: Page Research, 1978.

Pilichis, Dennis. *Night Siege: The Northern Ohio UFO-Creature Invasion,* Rome, OH: Page Research, 1982.

Stringfield, Leonard H. *Situation Red: The UFO Siege.* New York: Fawcett Crest, 1977.

Oklahoma

Farley, Gloria. *The Vikings Were Here.* Poteau: The Independent, 1970.

Landsverk, O. G. *Ancient Messages on American Stones.* Glendale, CA: Norseman, 1969.

Oregon

Hult, Ruby. *Lost Mines and Treasures of the Pacific Northwest.* Portland: Binford & Mort, 1957.

Jones, Suzi. *Oregon Folklore.* Eugene: University of Oregon, 1977.

Pennsylvania

Barach, Sally M. *Haunts of Adams and Other Counties.* Indiana PA: Halldin, 1972.

Jeffrey, Adi-Kent Thomas. *Ghosts in the Valley.* New Hope: New Hope Art, 1970.

Jeffrey, Adi-Kent Thomas. *More Ghosts in the Valley.* New Hope: New Hope Art, 1973.

Korson, George. *Black Rock: Mining Folklore of the Pennsylvania Dutch.* Baltimore: Johns Hopkins, 1960.

Korson, George. *Pennsylvania Songs and Legends.* Philadelphia: University of Pennsylvania, 1949.

Lewis, Arthur. *Hex.* New York: Trident, 1969.

Lyman, Robert R. *Amazing Indeed!* Coudersport: Potter Enterprise, 1973.

Lyman, Robert R. *Forbidden Land.* Coudersport: Potter Enterprise, 1971.

Rhode Island

Bacon, Edgar. *Narragansett Bay: Its Historic and Romantic Associations.* New York: Putnam, 1904.

Means, Philip. *The Newport Tower.* New York: Holt, 1942.

Weber, Ken. *Twenty-five Walks in Rhode Island.* Somersworth, NH: New Hampshire Publishing Co., 1978.

South Carolina

Kershaw, C. D. *The Gray Lady: A Legend of Old Camden.* Charleston: Walker, Evans & Coggswell, n.d.

Martin, Margaret Rhett. *Charleston Ghosts.* Columbia: University of South Carolina, 1963.

Roberts, Nancy and Bruce. *Ghosts of the Carolinas.* Charlotte: McNally & Loftin, 1962.

South Dakota

Bennett, Estalline. *Old Deadwood Days.* New York: Charles Scribner's Sons, 1935.

Tennessee

Bell, Charles B. *The Bell Witch: A Mysterious Spirit,* Nashville: Lark, 1934.

Faulkner, Charles H. *The Old Stone Fort.* Knoxville: University of Tennessee, 1968.

Windham, Kathryn Tucker. *Thirteen Tennessee Ghosts and Jeffrey.* Huntsville: Strode, 1977.

Texas

Abernathy, Francis. *Tales from the Big Thicket.* Austin: University of Texas, 1966.

Clarke, Sally Ann. *The Lake Worth Monster.* Fort Worth: The Author, 1969.

Dobie, J. Frank. *Tales of Old-Time Texas.* Boston: Little, Brown, 1955.

Miles, Elton. *Tales of the Big Bend.* College State: Texas A & M, 1976.

Wheeler, David R. *The Lubbock Lights.* New York: Award, 1977.

Utah

Lee, Hector. *The Three Nephites: The Substance and Significance of the Legend in Folklore.* Albuquerque: University of New Mexico, 1949.

Salisbury, Frank B. *The Utah UFO Display.* Old Greenwich, CT: Devin-Adair, 1974.

Vermont

Cook, Warren L. *Ancient Vermont.* Rutland: Academy, 1978.

Olcott, Henry S. *People from the Other World.* Rutland: Tuttle, 1972 (reprint).

Virginia

Tucker, George H. *Virginia Supernatural Tales.* Norfolk: Donning, 1977.

Washington

Arnold, Kenneth and Ray Palmer. *The Coming of the Saucers.* Boise: The Authors, 1952.

Beck, Fred and R.A. *I Fought the Apeman of Mt. St. Helens.* Washington State: The Authors, 1967.

Finke, Mary J. *Legends of Four High Mountains.* Portland: Portland Historical Journal, 1944.

West Virginia

Barker, Gray. *The Silver Bridge.* Clarksburg: Saucerian, 1970.

Keel, John A. *The Mothman Prophecies.* New York: Saturday Review Press/Dutton, 1975.

Musick, Ruth Ann. *Coffin Hollow.* Lexington: University of Kentucky, 1977.

Musick, Ruth Ann. *The Telltale Lilac Bush.* Lexington: University of Kentucky, 1965.

Wisconsin

Brown, Charles E. *Sea Serpents: Wisconsin Occurrences of These Weird Water Monsters.* Madison: Wisconsin Folklore Society, 1942.

Rath, Jay. *The W-Files: True Reports of Unexplained Phenomena in Wisconsin.* Madison, Wisconsin: Trailside, 1997.

Salisbury, Rollin D. and Wallace W. Atwood. *The Geography of the Region About Devil's Lake.* Madison: Wisconsin Geological and Natural History Survey, 1900.

Wells, Robert W. *Fire at Peshtigo.* Englewood Cliffs: Prentice-Hall, 1968.

Wyman, Walker D. *Wisconsin Folklore.* River Falls: University of Wisconsin, 1979.

Wyoming

Gebhard, David. *The Rock Art of Dinwoody, Wyoming.* Santa Barbara: Unversity of California, 1969.

Canada

Berton, Pierre. *The Mysterious North.* New York: Knopf, 1956.

Colombo, John Robert. *Colombo's Book of Marvels.* Toronto: NC Press, 1979.

Colombo, John Robert. *Mysterious Canada.* Toronto: Doubleday, 1988. (Colombo gave this book its title in tribute to my 1983 edition of *Mysterious America.*)

Fowke, Edith. *Folklore of Canada.* Toronto: McClelland & Stewart, 1976.

Garner, Betty Sanders. *Canada's Monsters.* Hamilton, Ont.: Potlatch, 1976.

Hervey, Shelia. *Some Canadian Ghosts.* Richmond Hill, Ont.: Pocket, 1973.

Lambert, R. S. *Exploring the Supernatural: The Weird in Canadian Folklore.* Toronto: McClelland & Stewart, 1955.

Owen, A. R. G. *Psychic Mysteries of the North.* New York: Harper & Row, 1975.

Skinner, Charles M. *Myths and Legends Beyond Our Borders.* Philadelphia: Lippincott, 1899.

Sonin, Eileen. *More Canadian Ghosts.* Richmond Hill, Ont.: Pocket, 1974.

British Columbia

Buckland, Frank M. *Story of Ogopogo.* Kelowna: Okanagan Historical Society, 1943.

Corner, John. *Pictograms in the Interior of British Columbia.* Vernon: Wayside, 1968.

Gaal, Arlene. *Ogopogo.* Surrey, B.C.: Hancock House, 1986.

LeBlond, Paul J. and John Sibert. *Observations of Large Unidentified Marine Animals in British Columbia and Adjacent Waters.* Vancouver: University of British Columbia, 1973.

Moon, Mary. *Ogopogo.* Vancouver: J. J. Douglas, 1977.

New Brunswick

Trueman, Stuart. *Ghosts, Pirates and Treasure Trove: The Phantoms that Haunt New Brunswick.* Toronto: McClelland & Stewart, 1975.

Truman, Stuart. *An Intimate History of New Brunswick.* Toronto: McClelland & Stewart, 1970.

Wright, Bruce S. *The Eastern Panther.* Toronto: Clark, Irwin, 1972.

Wright, Bruce S. *The Ghost of North America*. New York: Vantage, 1959.

Newfoundland
Mowat, Farley. *Westviking*. Totowa, NJ: Minerva, 1965.
Smallwood, Joseph. *The Book of Newfoundland*. St. John's: Newfoundland, 1937.

Nova Scotia
Creighton, Helen. *Bluenose Ghosts*. Toronto: Ryerson. 1957.
Fraser, Mary L. *Folklore of Nova Scotia*. Toronto: Catholic Truth, 1931.
Furneaux, Rupert. *The Money Pit Mystery*. New York: Dodd, Mead, 1972.
Sherwood, Roland H. *The Phantom Ship of Northumberland Strait*. Windsor, NS: Lancelot, 1975.

Ontario
Cochrane, Hugh. *Gateway to Oblivion: The Great Lakes' Bermuda Triangle*. New York: Avon, 1980.
Haisell, David. *The Missing Seven Hours*. Markham: Paperjacks, 1978.
Tushingham, A. D. *The Beardmore Relics: Hoax or History?* Toronto: Royal Ontario Museum, 1966.

Prince Edward Island
Ramsey, Sterling. *Folklore: Prince Edward Island*. Charlottetown: Square Deal, 1973.

Quebec
Davies, Blodwen. *Romantic Quebec,* New York: Dodd, Mead, 1932.
Gagnon, Claude and Michael Meurger. *Monsters in Quebec Lakes: Myths and Troublesome Realities*. Montreal: Alain Stanke, 1983. Published in French *(Monstres des Lacs du Quebec)* in 1982.

Looking for a handy way to find some of the above titles and get the latest on new titles discussing the wonders around Mysterious America? A special resource for those interested in recent and old books on regional mysteries are online booksellers. There are two major online book dealers that have their stock of books catalogued by states and provinces at their websites. They are:

Troy Taylor's
Ghosts of the Prairie
Whitechapel Productions Press
515 East Third Street
Alton, Illinois 62002
1-618-465-1086
1-888-Ghostly
http://www.prairieghosts.com/ghostbooks.html

Chris Woodyard's
Invisible Ink
1811 Stonewood Drive
Dayton, Ohio 45432
1-937-426-5110
1-800-31-GHOST
http://www.inkvink.com/inkvink1.html

Acknowledgments

I deeply appreciate permission given by *Fate, Flying Saucer Review, Boston Magazine, People's Almanac,* and *Occult* for the revised use of material previously published. Thanks also to *Fortean Times* for serving as a forum for many ideas expressed in *Mysterious America* through my column "On the Trail" published in that journal.

For the years of correspondence, information exchange, and intellectual stimulation, I would like to take a special moment to thank Mark A. Hall of Minnesota. Working away, unbeknownst to most of the rest of the world, Mark has painstakingly sorted through reams of material, checked into numerous Fortean mysteries, and thoughtfully ventured a few answers to these anomalies. Mark and I have carried on a dynamic interchange that many times propelled me into new Fortean directions. My long-distance friend, therefore, has been with me on many of my excursions across America, in spirit, and I appreciate his assistance in the essence of this book.

And likewise, a sincere and long thank you to Jerome Clark. Jerry and I worked closely, in the 1970s, sorting through material collected for over a decade before that. Jerry Clark must be credited with assisting my words to flow from the ideas in my head and the data in my hands. Jerry saw that river begin to flow and it still courses its way through *Mysterious America,* thanks in part to Jerry's encouragement. Some material in this book reflects work done with Jerry Clark, and I appreciate his permission to use it.

A leader in the field of cryptozoology, Dr. Bernard Heuvelmans has influenced my life since I read his book on unknown animals. He has become a person I now call "friend" and truly feel very close to him in words, deeds, and some ideas. Bernard may not share my total view of what's up with our monsters, but we do agree in post-fieldwork methodology and hard work to attempt to understand the facts. With sympathy, Bernard, part of this is for you.

Some departed individuals who have had a great impact on my investigative life, and whom I would like to thank, are Charles Fort, Ivan T. Sanderson, George F. Haas, and Carleton Coon. I was happy to have personally known the last three. Charles Fort, whom we have to thank for the examination of unexplained things, or Forteana, helped me from afar, and by his works.

The body of a book is filled with information, especially a Fortean one like this. Dedicated correspondents and fellow researchers who have consistently shared their Fortean data with me since the 1960s include Robert Rickard, Tom Adams, Lou Farish, John Green, Mr. X, Steve Hicks, Joseph Zarzynski, Warren Thompson, Larry Arnold, David Fideler, Bill Grimstad, Gary Mangicopra, John A. Keel, Robert Neeley, Dwight Whalen, Walt Webb, Jim McClarin, Paul Willis, and Jerry Coleman.

As the miles and days rolled by while I traveled about looking into the shadowy corners of this country, leads, clues, and hints which made my investigative work more complete have been forwarded to me by an ever-growing body of Forteans. Although I am certain I shall leave some-one out, I have found the following people helpful with these bits and pieces: Roy Mackal, Ted Bloecher, William Zeiser, Ron Westrum, Don Worley, Janet and Colin Bord, David Webb, Pat Bontempo, Doug Tarrant, Tom Bearden, Gray Barker, Jay Garon, Bob Betts, Vincent Gaddis, Peter Costello, Robert Downing, Terry Colvin, Dennis Pilichis, Mary Margaret and Curtis Fuller, George Earley, Randall Eaton, Roberta Payne, Peter Rodman, Berthold Schwarz, Roy Robinson, Peter Jordan, Joseph Nyman, Rene Dahinden, Betty Hill, Richard Crowe, Tim Church, James Moseley, Carol Michels, William Corliss, Ray Boeche, Bob Tarte, Curt Sutherly, Paul Bartholomew, Constance Cameron, Rod Dyke, Bob Jones, David Downs, Wayne Laporte, Joan Jeffers, Joel Hurd, Allen Greenfield, Ron Schaffner, Gene Duplantier, Ramona Hibner, Tom Miller, Joan Thomp-son, Graham Conway, Jim Auburn, Jacob Davidson, Len Aiken, Michael Anthony Hoffman, Thomas Archer, Stan Gordon, Ted Phillips, Michael Bershad, Hank Davis, Ron Dobbins, George Eberhart, Jerome Eden, and Bjorn Kurten. Organizations need to be mentioned also, and I am espe-cially happy with NEARA, MUFON, INFO, VESTIGA, SITU, and the International Society of Cryptozoology.

My editor for the first edition, Dennis Campbell, has been there when I needed him, and has assisted me in the birth of this project. Margaret Fitzpatrick's extra hours were filled with typing the manuscript, and I thank her.

I deeply appreciate the support and contributions to this work by Libbet Cone.

I am grateful to all of those mentioned and unmentioned who have assisted my efforts in exploring those secret places in time and space which fill this book. I could not have made my treks without them.

LOREN COLEMAN
June 1983

This new edition of *Mysterious America* is the direct outcome of an idea and the encouragement of one man who has become a great friend during the last twenty years, as well as a co-author, a close colleague, and, as it turns out, my editor: Patrick Huyghe. I thank him deeply for his assistance with this project.

For this 2001 revision and update of *Mysterious America,* I also wish to note my appreciation to the following people for their helpful comments, permissions, inclusions, and support: Leslie Abrons, Mark A. Hall, Jim Boyd, Richard Hendricks, Bill Rebsamen, William Gibbons, John Kirk, Matthew Johnson, Bob Rickard, Phyllis Galde, Harry Trumbore, Michael Goss, David P. Mikkelson, Brent O'Donnell, David Walsh, Stacy McArdle, Troy Taylor, Peter Hassall, Rachel Carthy, Richard Leshuk, Jim Lyding, Monte Ballard, Cosma Shalizi, Craig Heinselman, Andrew D. Gable, Tom Winebrenner, Curt Krumpe, Todd Roll, George Wagner, Chris Kraska, Zack Clothier, Karl Shuker, Chad Arment, Marcello Truzzi, Sunny Franson, Lee Fritzhugh, Sean Foley, Mark Dion, Alexis Rockman, Todd Lester, Pauline Strawn, Richard Brown, Gilbert Miller, Dolores Phelps, Laura Smyth, Dennis Jay Hall, Chris Woodyard, Malcolm Cone-Coleman, Caleb Cone-Coleman, Scott Norman, Richard Noll, Susan Hoey, Bill Coleman, Anna Atkins, and Gregg Hale.

L.C.
November 2000

Index

Hecht, Ben 12
Hendricks, Richard 156, 183, 325
Heuvelmans, Bernard 90, 94, 136, 210, 221, 223–230, 288
Hill, Barney and Betty 42
Hill, Earl 106, 129
Hitchcock, Harold 125
Hobbs Island, Alabama 278
Hobbs, Indiana 275
Hobbs, New Mexico 275
Hoccomocco, Massachusetts 29
Hockamik, New Jersey 29
Hockamin Creek, Minnesota 29
Hocking, Peter 139
Hockomock Swamp, Massachusetts 29, 33ff, 79
Hockomock, Maine 29
Hogarth, Todd 200
Holden, Massachusetts 60
Holland, Harold 210
Holmes, Oliver Wendell 12
Hoosac Tunnel, Massachusetts 31–32
Hopkinsville, Kentucky 245ff
Hopko, Pauline 79
Houston, Texas 257, 260–261
Humboldt County, Iowa 216
Huyghe, Patrick 5, 16, 230

Ice falls 16, 65, 66
Idaho 90
Iliamna Lake, Alaska 86ff
Illinois 8–9, 15, 19, 22, 24, 26, 34, 36, 58, 65, 69, 77, 81, 87, 91, 105ff, 115, 118, 124, 125, 129, 131–133, 141, 155, 160–161, 169–174, 198, 200, 214, 223, 226, 249, 251, 254, 258, 261–262, 269, 278–279, 287
"In Search Of" 8
Indiana 19, 29, 74, 81, 88, 105, 107, 109, 113, 115, 121, 124–125, 130–131, 153, 156, 161, 169, 172–173, 182, 190, 209, 217, 275–279
International Fortean Organization (INFO) 15, 16, 44, 177, 188, 287
International Society of Cryptozoology 141, 289

Iowa 134, 183–184, 216

Janesville, Wisconsin 69
Jay, Ricky 63, 64
Jefferson, G. T. 153, 154
Johnson, Charles 127
Johnson, Mrs. 88
Joliet, Illinois 132ff
Jolliet, Louis 92
Jones, Earl 200
Jones, Steve 200

Kane, Philip 39
Kansas 69, 81, 116, 167–168, 206, 267–268, 278
Kansas City, Kansas 267–268
Kansas City, Missouri 267–268
Kapuskasing, Ontario 132
Kearney, Bert 250ff
Keating, Don 200
Keel, John 80, 279, 280, 287, 288
Kelly Hill, Ohio 79
Kelly, Kentucky 55, 231ff
Kelly, Ringo 31
Kenton, Ohio 80
Kentucky 55, 80–81, 91, 115–116, 125, 140–141, 185, 209–210, 245ff
Kimble, Jeff 62
Kirkwood, Ohio 20
Knight, Damon 65
Kottmeyer, Martin S. 58–61
Kraska, Chris 200
Kraybill, Spencer 125
Kurten, Bjorn 151, 154

La Fayette, Pennsylvania 276
Lafayette Hill, Pennsylvania 276
Lafayette Square, Washington, D.C. 279
Lafayette, California 276
Lafayette, Indiana 182
Lafayette, Oregon 277
Lafayette, Wisconsin 276
Lake Brompton, Quebec 92
Lake Manitou, Indiana 29
Lake Massaswippi, Quebec 92
Lake Michigan 29, 87
Lake Minnetonka, Minnesota 81

Mireno, Jimmy 71
Mississippi 217
Missouri 9, 77, 93, 124, 157–158,
    191ff, 206ff, 249, 267–268, 279
Mitchell, Clarence 78
Moneymaker, Matt 200
Monkey Cave Hollow, Kentucky 210
Monmouth Beach, New Jersey 68
Montana 80–81, 88–90
Monticello, Illinois 105ff
Montreal, Quebec 77
Moose 58–61
Morgan, Robert W. 200
Morning Sun, Ohio 130–131
Mothman 23, 242, 280, 282, 283
Moul, George 75
Moundsville, West Virginia 282
Mt. Diablo, California 25, 121–122,
    226
Mt. Tamalpais, California 120
Myers, Paul G. 107
Mystery Hill, New Hampshire 13, 17

Nahant, Massachusetts 39
Nashville, Tennessee 80–81
Nebraska 81, 85, 113, 131, 134, 152,
    166–167, 282
Negus, Lucas 93, 95
Nelson-Miramichi, New Brunswick
    178–179
New Brunswick 84, 113, 116, 124, 129,
    131–132, 178–179
New Hampshire 13, 17, 27, 34, 60, 102,
    113
New Jersey 29, 68, 115, 164–165, 199,
    211, 223, 232ff, 279, 286
New Mexico 212, 275
New Richmond, Wisconsin 164
New Rochelle, New York 74
New York 12, 64, 68ff, 81, 85–87, 97ff,
    111, 115, 122, 126, 165, 190, 208,
    211, 239, 245, 270, 276, 280, 283
New York City, New York 70ff
Newcomerstown, Ohio 8, 189
North Carolina 81, 116, 125, 135, 141,
    181, 189, 209, 278
Norton, Massachusetts 34–36

Nova Scotia 9, 181ff, 217
Nyman, Joseph 44ff

O'Grady, R. J. P. 125
Oakland County, Michigan 112
Ohio 8, 19, 20, 22, 26, 67–68, 76, 78,
    80–81, 91, 93, 109, 113, 115–116,
    120, 125, 130–135, 143–144, 165,
    168, 185, 189, 198, 200, 206,
    276–278
Ohio River, West Virginia 81
Oklahoma 64, 81, 132, 175, 180–181,
    196, 209, 216, 223
Olive Branch, Illinois 110
Omaha, Nebraska 268
Ontario 81, 84, 85, 132, 178, 204
Onza 123–124
Oquawka, Illinois 107
Oregon 277
Orsini-Meinhard, Kirsten 64
Osborn, Chester 106, 129
Ottawa Valley, Ontario 81
Ottumwa, Wisconsin 183–184

Packer, Orland 80
Paint River, Michigan 88
Paris, Missouri 249
Parker, Gerry 113, 117
Parks, Betty 200
Parks, Leon 200
Paxton, Charles 91
Pennsylvania 36, 80, 115, 116,
    124–125, 142, 145, 149, 151, 190,
    208, 242, 268, 242, 268, 276, 282,
    303
Pentz, Peter 145ff
Peoria County, Illinois 131
Pepin County, Wisconsin 139
Pepperell, William 32
Persinger, Michael A. 15
Peru 139
Phoenix, Arizona 93
Pike County, Pennsylvania 142
Pilichis, Dennis 200
Pittsburgh, Pennsylvania 75, 268
Plano, Illinois 170ff
Plattsburgh, New York 98ff

Taylor, Billy Ray 245ff
Taylor, Troy 91, 111
Tennessee 80, 116, 158, 165
Texas 36, 69, 81, 93, 114, 135, 209,
   213, 217, 223, 284
Thayer, Tiffany 12
Thomas, Eugene P. 94
Thunderbird 19, 24, 165
Toledo, Ohio 20
Tolkien, J.R.R. 61
Toney, Ivan 130
Trail, Reid 77
Trento, Salvatore 15
Trenton, New Jersey 232ff
Trimble County, Kentucky 209
Trinity Alps, California 67
Truzzi, Marcello 66
Tulare Lake, California 67
Tulison, Glyan 106
Tulsa, Oklahoma 180
Turner, Arthur and Howard 130
Twain, Mark 92

Ufiti 218ff
Union Village, New York 74
Urbana, Illinois 19–20, 107, 109
Urbana, Ohio 20, 109
Utah 74, 179–180, 278

Vallee, Jacques 287
Vallejo, General 25
Vandike, James E. 157
Vaughn, Mrs. Roy 78–79
Ventura County, California 118ff
Vermont 60, 83ff, 125
Vineyard, Jerry 157
Virginia 77, 81, 115, 116, 142, 155,
   181, 185, 269, 280–283

Wagner, George 200
Wakely, Richard 53
Waldo County, Maine 112
Walnut Creek, California 120
Warrick County, Indiana 131
Warsaw, Indiana 88–89
Washington 135, 156, 167, 263, 269,
   279

Washington, D.C. 12
Waukesha, Wisconsin 175ff
Webb, David 121
Webb, Walter 42ff
Weed, Frank 125
Weir, Peter 65
Wellfleet, Massachusetts 32
Wellman, Iowa 183
West Virginia 81, 115, 116, 142, 155,
   269, 280–283, 325
Westerville, Ohio 19–20
Weston, Charles 99
Wetzel County, West Virginia 282–283
Wetzel, Charles (California) 273,
   280–282
Wetzel, Charles (Nebraska) 166–167,
   187, 282
Wetzel, Louis 283–284
Wilhelm, Charles 200
Wilkesboro, South Carolina 141
Wilkinston, Ken 93
Williamson, Jim 82
Winchester, New Hampshire 102
Winooski, Vermont 99–100
Wisconsin 26–27, 115, 123, 139,
   156–157, 164, 175ff, 183, 223, 269,
   271, 276, 278
Witherby, Jack 130
Woollcott, Alexander 12
Worley, Don 200
Wright, Bruce S. 105, 113, 125, 129,
   131
Wygle, Linda 200
Wyoming 28
Wyoming County, Pennsylvania 142

Yakin County, South Carolina 141
Yen, David 64

Zabolski, George 64
Zarzynski, Joseph 86, 97ff